John Harvey Treat

**Notes on the rubrics of the communion office**

Illustrating the history of the rubrics of the various prayer books

John Harvey Treat

**Notes on the rubrics of the communion office**
*Illustrating the history of the rubrics of the various prayer books*

ISBN/EAN: 9783337268374

Printed in Europe, USA, Canada, Australia, Japan

Cover: Foto ©Andreas Hilbeck / pixelio.de

More available books at **www.hansebooks.com**

# NOTES

ON THE

## Rubrics of the Communion Office;

ILLUSTRATING

THE HISTORY OF THE RUBRICS OF THE VARIOUS PRAYER BOOKS,
AND THEIR BEARING ON THE USE OF VESTMENTS, ALTAR
LIGHTS, THE EASTWARD POSITION, WAFER-BREAD,
AND THE MIXED CHALICE.

TOGETHER WITH A REVIEW OF

## THE DECISIONS OF THE PRIVY COUNCIL,

AND OBSERVATIONS ON

## MODERN RITUALISM.

BY

JOHN HARVEY TREAT.

WITH AN

INTRODUCTORY LETTER BY THE REV. MORGAN DIX, S.T.D.

**With Many Illustrations.**

"Ritual and ceremonial things move not God; but they exalt that devotion, and they conserve that order, which does move Him." — DR. DONNE: *Sermon 122, preached at St. Paul's Cross, May 6, 1627. Page 175, vol. 5.*

NEW YORK:
JAMES POTT, PUBLISHER,
12 ASTOR PLACE.
1882.

# Introductory Letter.

New York, July 14th, 1882.

John Harvey Treat, Esq.,

*My Dear Sir:*

A year, or more, must have elapsed since my attention was called to an incomplete pamphlet entitled "Loyalty to the Prayer Book." It looked like the beginning of a larger work; it bore no name of author; nor had it been offered for sale; but the friend who sent it to me disclosed the writer's name, and intimated that he was seeking for a publisher. You know,—for my correspondence with you since that time has made it clear,—how much interested I became in your work, and how glad I was to learn from you that you intended to complete it, adorn it with some illustrations, and present it to the public. I cheerfully complied with your request that I would write something for you by way of a preface; and this familiar letter will, I think, serve that purpose quite as well as an introduction in the usual formal style.

Let me say then to you, and, through you, to those who read your book,—I hope many will not only read, but study, mark, and inwardly digest its contents,—that on several accounts it appears to me to deserve a favorable reception. In the first place the subject matter commands respect and attention, as bearing on our rights to a share in the common heritage of the Holy Catholic Church. The day has gone by when men can be dissuaded by sneers and sarcastic jests from reverently studying the externals of our holy religion; nor can it be concealed that these hold an intimate relation to the Faith, as aids to the preservation and dissemination of orthodox teaching. Whatever bears on the worship of Almighty God in the Ritual and Ceremonial of His Church demands the respectful consideration of religious men. Liturgiology is not only a science, but one which is making a new literature for itself under the diligent labours of devout and critical scholars. Questions about the Prayer Book, its Order of Divine Service, for fixed days, seasons, and hours, and its sacramental offices; the Church edifice, its architectural style, and proper arrangement; the mode of performing rites and ceremonies; the Ornaments of the holy place and the Ministers in all times of their ministration; the Vestments to be worn by the divers grades of the hierarchy, their shape, material and color; the acts, position, and demeanour of Bishop, Priest, and Deacon in their several duties: —these are questions of great moment in their proper sphere, nor is the time wasted which we devote to their consideration. We mark, with pleasure, a healthful reaction from the contemptuous indifference to these subjects which marked a former generation, who never wearied of boasting that carelessness and rude simplicity should be held to be superior to order, beauty, and stateliness in the worship of the Lord. However widely men may depart from the old positions, they will return to them at length, constrained not only by argument but also by the demands of human nature. The answer to taunts about "ritualism," "man-millinery," "attitudinarianism," etc., is this:—That Almighty God, Creator of heaven and earth, thought it not beneath Him to give directions about the manner of His worship, but took pains to order, to its most minute particulars, the Service of the Ancient Church; that in the Holy Catholic Church it has always been considered a duty to follow that example; that indifference to these things, so far from being laudable, is, really, a sign of the pride of the human heart, as if it mattered not to illustrious and all-glorious Man how he chose to worship God, so long as he did God the favor to worship Him at all; and, notably, that whenever men have made a mock of the external beauty and attractiveness of religion, affecting to need no helps to devotion and alleging that worship is purest when most bald and unadorned, their hold on the Faith has relaxed. It may be demonstrated by historical evidence, that distaste for the solemn splendours and calm loveliness of Catholic Worship leads inevitably to rejection of the dogmas of our Creed and the revolt from that divine law which regulates the moral actions of men. You therefore have been doing a good work in giving much thought to the study of the Book of Common Prayer in its principles and history: and far from accusing you of having wasted your time in such investigation to the neglect of weightier matters, I assert that such labours tend to help forward the cause of true religion and to check the growth of error in doctrine and viciousness of life.

And, in the second place, your work interests me the more, because it is that of a layman. It is an auspicious sign when the laity are with the Clergy in their interest in whatever relates to the order of the Church; and nothing can put us in better heart than to find intelligent co-operation with us in that quarter. Happy indeed is any branch of the Church which has, among her lay members, men well learned in theology, in history, and in liturgical science, and qualified to aid and cheer her Priests in their efforts to enlighten the ignorance and overcome the prejudices of the day. In this particular, indeed, we have been favored, heretofore, in having, outside the clerical order, a line of distinguished and devout Sons of the Church, whose names will at once suggest themselves to the memory. You seem to me to have won your place in that worthy brotherhood; and while this work is an earnest of your ability, the mere fact that it is a layman's contribution to some questions of the day, will doubtless secure for it a reading in quarters in which nothing that a clergyman could say would be listened to. I wish the faithful laity were more fully awake to their responsibilities. The victories already won in England over the illiberal and domineering spirit of modern puritanism, to which the Catholic Faith and the Catholic Ritual are alike odious, were due as much to the hearty co-operation of the laity as to the zeal and devotion of the clergy; and to those united efforts do we look for the ultimate triumph which the present aspect of affairs encourages us to predict.

I have read, though hastily, the first part of your work; I promise myself profit as well as pleasure in perusing what you are now preparing for the press. From appreciative friends I have received accounts of your patience and diligence in your study; of the many days you have passed in libraries; of your industry in collecting and arranging your materials; of your conscientiousness in verifying every quotation you make and in taking nothing at second hand, but invariably examining the originals. Work done in that way is worth doing, and its results must be valuable.

With my best wishes, and a hearty God speed, I am, very sincerely yours,

MORGAN DIX.

# Contents.

| | | |
|---|---|---|
| | **LOYALTY TO THE PRAYER BOOK,** | 1–26 |
| I. | THE PURITANS AT THE TIME OF THE REFORMATION, | 4–5 |
| II. | THE PURITANS UNDER EDWARD VI., | 5–6 |
| III. | THE PURITANS UNDER QUEEN MARY, | 6–7 |
| IV. | THE PURITANS UNDER QUEEN ELIZABETH, | 7–14 |
| 1. | The Puritans were as yet few in number, and mostly confined to London, | 7 |
| 2. | The Puritan Reformers induced the Continental Reformers to write to the Queen in the interest of further reform, | 7–8 |
| 3. | The Puritans were advised by Foreigners to retain their Offices in the Church, though they did not believe in it, lest those who did should get the places vacated by them, | 8 |
| 4. | Even when the Puritan Preachers were forbidden to preach, they preached just the same, | 9 |
| 5. | The Puritans were really united only against the Church, whilst among themselves, most bitter quarrels raged, to the great decay of religion, | 9–11 |
| 6. | To such extremes did these men go, that Puritanism was declared to be as great an evil to the Church and State as Popery, | 11–13 |
| | HIGH CHURCH AND LOW CHURCH, | 14–19 |
| | SECESSION TO ROME, | 19–20 |
| | FAULT-FINDING, | 21–22 |
| | PERSECUTION, | 22–26 |

### I.
### THE VESTMENTS, 28–151

| | | |
|---|---|---|
| I. | PRAYER BOOK AND RUBRICS OF 1549, | 28–30 |
| II. | PRAYER BOOK AND RUBRIC OF 1552, | 30–35 |
| III. | PRAYER BOOK AND RUBRIC OF 1559, | 35–45 |

1. It was well understood that the Queen herself was in favor of High Ritual, and not inclined to Puritanism, which she detested,     37–38

2. The Catholic character of the revision of the Prayer Book, and the intention of the Queen to adopt Catholic usages, was so well known, that out of nearly 10,000 Clergy, who had officiated under Queen Mary, only about 200 to 250, refused to conform,     38–43

  (1) *We also have the testimony of the Puritans that most of the Clergy were " Papists," or, as we should say, Churchmen,*     39–40

  (2) *The Pope is said to have promised to confirm the English Liturgy, if Elizabeth would only acknowledge the claims of the Roman Pontiff,*     40

  (3) *For 10 or 11 years the great bulk of Roman Catholics frequented the English Church and were contented with her Services,*     40–42

  (4) *Pope Pius V. excommunicated Elizabeth, April 25, 1570. (Bulla, n. 5, p. 303, T. 5. Mag. Bull. Rom.)*     42–43

3. But the Queen had another class of persons to deal with, whom it was also necessary to conciliate,     43–45

  (1) *During Elizabeth's reign, as also during the latter part of Edward's, the Puritans were accustomed to officiate in their ordinary dress, not even using the Surplice, thereby wholly setting at naught the Rubrics of the Church and the Laws of the Realm,*     43–44

  (2) *Some of the Bishops upon their return from exile, both before and after they entered upon their ministry, incited by foreign Reformers, among whom they had lived, favored the Puritans, but the Queen and Parliament resisted,*     44–45

IV. QUEEN ELIZABETH TAKES "FURTHER ORDER" TO ENFORCE UNIFORMITY, IN 1560-1,     46–47

V. "INTERPRETATIONS AND FURTHER CONSIDERATIONS," DRAWN UP IN 1561,     48

VI. "GENERAL NOTES OF MATTERS TO BE MOVED BY THE [PURITAN] CLERGY IN THE NEXT PARLIAMENT AND SYNOD," 1562–3.     49

VII. THE ADVERTISEMENTS,     50–76

  1. Circumstances attending the drawing up of the Advertisements,     51–61

  2. The Advertisements were the work of the Bishops alone,     61–62

  3. The Advertisements were against no Law of the Realm,     62–63

4. Use made of the Advertisements in Official Documents,     63–66

5. The Advertisements were not the taking of "other Order" as authorized by the Act of Uniformity,     66–72

  (1) *In 1559, and in 1560-1, the Queen issued further orders to enforce uniformity in the Church,*     66–67

  (2) *There is quite a marked difference between the Advertisements of 1564 and those as finally published in 1566,*     67–68

  (3) *The Advertisements, as we have seen, were the work of the Bishops, though they were incited thereto by the Queen, "who could not satisfy her conscience without crushing the Puritans." (Speech of Cecil, cited by Oldmixon, Hist. of England, an. 1573, p. 451.*     68–72

6. It is now claimed by some that the Advertisements were directed against high ritual,     72–73

7. Summary,     73–76

  (1) *Circumstances attending the drawing up of the Advertisements,*     73–74

  (2) *The Queen never signed the Advertisements; therefore, they could not have repealed or modified the Rubric of 1559,*     74–75

  (3) *The Advertisements were not against High Ritual,*     75–76

But even if the Queen did sanction the Advertisements, and they did repeal the Rubric of 1559, they could not affect in the least the Rubric of 1662, adopted nearly a hundred years later,     76

VIII. PRAYER BOOK AND RUBRIC OF 1603–4,     76

IX. CANONS OF 1603–4,     76

X. THE HOUSE OF LORDS, 1640–1,     77

XI. PRAYER BOOK AND RUBRIC OF 1662,     77–79

XII. ATTEMPTED REVISION OF THE LITURGY IN 1689,     79–80

XIII. ATTEMPTED REVISION OF THE ORNAMENTS RUBRIC IN 1879,     80–82

Convocation of the Province of Canterbury,     80–82

Convocation of the Province of York,     82

XIV. THE USE OF VESTMENTS IN THE CHURCH OF ENGLAND SINCE THE REFORMATION,     82–151

The Jewish Priests used Vestments,     82

Names and description of the Vestments ordered to be used by the Church of England since the Reformation,     83

The Hooper Controversy,     83–84

|   |   |   |
|---|---|---|
| | The Calvinistic Reformers encouraged dissensions in England, | 84–85 |
| | A distinction has of late been made between the Cope and the Chasuble, on the ground the latter was the exclusive mass-garment, while the Cope was not used for that purpose, | 85 |
| 1. | History of the Chasuble—1. *The Pænula*; 2. *The Planeta*; 3. *The Casula*, | 86–87 |
| 2. | History of the Cope; originally identical with the Chasuble, | 87–89 |
| 3. | The early Puritans never made any distinction between the Vestments, but condemned them all alike, | 89 |
| 4. | The Cope, and the Surplice even, was sometimes used as a Mass-vestment by the Church of Rome, both before and since the Reformation, | 89–92 |
| (1) | *Use of the Cope before the Reformation*, | 89–91 |
| (2) | *Use of the Cope since the Reformation*, | 91 |
| (3) | *Use of the Surplice at Mass before the Reformation*, | 91–92 |
| 5. | The Armenians and Nestorians at this day use the Cope as the Eucharistic Vestment, | 92 |
| 6. | The use of the Cope by the Anglican Reformers, | 92–94 |
| | PLATES ILLUSTRATING THE VESTMENTS, | 95–107 |
| (I). | USE OF VESTMENTS UNDER THE PRAYER BOOK OF 1549, | 108–109 |
| (II). | USE OF VESTMENTS UNDER THE PRAYER BOOK OF 1552, | 109–117 |
| (III). | USE OF VESTMENTS UNDER THE PRAYER BOOKS OF 1559 AND 1662, | 117–142 |
| (IV). | THE USE OF COPES AND VESTMENTS IN PARISH CHURCHES, | 143–150 |
| (V). | SUMMARY, | 150–151 |

## II.
## HOLY TABLE OR ALTAR, 152–157

|   |   |   |
|---|---|---|
| I. | NAME, | 152–154 |
| II. | STONE OR WOODEN ALTARS, | 154–155 |
| III. | FORM OF ALTARS, | 155–157 |

## III.
## POSITION OF THE PRIEST AT THE ALTAR, 158–181

|   |   |   |
|---|---|---|
| I. | THE EARLY CHRISTIANS ALWAYS PRAYED TOWARDS THE EAST, | 158–159 |
| II. | POSITION OF ANCIENT CHURCHES, | 159–161 |

|     |     |     |
| --- | --- | --- |
| III. | THE PRIEST STOOD BEFORE THE ALTAR, | 161 |
| IV. | POSITION OF THE ALTAR AND OF THE PRIEST IN THE CHURCH OF ENGLAND SINCE THE REFORMATION, | 161–181 |
| 1. | The old Altars removed and Wooden Tables substituted, | 162–163 |
| 2. | The Table allowed to be moved at Communion time, | 163–165 |
| 3. | Altars or Tables placed table-wise, | 165–171 |
| 4. | Difference between end and side of the Holy Table or Altar, | 171–173 |
| 5. | The Rubrics of the Communion Office, | 173–174 |
| 6. | The word "before" the Table means in front of the Table, looking east, | 174–175 |
| 7. | In 1832, the House of Bishops, at the request of the House of Clerical and Lay Deputies in 1829, put forth the following Directions to insure Uniformity of Posture in the Celebration of the Holy Eucharist, | 175–176 |
| 8. | The Eastward Position. | 176–181 |

## IV.
## ORNAMENTS OF THE ALTAR, 181–206

|     |     |     |
| --- | --- | --- |
| I. | THE CROSS, | 183–185 |
| II. | ALTAR LIGHTS, | 186–205 |
| 1. | The use of Altar Lights in the Church of England since the Reformation, | 186–198 |
| 2. | The use of Altar Lights, Vestments, &c., among the Lutherans, | 199–205 |
| III. | FLOWERS, | 205–206 |

## V.
## THE EUCHARIST A MEMORIAL SACRIFICE, 206–208

## VI.
## REVERENCE FOR GOD'S HOUSE, 208–213

BOWING TOWARDS THE ALTAR, 209–213

## VII.
## THE PEOPLE KNEELING, 213

## VIII.
## THE APOSTLES' OR NICENE CREED, 213–217

|     |     |     |
| --- | --- | --- |
| I. | BOWING AT THE NAME OF JESUS, | 214 |
| II. | THE WORD CATHOLIC, | 214–217 |
| III. | BELIEF IN THE CREED, | 217 |

## IX.
### NOTICE OF HOLY DAYS, 217-218

## X.
### "THEN SHALL FOLLOW THE SERMON," 218

## XI.
### PRESENTATION OF OFFERINGS, 219

## XII.
### INVITATION TO THE HOLY COMMUNION, 219-220

## XIII.
### PLACING THE ELEMENTS UPON THE ALTAR, 220-224

I. THE MIXED CHALICE, 220-221
II. WAFER BREAD, 221-223

Wafer Bread used by the Calvinists at Geneva, and among all the Reformed upon the Continent at that time, and by the Lutherans to this day, 224

## XIV.
### DISPOSAL OF THE CONSECRATED ELEMENTS, 224-225

## XV.
### THE DECISIONS OF THE PRIVY COUNCIL, 226-241

1857.] LIDDELL v. WESTERTON, 227-228
1868.] MARTIN v. MACKONOCHIE, 228-230
1870-1.] HEBBERT v. PURCHAS, 230-235
1876.] CLIFTON AND OTHERS v. RIDSDALE, 235
1877.] RIDSDALE v. CLIFTON AND OTHERS; OR THE RIDSDALE APPEAL CASE, 235-240

Reasons why the Ritualists were condemned, 240-241
Reasons why Churchmen refused to obey the Decisions of a secular Court, 241

## XVI.
### RITUALISM NOT NECESSARILY ROMANISM, 242-244

## XVII.
### THE RITUALISTS, 244-248

## XVIII.
### WHY CHURCHMEN ARE TENACIOUS OF SMALL THINGS, 248-251

|  |  |  |
|---|---|---|
| XIX. CONCLUSION, | | 251–253 |
| INDEX OF AUTHORS, | | 254–264 |
| INDEX OF SUBJECTS, | | 265 |

# Illustrations.

| | |
|---|---|
| Plates illustrating the Vestments, | 95–107 |
| Representation of the Coronation of Queen Victoria in 1838, | 139 |
| " " a Pagan Altar, | 152 |
| " " an ancient Altar at Ravenna, | 156 |
| " " " " " " Rome, | 156 |
| " " " " " " Milan, | 157 |
| " " " " " " Auriol, | 157 |
| " " a modern Roman Catholic Altar at Paris, | 157 |
| " " an Altar or Table turned table-wise, | 169 |
| " " the Altar in St. Paul's in 1719, | 196 |
| " " " " " St. George's Chapel, Windsor, | 197 |
| " " a Lutheran Altar at Molmen, Norway, | 203 |

# Corrigenda.

Page 37, line 34, *for* ceremony in *read* ceremony appointed in
" 128, " 4, *for* THE *read* THE OLD
" 128, " 26, *for* PUBL. *read* PUBL. N. S.
" 129, " 48, *for* in Parish Churches. *read* elsewhere.
" 227, " 29, *for* spoke of *read* spoke . . . of
" 231, " 42, *for* he celebrate *read* he is to celebrate
" 191, " 28, for *Gloria Patria* read *Gloria Patri*

# Addenda.

Page 80, at the end of Chapter XII., insert:

In the Comprehension Bill of 1689, it was proposed:

"And Be it enacted by the authority aforesaid that from henceforth Noe Minister shall be obliged to wear a Surplice in the time of reading Prayers or performing any other Religious Office, Except onely to the King and Queens Ma^ties Chappells and in all Cathedral or Collegiate Churches and Chappells of this Realme of England and Dominion of Wales Provided alsoe that every Minister that shall not think fitt to wear a Surplice as aforesaid shall nevertheless be obliged to perform all y^e Publick Offices ot his Ministry in the Church in a Black Gowne suitable to his Degree." AN ACT FOR THE UNITING THEIR MAJESTYES PROTESTANT SUBJECTS. Cited in the REPORT OF HER MAJESTY'S COMMISSIONERS APPOINTED TO CONSIDER THE SUBSCRIPTION, DECLARATION, AND OATHS REQUIRED TO BE MADE AND TAKEN BY THE CLERGY OF THE UNITED CHURCH OF ENGLAND AND IRELAND. APP., P. 49.

Page 123, under WIBURN, line 21, after the word cope., insert:

And two other ministers formerly called deacon and subdeacon, must assist him to read the epistle and gospel.

Page 149, after line 39, insert:

This brass of Dyke (it should be Dykes) represents a Priest vested in Alb with apparels, Chasuble with orphreys, Amice, Stole, and Maniple. The date of this figure is of about the middle of the fourteenth century, and it originally belonged to the tomb of Symon de Wenslagh, but was appropriated by Dykes, who inserted his own epitaph above the head of the figure. Perhaps the original inscription had been broken or lost. We do not say that Dykes wore these Vestments, but he must have regarded them as legal, else he would not have chosen this brass.

Page 192, after line 19, insert:

1705.] At the Church Congress, at Derby, England, in 1882, there was on exhibition a curious old painting representing the interior of Westminster Abbey, showing the marble Altar-piece that was put up in 1705 under the advice of Sir Christopher Wren. On the Altar is a Crucifix and seven candles, three on one side of the Crucifix, and four on the other.

# Loyalty to the Prayer Book.

WE all profess to desire that the services of the Church should be conducted according to the Rubrics and the principles of the Reformation. The only question is, what is the correct interpretation of the Rubrics, and what are the principles upon which the Reformers acted. Very few people know anything at all about these matters. Very many have never read through their Prayer Book, much less studied it. They are even ignorant of the Creed which they are supposed to repeat every Sunday. It was related in a Sunday School Convention held in New York a few years since, "that a little girl asked her teacher what was the meaning of the word Catholic in the Creed. She replied that there was no such word there, and when it was pointed out to her, she looked a few moments, and then replied that she guessed that it was a mistake." I have observed many such instances myself.

Some, however, refuse to make any investigation. One man told me that "he was so prejudiced that he would not read the other side." Of course it is utterly impossible to convince such. Prejudice with them takes the place of argument. They have so little confidence in the justice of their cause that they are afraid to look into the grounds upon which they stand, lest they be converted in spite of themselves.

But the people are not always to blame for their ignorance. They have never been taught anything about the Church, nor have they the time, perhaps, or opportunities for study. The Clergy are sometimes as ignorant as the laity. I have known some fresh from the Divinity school, who had never read over the Baptismal service till they came to use it, and one forgot the water till he was about to baptise the child and found he had none. Had he only observed the Rubric:

"The Minister coming to the Font, (which is then to be filled with pure water,)" &c.
he never would have made such a mistake.

It is the paramount duty of the Clergy to be well instructed and grounded in the Church themselves, and then impart that knowledge to their flocks. The Bishops of our Church in their Pastoral, in 1874, well say:

"A long-established Canon reminds our Clergy, and the same duty is after their manner binding on the laity in their more limited spiritual cures, 'that they shall not only be diligent in instructing the children in the catechism, but shall also, by stated catechetical lectures and instruction, be diligent in informing the youth and others in the Doctrines, Constitution, and Liturgy of the Church.' For the Church maintains the Faith in its purity and integrity as taught in the Holy Scriptures, held by the primitive Church, summed up in the Creeds, and affirmed by the undisputed General Councils; her Constitution, attested by Holy Scripture and ancient authors, she has not invented, but inherited from the days of old; her Liturgy was moulded by the breath of many saintly men. Your children should know the value of these precious gifts, and the grounds on which we receive and love them. In an age of indifferentism, when so many seek to reduce all religion to a sentiment, it is cruel to expose a child to the solicitations of varient systems of belief and practice without a knowledge of the origin and history of the Church of Christ, and an intelligent understanding of the authority on which she relies for her doctrine and order." DAILY CHURCHMAN, P. 251.

It is sheer ignorance about what the Church teaches that causes most of our real trouble. I propose, therefore, to fully examine the doctrines, practices, and ceremonies, even the most extreme, which have been objected against, solely from an historical point of view. I am not advocating, mark that, the restoration of practices which were to a great extent laid aside owing to Puritan influence and prejudice, but never abolished. Whether such things are right or wrong, whether the Rubrics and Canons of the Church are wrong and need revision, and whether the Clergy who have promised to take the Prayer Book for their guide, do so take it, that does not concern me in the least. I merely propose to show that High Churchmen, and they alone, are faithful to the principles of the Reformation, and the Prayer Book in its plain, literal, and grammatical sense. In its entirety, without any mental reservation, they accept that book which was compiled by such great men as Cranmer and the other Reformers, who were men of caution, prudence and wisdom, noted not only for their knowledge of Christian antiquities, but for their zeal and piety. To Cranmer we are indebted for our admirable Liturgy, upon which he labored for two years. He sought to reform what had been corrupted, not to destroy.

The Reformers sacrificed their lives in defence of the doctrines contained in the Prayer Book, literally sealing its pages with their blood. Those who in our days seek to pour contempt upon their great work by stigmatizing it as "Popery," show themselves wholly ignorant of history. Men who were burnt at the stake by "Papists" could not have been very great "Papists" themselves. Can we blame a Churchman, then, for fondly clinging to a certain Ritual which has ever been in the Church, was sanctioned by our martyr Reformers, required even by the Rubrics and Canons of the Church of England, and acknowledged by the General Convention of our Church in 1874? To be sure, the Reformers may have been but half reformed and only Papists in disguise, but that does not concern us at all. The question with us, who profess to follow their teachings, is not what they ought to have taught, but what they actually did teach.

After the Church had been suppressed nearly twenty years, at the Great Rebellion, it was impossible to restore at once many practices which from long disuse had become extinct or forgotten, but, as a matter of fact, many more things still remained in the Church of England, and have remained ever since the Reformation, than any one unacquainted with the subject ever dreamed of. To such as wish to inform themselves, I would recommend HIERURGIA ANGLICANA, LOND., 1848. This book consists of Documents and extracts from contemporary writers, with some plates, illustrative of the Ritual of the Church. Although published more than thirty years since, before much attention had been paid to ritual, it consists of nearly 400 pp., and might readily now be increased to double that size.

Some will perhaps say, "we care not what the Church and the Prayer Book teach, we do not like such things," that is, they prefer their own human ideas to Christ's teaching. Our Lord says:

"If he neglect to hear the Church, let him be unto thee as a heathen man and a publican." MATT. 18 : 17.

ART. XX.,—and Low Churchmen profess great admiration for the Articles,—tells us that:

"The Church hath power to decree Rites or Ceremonies, and authority in Controversies of Faith."

The question is not what we like or dislike, but what God commands.

The men who wrought all the mischief in the Church were not generally those who suffered for her, but those who, like cowards, fled in time of persecution under Queen Mary to the Continent, and imbibed at Geneva and elsewhere sentiments hostile to the Church. Upon their return they sought to propagate their heresies. These men had been quite restless under Edward VI., but under Elizabeth and during the succeeding reigns they became very troublesome, and for a time actually overthrew the Church. Let me give you a specimen of the teachings of the Puritans and Presbyterians. Like many, now, they called everything they objected to "Popery;" put forth a spurious Prayer Book in order to evade conformity; denounced religious toleration as the "Devil's masterpiece;" refused to stand at the Creed, and considered bowing at the name of JESUS as bad as drunkenness; sat in Church with their hats on, but if some great personage came in whose presence they seemed to value more than that of the Almighty, they honored him by removing their hats; they also removed their hats when the Psalms in metre, human compositions, were sung, but refused to do so when the inspired words of David were used; would not use fonts but basins for Baptisms; despised the sign of the Cross; called Organs "Popery," and cast them out of the Churches; would not use the old Pulpits, from which "Popery" had been preached, but destroyed them and erected new ones; called the Prayer Book "Porridge" and an "Idol," and frequently burnt it; refused to attend Public Prayer, alleging it cut short the sermon, and walked the churchyard till sermon time, when they went in; regarded funeral sermons as "Popish" at first (see ROBERTSON, HOW SHALL WE CONFORM, &c., c. 20, p. 252; c. 21, p. 228, 3D ED.), but after a few years made great use of them; sometimes they walked, smoked, or engaged in knitting or sewing in Church. By the Act of Uniformity they were obliged to wear a Surplice, which they called "a Babylonish garment," but the Wardens were obliged to furnish it. The Puritan Clergy would persuade the Wardens not to furnish one, and when complained of for non-conformity, allege as an excuse that none were furnished them. Baxter, a nominal Conformist, acknowledged that he had not worn a Surplice for twenty years. To this day the Church has not recovered from the blight of Puritanism. (See LATHBURY'S HISTORY OF THE BOOK OF COMMON PRAYER.)

## I. The Puritans at the time of the Reformation.

A GREAT many joined in the Reformation, not to promote the glory of God, but to enrich themselves. Lands, Altar Cloths, Vestments, gold and silver Chalices, and other articles of Church furniture, which had been devoted to "superstitious uses"—for thus they spoke of things which their pious ancestors had given to the Church of God,—were taken without scruple, and rich Copes and Church plate served to ornament their banquet rooms. (COLLIER, ECCL. HIST., B. 4, P. 494. Vol. 5.)

Just so now, very bad and unprincipled men "join the church," to gain their own ends, thereby preventing thousands of good men from having anything to do with religion. We can have great respect for Luther or Calvin, and men of that stamp, though we may differ very widely from them, but miscreants who stole from and pillaged the Church, over which they were appointed guardians, we can but abhor.

## II. The Puritans under Edward VI.

SO rapacious were those who clamored for reformation, that Cranmer was forced to part with more than half the possessions of his See (STRYPE, MEM. OF CRANMER, B. 2, C. 29, P. 404-406. VOL. 1), and Ridley was obliged to give away in one day four of his best manors (STOWE, SURVEY OF LOND., P. 909, 910; STRYPE, ECCL. MEM., B. 1, C. 27, P. 339-341. VOL. 2). The Universities were called a "seat of Blockheads," and their revenues were so invaded, that in a short time there was a general complaint of the great dearth of learned men. (STRYPE, ECCL. MEM., B. 2, C. 8, P. 100; B. 1, C. 31, P. 404-409. VOL. 2, PT. 1; B. 2, C. 15, P. 29. VOL. 2, PT. 2; COLLIER, ECCL. HIST., B. 4, P. 238, 239, 490. VOL. 5; FROUDE, HIST. OF ENG., C. 27, AN. 1550, P. 270-272, 278. VOL. 5.) FAGIUS, EP. 22, TO WISBACH, GORHAM, GLEANINGS, &C., P. 78, complains of the seizure of Ecclesiastical property.

In the churches sometimes the knave of Clubs was hung up in place of the Sacrament, the legs and face of the Crucifix were cut and scratched, and other sacrilegious acts were committed, which only served to wound the feelings and excite the anger of those who, rightly or wrongly, reverenced such things. (CARDWELL, HIST. OF CONF., C. 2, N. 8, P. 103.) At this day, we can scarcely conceive to what extent ridicule for religion went. People went from one extreme to another. As early as Dec. 27, 1547, the King was obliged to issue a Proclamation against irreverent language towards the Sacrament (CRANMER, MISS. WRITINGS AND LETTERS, APPEND., N. 27, P. 505, 506). The Rubrics of the Prayer Book were not obeyed, and the surplice was not worn by many, and general lawlessness prevailed. It was the intention of the Puritans to make a much further reformation, had not the death of Edward prevented their plans from being fully carried out.

1549.] FRANCIS DRYANDER. "For I have seen a public edict proclaimed by royal authority, and printed, in which is not only confirmed the reformation of which I sent you an account, but it declares that some other matters, yet untouched, shall be reformed according to the tenor of the gospel." EP. 173, TO BULLINGER, DEC. 3, P. 353, 354. ORIG. LET. VOL. 1.

The King even threatened to effect a further reformation, in spite of the Bishops, by the exercise of his royal authority, if necessary, when Parliament met:

1551.] PETER MARTYR.

Verum hoc me parum recreat, quod mihi, D. Checus indicavit; si noluerint ipsi [episcopi] ait, efficere, ut quae mutanda sint mutentur, Rex per seipsum id faciet; et cum ad parliamentum ventum fuerit ipse suae Majestatis authoritatem interponet. Ep. AD BUCER. Cited by STRYPE, MEMORIALS OF CRANMER. APPEND. N. 61. P. 899. VOL. 2.

But what Mr. Cheke informed me pleases me not a little. If, he says, the Bishops refuse to make the necessary changes, the King will do it himself, and when the matter comes before Parliament, he will interpose the authority of his Majesty.

Circa 1566.] GEORGE WITHERS. "What he [Edward VI.] retained however was left so free, that no man who objected to them was compelled to observe them. But the king, who truly feared God, not being yet satisfied with these improvements, was about to put the last finish to this work, and appointed a day for the assembling of both houses of parliament. All were full of hope and expectation; but in the mean time our most excellent king was taken away by an untimely death." Ep. 62, TO THE PRINCE ELECTOR PALATINE, P. 159, 160. ZURICH LETTERS, SECOND SERIES.

## III. The Puritans under Queen Mary.

**D**URING the reign of Mary, many—the number is estimated at from 300 to 800—fled to Frankfort, Zurich, Geneva, &c. At Frankfort the exiles made considerable alteration in the Prayer Book, and gave in to French and German novelties. This was very displeasing to other English exiles, but by the advice of Calvin, this party, among whom were Knox and Foxe, continued to oppose the English Liturgy. When Dr. Cox came to Frankfort, finding it impossible to restore the Prayer Book of Edward while Knox and his party were in power, he accused the former of high treason. Knox was obliged to depart, and take refuge at Geneva, whither he was soon followed by others who were great admirers of Calvin. But the new party could not long agree among themselves, and their brawls became so notorious as to shame and grieve all good Englishmen, and cause the State of Frankfort to take notice of them. Finally, when they returned home upon the death of the Queen, they brought over with them their quarrelsome dispositions, which their descendants still retain. See a full account of this affair in

"A Brief discours of the troubles begonne at Franckford in Germany Anno Domini 1554. Abowte the Booke off common prayer and Ceremonies," &c., 1575, by WHITTINGHAM, an active participant in the affair; STRYPE, MEM. OF CRANMER, B. 3, C. 15, P. 509-513. VOL. 1.

## IV. The Puritans under Queen Elizabeth.

EVERY effort was made by the Puritans to induce Elizabeth to espouse their side, but she was more disposed towards the Church party. Yet as the Puritans were very noisy and energetic, and had powerful friends at Court, as well as holding high positions in the Church, she had to be very politic and cautious. She also had to keep on good terms with the Roman Catholics, a much more numerous body:

1562.] ROGER ASCHAM. "First of all, she dedicated her earliest endeavours to God, by nobly purifying the religion which she found miserably polluted; in the accomplishment of which object she exercised such moderation, that the papists themselves have no complaint to make of having been severely dealt with." EP. 30, TO STRUMIUS, P. 66. Z. L. 2D.

1. THE PURITANS WERE AS YET FEW IN NUMBER, AND MOSTLY CONFINED TO LONDON.

1559.] RICHARD COX, BISHOP OF ELY. "Meanwhile we, that little flock." EP. 11, TO WEIDNER, P. 27. Z. L.

1564-5.] MATTHEW PARKER, ABP. OF CANTERBURY. "He [the Bishop of London] saith, if he be so charged, he will out of hand see reformation in all London; and ye know there is the most disorder." EP. 175, TO CECIL, P. 233. PARKER CORRESPONDENCE.

1565.] ROBERT HORN, BISHOP OF WINCHESTER. "Our little flock." EP. 64, TO GUALTER, P. 142. Z. L.

1566.] THEODORE BEZA. "Those very few teachers of the pure gospel." EP. 53, TO BULLINGER, P. 130. IB. 2D.

2. THE PURITAN REFORMERS INDUCED THE CONTINENTAL REFORMERS TO WRITE TO THE QUEEN IN THE INTEREST OF FURTHER REFORM.

1560.] THOMAS SAMPSON. "P. S. If either yourself or masters Bernardine or Bullinger should think of writing to the queen's majesty, you are well aware that it must not seem as if you had been urged by any one to do so." EP. 27, TO P. MARTYR, P. 65. Z. L.

1569.] PETER MARTYR. "As to writing a letter to the queen upon this matter, you must understand that I am now so overwhelmed with business, that were I ever so willing, I should not have it in my power. . . . Besides this, I do not think that any letter of mine will have much weight. I have already written twice, publicly and privately, and have been unable to discover whether my letters were received." Ep. 20, to Sampson, p. 48. Ib. 2d.

1566.] THEODORE BEZA. "As to our own church, I would have you know that it is so hateful to that queen, that on this account she has never said a single word in acknowledgement of the gift of my Annotations." Ep. 53, to Bullinger, p. 131. Ib.

1566.] RODOLPH GUALTER. "It would be useless to write to the queen herself. . . . Nor indeed can we promise ourselves much from her, as she has never answered any of our letters." Ep. 57, to Beza, p. 145, Ib.

Circa 1566.] GEORGE WITHERS. "Wherefore if you possess any interest or influence with our most serene queen, we beg and intreat you to make use of it, in so godly a cause. . . . If you cannot, as we desire, obtain a more complete reformation of the whole church," &c. Ep. 62, to the Pr. Elect. Palat., p. 163. Ib.

ZANCHIUS, in 1571, wrote a Letter to Elizabeth to induce her to give up the Vestments. Append., p. 339-353. Ib.

3. THE PURITANS WERE ADVISED BY FOREIGNERS TO RETAIN THEIR OFFICES IN THE CHURCH, THOUGH THEY DID NOT BELIEVE IN IT, LEST THOSE WHO DID SHOULD GET THE PLACES VACATED BY THEM.

They seem to have adopted the motto afterwards attributed to the Jesuits,—"The end justifies the means."

1560.] PETER MARTYR. "In the first place, I exhort you, by reason of the great want of ministers in your country, not to withdraw yourself from the function offered you: for if you, who are as it were pillars, shall decline taking upon yourselves the performance of ecclesiastical offices, not only will the churches be destitute of pastors, but you will give place to wolves and antichrists. . . . You may therefore use those habits either in preaching, or in the administration of the Lord's supper, provided however you persist in speaking and teaching against the use of them." Ep. 17, to Sampson, p. 38, 39. Z. L. 2d. See Ep. 14, p. 32, 33. Ib.

1565.] ROBERT HORN, Bishop of Winchester. "It was enjoined us, (who had not then any authority either to make laws or repeal them,) either to wear caps and surplices, or to give place to others. We complied with this injunction, lest our enemies should take possession of the places deserted by ourselves." Ep. 64, to Gualter, p. 142. Z. L.

See also the Letter of Bullinger to Coverdale, in 1566, Ep. 54. Ib. 2d.

4. EVEN WHEN THE PURITAN PREACHERS WERE FORBIDDEN TO PREACH, THEY PREACHED JUST THE SAME.

1566.] JOHN ABEL. "These five preachers had been interdicted from preaching, but notwithstanding the prohibition, they again preached in their respective churches, in consequence of which our queen and privy council are much displeased." Ep. 49, TO BULLINGER, P. 119. Z. L. 2D.

5. THE PURITANS WERE REALLY UNITED ONLY AGAINST THE CHURCH, WHILST AMONG THEMSELVES, MOST BITTER QUARRELS RAGED, TO THE GREAT DECAY OF RELIGION.

The Bible alone was not enough to restrain them, because every one interpreted it to suit himself.

1560.] EDWIN SANDYS, BISHOP OF WORCESTER. "This pretence of unity is daily giving rise to many divisions." Ep. 31, TO P. MARTYR, P. 74. Z. L.

1562.] JOHN PARKHURST, BISHOP OF NORWICH. "For almost all are covetous, all love gifts. There is no truth, no liberality, no knowledge of God. Men have broken forth to curse and to lie, and murder, and steal, and commit adultery." Ep. 46, TO BULLINGER, P. 108. IB.

"It is the inconsistency of the lives of the English with the gospel, that alone displeases me. The gospel was never preached among us more sincerely or with greater zeal." Ep. 47, TO SIMLER, P. 109. IB.

1566.] THEODORE BEZA. "Some of them [the Puritans], I admit, are rather hard to please." Ep. 53, TO BULLINGER, P. 128. Z. L. 2D.

1566.] RODOLPH GUALTER. "Some of those brethren are, I grant, somewhat hard to please." Ep. 56, TO PARKHURST, P. 141. IB.

1571.] RICHARD COX, BISHOP OF ELY. "You candidly and truly confess, master Gualter, that there are some among those brethren who are a little morose; and you might add too, obstreperous, contentious, rending asunder the unity of a well-constituted church, and everywhere handing up and down among the people a form of divine worship concocted out of their own heads; that book, in the mean time, composed by godly fathers, and set forth by lawful authority, being altogether despised and trodden under foot. . . . Nothing moves them, neither the authority of the state, nor of our church, nor of her most serene majesty, nor of brotherly warning, nor of pious exhortation." Ep. 94, TO GUALTER, P. 237. Z. L.

1573.] They cannot endure the reading of the holy scriptures in the Church. . . . Satan is envious of our prosperity. It is not enough to have the papists our enemies, without stirring up men of their opinion who are labouring to bring about a revolution in the church." Ep. 107, TO GUALTER, P. 281. IB.

1574.] "It is indeed to be lamented that so many dissensions exist in the reformed churches, as that they seem to be destroying themselves with their own weapons." Ep. 120, p. 307. In.

1572.] HENRY BULLINGER.

Dolet autem nobis non mediocriter, quod in propaganda veritate, inque dilatandis Ecclesiae Christi pomaeriis, tot vobis se objiciunt obstacula atque remorae; ab illis quoque exortae, qui maxime Evangelici volunt videri. Verum per initia reformationis Ecclesiae nostrae, eadem nos exercuit molestia. Erant enim quibus nihil in reformando satis purum videbatur; unde et ab Ecclesia segregabunt, et conventicula peculiaria constituebant, quae mox sequebantur schismata et sectae variae. Quae jucundum spectaculum exhibebant hostibus Papisticis. Sed innotuit ipsorum hypocrasis et ataxia, suaque sponte diffluxere. LETTER TO HORN. Cited by STRYPE, LIFE OF PARKER, APPEND., B. 4, N. 67, P. 196. VOL. 3.

But it grieves us not a little, that in propagating the truth and in extending the bounds of Christ's Church, so many obstacles and hindrances are opposed to you, originating from those also, who would seem to be particularly Evangelical. But at the beginning of the reformation of our Church, the same annoyances troubled us. For there were some to whom nothing seemed pure enough in reforming; whence also they separated from the Church, and set up conventicles of their own. Soon schisms and various sects followed. These presented a pleasant spectacle to our enemies the Papists. But after awhile, their hypocrisy and insubordination became known, and of their own accord they ceased to exist.

1574.] "These things are doubtless owing to the wiles of Satan, who, when he perceives that he is unable to destroy the churches by threatenings, violence, and persecutions, from without, has recourse to other artifices, and meditates the overthrow of the church by domestic broils and the mutual attacks of brethren upon each other." EP. 98, TO SANDYS, P. 241. Z. L. 2D.

NEAL says of the later Puritans:

"Accordingly, they [the Brownists, afterwards called Congregationalists] were involved in frequent quarrels and divisions; but their chief crime was their uncharitableness, in unchurching the whole Christian world." HIST. OF THE PURITANS, C. 6, P. 150. VOL. 1.

I will supplement the testimony from Puritan writers, by that of CHARLES WESLEY:

"This is of the last importance to the cause we maintain, which suffered so much, as you well observe, by the dissensions of the first Reformers. Erasmus gave that as a reason why he would not turn Protestant,—the Protestants could not agree among themselves. Their divisions stopped the work of God then, and in the next age destroyed it." EP. 1, TO WHITEFIELD, P. 169. VOL. 2.

The state of religion in those times, in many places, was deplorable. Baptism was administered irregularly; the Holy Communion was celebrated only a few times in a year, and often in a most irreverent and slovenly manner, sometimes in vessels brought from neighboring houses, and the communicants took their seats at a table made by placing boards on tressels, which Roman Catholics called "oyster boards" in derision; the daily service was omitted; the feast and fast days of the Church were not observed; many of the Churches had no regular service, nor any regular clergyman; the Clergy, and even Bishops, did not scruple to alienate the estates of the Church to their own gain; some of the Clergy, even in large Parish Churches, refused to wear a Surplice, but officiated in their ordinary clothes; the old customs and habits of the people, deeply rooted, were harshly dealt with and ridiculed; the ceremonies of the Church were done away with; the beautiful paintings, the ornamental brasses, the stained-glass windows, the elegant embroideries, the Vestments, and the sacred vessels, were ruthlessly defaced, destroyed, or stolen away, so that the churches speedily fell into shameful neglect and ruin. ' Bare white-washed walls, and bald, plain services, instead of beauty and stately ceremonies, did not attract the multitude. There was no encouragement to repair the churches, or to restore the ornaments which had been destroyed, for what had once happened would probably happen again.

Rank Papist contended with rank Puritan—both parties terribly in earnest and equally sincere. The one would not attend Puritan services which had nothing to interest him, and which he regarded as heretical; the other looked upon everything the Church of Rome had with suspicion and hatred. So that between the two, moderate men, who clung to what was primitive and Catholic, whether it existed in the Church of Rome or not, were almost powerless. The only wonder is that religion itself survived such rude shocks. See "A description of the state, civil and ecclesiastical, of the County of Lancaster, by some of the Clergy of the Diocese of Chester," PAGE 1–48, CHETHAM SOC. PUBL. VOL. 96; BARNES, VISITATION, 1577–86, SURTEES SOC. PUBL. VOL. 22; FROUDE, HIST. OF ENG., c. 6, AN. 1561, P. 467-470. VOL. 7; c. 8, P. 93, 132, 133. VOL. 8., and c. 18, AN. 1567, NOTE, P. 506, 507. VOL. 9., for an account of the "Disorders in the Diocese of Chichester, Dec., 1569."

6. TO SUCH EXTREMES DID THESE MEN GO, THAT PURITANISM WAS AT LENGTH REGARDED AS GREAT AN EVIL TO THE CHURCH AND STATE AS POPERY.

Even those who once favored the Puritans, now, when too late, denounced them.

1573.] MATTHEW PARKER AND EDWIN SANDYS. "The church is sore assaulted; but not so much of open enemies, who can less hurt, as of pretended favourers and false brethren, who under colour of reformation seek the ruin and subversion both of learning and religion.

"In the platform set down by these new builders, we evidently see the spoliation of the patrimony of Christ, a popular state to be sought. The end will be ruin to religion, and confusion to our country." EP. 331, P. 434. P. C.

1573.] MATTHEW PARKER, ABP. OF CANTERBURY. "Both papists and precisians have one mark to shoot at, plain disobedience." EP. 333, TO LORD BURGHLEY, P. 437. IB.

1573.] JAMES PILKINGTON, BISHOP OF DURHAM. "That which heretofore lurked in dissimulation has now so openly discovered itself, that not only the habits, but our whole ecclesiastical polity, discipline, the revenues of the bishops, ceremonies or public forms of worship, liturgies, vocation of ministers, or the ministration of the sacraments,—all these things are now openly attacked from the press, and it is contended with the greatest bitterness, that they are not to be endured in the church of Christ." EP. 110, TO GUALTER, P. 287. Z. L.

1575.] RICHARD COX, BISHOP OF ELY. "They [the Puritans] complain that we treat them with severity, while in the meantime they attack us with the most bitter abuse, both in public and private; and everywhere calumniate us in their sermons and printed writings." EP. 126, TO GUALTER, P. 315. IB.

1576.] ROBERT HORN, BISHOP OF WINCHESTER. "But those contentious, or, if you choose, vainglorious, and certainly mischievous men, who by their ungovernable zeal for discord were retarding the free progress of the gospel among us, and drawing away the people, maddened by their follies, through every vain variety of opinion, or rather madness of error, into what they call *purity*, are now silenced, skulk about, and are become of no importance." EP. 129, TO GUALTER, P. 320. IB.

1579.] EDWIN SANDYS, ABP. OF YORK. "For although we are unable altogether to banish from the church, so as to prevent the appearance of a remarkable variety of names and opinions, those *new* men whom we call Puritans, who tread all authority under foot; or the *veteran* papists," &c. EP. 194, TO GUALTER, P. 332. IB.

1588.] A Letter was written about this time by Sir Francis Walsingham to Mons. Critoy, a French gentleman, wherein Puritanism is declared to be as great an evil to the State as Popery. (BURNET, HIST. OF THE REFORM., PT. 2, B. 3, P. 661-665. VOL. 2; COLLIER, ECCL. HIST., B. 7, P. 79-84. VOL. 7.) Their behaviour when the Spanish Armada was threatening England "lost them the friendship of the Earl of Leicester and Sir Francis Walsingham." IB. P. 79.

1591.] In 1591, the Queen told Sir Francis Knollys "that she was in as much danger from Puritans as Papists." STRYPE, LIFE OF WHITGIFT, B. 4, C. 5, P. 73. VOL. 2.

She had frequent occasion to rebuke Knollys for his Puritanism.

CARDWELL, speaking of Archbishop Parker's Articles of Visitation in 1567, says:

" Puritanism and not Popery was now the opponent to be dreaded." Doc. ANNAL., N. 68, P. 338. VOL. 1.

That the Puritans, as a body, were sincere, as are members of all religious bodies, especially at first, I do not for a moment doubt. What I object to, is that they willingly and knowingly took Orders in a Church which clearly prescribed certain things, and yet not only refused to comply with its regulations, but, like their descendants, called those who did, "Papists." To wear the Surplice for the sake of the office, and at the same time to preach against and ridicule it, does not seem to be honest, and, as they must have known, could only result in confusion and discord. Some refused promotion and offices in a Church to which they could not conscientiously conform. All honor to such.

1566.] JOHN ABEL. "Some persons however, are not satisfied with it, those namely, who have thought fit rather to give up the office of a preacher and minister rather than wear a surplice in the administration of the holy sacraments, or put on a clerical cap. So rigid are they in their opinion, that they have altogether given up their ecclesiastical vocation, and are therefore deposed from their ministry." EP. 49, TO BULLINGER, P. 118. Z. L. 2D.

Strange as it may seem, at the present day, Puritans outside of the Church are less bigoted and narrow minded, and more open to conviction, generally, than Puritans within the Church.

Some of the Bishops, and their friends in the State, at first connived at and abetted disloyalty to the Church, which they afterwards, when too late, strove to suppress by harsh measures. Then the State did wrong in trying to enforce outward uniformity; for it is impossible to persuade and convince a man against his will, and to oblige him to say that he believes what he does not believe, is not Christianity. It would have been better had they been allowed to go in the beginning and form new sects, as they afterwards did. If you cannot convince a man by argument and reason, you cannot by force; you may make a *hypocrite of him.

---

*This idea is well expressed by Mr. Adkinson, a Member of the House of Commons, in a speech against the Oath of Supremacy, made March 10, 1563:

"But, suppose the bulk of the people should not decline the oath, can you imagine all that would take it will change their opinion? No: menacing and terror may command the practice, but not the persuasion; violence may make a coward, but never a convert; and thus many a man will lay his hand upon the book when his heart keeps off at a distance. Besides, this frightening people out of their sentiment, and starving them into perjury, does but heighten their disaffection, and push them forward to revenge at the first opportunity." COLLIER, ECCL. HIST., B. 6, P. 354, 355. VOL. 6.

It is idle to expect that men who do not believe in a Liturgical form of worship, will be satisfied with mere verbal changes in the Prayers; that those who reject Episcopacy will be content with conditional ordination; or that those who refuse all Ministerial Habits from principle, will submit to the use of a Surplice as a compromise. Extermination, or free toleration, are the only alternatives. EDWARD HYDE, Earl of Clarendon, made this very sensible observation at the time that the Prayer Book of 1662 was being drawn up:

"It is an unhappy Policy, and always unhappily applied, to imagine that that *Classis* of Men can be recovered and reconciled by partial concessions, or granting less than They demand. And if all were granted, They would have more to ask, somewhat as a security for the Enjoyment of what is granted, that shall preserve their Power, and shake the whole Frame of the Government. Their Faction is their Religion: Nor are those Combinations ever entered into upon real and substantial Motives of Conscience how erroneous soever, but consist of many glutenous Materials, of Will, and Humor, and Folly, and Knavery, and Ambition, and Malice, which make Men cling inseperably together, till They have Satisfaction in all their Pretences, or till They are absolutely broken and subdued, which may always be more easily done than the other. And if some few, how signal soever (which often deceives us), are separated and divided from the Head upon reasonable Overtures, and secret Rewards which make the Overtures look the more reasonable; They are but so many single Men, and have no more Credit and Authority (whatever they may have had) with their Companions, than if they had never known them, rather less; being less mad than they were makes them thought less fit to be believed. And They, whom You think You have recovered, carry always a Chagrin about them, which makes them good for nothing, but for Instances to divert you from any more of that kind of Traffick." THE CONTINUATION OF THE LIFE, &c., P. 280, 281.

The Puritans were intolerant in their turn, as soon as they had an opportunity, not merely depriving Churchmen of their offices, but even barbarously defacing and breaking the very structures of the Churches, which their ancestors had erected with so much labor and cost. Even in America, to which they fled to enjoy freedom of conscience, they hung, burnt, drove off, and in other ways annoyed, contrary to their professed principles, all who differed from them.

## High Church and Low Church.

I VERY much dislike the terms High and Low Churchmen. A person is either a Churchman, or he is not one; there is really no such thing as High or Low. But since these words are in common use, it is frequently convenient to employ them. A true Churchman, or a High Churchman, as he is commonly called, believes "in the Holy Catholic Church," as he declares every time he recites the Creed, and accepts all that she teaches. A true Low Churchman believes all the Church teaches, but has a dislike for any ceremonies or ritual, and prefers a plain, bare service. He has been accustomed, perhaps, to such a mode of worship, and it may be, he has a natural dislike to what he regards as display. We do not blame such. People differ in their tastes.

But there is another, and a very common class, calling themselves Low Churchmen, who by their own acknowledgment are no Churchmen at all. They repeat the Creed like the others and solemnly declare before God that they "believe one Catholic and Apostolic Church," and "acknowledge one Baptism for the remission of sins." Yet as soon as they get out of Church, they scout the very idea of believing any such thing. Men of this class, and prominent leaders too, have told me that they " did not believe in one Church, that one denomination was as good as another, and that it did not make any difference what a man believed, that Baptism did not amount to anything;" and one went so far as to say that "Prayer was of no avail to move God," and wound up by saying that he "didn't know what he believed;" and yet that man Sunday after Sunday repeated the Creed, "I believe," &c. His excuse, when his inconsistency was pointed out, was "that some of the Clergy who are supposed to set an example in honesty, repeated the same Creed, and yet didn't believe it any more than he did." How men can tell Almighty God that they believe what they do not believe, passes my comprehension.

Why do those who hold that it makes no difference what a man believes, find so much fault with those who differ from them? If, as they say, "all men cannot think alike," why do they blame those who think otherwise than they do? They claim the largest liberty for themselves, but refuse the least even to others. Almost invariably those who make the greatest pretensions to liberality, are the most intolerant and fault-finding.

There are also spurious High Churchmen. They are not so narrow-minded as the preceding class, and nothing in the way of ceremonies troubles them—not Romanism itself. If they can not have the ritual they want in their own Church, they are continually saying that they "will go to the Roman Church," but the moment they lose their influence by reason of the course they adopt, they turn around and denounce what they have previously upheld. Self-interest, and not principle is their motive. These extreme men are always frightening timid people, and grieving true Churchmen by their intemperate remarks and actions.

I must say a word for the poor Ritualists. Not that I think that a Ritualist is necessarily a good man, for some of the most unprincipled persons I was ever acquainted with were professed Ritualists —hypocrisy being confined to no body of Christians, all being infected with it alike,—but it is of Ritualists as a class, and not as individuals, that I wish to speak.

Personally, I do not care for a very ornate service, but I am not such a "rigid Ritualist," as to find the least fault with those who prefer a more, or a less ornate service than I like myself. Not being narrow-minded, nor infallible, I do not require every one to think just as I do, but allow others the same liberty that I claim for myself. I look upon Rationalism, Sectarianism, and Romanism, as equally pernicious errors. I know that in defending this class of men, I do what is now unpopular, but I also know that at the judgment-day, it will not be asked whether my course has been popular or not, but whether to the best of my abilities, I have done what seemed to be right. We can find fault with many things in the Ritualistic movement, which are mainly due to energy and enthusiasm; but can we not find fault with many on the other side, whose energy is directed to the sole end of "stamping out Ritualism," but who do nothing whatever to replace it with something better? I have no patience with those professed Christians who never do a particle of work to reform the outcast, but sit in their comfortable homes and talk against the Ritualists and others who do; doing nothing themselves to "advance their dear Master's kingdom," and hindering those who are willing to work. Better to be in a Ritualistic Church than an inmate of a State Prison, and even a Ritualist is preferable to an immoral person, a profane swearer, a thief, or a drunkard. Of course, it is easier to talk than to work, but why do those who prefer to talk, find fault with those who prefer to work?

Surely, it is no more lawless to do things which are not indeed now sanctioned by express Rubric, but are commanded or allowed by old Rubrics, the practice of the Church, and were never forbidden; than it is to leave undone things plainly commanded by existing Rubrics?

The word Ritualist properly denotes a person well versed in the rites of the Church, but like the word regeneration, an entirely new meaning has been attached to it of late years. No one seems able to define what Ritualism is. It certainly is not Romish doctrine. The Universalists of this vicinity on Easter Sunday are accustomed to deck their House with flowers and illuminate it with candles in the day time; but no one accuses them of Ritualism. Once they placed a picture of the Madonna, which many did not know was but another name for the Virgin, over the pulpit; yet no one raised the cry of "Popery,"—on the contrary, every one was delighted. The same people who are very fond of Ritualism in the Lodge, find fault with it in a Church. Where is their consistency? A Ritualist may perhaps be defined as a person who endeavors, by every lawful means, to make the services of the Church attractive and interesting, by means of a more or less elaborate ceremonial, hearty choral services, great reverence for holy things, and by frequent services and celebrations of the Holy Eucharist, to build up his flock in the spiritual life. Some, it is true, go to extremes, but they are few in number, and if not persecuted, the evil will in time correct itself. But there are extremes on the other side as well, some even denying our Lord's Divinity, and the inspiration of the Scriptures, errors much greater than those held by the Ritualist, who only errs in having too much reverence, instead of too little. Be consistent and treat both sides alike. Some, I fear, cannot do this without condemning themselves.

Our Bishops in their Pastoral in 1874, rebuke both extremes:

"Our Clergy have large liberty; shall they abuse the gentleness of Christ and the patience of their Mother, by pressing their own fancies and self-conceits to the utmost verge of canonical endurance? Shall they usurp the functions of the body that commissions them, and seek to make that Church more Evangelical or more Catholic than her own formularies and Ritual affect to be?" DAILY CHURCHMAN, P. 251.

Every one acknowledges that, as a class, these men are the hardest workers in the Church. The Church has greatly increased in the number of communicants, since she has been "cursed by Ritualism." In 10 years, from 1860 to 1870, the population of the country increased 22 per cent., but in 9 years, from 1859 to 1868, our communicants increased 43 per cent. The growth of the Church in 5 years, from 1868 to 1873, has been 29 per cent. Bishop Ellicott, of Gloucester, an enemy of the Ritualists, recently declared that the efficiency of the Church of England was at least double what it was in 1864. The number of Clergy in 1801, in England, was 10,307; in 1841, 14,612; in 1871, 20,694.

Bishop Whipple, at the Church Congress in 1874, related that when in England some years since, he asked a Bishop who was far from being a Ritualist, how he permitted certain things done by these men. "The tears came into his eyes: Bishop," he replied, "those men are the only men that seem to have found out that those poor people have souls to be saved." He also related, how in the veriest slums of London, among the most abandoned creatures, he found a daughter of the richest nobleman in England doing the work of a Sister. I have seen just such scenes myself. When I went to

England, I was as much prejudiced against these men as any one of Puritan ancestry, and brought up as one, could be, but their self-denying devotion in giving up all—wealth, position in society, and life itself,—with nothing to reward them in this life, but the sneers and rebuffs of those whom they would benefit, led me to change my mind.

The question of Ritualism was settled for us in the General Convention of 1874. For some six months, men had been perfectly frantic upon this subject, and when the Convention assembled, petitions from various quarters poured in upon it. The following are some of the practices, which it was proposed to condemn:

1. The use of Incense. 2. A Crucifix in any part of the Church. 3. Carrying a Cross in procession in Church. 4. Use of Lights on or about the Holy Table except when necessary for light. 5. Elevation of the Elements in the Holy Communion, for adoration. 6. Mixing water with the wine as part of the Service. 7. Ablution of the vessels in the presence of the Congregation. 8. Bowings, crossings, &c., except as directed by Rubric or Canon. 9. Allowing persons not in Holy Orders, to assist at the Holy Communion. 10. Use of Wafer-Bread. 11. The practice of auricular Confession, and private absolution. 12. The use of any clerical Vestment, except the present Episcopal robes, a white Surplice, a black or white Stole, a black Cassock, a black Gown and Bands.

A Committee of thirteen wise and discreet men was chosen, to whom the whole matter was referred. When they came to investigate the subject prayerfully and impartially, they found that in the whole country, there was less than a dozen Ritualistic churches, strictly speaking, and these, with two exceptions, were insignificant. They also found that there was all over our land a growing æsthetic tendency, and that there had been a vast increase of reverence and devotion of late years in our Church, and they could not have the slightest desire to crush out this state of affairs. Finally, after sitting some five or six times before putting a word to paper, after carefully examining all those things which some desired to condemn, they made their Report. Dr. Fulton, in his introductory speech, remarked:

"You will observe that the Canon as it is before you in printed form is exceedingly careful to touch no ceremonial except that which belongs to the order of the celebration of the Holy Communion — none other. Processional hymns; recessional hymns; Sunday-school children's crosses; vestments of more or less beauty —these things are left entirely out. I trust the time has gone by when this Church can be pestered out of its dignity by proposed legislation on any such subjects as these. We have confined everything that we have proposed to this Convention to the single subject of the doctrine touching the Holy Communion, and here I rest our cause upon that subject." DAILY CHURCHMAN, P. 120.

Now out of the many practices objected against, they condemned just four things:

"*a.* The use of Incense. *b.* The placing, or carrying, or retaining a Crucifix in any part of the place of public worship. *c.* The elevation of the Elements in the Holy Communion in such a manner as to expose them to the view of the people as objects towards which adoration is to be made. *d.* Any act of adoration of or towards the elements in the Holy Communion, such as bowings, prostrations, genuflections, and all such like acts not authorized or allowed by the Rubrics of the Book of Common Prayer." DAILY CHURCHMAN, P. 136, 147.

The Canon passed the Lower House without much opposition. But the House of Bishops struck out the clause relating to Incense, because they could not condemn what God Himself had ordained; as also that relating to the Crucifix, which symbolizes our Lord's death. The Canon as passed by both Houses condemns;

"*a.* The elevation of the Elements in the Holy Communion in such manner as to expose them to the view of the people as objects towards which adoration is to be made; *b.* Any act of adoration of or towards the Elements in the Holy Communion, such as bowings, prostrations, or genuflections; and *c.* All other like acts, not authorized or allowed by the Rubrics of the Book of Common Prayer." DAILY CHURCHMAN, P. 208, 209.

The late Bishop Cummins, in a sermon, Oct. 18, 1874, said that "the Convention only condemned Eucharistic Adoration, which is not Ritualism at all."

Hereafter, if any one objects against things that the Church, in her highest representative body, has refused to condemn, he sets himself right against the Church—he condemns her and rejects her authority.

## Secession to Rome.

SOME people seem to be ever in a perfect panic for fear lest any one should go over to Rome. If you ask them who have gone, some will tell you that they don't know of any, while others can at most mention but two or three. Very few go from the Church to Rome willingly. They go there generally, for the sake of peace. For years they have been called "Romanists," "Jesuits," and similar names, by people who call themselves Christians, and told to "go to Rome, where they belong," and at length, they accept an invitation which they would have never thought of, had it not been constantly suggested to them. They are driven from their Church, and being unable to accept either Infidelity or Protestantism, they adopt what seems to them to be the next best course.

Ask these same persons how many, who claim to have been brought up in the Church, have gone over to all kinds of Dissent— Unitarianism, Universalism, and Spiritualism even, to say nothing of utter indifference and open infidelity—and they can enumerate hundreds. Where one goes to Rome, hundreds go to the other extreme. A well informed Churchman has nothing whatever to fear from a Romanist, because he knows that the History of the Church is wholly in his favor, while Rome's peculiar doctrines are of modern origin. When a person goes over to Rome from conviction, it is not because our Church is already so near that there is scarcely any difference between the two; but he denies that we are a part of the Catholic Church at all. He denies that we have a valid Ministry, or valid Sacraments. He claims that we reject a part of the Old Testament as apocryphal, refuse due honor and worship to the Virgin, reject the Pope's Infallibility, &c. An intelligent Romanist has often remarked to me: "It is very difficult to get you who *seem* so near to us, but we get plenty of Unitarians and others who are far removed from us." I always told him that we were already Catholic, and had no need to engraft upon the ancient Creeds Rome's modern doctrines. Another told me that a few Sundays since, while coming out of his little church in Boston, he counted more than a hundred converts from Unitarianism. No one of any account goes over to Rome from us now, and many who went years ago are returning. What is the loss to us of such nominal Churchmen, as a Marquis of Bute, or Ripon, compared with the loss of a Döllinger and the Old Catholics to Rome? When a person leaves us for Rome, he leaves us for good, and does not "hang around,"—to his credit be it said,—troubling us and stirring up strife, as do perverts to Sectarianism.

Archbishop PARKER, in 1572, thought that the increase of "Papists" was greatly owing to people being "exasperated by the disordered preachings and writings of some puritans." EP. 304, TO LORD BURGHLEY, P. 398. P. C.

RICHARD BAXTER, a Puritan, says:

"I am persuaded that all the arguments else in Bellarmine and all other books that ever were written, have not done so much to make papists in England as the multitude of sects among us." DEFENCE OF THE PRINCIPLES OF LOVE, PART 1, P. 52, 53. Cited by LATHBURY, HIST. OF THE BOOK OF COMMON PRAYER, C. 12, P. 264, 265.

## Fault-Finding.

"BLESSED are the peacemakers," says our Lord. (MATT. 5:9.) Yet there are some of the professed disciples of "the Prince of Peace," who are constantly stirring up strife about the most insignificant trifles. Nine-tenths of all our troubles are utterly puerile. No sooner is one imaginary trouble satisfactorily explained and done away with, than another arises. The same persons will one day say one thing, and the next day the very opposite. No dependence whatever can be placed upon them. Such persons are constantly making troubles in the Church. They talk about "peace in believing," but as they give none to others, their professions are looked upon as shams. Many go to church solely to watch the Minister, to see if they cannot discover something out of the way to talk about. Again, A. is jealous of B., and is afraid he has too much influence, and so the poor Church has to suffer. If such would spend one-tenth only of the time in smoothing over and explaining difficulties, that they more than waste in stirring up strife, we should live in peace. It is not the thing done, generally, that makes trouble, but the person who does it. I have known things to be done by those who are "truly Evangelical," which many High Churchmen would not dare to do. I have known the *Agnus Dei* sung at the Celebration, and Lights constantly burnt before the Altar, "when not necessary for light," in Churches called very Low. I have known those who did much for a Church, turn right round and do as much against it, when they thought that their influence was not what it should be. I know of a Parish that had in succession Low, Broad, and High Church Rectors, and yet the same persons supported or opposed the various Rectors, according as their views were in the ascendancy or not. In the Church, fault-finders have a great advantage. To denounce Ritualism is popular, but to parade one's private grudges before the public, is not so popular. Therefore, Ritualism is made the scape-goat when any one is dissatisfied. But as such persons seldom or never attend any services except those at which Ritual is used, and some never go to Church at all, and are always making trouble in matters which have no connection whatever with Ritual, their excuse amounts to nothing. We are constantly wondering at the ungrateful and rebellious dispositions of the Jews, but, perhaps, they only objected to the Ritualism which God imposed upon them, and were not so bad, after all. They crucified the Son of God but once, and that ignorantly, for our Saviour says from the Cross: "Father forgive them; for they know not what they do." (LUKE 23:34.) But now His professed followers knowingly "crucify to themselves the Son of

God afresh, and put Him to an open shame." (HEB. 6:6.) Who are the worst of the two, the ignorant Jews, or enlightened Christians!

If people do not understand certain things they ought to go to some competent person for information. Nine-tenths of all the stories circulating about a Parish are without any foundation whatever. No one thing has so utterly disgusted people with the whole subject of religion, as this interminable and senseless talk about *nothing. Nothing has so promoted the cause of Infidelity, or driven so many from Church, as these constant Church quarrels, which generally have their origin in jealousy. If Christians ever expect to convert the world, they must lay aside such things, and work in earnest. The inconsistency of Christians with their professions, is the only real and unanswerable argument against religion. It is impossible to persuade the "unconverted" that those whose sole mission here seems to be to stir up strife, ever really expect to go to a Heaven of quiet;—they would be out of their sphere there.

But you cannot please every one; human nature is the same now that it was eighteen hundred years ago. "For John the Baptist," says our Lord, "came neither eating bread nor drinking wine; and ye say, he hath a devil. The Son of man is come eating and drinking; and ye say, Behold a gluttonous man, and a wine-bibber, a friend of publicans and sinners!" (LUKE 7:33, 34.) Then, as now, people were bound to find fault about something.

## Persecution.

IT WILL not do now to put people to death for their religion, as the Romanists and Puritans did a few centuries ago, so we have to resort to the more polite method, though fully as effectual in the end, of slander and misrepresentation. In primitive times, as we learn from Christian writers, the bare fact of being a Christian was enough to condemn a man. "But," says a friend, "what evil has he done; whereas once he was a murderer, a robber, a drunkard, and an abuser of his family, now, since his conversion, he has become a sober, industrious and

---

*A person having written to Bishop Wordsworth, of Lincoln, finding fault because he turned to the East at the conclusion of his sermon, he replied:

"I was not aware of having done what you say was the case, and may I be allowed to add that it would not have been worth noticing if I had done it. However, life is not long enough for debates on such trivialities." Cited in the *Rock*, Nov. 23, 1877. P. 993.

model citizen." "That is all very well," the persecutor would reply, "but he is a Christian,—away with him to the lions." (See TERTULLIAN, APOL., c. 2, 3, 40, p. 56-115. T. I.) Just so now. A man may be a free-thinking Unitarian, a Universalist, or anything else, but he is perfectly respectable,—you never hear a word against him, or.against the rapid spread of utter indifference and infidelity in our land. On the other hand, let a man be only charged with being a High Churchman, or a Ritualist, and he is shunned and avoided by professed Evangelical Christians who would think themselves honored by the acquaintance of those to whom they refuse the title of Evangelical, though they are forced to acknowledge that the High Churchman works harder in the Church than they do; attends the week-day services ordered by the Prayer Book, as well as those for Sunday merely; is more liberal with his money; never makes trouble in the Church,—but that is nothing, he is "High Church," and that is enough. Ask them what they mean by that expression, and they cannot tell you; they only know that it must mean something dreadful. It is just like the ancient cry: "The Christians to the lions." Reverence is everywhere frowned upon, while irreverence is everywhere encouraged, even by professed Christians. The question now seems to be not how we shall worship Christ, but whether we shall worship Him at all.

Such persons should remember that very many have come into the Church solely from conviction. It was not because their friends attended there, or because it was fashionable and they would thereby better their condition, or because they merely preferred a Liturgical Service. It was because they took the Church at her word. After long study and investigation they were convinced that the Church was, as she professed in her Creeds and elsewhere, a Catholic Church, and that her practices and teachings were primitive. They never thought that they must consult the various opinions and whims of A, B, and C. In good faith they professed to take the Church, not the opinions of fallible men, and to believe in her. Then to have persons who, contrary to their professions, do not believe in their Church, and who are profoundly ignorant of its teachings and of their Prayer Book even, denounce them as "Papists" for merely believing as they profess, every time they recite the Creed, very much shakes their belief in the sincerity and honesty of Christians. They find, after all, that it is not the teachings of the Church that people care for, but their own notions, which they put above the Church.

Calling offensive names, and the use of ridicule, only shows that the person resorting to such means has no argument to offer, and injures his cause with thinking people. Christians make great objections when irreligious persons use the same tactics which many of them employ. Where is their consistency? By such a course you may, and you do, drive out all reverent feelings, and disgust many with the whole subject of religion. But, remember, you never convert any one, or make him a better man. It is a very dangerous thing to disturb one's faith, without giving him a better one at the same time. Far better is a man who erroneously worships God by praying to the Virgin, or to Idols even, if that will only make him a good citizen, than a man who, having no religious principles, is a curse to the community. Some, I know, think differently, and if they can only break up a person's religion, they are perfectly happy; they tear down but never build. God will judge which is right.

But earnest and faithful men must expect persecution. They must find consolation in our Lord's words:

"Blessed are ye, when men shall revile you, and persecute you, and shall say all manner of evil against you falsely, for My sake. Rejoice, and be exceeding glad: for great is your reward in heaven: for so persecuted they the prophets which were before you." MATT. 5:11, 12.

Good John Wesley, who, were he living to-day, would be stigmatized as a Ritualist, was in his time denounced as a "Papist" and a "Jesuit." Substitute Ritualist for Methodist, in the newspaper paragraphs of those times, and they read wonderfully like what we find in the papers now. Take the following from the *St. James' Chronicle*, afterwards published in the *Canterbury Journal*:

"The Popish party boast much of the increase of the Methodists [Ritualists], and talk of that sect with rapture; how far the Methodists [Ritualists], and Papists stand connected in principles I know not; but I believe it is beyond a doubt that they are in constant correspondence with each other." Cited by J. WESLEY, JOURNAL, DEC. 20, 1769, P. 332. VOL. 3.

No one now accuses the Methodists of being Papists. Have they changed, or are they too numerous and respectable now to be nicknamed?

In his JOURNAL, WESLEY thus speaks of his persecutions:

"Indeed the report now current in Bristol was, that I was a Papist, if not a Jesuit. Some added, that I was born and bred at Rome; which many cordially believed. . . . I have often inquired who are the authors of this report; and have generally found that they were either bigoted Dissenters, or (I speak without fear or favor) Ministers of our Church. . . . I can no otherwise think, than that either they spoke thus (to put the most favorable construction upon it) from gross ignorance; they knew not what Popery was; they knew not what doctrines those are which the Papists teach;

or they wilfully spoke what they knew to be false: probably 'thinking' thereby 'to do God service.' Now take this to yourselves whosoever ye are, high or low, Dissenters or Churchmen, Clergy or laity, who have advanced this shameless charge; and digest it how you can." AUG. 27, 1739, P. 206, 207. VOL. 1.

"Besides, it is but two or three nights since, as I was just setting out to come to the room, Miss Gr— met me, and said 'my dear friend, you sha'nt go; indeed you sha'nt; you don't know what you do. I assure you, Mr. W. is a Papist, and so am I; he converted me. You know I used to pray to Saints and to the Virgin Mary; it was Mr. W. taught me when I was in the bands. And I saw him rock the cradle on Christmas-eve: you know I scorn to tell a lie.'" SEPT. 24, 1742, P. 375. IB.

Just so now; many who would "scorn to tell a lie, you know," do not hesitate for a moment to call a person a "Papist," when they know very well, or could know if they were so disposed, that the person so called is no more a "Papist," than they are themselves. I have known Clergymen, who were notorious for breaking many of the Rubrics, to engage in this un-Christian business.

CHARLES WESLEY, in his JOURNAL, says:

"Every Sunday damnation is denounced against all who hear us Papists, as Jesuits, as seducers, as bringers in of the Pretender." SEPT. 28, 1739, P. 182. VOL. 1.

In the mobs raised by Protestants, and often by Protestants and Papists combined, the former were far more violent than the latter.

Says JOHN WESLEY in his JOURNAL:

"I preached on the floor of the late house, (which the good Protestant mob had just pulled down,) to the largest and one of the quietest congregations I ever remember to have seen there." MAY 29, 1745, P. 466. VOL. 1.

"Nor is it any wonder that those who are born Papists generally live and die such, when the Protestants can find no better ways to convert them than Penal Laws and Acts of Parliament." AUG. 15, 1747, P. 67. VOL. 2.

"O what a harvest might be in Ireland, did not the poor Protestants hate Christianity worse than either Popery or Heathenism!" MAY 13, 1750, P. 178. IB.

"I preached in the evening at Ahaskra, where the bulk of the congregation were Papists. Yet the decency of their behaviour was such as might have made many Protestants ashamed." JUNE 6, 1760, P. 5. VOL. 3.

I take the following from the JOURNAL of CHARLES WESLEY:

"The Popish mob, encouraged and assisted by the Protestant. ... A mixed rabble of Papists and Protestants broke open our room," &c. SEPT. 9, 1747, P. 457. VOL. 1.

"A mob of Papists and Protestants assaulted the house." SEPT. 17, 1747, P. 459. IB.

"So far beyond the Papists are these *moderate men* [Protestants] advanced in persecution." SEPT. 17, 1748, P. 34. VOL. 2.

John Wesley lived and died a true member of the Church of England. To such as are not aware that his views are identical, in the main, with those now held by High Churchmen, I would recommend the perusal of a book entitled: JOHN WESLEY IN COMPANY WITH HIGH CHURCHMEN. LONDON, 1872.

Simeon, the leader of the great Evangelical movement half a century ago, often had the Church doors closed against him, and was most intensely hated by the indolent and worldly Churchmen of his day. John Newman, and others, were actually driven out of the Church of England by persecution.

There is no reason why people of different views should not live together in peace. In Foreign Missions, all sects keep out of sight, as much as possible, their differences and live in peace, in order to present to the Heathen the best side of Christianity. If, under certain circumstances, Christians can live in peace, would it not be better to do so always? Because there are no Heathen here to fear or convert, Christians need not tear each other in pieces for want of something to do. We should never speak unkindly of others, or impugn their motives, or call them hard names, when they differ from us. Let us rather adopt the motto commonly attributed to *St. Augustine, that great Doctor of the Church: "In essentials unity; in non-essentials liberty; and in all things charity." Such was the charity of this holy man, that he never allowed foolish talking to the disparagement of others, in their absence; and so strict was he in the observance of this rule, which he had caused to be written out on his table, that upon a certain occasion when it was infringed upon by a party of Bishops, his intimate friends, he rose up and reminding them of the rule before them, firmly told them that it must be obeyed, or he must leave the room. (POSSIDIUS, VIT. AUG., C. 22, COL. 52. PAT. LAT. T. 32.)

> "That it may please Thee to forgive our enemies, persecutors, and slanderers, and to turn their hearts; We beseech Thee to hear us, good Lord."

---

*I have never been able to find these words in the works of St. Augustine. BAXTER cites the following sentence from RUPERTUS MELDENIUS, a German Theologian of the 17th century, and perhaps he is the author of this famous saying:

"And with *R. Meldenius Parœn. f. F. 2. Verbo dicam: si nos servaremus in necessariis Unitatem, in non necessariis Libertatem, in utrisque Charitatem; optimo certe loco essent res nostrae.*" THE SAINTS EVERLASTING REST, PT. 3, C. 14, SECT. 10, P. 560.

See M'CLINTOCK AND STRONG'S CYCLOPEDIA, ART. MELDENIUS.

THE Preface to our Prayer Book declares:

"That this Church is far from intending to depart from the Church of England in any essential point of doctrine, discipline, or worship; or further than local circumstances require."

In 1814, the House of Bishops declared:

"But that when the severance alluded to took place, and ever since, this Church conceives of herself, as professing and acting on the principles of the Church of England, is evident from the organization of our Convention," &c. JOURNAL OF THE GENERAL CONVENTION, p. 431. VOL. 1.

The House of Deputies concurred in this declaration:

"A message was received from the House of Bishops, communicating a declaration, proposed to be made by this Convention, of the identity of the Protestant Episcopal Church, in the United States of America, with the body heretofore known by the name of the Church of England, . . . which declaration was concurred in and returned to the House of Bishops." IB. P. 409. IB.

Therefore, where there is no express legislation to the contrary, and local circumstances do not interfere, we must appeal to the Laws and Canons of the Church of England for guidance.

I propose to speak here only of Rites pertaining to the Holy Communion; that being the only Act of worship instituted and enjoined by Christ Himself for His Church for all time.

It has been customary to use three distinct Offices,—Morning Prayer, the Litany, and the Communion Office,—as one Service. They can be used separately, or independent of each other. In the General Convention of 1874, this Resolution was passed, the House of Bishops concurring:

"Resolved (the House of Bishops concurring), That it is the sense of this Convention that nothing in the present Order of Common Prayer prohibits the separation, when desirable, of the Morning Prayer, the Litany, and the Order for the Administration of the Lord's Supper, into distinct services, which may be used independently of each other, and either of them without the others. Provided, that, when used together, they be used in the same order as that in which they have commonly been used and in which they stand in the Book of Common Prayer." DAILY CHURCHMAN, p. 229, 234.

# E.
# The Vestments.

INASMUCH as there are no directions whatever in our Prayer Book, as to what Vestments the Clergy shall wear in their ministrations, we must, therefore, refer to the Rubrics of the Church of England for information.

## E. Prayer Book and Rubrics of 1549.

THE Reformers knowing well what Romanism was, did not intend to make a new religion, but only to amend the old, and always professed to refer to the primitive and Catholic Church for guidance.

A Committee was appointed in 1548, and these "by the aid of the Holy Ghost" (see Proclamation of Edward VI., 2 & 3 EDW. VI., c. 1, p. 287. STATUTES AT LARGE. VOL. 5), drew up a "Godly order" of worship. The reformed Book was laid before Parliament, Dec. 9, 1548, passed the House of Lords the 15th, the House of Commons the 21st of the following January, and came into general use the following Whitsun-Day, June 9, 1549. The first edition was published by Whitechurch, March 7, 1548-9.

Yet it is very probable that this Book was never used over a large part of England. There was great diversity in celebrating Service. Some used the new Book, some used it in part, while others used the old Books. Neither this Book, nor that of 1552, were used in the Diocese of Durham, and probably not in the Northern Counties; and as to the Diocese of London even, we are told in a Letter by the King and his Council to Bishop Bonner, July 23, 1549, that:

"Our said book so much travailed for, and also sincerely set forth (as is aforesaid) remaineth in many places of this our realm either not known at all, or not used, or at least, if it be used, very seldom." CARDWELL, DOC. ANNAL., N. 14, P. 78. VOL. 1.

The same Letter was sent to Thirleby, Bishop of Westminster, and probably to all the Bishops. (STRYPE, ECCL. MEM., B. 1, C. 25, P. 329-331. VOL. 2, PT. 1.)

CRANMER, writing against Gardiner, Bishop of Winchester, in 1551, says of the Book of 1549:

"I in no point improve that godly book, nor vary from it. But yet glad am I to hear that the said book liketh you so well, as no man can mislike it, that hath any godliness in him joined with knowledge." AN AUNSWER UNTO A CRAFTIE AND SOPHISTICAL CAVILLATION, &c., B. 3, p. 56. WRITINGS AND DISPUTATIONS.

Upon the whole, the Book of 1549 gave satisfaction to all except the extremes on both sides, to whom it was either too much, or too little reformed. DRYANDER, a Calvinist, says of this Book—though he objected to some "trifling puerilities" which he hoped would shortly be amended:—

"A book has now been published, a month or two back, which the English churches received with the greatest satisfaction." EP. 171, TO BULLINGER, P. 350, 351. ORIG. LET. VOL. 1. See EP. 170.

In the first Book of Edward VI., put forth in 1549, we find these Rubrics. The word Vestment is used for Chasuble, Stole, and the other appurtenances.

"Upon the day, and at the time appointed for the ministration of the holy Communion, the Priest that shall execute the holy ministry, shall put upon him the vesture appointed for that ministration, that is to say: a white Albe plain, with a vestment or Cope. And where there be many Priests or Deacons, there so many shall be ready to help the Priest, in the ministration, as shall be requisite: And shall have upon them likewise the vestures appointed for their ministry, that is to say, Albes with tunicles." PAGE 76.

"Upon Wednesdays and Fridays, the English Liturgy shall be said or sung in all places, &c. . . . And though there be none to communicate with the Priest, yet these days (after the Litany ended) the Priest shall put upon him a plain Albe or surplice, with a cope, and say all things at the Altar (appointed to be said at the celebration of the Lord's supper,) until after the offertory." PAGE 97.

"In the saying or singing of Matins and Evensong, Baptizing and Burying, the minister, in parish churches and chapels annexed to the same, shall use a Surplice."

"And whensoever the Bishop shall celebrate the holy communion in church, or execute any other public ministration, he shall have upon him, besides his rochette, a Surplice or albe, and a cope or vestment, and also his pastoral staff in his hand, or else borne or holden by his Chaplain." PAGE 157.

In THE FORME AND MANER OF MAKYNG AND CONSECRATYNG ARCHEBISHOPPES, BISHOPPES, PRIESTES AND DEACONS, published in 1549, Tunicles, Surplices, Copes, and Pastoral Staves, are required.

The Rubrics in the Form for the Ordering of Deacons are:

"After the exhortation ended, the Archdeacon, or his deputy, shall present such as come to be admitted, to the Bishop; every one of them, that are presented having upon him a plain Albe."

"Then one of them, appointed by the Bishop, putting on a tunicle, shall read the Gospel of that day." PAGE 162, 170.

The Rubric in the Form for the Ordering of Priests is:

"And then the Archdeacon shall present unto the Bishop all them that shall receive the order of Priesthood that day, every one of them having upon him a plain Albe." PAGE 174.

The Rubric in the Form for the Consecration of Bishops is:

"After the Gospel and Credo ended, first the elected Bishop, having upon him a surplice and a cope, shall be presented by two Bishops (being also in surplices and copes, and having their pastoral staves in their hands) unto the Archbishop of the Province, or some other Bishop appointed by his commission." PAGE 182.

## II. Prayer Book and Rubric of 1552.

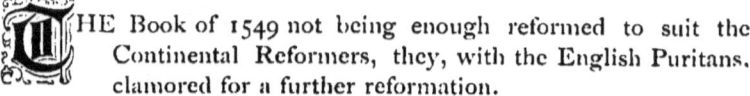HE Book of 1549 not being enough reformed to suit the Continental Reformers, they, with the English Puritans, clamored for a further reformation.

HOOPER, writing to Bullinger, a Calvinist, in 1550, says of that Book:

"I am so much offended with that book, and that not without abundant reason, that if it be not corrected, I neither can nor will communicate with the church in the administration of the [Lord's] supper." EP. 38, P. 79. ORIG. LET. VOL. 1.

See also the Letters from the following foreign Reformers to Bullinger, all hoping and laboring for a further reformation: HADDON, EP. 130, P. 281, 282; DRYANDER, EP. 170, 173, PP. 350, 353, 354. ORIG. LET. VOL. 1; PETER MARTYR, EP. 227, 230, PP. 480, 486, 487, 488; MICRONIUS, EP. 267, P. 580; BURCHER, EP. 312, 318, PP. 665, 674. IB. VOL. 2.

Martin Bucer and Peter Martyr, (who was so loyal to the Church, that all the while he was Canon of Christ Church, Oxford, he refused to wear a Surplice, though required by law to do so),—meddlesome foreigners, for whom a *Latin translation of the Prayer Book was made, as they did not understand English, were the leading spirits in this movement; assisted by Calvin, and John à Lasco, a Polish refugee, who alone of foreigners of any note, upheld Hooper in his refusal to wear the Vestments, and who afterwards set up a conventicle in London. JOHN BURCHER, a rigid

---

* STRYPE says that the translation was made by Sir John Cheke. LIFE OF CHEKE, C. 3. SECT. 6, P. 54. Others think they made use of the translation of Aless.

Calvinist, thus expresses his opinion of Bucer in his Letters to Bullinger:

"In case of his [Bucer's] death, England will be happy, and more favoured than all other countries, in having been delivered in the same year from two men of most pernicious talent, namely, Paul [Fagins] and Bucer. From these sources new sects are daily arising among us, and religion is always assuming a new appearance. I really think that our men of learning delight in novelty and change.... What do you think will take place a hundred years hence, if you are now blundering in open day-light?" EP. 311, AN, 1550, P. 662, 663. ORIG. LET. VOL. 2.

"Bucer is more than licentious on the subject of marriage. I heard him once disputing at table upon this question, when he asserted that a divorce should be allowed for any reason, however trifling; so that he is considered, not without cause, by our bishop of Winchester as the author of the book published in defence of the Landgrave. I am ignorant as to what the hireling Bucer, who fled from this church before the wolf came in sight, is plotting in England. He is an invalid, and (as report says) is either becoming childish, or is almost in his dotage, which is the usual result of a wandering and inconstant mind." EP. 312. AN. 1550, P. 665, 666. IB.

Philip, Landgrave of Hesse, married in 1540, though he already had a wife and a large family still living; and this he did with the sanction of Luther, Melancthon, and Bucer.

"The death of Bucer affords England the greatest possible opportunity of concord. The leading men of England are desirous of a successor not less learned than himself, to supply his place. For my own part I desire one who may be more sincere and steady." EP. 321, AN. 1551, P. 678. IB.

The constant disputes among learned men led to similar unseemly quarrels among the people. BURCHER says:

"Fightings have frequently taken place among the common people, on account of their diversity of opinion, even during the sermons." EP. 298, P. 643. IB.

The result of these constant quarrels and love of novelty, led to what we might expect,—great decline in religion:

"Yet in the mean time those very persons who wish to be, so to speak, most evangelical, imitate carnal licentiousness, under the pretext of religion and liberty. Every kind of vice, alas! is rife among them, and especially that of adultery and fornication, which, he tells me, they do not consider a sin. Unless this evil be corrected, we are undone." BURCHER, EP. 300, P. 647. IB.

THOMAS BECON, one of Abp. Cranmer's Chaplains, in the PREFACE to his JEWEL OF JOY, makes a similar complaint:

"What a number of false Christians live there at this present day, unto the exceeding dishonour of the christian profession, which 'with their mouth confess that they know God, but with their deeds they utterly deny him, and are abominable, disobedient to the word of God, and utterly estranged from all good works!' What a swarm of gross gospellers have we also among us, which can prattle of the gospel very finely, talk much of the justification of faith, crack very stoutly of the free remission of all their sins by Christ's blood, avance themselves to be of the number of those which are predestinate unto eternal glory, &c.; but how far doth their life differ from all true Christianity! They are puffed up with all kind of pride: they swell with all kind of envy, malice, hatred and enmity against their neighbor: they bren with unquenchable lusts of carnal concupiscence: they wallow and tumble in all kind of beastly pleasures: their greedy covetous affects are insatiable, the enlarging of their lordships, the increasing of their substance, the scraping together of their worldly possessions infinite and knoweth no end. In fine, all their endeavours tend unto this end, to shew themselves very ethnicks, and utterly estranged from God in their conversation, although in words they otherwise pretend. As for their alms-deeds, their praying, their watching, their fasting, and such other godly exercises of the Spirit, they are utterly banished from these rude and gross gospellers. All their religion consisteth in words and disputations; in christian acts and godly deeds nothing at all." WORKS, P. 416, 417.

LATIMER says:

"The English are infamous for whoredom beyond any other part of the world. Besides, they glory in their shame, and make a diversion of being wicked." SERMON cited by COLLIER, ECCL. HIST., B. 4, P. 383. VOL. 5.

See also BURNET, HIST. OF THE REF., PT. 3. B. 4, P. 378-380. VOL. 3; FROUDE, HIST. OF ENG., C. 27. P. 323-324. VOL. 5.

PETER MARTYR, in 1550, enumerates among the hindrances to the progress of the Gospel:

"the gross vices of those who profess the gospel." EP. 228, TO BULLINGER, P. 482. ORIG. LET. VOL. 2.

Purity in ceremonies was what they aimed at, but purity of life was made of no account.

As early as 1537, at the very dawn of the Reformation, Archbishop CRANMER had been forced to say:

"We should easily convert even the Turks to the obedience of our gospel, if only we would agree among ourselves, and unite in some holy confedracy. But if we go on in this way to 'bite and devour each other,' there will be reason to fear, lest (what I abhor the mention of), according to the warning of the apostle, we 'be consumed one of another.'" EP. 7, TO VIDIAN, P. 14. ORIG. LET. VOL. 1.

Remember, that these pictures of the men who clamored for a further and "purer" reformation, are drawn, not by their enemies, but by their friends, who looked upon such a state of affairs with fear and dismay, surely expecting that a change would follow, and this happened shortly after, when "Popery" was restored under Queen Mary. This event was looked upon by many as a judgment from God, as a punishment for the wickedness of the times. Why should men who regarded themselves as "predestinate unto eternal glory" submit longer to the restraints of the Church? Why should they not pillage the Goods of the Church and convert them to their own use? Again, why should we wonder at men who only carried out their belief logically and consistently, if they let their religion "consist in words,"—like many Christians at the present day,—and not in " Christian acts and Godly deeds?" But we may well wonder that such a horrid religion could be embraced by any sane man.

The King, a mere boy, and wholly under Puritan control, was written to by the Continental reformers, flattered in every way, called "a second Josiah," (see CRANMER'S SPEECH at his Coronation, P. 127. MISS. WRITINGS), and urged by every means to make the English Church like the Calvinistic. Lutheranism was regarded as being about as bad as Popery. CALVIN thus wrote to the King:

1551.] "For with respect to the general reformation, it is not so well established, as not to make it desirable to carry it still farther." EP. 336, P. 708. ORIG. LET. VOL. 2.

1552.] "As far as I am concerned, if I can be of any service, I shall not shrink from crossing ten seas, if need be, for that object. If the rendering a helping hand to the kingdom of England were the only point at issue, that of itself would be a sufficient motive to me." EP. 337, TO CRANMER, P. 713. IB.

The Book of 1552, sometimes called the "Foreigners' Book," was sanctioned by the Act of Uniformity, April 6, 1552, but was first used by Ridley on All Saints Day, Nov. 1, the same year, at St. Paul's, London.

There is no proof that the new Book, which was of foreign origin, was ever submitted to Convocation; and we can only judge from the Letters of Dryander, Peter Martyr, and Withers, cited on pages 5, 6, and that of Micronius, (EP. 267, AN. 1552, P. 580. ORIG. LET. VOL. 2), that the reforms contemplated, had not yet been completed. Edward VI. died July 6, 1553, so that this Book was in actual use about eight months.

It was not because the Book of 1549 contained anything erroneous, that it was superseded; for in the Preface to, or rather *apology for, the Book of 1552, we read thus:

---

*In fact, it is acknowledged that there was no worthy cause for a revision, but it was to satisfy the "curiosity"—or meddlesomeness—of some, and to gratify and keep quiet "mistakers"—that is, ignorant people—that these changes, which after all did not satisfy them, were made.

"Where there hath been a very Godly order set forth by authority of Parliament, for common prayer and administration of the Sacraments, to be used in the mother tongue within this Church of England, agreeable to the word of God, and the primitive Church, very comfortable to all good people, desiring to live in Christian conversation, and most profitable to the state of this realm;" &c.

"And because there hath arisen in the use and exercise of the foresaid common service in the Church heretofore set forth, diverse doubts for the fashion and manner of the ministration of the same, rather by the curiosity of the minister and mistakers, than of any other worthy cause: therefore," &c. PAGE 213, 214.

Moreover, in the Proclamation of Edward VI., just cited, the Book of 1549 is said to have been composed: "by the aid of the Holy Ghost,"—perhaps in allusion to the fact that it came into use on Whitsun-Day.

At the Disputation at Oxford in the year 1554, in Latimer's reply to Weston, speaking of the Communion Offices of the Books of 1549 and 1552, the following colloquy occurs:

"*Latimer:*—'I find no great diversity in them.'"
"*Prolocutor:*—'Then the first was naught, belike?'"
"*Latimer:*—'I do not remember wherein they differ.'"
DISPUT. HABIT. OXONIAE, P. 483. WORKS OF LATIMER. VOL. 2.

It was hoped that by some change and concession the Puritans would be satisfied and quieted. This hope was vain, as the event proved; for, as is always the case, the more concessions were made to these pestilent men, so much the more they clamored for changes, and never would have been satisfied, till they had totally overthrown the ancient religion, had not Elizabeth, in her reign, firmly determined to yield no more to them.

By the Rubric of this Book, the Albe, Vestment, and Cope, were forbidden, and the Surplice and Rochet alone allowed. No mention whatever is made of the Black Gown:

"And here it is to be noted, that the Minister at the time of the communion, and at all other times of his ministration, shall use neither Albe, Vestment, nor Cope; but being Archbishop, or Bishop, he shall have and wear a rochet: and being a priest or Deacon, he shall have and wear a Surplice only." PAGE 217.

Very little alteration was made in the Ordinal except that the use of the Cope, Albe and Tunicle is not required, nor is there any mention of any garment whatever, the above Rubric, probably, being thought to be sufficient.

CRANMER in a Letter to the Council, Oct. 7, 1552, in reply to a Royal mandate to peruse and report on the new Prayer Book, says:

"I know your Lordship's wisdom to be such that I trust ye will not be moved with these glorious and unquiet spirits which can like nothing but that is after their own fancy; and cease not to make trouble when things be most quiet and in good order. If such men should be heard, although the Book were made every year anew, yet it should not lack faults in their opinion." STATE PAPERS, DOMESTIC. EDW. VI., xv., 15. Cited by MACCOLL, LAWLESSNESS, &c., LET. 1, P. 28; BLUNT, ANNOTATED BOOK OF COMMON PRAYER, P. XXXI, XXXII.

The new Prayer Book had not yet come into actual legal use, before these "unquiet spirits" again began to tamper with it. The word "peruse" meant not only to correct printer's errors, but also to make changes and alterations, as is evident from the language used. This was in accordance with the plans of the foreign Reformers, whose intention was to gradually make the Church of England in doctrine and ceremonies like that of Calvin. Thus PETER MARTYR, in writing to Bullinger, Jan. 28, 1551, says:

"In fact we all of us agree that this use of ecclesiastical vestments should be abolished, though we do not all of us allege the same reasons. And though we may not obtain all we wish, I am nevertheless easily led to believe that we shall obtain greater simplicity than has hitherto been allowed. All things cannot be done in a moment, and there must be labour and time for this misshapen embryo to attain its proper symmetry and shape." EP. 230, P. 488. ORIG. LET. VOL. 2.

The death of King Edward, and the accession of Queen Mary to the throne, providentially put an end to this state of things for a time. Queen Elizabeth had a will of her own, and detested Calvinism. But, at the beginning of her reign, as she afterwards acknowledged, she "temporised," and allowed it to get so deeply rooted that in less than a century this "misshapen embryo" was able to overthrow both Church and State.

### III. Prayer Book and Rubric of 1559.

QUEEN Mary succeeded to Edward VI., and abolished the new services. Under Elizabeth, in 1559, a new edition was put forth. The Act authorising the Book was passed April 28, 1559. It was first used in the Queen's chapel, Sunday, May 12, and the following Wednesday, May 15, began to be used in St. Paul's, London, though by the Act of Uniformity it was not required to be used till the Feast of the Nativity of St. John Baptist, June 24.

The Rubric of 1552 was not restored, but deliberately passed over, and such Vestments and *Ornaments adopted as were in use in 1549, the second year of Edward VI., which are enumerated in the Rubric cited above:

"And here it is to be noted, that the minister at the time of the communion, and at all other times in his ministration, shall use such ornaments in the church as were in use by authority of Parliament in the second year of king Edward VI., according to the act of parliament set in the beginning of this book." PAGE 53.

The Act for Uniformity, according to the Act of Parliament, prefixed to this Book, says:

"Provided always and be it enacted, that such ornaments of the Church, and of the ministers thereof, shall be retained and be in use as was in this Church of England, by authority of Parliament, in the second year of the reign of King Edward the VI., until other order shall be therein taken by the authority of the Queen's Majesty, with the advice of her Commissioners appointed and authorized under the great seal of England, for causes ecclesiastical, or the Metropolitan of this realm. And also that if there shall happen any contempt or irreverence to be used in the ceremonies or rites of the Church, by the misusing of the orders appointed in this book: The Queen's Majesty may by like advice of the said commissioners, or Metropolitan, ordain and publish such further ceremonies or rites as may be most for the advancement of God's glory, the edifying of his Church, and the due reverence of Christ's holy mysteries and Sacraments." PAGE 32.

CARDWELL speaks as follows of the Rubric of 1559:

"But the rubric of 1559, that restored the ornaments and vestments of the second year of King Edward, was extremely galling to the exiles, and would probably have prevented the greater number of them from becoming ministers of the Church, had not the act of uniformity furnished them with a plea for complying. It had been enacted that the queen, with the advice of her commissioners or the metropolitan, might make such changes in the rubrics as might afterwards be found requisite. The reformers therefore were not without some reason for hoping that their brethren who might be advanced to high stations in the Church would retain their present spirit of moderation, and exercise a salutary influence on the future proceedings of the court. But the clauses in question, however available for such purposes, were probably introduced with very different designs. It appears that they were added to the bill at the express direction of the queen, and were intended to assist her in carrying forward the high views of doctrine and authority which she was known to entertain." HIST. OF CONF., c. 1, p. 36.

---

*The meaning of the word "ornaments" is equipment or furniture. It is the Latin word *ornamentum*. The second year of King Edward VI. ended Jan. 27, 1549.

This is the view which Dr. SANDYS, soon afterwards made Bishop of Worcester, a Puritan, took of the Rubric:

"The last book of service is gone through with a proviso to retain the ornaments which were used in the first and second year of King Edward, until it please the Queen to take other order for them. Our gloss upon this text is, that we shall not be forced to use them, but that others in the meantime shall not convey them away, but that they may remain for the Queen." EP. 49, APR. 30, 1559, TO PARKER, P. 65. P. C.

STRYPE remarks upon this gloss:

"But this must be looked upon as the conjecture of a private man." ANNALS, C. 4, P. 122. VOL. 1, PT. 1.

As a matter of fact, Sandys was about right.

The Ordinal of 1552 was adopted with a little variation in regard to the form of the oath.

Had the Queen designed to do away with the Vestments, she would have re-enacted the Rubric of 1552, and abolished the use of them in own Chapel. By the testimony of the Puritans, cited in SECTION 2, (1), the vast body of the Clergy were "Papists," and they would not have objected to the Vestments. Though the Puritans of those times were frequently brought to account for refusing to wear the Surplice, I have nowhere read of similar proceedings being taken against those who complied with the Rubric.

1. IT WAS WELL UNDERSTOOD THAT THE QUEEN HERSELF WAS IN FAVOR OF HIGH RITUAL, AND NOT INCLINED TO PURITANISM, WHICH SHE DETESTED.

How the Services were conducted in her own Chapel may be seen by referring to Section xib, (iii). The Puritans knew that by the Act of Uniformity the Queen retained the power of adding further ceremonies or rites, and feared lest she should exercise it. The Queen expressly claimed this right in 1560-1:

"Letting you to understand, that where it is provided by act of parliament, holden in the first year of our reign, that whensoever we shall see cause to take further order in any rite or ceremony in the Book of Common Prayer, and our pleasure known therein, either to our commissioners for causes ecclesiastical, or to the metropolitan, that then eftsoons consideration should be had therein." EP. 94, TO PARKER, P. 132. P. C.

1570-1.] MATTHEW PARKER, ARCHBISHOP OF CANTERBURY. "Her Highness talked with me once or twice in that point, and signified that there was one proviso in the act of uniformity of Common Prayer, that by law is granted unto her, that if there be any contempt or irreverence used in the ceremonies or rites of the Church by the misusing of the orders appointed in the book, the Queen's Majesty may, by the advice of her commissioners, or metropolitan, ordain and publish such further ceremonies, or rites, as may be most for the reverence of Christ's holy mysteries and sacraments, and but for which law her Highness would not have agreed to divers orders of the book. And by virtue of which law she published further order in her injunctions both for the communion-bread, and for the placing of the tables within the quire." Ep. 283, to Cecil, p. 375, 376. P. C.

1566.] THEODORE BEZA. "Nor is this the end of their miseries; but it is also expressly provided that whenever it may please the queen's majesty, with the sole concurrence of the archbishop of Canterbury, to establish, alter, or take away, with respect to the rites of the church, it shall forthwith be considered as having the force of law." Ep. 53, to Bullinger, p. 130. Z. L. 2d.

1566.] HENRY BULLINGER. "In my opinion great caution is to be observed lest this dispute, and clamour, and contention respecting the habits should be conducted with too much bitterness, and by this importunity a handle should be afforded to the queen's majesty to leave that no longer a matter of choice to those who have abused their liberty; but being irritated by these needless clamours, she may issue her orders, that either these habits must be adopted, or the ministry relinquished." Ep. 3, to Humphrey & Sampson, p. 349. Appendix, Z. L.

1567.] G. WITHERS & J. BARTHELOT. "Moreover, there is power given by act of parliament, to the queen and archbishop to introduce whatever ceremonies they please into every church in the kingdom." Ep. 58, to Bullinger, p. 150. Z. L. 2d.

Circa 1566.] GEORGE WITHERS. "Power, moreover, was given to the queen and the archbishop, to introduce whatever additional ceremonies they might think proper; and they immediately afterwards both discontinued the ordinary bread heretofore used in the administration of the Lord's supper, and, for the sake of a newer reformation, adopted the round wafer, after the pattern of that used by the papists." Ep. 62, to the Pr. Elect Palat. p. 161. Ib.

——] PERCIVAL WIBURN. "The queen's majesty, with the advice of the archbishop of Canterbury, may order, change, and remove anything in that church at her pleasure." State of the Church of England, n. 30, p. 361, 362. Ib.

2. The Catholic character of the revision of the Prayer Book, and the intention of the Queen to adopt Catholic usages, was so well known, that out of nearly 10,000 Clergy, who had officiated under Queen Mary, only about 200 to 250, refused to conform.

It was well known that the Queen was more likely to add to, than subtract from, the ritual and rites of the Church. We also have testimony as to the Catholic character of the Prayer Book.

De Quadra wrote to the Spanish Minister at Rome, begging him to ask the Pope in the name of the English Romanists whether they might without sin be present at "the Common prayers."

"The case," de Quadra said, "was a new and not an easy one, for the Prayer-book contained neither impiety or false doctrine." LET. TO VARGAS, AUG. 7. MS. FROUDE, HIST. OF ENG., C. 6, AN. 1562, P. 471, 472. VOL. 7.

Archbishop PARKER, in 1572, says:

"I have heard say, that when cardinal Lorrain saw our Prayer-book in Latin, or in French, he should answer, that he liked well of that order, 'if,' said he, 'they would go no further.' I beseech God to hold his hand over us." EP. 304, TO LORD BURGHLEY, P. 398. P. C.

It was the Queen's great desire to induce Roman Catholics to continue in the English Church, and for many years, till her excommunication by the Pope, she was successful. She also wished to retain the Puritans and engraft all her people into one National Church. She was for restoring the Book of 1549, but her Puritan advisers wanted that of 1552. She made a compromise, taking the Book of 1552, yet making certain changes. The most important was in restoring the Vestments and Ornaments. Moreover, in the Act of Uniformity, the Queen provided for ordering and publishing "further ceremonies or rites." But for this proviso, Archbishop Parker tells us, she would not have accepted the Book of 1559.

(1) *We also have the testimony of the Puritans that most of the Clergy were "Papists," or, as we should say, Churchmen.*

1559.] RICHARD COX, BISHOP OF ELY. "At length many of the nobility, and vast numbers of the people, began by degrees to return to their senses; but of the clergy none at all." EP. 11, TO WEIDNER, P. 27. Z. L.

1566.] THEODORE BEZA. "What must we say, when not only the papists are left in possession of the revenues of their benefices, but even of their ecclesiastical offices, upon merely taking an oath to maintain the reformation." EP. 53, TO BULLINGER, P. 130. Z. L. 2D.

1566.] RODOLPH GUALTER. "For we well knew that either avowed papists, or Lutherans, would succeed into their [Puritan's] places, and introduce greater follies, and corruption of doctrine at the same time." EP. 57, BEZA, P. 143. ID.

Circa 1566. GEORGE WITHERS. "What must we say, when most of them [the Clergy] are popish priests, consecrated to perform mass." EP. 62, P. 163. ID.

——] PERCIVAL WIBURN. "The English clergy consist, partly of the popish priests, who still retain their former office, and partly of ministers lately ordered and admitted."

"This book of prayers is filled with many absurdities (to say no worse of them) and silly superfluities, and seems entirely to be composed after the model and in the manner of the papists, the grosser superstitions, however, being taken away." STATE OF THE CHURCH OF ENGLAND, N. 1, 9, P. 358, 359. IB.

(2) *The Pope is said to have even promised to confirm the English Liturgy, if Elizabeth would only acknowledge the claims of the Roman Pontiff.*

1606.] SIR EDWARD COKE. "That Pius Quintus whome those of their side doe account to have beene a good Pope (though by false perswasions too much misled) before the time of his excommunication against Queene Elizabeth denounced, sent his letter unto her Majesty, in which hee did allowe the Bible, and Book of Divine Service, as it is now used amongst us, to bee authenticke, and not repugnant to truth. But that therein was contayned enough necessary to salvation, though there was not in it, so much as might conveniently be) and that hee would also alowe it unto us, without changing any parte: so as her Majestie would acknowledge to receive it from him the Pope, and by his allowance) which her Majestie denying to do, she was then presently by the same Pope excommunicated. And this is the truth concerning Pope Pius Quintus, as I have faith to God and men. I have oftentimes heard avowed by the late Queene her own words: And I have conferred with some Lords that were of greatest reckoning in the State, who had seene and read the letter, which the Pope sent to that effect: as have been by me specified. And this upon my credit, as I am an honest man, is most true." SPEECH DELIVERED AT THE ASSIZES HELD AT NORWICH, AUG. 4, 1606. [Not paged.]

1613.] ROBERT ABBOT, afterwards BISHOP OF SALISBURY.

| | |
|---|---|
| Memoratae quoque illae in concionibus praesente Regina ipsa, quin et Teste advocata, nec tamen quisquam unquam e vestris sive privatim sive publice mutire in contrarium ausus est. ANTILOQ. ADV. APOL., C. 2, FOL. 15, 16. | These Letters were also mentioned in discussions in the presence of the Queen herself, yea even, when summoned as a witness, nor yet has any one of you ever, either in private or public, dared to mutter anything to the contrary. |

See also the testimony of CAMDEN, ANNAL. ELIZ., AN. 1560, P. 58, 59; TWYSDEN, HISTORICAL VINDICATION, C. 9, N. 3-5, P. 175-178; BRAMHALL, JUST VINDICATION, PART I. DISC. 3. C. 2, P. 85. VOL. 2.

(3) *For 10 or 11 years the great bulk of Roman Catholics frequented the English Church and were contented with her Services.*

Circa 1580.] NICHOLAS SANDERS, (Jesuit).

| | |
|---|---|
| Atque ita vel vi vel arte factum est, ut maxima catholicorum pars, usque adeo his primis initiis non perspecto rei periculo, | And thus either by force or by craft, it was brought about, that the greatest part of the Catholics, so little in these be- |

hostibus paulatim cederet, ut schismaticorum ecclesias, conciones, communionem ac conventicula, aliquando publice adire non recusarent. Ita tamen ut interim missas secreto domi per eosdem saepe presbyteros, qui adulterina haereticorum sacra in templis publice peragebant, aliquando per alios non ita schismate contaminatos, celebrari curaverunt; saepeque et mensae domini, ac calicis daemoniorum, hoc est, sacrosanctae Eucharistiae, et coenae Calvinicae, uno eodemque die, illo luctuoso tempore participes fierent. Imo quod mirum ac miserum erat, sacerdos nonunquam prius rem sacram domi faciens, deferebat pro Catholicis, quos ipse id desiderare cognoverat, hostias secundum formam ab ecclesia usitatam consecratas, quas eodem tempore iisdem dispensabat, quo panes haereticorum ritu confectos, caeteris Catholicae fidei minus studiosis, distribuebat. DE ORIG. ET PROGRESS. SCHIS. ANGL., L. 3, P. 292.

ginnings did they perceive the peril of the thing, yielded by degrees to the enemy, so that they did not refuse sometimes to publicly attend the churches, sermons, communion and conventicles of the schismatics. Yet, in such a manner that meanwhile they were careful to have Masses secretly celebrated at home, often by those same Priests who publicly performed the corrupted consecrations of the heretics in the churches, and sometimes by others who were not thus contaminated with schism; and often, in those mournful times, they were partakers, on one and the same day, of the Lord's table, and the cup of devils, that is, of the Holy Eucharist, and the Calvinistic supper. Yea even what was more wonderful and miserable, the Priest sometimes first consecrating at home, brought away for the Catholics, whom he himself had known to desire it, hosts consecrated according to the form employed by the church, which he dispensed to the same at the same time that he distributed to the rest, who were less zealous for the Catholic faith, bread consecrated by the rite of the heretics.

Note two things: he calls the Altar "the Lord's Table," and also proves the general use in those times of Wafer-Bread, or Hosts, in the Church of England.

1606.] SIR EDWARD COKE. "And thus they all Continued, not one refusing to Come to our Churches, during the first tenne years of her Majesties government." SPEECH DELIVERED AT THE ASSIZES HELD AT NORWICH, AUG. 4, 1606, P.—

"For (as hath already in the former arraignments been touched) before the Bull of the Impins Pius Quintus, in the eleventh year of the Queen, wherein her majesty was excommunicated and deposed, and all they accursed who should yield any obedience unto her, &c. there were no Recusants in England, all came to church (howsoever popishly inclined, or persuaded in most Points) to the same divine Service we now use; but thereupon presently they refused to assemble in our churches or join with us in public Service, not for conscience of any thing there done, against which they might justly except out of the Word of God, but because the Pope had excommunicated and deposed her majesty, and cursed those who should obey her: and so upon this Bull ensued open Rebellion in the North, and many garboils." TRIAL OF HENRY GARNET, AN. 1606, P. 250. STATE TRIALS. VOL. 1.

1606.] ROBERT PARSONS, (Jesuit), after enumerating the Bishops, and others of the Clergy, together with many of the Nobility and Gentry, who suffered for their religion at the beginning of Elizabeth's reign, continues as follows:

"All which did refuse to go to the Protestant service, even in those first dayes; which is testimony enough, to convince the open and notorious falsity of *M. Attornys* assertion, *that no person of what persuasion soever in Christian religion, did at any time refuse to goe to church:* though I deny not, but that many other besides these, throughout the Realme, though otherwise Catholicks in heart (as most men then were) did at that tyme and after, as also now, either upon feare, or lacke of better instruction, or both, repaire to Protestant churches; &c." ANS. TO THE 5TH PART OF COOKE'S REPORTS, C. 16, N. 7, P. 371.

"I do well remember (quoth shee) the first douzen years of her highnesse raigne, how happy, pleasant, and quiet they were, with all manner of comfort and consolation. There was no mention then of factions in religion, neither was any man much noted or rejected for that cause: so otherwise his conversation were civill and courteous. No suspition of treason, no talke of bloudshed, no complaint of troubles, miseries or vexations." LEYCESTER'S COMMONWEALTH, P. 161.

See also the testimony of HEYLIN. HIST. OF THE PRESBYTERIANS, L. 6, N. 31. P. 260; BRAMHALL. JUST VINDICATION. PART 1, DISC. 3, C. 8. P. 245, 246. VOL. 2.

(4) *Pope Pius V. excommunicated Elizabeth, April 25, 1570.* (*Bulla. n. 5, p. 303, T. 5. Mag. Bull. Rom.*)

The issuing of this Bull, which caused the Roman schism in England, was very generally deprecated by the intelligent and liberal among the Roman party:

JOHN LINGARD. (Roman Catholic.) "If the Pontiff promised himself any particular benefit from this measure, the result must have disappointed his expectations. The time was gone by when the thunders of the Vatican could shake the thrones of princes. By foreign powers the bull was suffered to sleep in silence; among the English Catholics, it served only to breed doubts, dissension and dismay. Many contended that it had been issued by an incompetent authority; others that it could not bind the natives, till it should be carried into actual execution by some foreign power; all agreed that it was in their regard an imprudent and cruel expedient, which rendered them liable to the suspicion of disloyalty, and afforded their enemies a pretence to brand them with the name of traitors." HIST. OF ENGLAND, AN. 1570, C. 1, P. 61. VOL. 8.

See also CAMDEN, ANNAL. ELIZ., AN. 1570, P. 182.

3. BUT THE QUEEN HAD ANOTHER CLASS OF PERSONS TO DEAL WITH, WHOM IT WAS ALSO NECESSARY TO CONCILIATE.

(1) *During Elizabeth's reign, as also during the latter part of Edward's, the Puritans were accustomed to officiate in their ordinary dress, not even using the Surplice, thereby wholly setting at naught the Rubrics of the Church and the Laws of the Realm.*

PETER MARTYR thus writes to Sampson:

1559.] "As to myself, when I was at Oxford, I would never wear the surplice in the choir, although I was a canon, and I had my own reasons for doing so." EP. 14, P. 33. Z. L. 2D.

He also advises his friend Sampson to abstain from officiating till the Vestments are removed, in EP. 11, 14. IB. In EP. 17, he allows him to wear them upon certain conditions. See page 8.

1561.] SIR WILLIAM CECIL. "The bishop of Norwich [Parkhurst] is blamed even of the best sort for his remissness in ordering his clergy. He winketh at schismatics and anabaptists, as I am informed. Surely I see great variety in ministration. A surplice may not be borne with here. And the ministers follow the folly of the people, calling it charity to feed their fond humor." EP. 107, TO PARKER, P. 149. P. C..

1566.] MATTHEW PARKER, ABP. OF CANTERBURY. "I have sent divers days three and four of my chaplains to serve in the greatest parishes [in London], what for lack of surplice and waferbread, they did mostly but preach. . . . And divers churchwardens to make a trouble and a difficulty, will provide neither surplice nor bread." EP. 213, TO CECIL, P. 277, 278. IB.

1566.] L. HUMPHREY & T. SAMPSON. "In the time of the most serene king Edward the Sixth, the Lord's supper was celebrated in simplicity in many places without the surplice." EP. 71, TO BULLINGER, P. 158. Z. L.

See also the testimony of WITHERS, cited on page 6.

1567.] AN EXAMINATION OF CERTAYNE LONDONNERS BEFORE THE COMMISSIONERS, ABOUT ANNO 1567.

"*Deane* . . . . We holde the reformation that was in King Edwards dayes.

". . . *Nixson*. Yet they neuer came so farre as ye haue done to make a law that none should Preach or minister without these garments." PARTE OF A REGISTER, P. 33, 34.

1571.] HIEROME ZANCHIUS. "The dispute itself teaches

us that they [the Puritans] are disturbed beyond measure by the order about wearing the linen surplice. For their complaints are so vehement, that their querulous lamentations and groans penetrate into and are heard even in Germany." EP. 1, TO ELIZ., P. 349, 350. APPENDIX. Z. L. 2D.

————] DANIEL NEAL. "The parochial clergy, both in city and country, had an aversion to the habits; they wore them sometimes in obedience to the law, but more frequently administered without them." HIST. OF THE PURITANS, C. 4, P. 90. VOL. 1.

The Abbé GUERANGER informs us that the more liberal among the Roman Catholic clergy in Germany, sometimes officiate in ordinary dress,—"célèbrent la Messe avec les vêtements plus ou moins profanes dont ils se trouvent pour le moment revêtus." INSTITUT. LITURG., P. 707. T. 2.

(2) *Some of the Bishops upon their return from exile, both before and after they entered upon their ministry, incited by foreign Reformers, among whom they had lived, favored the Puritans, but the Queen and Parliament resisted.*

They themselves complied with the laws in order to retain their places, wearing the habits which they condemned, hoping meanwhile to obtain some concessions for their friends. But when they found that the Puritans were gradually undermining the whole structure of the Church, and would eventually destroy the very offices which they held, they then, when too late, opposed them. The Queen made a great mistake in appointing such men. See pages 11-13.

SANDYS, BISHOP OF WORCESTER, an. 1560, was too active in reforming:

"I was very near being deposed from my office, and incurring the displeasure of the queen." EP. 31, TO P. MARTYR, P. 74. Z. L.

1565.] ROBERT HORN, BISHOP OF WINCHESTER. "It was enjoined us, (who had not then any authority either to make laws or repeal them,) either to wear the caps and surplices, or to give place to others. We complied with this injunction, lest our enemies should take possession of the places deserted by ourselves. . . . We certainly hope to repeal this clause of the act [of Uniformity] next session; but if this cannot be effected," &c. EP. 64, TO GUALTER, P. 142, 143. Z. L.

1562.] JOHN JEWELL, BISHOP OF SALISBURY. "And I wish we could effect this [removal] in respect to that linen surplice." EP. 43, TO P. MARTYR, P. 100. IB.

1566.] "The contest respecting the linen surplice, about which I doubt not but you have heard either from our friend Abel or Parkhurst, is not yet at rest. The matter still somewhat disturbs weak minds, and I wish that all, even the slightest vestige of popery might be removed from our churches, and above all from our minds. But the Queen at this time is unable to endure the least alteration in matters of religion." EP. 67, TO BULLINGER, P. 148, 149. IB.

Circa 1566.] GEORGE WITHERS. "These [Bishops] at first began to oppose the ceremonies; but afterwards, when there was no hope otherwise of obtaining a bishoprick, they yielded, and, as one of them openly acknowledged, undertook the office against their conscience. In the mean while they comforted their brethren, whom they perceived to be still struggling against these things, by promising them free liberty in the government of their churches; and for some years they kept this promise. On the obtaining of which liberty, they diligently purified their churches from all blemishes and defilements of popery. Others, who had at first yielded, incited by their example, began to reform their churches in the like manner. But when the bishops perceived that the number and influence of these parties was increasing among the people, they thought their dignity would come to nought unless they compelled the inferior clergy to adopt the same usages as they did themselves. They took up the matter therefore at the queen's command." EP. 62, TO THE PR. ELECT. PALAT, P. 161. Z. L. 2D.

1566.] EDMUND GRINDAL, BISHOP OF LONDON. "We, who are now bishops, on our first return, and before we entered upon our ministry, contended long and earnestly for the removal of those things that have occasioned the present dispute; but as we were unable to prevail, either with the queen or the parliament," &c. EP. 73, TO BULLINGER, P. 169. Z. L.

1567.] EDMUND GRINDAL & ROBERT HORN. "We hold that the ministers of the church of England may adopt without impiety the distinction of habits now prescribed by public authority, both in the administration of divine worship, and for common use. . . . This dissension has not been occasioned by any fault of ours, nor is it owing to us that vestments of this kind have not been altogether done away with." EP. 75, TO BULLINGER & GUALTER, 176, 177. IB.

Grindal, while Archbishop of Canterbury, was confined and sequestered in June 1577, for non-compliance with the Queen's command to redress the disorders of Puritanism, and kept in disgrace and inactivity nearly to the end of his life. He resigned his see in 1582, and died in 1583. See SANDYS, EP. 134, TO GUALTER, P. 332. Z. L; STRYPE, HIST. OF THE LIFE AND ACTS OF GRINDAL, B. 2, C. 9, P. 13-15.

1571.] RICHARD COX, BISHOP OF ELY. "The popish dress, which we seriously reject and condemn equally with themselves." EP. 94, TO GAULTER, P. 236. Z. L.

See also HORN, EP. 98, AN. 1571, P. 248, 249. IB; and PILKINGTON, EP. 110, AN. 1573, P. 287. IB.

# IV. Queen Elizabeth takes "further order" to enforce Uniformity, in 1560-1.

JAN. 22, 1560–1, the Queen issued "Letters under the Great Seal" to her Commissioners:

"Most reverend father in God right trusty and right well-beloved, right reverend father in God right trusty and well-beloved, trusty and right well-beloved, and trusty and well-beloved, we greet you well. Letting you to understand, that where it is provided by act of parliament, holden in the first year of our reign, that whensoever we shall see cause to take further order in any rite or ceremony appointed in the Book of Common Prayer, and our pleasure known therein, either to our commissioners for causes ecclesiastical, or to the metropolitan, that then eftsoons consideration should be had therein. We therefore understanding that there be in the said book certain chapters for lessons and other things appointed to be read, which might be supplied with other chapters or parcels of scripture, tending in the hearing of the unlearned or lay people more to their edification; and that furthermore in sundry churches and chapels where divine service, as prayer, preaching and ministration of the sacraments be used, there is such negligence and lack of convenient reverence used towards the comely keeping and order of the said churches, and specially of the upper part, called the chancels, that it breedeth no small offence and slander to see and consider, on the one part the curiosity and costs bestowed by all sorts of men upon their private houses, and on the other part the unclean or negligent order and spare-keeping of the house of prayer, by permitting open decays and ruins of coverings, walls and windows, and by appointing unmeet and unseemly tables with foul cloths for the communion of the sacraments, and generally leaving the place of prayers desolate of all cleanliness and meet ornaments for such a place, whereby it might be known a place provided for divine service; have thought it good to require you, our commissioners so authorized by our great seal for causes ecclesiastical, or four of you, whereof we will you, Matthew, archbishop of Canterbury, Edmund, bishop of London, William Bill, our almoner, and Walter Haddon, one of the masters of our request, to be always two, to peruse the order of the said lessons throughout the whole year, and to cause some new calenders to be imprinted, whereby such chapters or parcels of less edification may be removed, and other more profitable may supply their rooms; and further also to consider, as becometh, the foresaid great disorders in the decays of churches, and in the unseemly keeping and order of the chancels, and such like, and according to your discretions to determine upon some good and speedy means of reformation, and, amongst other things, to order that the tables of the commandments may be comely set or hung up in the east end of the chancel, to be not only read for edification, but also to give some comely ornament and demonstration that the same is a place of religion and prayer; and diligently to provide, that whatsoever ye shall devise, either in this or any other like point, to the reformation of this disorder, that the order and reformation be of one sort and fashion, and that the things prescribed may accord in one form as nigh as ye may; specially that in all collegiate and cathedral churches, where cost may be more probably allowed, one manner to be used; and in all parish-churches also, either the same, or at the least the like, and one manner throughout our realm: and further, we will that where we have caused our Book of Common Service to be translated into the Latin tongue, for the use and exercise of such students and other learned in the Latin tongue, we will also that by your wisdoms and discretions ye prescribe some good orders to the collegiate churches, to which we have permitted the use of divine service and prayer in the Latin tongue, in such sort as ye shall consider to be most meet to be used, in respect of their companies, or of resort of our lay subjects to the said churches, so that our good purpose in the said translation be not frustrated, nor be corruptly abused, contrary to the effect of our meaning. And for the publication of that which you shall order, we will and require you, the archbishop of Canterbury, to see the same put in execution throughout your province, and that you, with the rest of our commissioners before mentioned, prescribe the same to the archbishop now nominated of York, to be in like manner set forth in that province, and that the alteration of any thing hereby ensuing be quietly done, without show of any innovation in the church. And these our letters shall be your sufficient warrant in this behalf. Given under our signet at our palace of Westminster, the two and twentieth of January, the third year of our reign." EP. 94, TO PARKER, P. 132-134. P. C.

This document fulfills every requirement in the Act of Uniformity. It was issued under the Queen's signet, and is filed among the State Papers in the Record Office, and engrossed in due form. The order for new Lessons was published in every subsequent edition of the Prayer Book, and for Books still in use, a cancel of ten leaves was issued at once. This order made no provision whatever for the Vestments of the Clergy.

Feb. 15, 1560-1, Archbishop PARKER sends a Letter to Grindal, Bishop of London, announcing that the Queen had issued a Letter to him requiring certain reforms to be made and published throughout his Province of Canterbury,—"per totam provinciam nostram Cantuariensem,"—and commanding him with all speed to carry out the said mandate. EP. 95, P. 134-136. P. C.

1763.] DR. RICHARD BURN. "Two years afterwards, by virtue of this clause [in the Act of Uniformity], the queen issued her commission to the archbishop and three others to peruse the order of the lessons throughout the whole year," &c. ECCL. LAW, word PUBLIC WORSHIP, N. 1, SECT. 5, P. 242. VOL. 3.

## V. "Interpretations and further Considerations," drawn up in 1561.

STRYPE, under the date of 1561, says:

"Another thing also was now drawn up in writing by the archbishop and bishops, for the further regulation of the inferior clergy. This paper consisted of *interpretations and further considerations* of certain of the queen's *injunctions*, for the better direction of the clergy, and for keeping good order in the church. It was framed, as it seems to me, by the pen of Cox, bishop of Ely, and revised by the archbishop, and was as followeth.

"That there be used only but one apparel; as the Cope in the ministration of the Lord's supper, and the Surplice in all other ministrations; and that there be no other manner and form of ministering the sacraments, but as the service book doth precisely prescribe, with the declaration of the Injunctions; as for example, the common [communion?] bread." ANNALS, c. 17, p. 318, 320. VOL. 1, PT. 1; CARDWELL, DOC. ANN., N. 43, p. 238. VOL. 1.

The Queen in her letter to Parker, cited on page 47, was very desirous of Uniformity in the services of Cathedral and Parish Churches, if possible, and especially in all Collegiate and Cathedral churches, which could better bear the expense.

Probably this fact was the cause why the "Interpretations" were drawn up. From them it appears that Cathedral and Parish churches were to be on the same footing, and that a variety of Vestments was to be disused. The word "as" seems to imply that a Cope and Surplice was sufficient, and that it would not be required to wear an Alb and Chasuble as required by the Rubric. However they were not forbidden. Why the Cope was preferred to the Chasuble, we cannot now tell. Perhaps it was because the former was much more showy and costly than the latter, and was worn in the Queen's Chapel. Or it may have been from merely personal preference, or perhaps, the Chasuble was made in such shape that it was often confounded with the Cope, of which we have numerous examples, and especially in the case of the Copes at Durham Cathedral, in 1627. See Section xib, (iii). At any rate we have clear evidence that the Church Reformers desired a distinctive garment for the Holy Eucharist.

These "Interpretations" were never issued, but were found among Archbishop Parker's papers, which are preserved at Cambridge.

## VI. "General notes of matters to be moved by the [Puritan] Clergy in the next Parliament and Synod," 1562-63.

THE Queen's Letter and "further order" for Uniformity, and the efforts of the Bishops, seem to have had no effect. In the Synod which began January 13, 1562-3, it was proposed:

"That the use of vestments, copes and surplices be from henceforth taken away." Ap. STRYPE, ANNALS, c. 27, p. 475. VOL. 1, PT. 1.

Besides, it was proposed in a Paper signed by 33 Members of the Lower House:

"IV. That the use of Copes and Surplices may be taken away; so that all ministers in their ministry use a grave, comely, and side-garment, as commonly they do in preaching." IB. P. 500, 501. IB.

This proposal was afterwards modified as follows:

"V. That it be sufficient for the minister, in the time of saying of divine service, and the ministering of the sacraments, to use a Surplice: and that no minister say service, or minister the sacraments, but in a comely garment or habit." IB. P. 503. IB.

This proposal was lost, after a warm debate, Feb. 13, 1562-3, by a vote of 59 to 58. (IB. P. 504-506; BURNET, HIST. OF THE REF., PT. 3, B. 6, N. 74, P. 480-482. VOL. 6; CARDWELL, HIST. OF CONF., C. 2, N. 10, P. 117-120.) Thus the Vestments were retained, in spite of the strenuous efforts of the Puritan party, though by a bare majority of one. We have clear evidence from these proceedings, that all the Vestments,—Alb, Chasuble, Cope, and Surplice,—were still in legal use in 1563; that the cope at least, was in extensive actual use, and that there was quite a large number of Clergy in the Lower House of Convocation, who not only wished to do away with the Vestments, but the Surplice even. They were were not successful, however.

Nevertheless the Puritans persevered, and were encouraged by some of the Bishops. GRINDAL, Bishop of London, and HORN, Bishop of Winchester, in a Letter dated Feb. 6, 1566, say:

"Continue therefore to love, to advise, and to assist us, that the flame which has been stirred up amongst us solely on account of this affair of the habits, may be extinguished; and we will endeavor, to the utmost of our power, as we did at the last convocation, even although we could obtain nothing, that all errors and abuses may be corrected, amended and purified, according to the word of God." EP. 75, TO BULLINGER AND GAULTER, P. 181. Z. L.

## VII. The Advertisements of 1564 and 1566.

THE Puritans were utterly lawless, laying aside all Vestments. It was impossible to enforce the Rubric, but there it was, bearing silent witness all the while to the teaching of the Church. The use of the Surplice was hardly maintained. In 1564, Advertisements were drawn up, not published and issued till 1566, which were not binding in law, moderating the ancient Rubric,— though the Puritans looked upon them with dismay, as they required the use of the Surplice, which many of them had discontinued,—leaving the use of the Vestments optional, with certain exceptions, and ordering that:

*"In ministration of the Holy Communion in the Cathedrall and Collegiate Churches, the principal Minister shall use a Cope with Gospeller and Epistoler agreeably; and at all other prayers to be sayde at the Communion Table, to use no Copes but Surplesses.

"That every Minister sayinge any publique prayers, or ministeringe the Sacramentes or other rites of the Churche, shall weare a comely surples with sleeves, to bee provided at the charges of the parishe." CARDWELL, DOC. ANNALS, N. 65, P. 326. VOL. 1.

What gives the Advertisements special importance, is the fact that they are now claimed to be the "further" or "other order" put forth by the Queen:

"But their lordships are clearly of opinion that the Advertisements (a word which in the language of the time was equivalent to "admonitions" or "injunctions") of Elizabeth, issued in 1566, were a "taking of order," within the Act of Parliament, by the Queen, with the advice of the Metropolitan." JUDGMENT IN THE RISDALE APPEAL CASE, P. 49.

They modified the Rubric, which required the use of the Vestments everywhere, and only required the Cope in Cathedrals and Collegiate Churches, and the Surplice in Parish churches. The Rubric of 1662, which orders the same Vestments as were used in the 2d year of Edward VI., was once said to be very obscure, ambiguous, or difficult. Thus the judges in the Purchas case said in 1871:

"Their Lordships are now called on to determine the force of the Rubric of 1662, and its effects upon other regulations, such as the

---

* In the first draft of the Advertisements, as they appeared in 1564, these sections read as follows:

"*Item.* In the mynystracion of the Communyon in cathedral and collegiate churches, the Executor, with Pistoler and Gospeller, mynyster the same in coopes; and at other praiers to be said at the communyon table, to have no coopes, but surplices.

"*Item.* That everic Mynyster, sayinge anye publique prayers, or mynysteringe the Sacramentes, or other rites of the Churche, shall wear a comelye surples with sleves, to be provided at the chargis of the parishe." Cited by STRYPE, LIFE OF PARKER, APPENDIX, B. 2, N. 28, P. 87, 88. VOL. 3.

Canons of 1603-4. They do not disguise from themselves that the task is difficult." PRIVY COUNCIL JUDGMENTS, P. 177.

But that plea is now abandoned by the Judicial Committee in the Risdale Appeal Case:

"In the opinion of their lordships, if the only law as to the vesture of the clergy is to be found in the Ornaments Rubric, the use of the vestments of the First Edwardian Prayer-book is not merely authorised, it is enjoined. It is not an enactment ordering the accomplishment of a particular result, and suggesting or directing a mode by which the proposed result may be attained. The sole object of the rubric is to define the mode of performing an existing ministration. If the rubric is taken alone, the words in it are not optional, they are imperative; and every clergyman who, since 1662, has failed, or who may hereafter fail, to use in the administration of the Holy Communion the vestments of the First Edwardian Prayer-book, has been, and will be, guilty of ecclesiastical offence rendering him liable to heavy penalties." PAGE 47.

Their Lordships next proceed to read the Advertisements into the Rubric of 1662:

"Reading, then, as their lordships consider they are bound to do, the orders as to vestures in the Book of Advertisements, into the 25th section of the 1st of Elizabeth, cap. 2, and omitting (for the sake of brevity) all reference to hoods, it will appear that that section, from the year 1566 to 1662, had the same operation in law as if it had been expressed in these words:—'Provided always that such ornaments of the Church and of the ministers thereof shall be retained and be in use as were in this Church of England by authority of Parliament in the second year of King Edward VI., except that the surplice shall be used by the ministers of the Church at all times of their public ministrations, and the alb, vestment, or tunicle shall not be used, nor shall a cope be used except at the administration of the Holy Communion in cathedral and collegiate churches.'" PAGE 54.

That is, the Rubric of 1662 is now regarded as so clear, plain and unambiguous, that unless modified by the Advertisements, which are the "other order" taken by the Queen as authorized by the Act of Uniformity, the use of the Vestments would be obligatory.

We intend to prove that the only "further" or "other order" taken by the Queen, was taken as Abp. Parker expressly says (see page 38), in the Injunctions of 1559,—and it is well to notice that though his letter was written as late as 1570-1, the Advertisements are not even mentioned—and in 1560-1 (see page 46-47); and that the present Book of Advertisements, was the sole work of the Bishops, though incited thereto by the Queen, and never received the Royal sanction, and is consequently, of no binding force in law.

1. CIRCUMSTANCES ATTENDING THE DRAWING UP OF THE ADVERTISEMENTS.

1563.] Shortly after April 14, Abp. PARKER addressed a Letter to Cecil, consulting him as to the advisability of sending a letter to the Bishops to prevent their use of the Queen's name in pressing the act requiring the Clergy to take the oath of the Queen's supremacy which had recently passed Parliament with some opposition:

"In consideration of yesternight's talk, calling to remembrance [what] the qualities of all my brethren be in experience of our convocation societies, I see some of them to be *pleni rimarum, hac atque illac effluunt*. . . . And where the Queen's Highness doth note me to be too soft and easy, I think divers of my brethren will rather note me, if they were asked, too sharp and too earnest in moderation, which towards them I have used, and will still do, till mediocrity shall be received amongst us. . . . I have thought to use this kind of writing to my brethren already departed home, not to recite the Queen's Majesty's name, which I would not have rehearsed to the discouragement of the honest Protestant, nor known too easy, to the rejoice too much of the adversaries, *her* enemies indeed. I had rather bear the burthen myself. . . . Whereupon though I shall thus write, as having no warrant in writing, to stay full execution of the imperial laws, as it may be so far forced, yet if the jeoparding of my private estimation may do good, that the purpose itself be performed that the Queen would have done, it shall suffice, I think. If ye shall allow this device, I pray your honour to return it me again with your corrections as ye shall think meet." Ep. 127, TO CECIL, P. 173, 174. P. C.

Enclosed was a draft of a letter, for Cecil's approbation, in which he made several corrections, as is evident from the copy still extant. Cecil also added the following paragraph to his Letter:

"And I also pray to assure and persuade yourself, that this manner of my sudden writing at this time is grounded upon great and necessary consideration, for the weal and credit of us that are governers of the church under the Queen's Majesty, and yet for divers respects meet to be kept secret to yourselves, as I doubt not but your wisdoms will easily see and judge." Ep. 128, P. 174, 175. IB.

1564.] Jan. 15, 1564-5, CECIL drew up a Letter in the name of the Queen, and sent it to Parker with the following note:

"It may please your grace. I do send herewith a form of a letter, which at the beginning to write the same I thought should have been meet for to have procured from the Queen's Majesty to your grace, but after that I had caused it to be new written, I misliked the same chiefly for length. But yet, before I would alter anything, I thought meet to remit it to your grace's consideration, praying the same to alter or abridge any part thereof. The next doubt I have is, whether the Queen's Majesty will not be provoked to some offence that there is such cause of reformation, and whether she will not have more added than I shall allow. Upon your grace's correction hereof I will follow your advice." Ep. 169, TO PARKER, P. 223. IB.

Two copies of the enclosed letter still exist.—a rough, and the fair copy. The rough copy, with Cecil's numerous corrections in his own hand-writing, is reprinted by PARKER, DID QUEEN ELIZABETH TAKE OTHER ORDER IN THE ADVERTISEMENTS OF 1566? A POSTSCRIPT TO A LETTER TO LORD SELBORNE, P. 127-130.

This Letter which Cecil was afraid to show to the Queen, it is now claimed, is the authority to " take other order."

Below is the fair copy, dated Jan. 25, 1564-5, addressed to Abp. Parker:

"Most reverend Father in God, &c. We greet you well. Like as no one thing, in the government and charge committed unto us by the favourable goodness of Almighty God, doth more profit and beautify the same to his pleasure and acceptation, to our comfort and ease of our government, and, finally, to the universal weal and repose of our people and countries, than unity, quietness, and concord, as well amongst the public ministers having charge under us, as in the multitude of the people by us and them ruled; so, contrawise, diversity, variety, contention, and vain love of singularity, either in our ministers or in the people, must needs provoke the displeasure of Almighty God, and be to us, having the burden of government, discomfortable, heavy, and troublesome; and, finally, must needs bring danger of ruin to our people and country. Wherefore, although our earnest care and inward desire hath always been, from the beginning of our reign, to provide that by *laws and ordinances* agreeable to truth and justice, and consonant to good order, this our realm should be directed and governed, both in the ecclesiastical and civil policy, by public officers and ministers following, as near as possible might be, one rule, form, and manner of order in all their actions, and directing our people to obey humbly and live godly, according to their several callings, in unity and concord, without diversities of opinions or novelties of rites and manners, or without maintenance or breeding of any contentions about the same; yet we, to our no small grief and discomfort do hear, that where, of the two manner of governments without which no manner of people is well ruled, the ecclesiastical should be the more perfect, and should give example and be as it were a light and guide to allure, direct, and lead all officers in civil policy; yet in sundry places of our realm of late, for *lack of regard* given thereto in due time, by such superior and principal officers as you are, being the primate and *other the bishops of your province*, with sufferance of sundry varieties and novelties, not only in opinions but in external ceremonies and rites, there is crept and brought into the church by some few persons, abounding more in their own senses than wisdom would, and delighting with singularities and changes, an open and manifest disorder and offence to the godly wise and obedient persons, by diversity of opinions and specially in the external, decent, and lawful rites and ceremonies to be used in the churches, so as except the same should be speedily withstand, stayed, and reformed the inconvenience thereof were like to grow from from place to place, as it were by an infection, to a great annoyance, trouble, and deformity to the rest of the whole body of the realm, and thereby impair, deface, and disturb Christian charity, union and concord, being the very bands of our religion; which we do so much desire to increase and continue amongst our people, and by and with which our Lord God, being the God of peace and not of dissension, will continue his blessings and graces over us and his people. And although we have now a good while heard to our grief sundry reports hereof, hoping that all cannot be true, but rather mistrusting that the adversaries of the truth might of their evil disposition increase their reports of the same: yet we thought, until this present, that by the regard which you, being the primate and metropolitan would have had hereto according to your office, with the assistance of the bishops your brethren in their several dioceses, (*having also received of us hertofore charge for the same purpose,*) these errors, tending to breed some schism or deformity in the church, should have been stayed and appeased. But perceiving very lately, and also certainly, that the same doth rather begin to increase than to stay or diminish, *We, considering the authority given to us of Almighty God* for defence of the public peace, concord, and truth of this his Church, and how we are answerable for the same to the seat of his high justice, mean not to endure or suffer any longer these evils thus to proceed, spread, and increase in our realm, *but have certainly determined to have all such diversities, varieties, and novelties* amongst them of the clergy and our people as breed nothing but contention, offence, and breach of common charity, *and are also against the laws, good usages, and ordinances of our realm*, to be reformed and repressed and brought to *one manner of uniformity thoughout our whole realm and dominions*, that our people may thereby quietly honour and serve Almighty God in truth, concord, peace and quietness, and thereby also avoid the slanders that are spread abroad hereupon in foreign countries.

"And therefore, We do by these our present letters require, enjoin, and straitly charge you, being the metropolitan, according to the power and authority which you have under us over the *province of Canterbury*, (as the like we will order for the province of York,) to confer with the bishops your brethren, namely such as be in commission for causes ecclesiastical, and also all other head officers having jurisdiction ecclesiastical, as well in both our Universities as in any other places, collegiate, cathedral, or whatsoever the same be, exempt or not exempt, either by calling to you from thence whom you shall think meet, to have assistance or conference, or by message, process, or letters, as you shall see most convenient, and cause to be truly understand [sic] what varieties, novelties and diversities there are in our clergy or amongst our people within every of the said jurisdictions, either in doctrine or in ceremonies and rites of the Church, or in the manners, usages, or behaviour of the clergy themselves, by what name soever any of them be called. And thereupon, as the several cases shall appear to require reformation, so to proceed by *order, injunction*, or *censure*, according to the order and appointment of such *laws and ordinances as are provided by act of Parliament*, and the true meaning thereof, so as uniformity of order may be kept in every church, and without variety and contention.

"And for the time to come, we will and straitly charge you to provide and enjoin in our name, in all and every places of *your province*, as well in places exempt as otherwise, that none be hereafter admitted or allowed to any office, room, cure, or place ecclesiastical, either having cure of souls, or without cure, but such as shall be found disposed and well and advisedly given to common order; and shall also, before their admittance to the same, orderly and formally promise to use and exercise the same office, room, or place, to the honour of God [and] the edification of our people under their charge, in truth, concord, and unity; and also to observe, keep, and maintain *such order and uniformity in all the external rites and ceremonies, both for the Church and for their own persons, as by laws, good usages, and orders, are already allowed, well provided, and established.* And if any superior officers shall be found hereto disagreeable, if otherwise your discretion or authority shall not serve to reform, We will that you shall duly inform us thereof, to the end we may give indelayed order for the same; for we intend to have no dissension or variety grow by suffering of persons which maintain dissension to remain in authority; for so the sovereign authority which we have under Almighty God should be violate and made frustrate, and we might be well thought to bear the sword in vain.

"And in the execution hereof we require you to use all expedition that, to such a cause as this is, shall seem necessary, that hereafter we be not occasioned, for lack of your diligence, to provide such further remedy, by some other sharp proceedings, as shall percase not be easy to be borne by such as shall be disordered: and therewith also we shall impute to you the cause thereof." EP. 170, TO PARKER, P. 223-227. P. C.

I have given the above Letter in full. It is so verbose that I have *italicized* the most important words, as also in some of the following documents.

The reader is requested to compare this Letter with the Queen's Letter, cited on pages 46–47. It will be seen that no allusion is here made to "further order," as in the Letter of 1560-1, nor is there any wish expressed to have any Rubric or order changed, but only to have novelties and disorders repressed by "laws already established." No allusion whatever is made to Vestments. This Letter was never signed by the Queen, and was found among Cecil's private papers.

1564-5.] Abp. PARKER writes to Grindal, Bishop of London, January 30, 1564-5:

"Whereupon her Majesty hath straitly charged me, according to *such power and authority as I have under her*, to have consideration of the same in such form as by her said letters is expressed, &c. .... I do by these my letters desire your lordship, and in her name straitly charge you, to expend and execute the premises; and also to signify the same with charge to the rest of our brethren *in my province*, that they inviolably see the *laws and ordinances already stablished* to be without delay and colour executed in their particular jurisdictions, with proceeding against offenders by the censures of the Church &c., and such as be incorrigible to send up hither the causes and demerits of those persons; as they the said bishops to charge their inferiors having any jurisdiction, to do the same. And also, that you and they severally calling the most apt grave men to confer with in your and their diocese, to certify me what varieties and disorder there be, either in doctrine or in ceremonies of the Church and behaviour of the clergy themselves, by what names soever they be called. Which certificate to be returned by the last day of February next to come at the farthest. And that you and they thereof fail not, as ye and they will answer to the contrary at your and their peril." EP. 171, p. 228–230. P. C.

1564–5, March 3.] Abp. PARKER. "I send your honour a book of articles, partly of *old* agreed on *amongst us*, and partly of late these three or four days considered, which be either in papers fasted on, as ye see, or new written by secretary hand. Because it is the first view, not fully digested, I thought good to send it to your honour to peruse, to know your judgment, and so to return it, that it may be fair written and presented. The *devisers were only* the bishops of London [Grindal], Winchester [Horn], Ely [Cox], Lincoln [Bullingham] and myself. . . . . Furthermore, I must earnestly pray your honour to obtain a private letter from the Queen's Majesty to my lord of London, *to execute laws and injunctions;* which he saith, if he be so charged, he will out of hand see reformation in all London; and ye know there is the most disorder, and then is the matter almost won through the realm. I pray you earnestly, expeditely to procure these letters, for he is now in a good mood to execute the *laws*, and it will work much more than ye would think." EP. 175, to CECIL, p. 233, 234. IB.

1564–5, March 8.] Abp. PARKER. "I send your honour *our book* which is subscribed to by the bishops conferers, which I keep by myself. I trust your honour will present it upon opportunity which ye can take in removing offences that might grow by mine imprudent talk. *If the Queen's Majesty will not authorise them*, the most part be like to lie in the dust for execution of our parties, *laws be so much against our private doings.* 'The Queen's Majesty, with consent, &c.' I trust shall be obeyed. . . . . If this ball shall be tossed unto us, and then have no *authority by the Queen's Majesty's hand*, we will set still. I marvel that not six words were spoken from the Queen's Majesty to my lord of London, for uniformity of his London, as himself told me; if the remedy is not by letter, I will no more strive against the stream, fume or chide who will." EP. 176, TO CECIL, p. 234, 235. IB.

From this letter, and from the two next, it is evident that the Queen would not sanction his book. He complains of her sudden coldness, and that the whole blame is laid on him, and wishes that he had not entered upon the work.

1564–5, March 24.] "I would ye had not have stirred *istam camarinam*, or else have to set on it to some order at the beginning. This delaying works daily more inconvenience." EP. 178, TO CECIL, p. 236. IB.

1565, April 7.] "The talk, as I am informed, is much increased, and unrestful they be, and *I alone they say am in fault.* For as for the Queen's Majesty's part, in my expostulation with many of them I signify their disobedience, wherein, because they see the danger, they cease to impute it to her Majesty, for they say, *but for my calling on, she is indifferent.* Again, most of them dare not name your honour in this tragedy, for many must have your help in their suits, &c. My lord of London is their own, say they, and is but brought in against his will. *I only am the stirrer and incenser.* And my lord of Durham will be against us all: and will give over his bishopric rather than it shall take place in his diocese." Ep. 179, TO CECIL, P. 237. IB.

Nearly a year passed before Parker again makes reference to the Advertisements in his Letters. Meanwhile, perhaps, he hoped that the Queen would authorise them. March 12, 1565-6, he addressed another letter to Cecil.

1565-6.] "I am much astonied, and in great perplexity to think what event this cause will have in the proceeding to an end. Where I have endeavored myself to enforce the Queen's Majesty's pleasure upon all my brothers, and have desired that others should not hinder such proceedings by secret aiding and comforting, I see my service but defeated: and then again otherwiles dulled by variable considerations of the state of the times, and of doubtfulness in discouraging some good protestants if this order should be vehemently prosecuted. *I have stayed upon such advertisements*; but I alway perceived much hurt might come of such tolerations (the parties hardened in their disobedience), and at the last the Queen's Majesty's displeasure, to see how her commandment take little effect, where yet order for all other men's apparel, and laws for abstinence, so much forced and well set to, may induce an obedience, howsoever a great number may be offended; and therefore they who think that disorder of our state were as soon reformed if we had like helps, seem to me to speak reasonably. I have written to the Queen's Majesty, as you see. *I pray your honour use your opportunity. And where once this last year certain of us* consulted and agreed upon some *particularities in apparel* (where the *Queen's Majesty's letters were very general*), and for that by statute *we be inhibited* to set out any constitutions without license obtained of the prince, *I sent them to your honour to be presented* [March 8, 1564-5]; they could not be allowed *then*, I cannot tell of what meaning; which I now send *again*, humbly praying that *if not all yet so many as be thought good*, may be returned *with some authority*, at the least way for *particular apparel:* or else we shall not be able to do so much as the Queen's Majesty expected for, of us to be done. And surely if I draw forward, and others draw backwards, what shall it avail, but raise exclamations and privy mutterings against your honour and against me, by whom they think these matters be stirred? I see how other men get their heads out of the collar, and convey the envy otherwhere." EP. 203, P. 262, 263. IB.

1565-6, March 20.] Abp. PARKER, and GRINDAL, Bishop of London, join in a letter to Cecil, stating how they propose to enforce uniformity :

"2. Item after the general propositions made (as afore) to the whole number, we intend particularly to examine every of them, whether they *will promise conformity in their ministrations and outward apparel, stablished by law and Injunction*, and testify the same by subscriptions of their hands." Ep. 205, p. 268. IB.

1566, March 26.] Abp. PARKER informs Cecil of the result of his examination of certain of the Clergy:

"I must signify to your honour what we have done in the examination of London ministers. Sixty-one promised conformity; nine or ten were absent; thirty-seven denied, of which number were the best, and some preachers; six or seven convenient sober men, pretending a conscience, divers of them but zealous, and of little learning and judgment." Ep. 207, p. 269, 270. IB.

1566, March 28.] Abp. PARKER. "I pray your honour to peruse this draft of letters, and the *Book of Advertisements* with your pen, which I mean to send to my lord of London. This form is but *newly printed*, and *yet stayed* till I may hear your advice. *I am* now fully bent to prosecute this order, and to delay no longer, and *I have weeded out of these articles all such of doctrine*, &c., *which peradventure stayed the book from the Queen's Majesty's approbation*, and have put in but things advouchable, and, as I take them, *against no law of the realm*. And where the Queen's Highness will needs have *me* assay with *mine own authority* what I can do for order, I trust I shall not be stayed hereafter, saving that I would pray your honour to have your advice to do that more prudently in common cause which must needs be done.

"Some of these silly recusants [referred to in Ep. 207, p. 269, 270, just cited above] say now that they thought not that ever the matter (in such scarcity of ministers) should have been forced, and some begin to repent; and one of them was with me this day to be admitted again to his parish, and now promiseth conformity, whom I repelled till I had him bound with two good sureties of his own parish, and so I have, and he now saith there will come more to that point, whom I will so order. For as for the most part of these recusants, I would wish them out of the ministry, as mere ignorant and vain heads." Ep. 209, TO CECIL, p. 271, 272. IB.

1566, March 28.] Abp. PARKER. "And whereas the whole state of the realm, by act of Parliament openly published, doth most earnestly in God's name require us all to endeavour ourselves, to the uttermost of our knowledge, duly and truly to execute the said laws, as we will answer before God. By the which act also we have full power and authority to reform, and punish by censures of the church, all and singular persons which shall offend. And whereas also the Queen's most excellent Majesty, now a year past and more, addressed her Highness' letters enforcing the same charge, the contents whereof I sent your lordship in her name and authority, to admonish them to obedience, and so I doubt not but your lordship have distributed the same unto others of our brethren within this province of Canterbury; whereupon hath ensued in the most part of the realm an humble and obedient conformity, and yet some few persons, I fear more scrupulous than godly prudent, have not conformed themselves; peradventure some of them for *lack of particular description of orders* to be followed, which as your lordship doth know, were *agreed upon among us* long ago, and *yet in certain respects not published.* Now for the speedy reformation of the same, as the Queen's Highness hath expressly charged both you and me, of late *being therefore called to her presence, to see her laws executed,* and *good orders decreed* and observed, I can no less do of my obedience to Almighty God, of my allegiance to her princely estate, and of sincere zeal to the truth and promotion of Christian religion now established, but require and charge you, as you will answer to God, and to her Majesty, to see *her Majesty's laws and injunctions* duly observed within your diocese, and *also these our convenient orders* described *in these books* at this present sent unto your lordship. And furthermore, to transmit the same books with your letters (according as hath been heretofore used) unto all others of our brethren *within this province,* to cause the same to be performed in their several jurisdictions and charges." EP. 210, TO GRINDAL, P. 273, 274. IB.

1566, March 28.] Abp. PARKER. "I commende me hartely unto you, and whereas I am informid that diverse parsons, vicares and curats, within my peculiar Jurisdiction of the deanrie of Bockinge (beinge as I feare more scrupulouse then godly prudente) have not conformed them selves to the Quenes Majesties *Lawes and Injunctions* in thadministracion of publike prayers and Sacraments, and in outwarde *apparell* agreable in Regarde of order for them to weare, notwithstanding the said Lawes injunctions and ordinances prescribed *for the same.* In which disorder appeareth (as yt ys commonly interpreted) a manifest violation and contempte of the Quenes Majestie authoritie and abusinge her princely clemencye in so longe bearinge with the same withowte execution of condigne severitie for there due correction, yf the Lawes weare extended uppon them. I have sente you herewith *a booke of certeine orders agreed uppon by me and other of my bretherne of my province of Canturburie,* and hitherto *not published,* wyllinge and requiringe you with all spede to call before you all and singler the parsons vicars and curats of my said peculiar Jurisdiction of Bockinge, *to publishe* to them the said orders prescribed *in this boke,* and also to more persuade and commaunde them and every of them as they will answer at there peril, duely to observe as well *her Majesties said Lawes and injunctions* in thadministracion of publique prayer and the Sacramentes and in there externe apparell, *as also these orders* sente unto you herewith, and such as will obstinately refuse to conforme themselves to said Lawes injunctions and orders that you do forthwith suspende them and everie of them from there publique ministracions whatsoever, and also do sequester all the fructe of there benefice, &c." EP. TO DR. COLE, DEAN OF BOCKING. Cited by PARKER, DID QUEEN ELIZABETH TAKE OTHER ORDER IN THE ADVERTISEMENTS OF 1566? C. 4, P. 49, 50.

This letter was printed in full for the first time by MR. PARKER, from Abp. PARKER'S REGISTER at Lambeth. FOL. 257, VOL. 1.

In the Register, the following notes are appended, written in the same hand:

"A like letter was written to Mr. Denne, Commissarie of Canterbury.

"Another like Letter to the Busshoppe of Chichester, Commissarie of the peculiar jurisdiction of South Mallinge Pagh[a]m and Terringe.

"Another like letter to Mr. Doctr. Weston, Dean of Tharches, Shoreh[a]m and Croyden, with severall *bookes above mentioned inclosed* severally in the same L[ett]res." In. See STRYPE, LIFE AND ACTS OF PARKER, B. 3, c. 9, p. 431, 432. VOL. 2.

1566.] JOHN STOWE. A very important document has just been discovered in the handwriting of Stowe, the Antiquary, in Lambeth MS., No. 306. which not only determines the time when the Advertisements were published, about March 28, but shows that they were issued to put in force the Queen's Injunctions, and that they were not intended to do away with the Cope or Vestment, but to enforce the Surplice, Gown, and Square Cap, all of which were most cordially hated by the Puritans:

"The xvvj. day of Marche, in anno 1566, beying Twesday, y$^e$ parsons and mynysters of y$^e$ churches in and aboughte London were (by commaundyment) at Lambethe, before y$^e$ Archebyshoppe of Caunterbury and othar of y$^e$ cownsell, wher charge was gyven to them to sarve theyr churchis and were thayr apparayl accordyng to y$^e$ quens injunctions, or ells to do no sarvyce. And that same weke or y$^e$ begynyng of y$^e$ next came forthe a boke in print subscribyd by y$^e$ Archebyshope of Cauntorbury, y$^e$ Byshopps of London, Wynchester, Elii, and divers othar, whiche apoyntyd y$^e$ sayd mynistars to were theyre gounes and clokes with standynge colars and corneryd capse, and at theyr servyce to were syrplysys, or els not to mynystar, &c. Afftar this followyd myche troble with y$^e$ mynistar of y$^e$ citie of London; for in moost paryshis y$^e$ sextyn of y$^e$ churche dyd all shuche servys as was done, and that in his coate or gonne, as he comonly went about othar busynes." MEMORANDA, P. 135. CAMDEN SOCIETY PUBLICATIONS, NEW SERIES. VOL. 28.

On pages 135-140, are accounts of the great disturbances which arose from the attempted enforcement of the Advertisements. When the Bishop of London, a friend of the Puritans, preached at St. Margaret's, Old Fish Street, on the following January 26, many of the people, especially the women, hooted at him. and cried out "Ware horns," because he wore a cornered cap as required by law. (PAGE 140. IB.)

1566.] COVERDALE. HUMPHREY & SAMPSON wrote a letter to Farell, Viret, Beza and others in July. 1566. wherein they say, alluding to the Advertisements:

"For it is now settled and determined, that .... the white surplice and cope are to be retained in divine service." EP. 50, P. 121. Z. L. 2D.

The Advertisements were published about March 28. PARKER

again writes to Cecil April 28, 1566, still complaining that no aid is afforded him to put in operation the Act for Uniformity:

"The Queen's Majesty willed my lord of York to declare her pleasure determinately to have the order go forward. I trust her Highness hath devised how it may be performed. I utterly despair therein as of myself, and therefore must sit still, as I have now done, always waiting either her toleration, or else further aid. Mr. Secretary, can it be thought, that I alone, having sun and moon against me, can compass this difficulty? If you of her Majesty's Council provide no otherwise for this matter than as it appeareth openly, what the sequel will be *horresco vel reminiscendo cogitare.* In King Edward's days the whole body of the council travailed in Hooper's attempt. My predecessor, Dr. Cranmer, labouring in vain with bishop Farrar, the council took it in hand; and shall I hope to do that the Queen's Majesty will have done? What I hear and see, what complaints be brought unto me, I shall not report; how I am used of many men's hands. I commit all to God. If I die in the cause (malice so far prevailing) I shall commit my soul to God in a good conscience. If the Queen's Majesty be no more considered, I shall not marvel what be said, or done to me." Ep. 215, p. 280, 280. P. C.

And here the matter appears to have rested for many years.

2. THE ADVERTISEMENTS WERE THE WORK OF THE BISHOPS ALONE.

Archbishop Parker frequently speaks of them as "our advertisements," "our book," &c., and says expressly that it was composed by him and other Bishops. He frequently complains that although he was incited to this proceeding by the Queen, he was not supported by her, and could not get her to approve of the Advertisements, and that he was bound to "prosecute this order" by his "own authority." (See Ep. 175, 176, 209, 210, 212, and EP. TO THE DEAN OF BOCKING.)

1564–5.] On the 8th March, 1564–5, Abp. PARKER sent Cecil a copy of his book of Advertisements, which he soon returned with the following indorsement, according to STRYPE, who says:

"For these are the words written upon them by the Secretary's own hand, Mar. 1564. *Ordinances accorded by the Archbishop of Cant, &c. in his province. These were not authorised nor published.* . . . . But because the book wanted the Queen's authority, they thought fit not to term the contents thereof *Articles* or *Ordinances,* by which names they at first went, but by a modester denomination, viz. *Advertisements.*" LIFE OF PARKER, B. 2, c. 20, AN. 1564, P. 314. VOL. 1.

1567.] GEORGE WITHERS AND JOHN BARTHELOT. "The *Advertisements* of the bishops . . . . For all that we have above treated of is manifest from the advertisements of the bishops, from certain royal injunctions, &c." EP. 58, TO BULLINGER AND GUALTER, P. 149, 151. Z. L. 2D.

Circa 1567.] GEORGE WITHERS. "The royal injunctions, and the admonitions, or (as they call them) the advertisements of the Bishops." EP. 62, TO THE PRINCE ELECTOR PALATINE, P. 163. IB.

JOHN OLDMIXON. "The Archbishop of Canterbury, the Bishops of London, Ely, Winchester and Lincoln, framed several Articles to inforce the Habits, which were stiled Advertisements. The Archbishop carryed them to the Court, but the Queen as yet, refused to give them her sanction. The Archbishop chafed at the disappointment, said, the Court had put them upon framing them, and if they would not go on and give them the Royal sanction, they had better never have done anything; nay, if the Council would not lend their helping hand against Nonconformists, as they had done heretofore in Hooper's days, they should be but laughed at for what they had done; but still the Queen was so cold, that when the Bishop of London came to Court, she spoke not a word to him about the redressing the neglect of conformity in the City of London, where it was most disregarded, upon which the Archbishop writ to the Secretary, desiring another Letter from the Queen, to back up their endeavours for Conformity; adding, in some heat, If you remedy it not by Letter, I will no more strive against the stream, fume or chide who will. Which shews us, that the Bishops incited the severe measures against the Puritans, and that the Statesmen did not care to meddle in the matter, since it must be their backwardness which made the Queen cool in an affair she had put the Bishops upon." HIST. OF ENGLAND, AN. 1564, P. 340.

DANIEL NEAL. "The Archbishop, with the Bishops of London, Ely, Winchester, and Lincoln, framed sundry articles to enforce the habits, which were afterwards published under the title of Advertisements. But the Queen refused to give them her sanction." HISTORY OF THE PURITANS, C. 4, P. 91. VOL. 1.

JOHN STRYPE. "But she was persuaded not to add her own immediate authority to the book by some great persons at court, because, upon their suggestion, she said, the archbishop's authority and the commissioners alone were sufficient. And so instead of calling them *articles* or *ordinances*, they only named them *advertisements*." ANNALS OF THE REFORMATION, C. 41, AN. 1564, P. 130, 131. VOL. 1, PT. 2.

3. THE ADVERTISEMENTS WERE AGAINST NO LAW OF THE REALM.

Having no force of law, they could not repeal or do away with the Rubric of 1559, for as Bishop HORN, who helped draw them up, remarks in speaking of certain habits enjoined by Act of Parliament:

"This act cannot be repealed unless by the agreement and consent of all the estates of the kingdom, by whose concurrence it was enacted. .... We certainly hope to repeal this clause next session." EP. 64, TO GUALTER, AN. 1565, P. 142, 143. Z. L.

HORN appears to confuse Elizabeth's Injunctions with the Act of Uniformity. But his testimony serves to show that the Rubric of 1559 could only be repealed by Parliament.

1566.] ABP. PARKER. "I have weeded out of these articles all such of doctrine, &c., which peradventure stayed the book from the Queen's Majesty's approbation, and have put in but things advouchable, and, as I take them, against no law of the realm." EP. 209, TO CECIL, P. 272. P. C.

In fact, the Advertisements were drawn up to enforce "laws and ordinances already established." (See PARKER, EP. 171, 203, 205, 209, 210, cited above.)

Circa 1572.] EDMUND GRINDAL, ARCHBISHOP OF YORK.

Quare in hac ipsa, de qua jam dixi olim a Rege Edwardo conscriptae religionis. Forma multa de vestiendi ratione ad ecclesiae ministros proprie accomodata praecipiantur; deque rebus aliis quae vel aboleri vel emendari nonnulli viri boni cuperent, quo minus hoc operi manum quispiam admovere potuit, legis authoritate prohibebatur. Regiae vero Majestatis, ut ex episcoporum quorumdam consilio, quaedam immutare possit, lex ipsa concedit. At vero de lege nihil nec mutatum nec imminutum est, nec sane episcoporum quod sciam quisquam reperitur, qui non et ipse praescriptis pareat institutis, et caeteris, ut idem faciant, ducem se suasoremque praebeant." EP. AD ZANCH. Cited by STRYPE, LIFE OF GRINDAL, B. 1, C. 12, P. 494.

Whereas, in this very form of religion formerly drawn up by King Edward, of which I have spoken before, many things are commended respecting the manner of dress properly adapted to the ministers of the Church, and also concerning other matters, which some good men wished to abolish or mend, it was forbidden by the authority of law that any one should meddle in this matter. But the law itself allowed the Queen's Majesty, with the advice of some of the bishops, to make some changes. But nothing of the law is either changed or diminished; nor so far as I know, is there any bishop to be found, who does not himself obey the prescribed rules, and lead and persuade the rest to do the same.

4. USE MADE OF THE ADVERTISEMENTS IN OFFICIAL DOCUMENTS.

A distinction is made between "the Queen's Laws and Injunctions" and the "Advertisements" or "Laws set out by public authority."

1566.] EDMUND GRINDAL, BISHOP OF LONDON. "After my hartie commendacyons, these are to require .... that you enjoyne everie [minister, &c.] upon payne of deprivacion to prepare forthwith and to weare *such* habitt and *apparell as is ordeyned by the*

*Queenes Majesties authoritie, expressed* in the treaty intituled the advertisem<sup>ts</sup>, &c., which I send heerein inclosed unto yo<sup>u</sup>, and in like to injoyne every of them under the said payne of deprivacion as well to observe the order of mynistracion in the church w<sup>th</sup> *surples*, and in such forme as is sett forth in the saide treatie, as alsoe to require the subscription of every of them to the said Advertism<sup>nts</sup>." STATE PAPERS, DOMESTIC, ELIZABETH, VOL. 39, No. 76. Cited by PARKER, DID QUEEN ELIZABETH, &c., SEC. 5, P. 56.

The Queen's Injunctions contained certain orders as to habits and apparel, which were "expressed," that is, more fully set forth and explained in the Advertisements.

1567.] MATTHEW PARKER, ARCHBISHOP OF CANTERBURY. In his VISITATION ARTICLES, in 1567, he says nothing of the Advertisements, but only of the "quenes majesties injunctions," or of her "laws and injunctions." CARDWELL, DOC. ANNALS, N. 68. ART. N. 1, 3, P. 338, 339. VOL. I.

1569.] "Imprimis whether divine service be sayde or songe by youre minister or ministers in your severall churches duely and reverently as it is set forth by the laws of this realme without any kinde of variations.

"And whether the holy sacramentes be likewise ministered reverently in such manner, as by the lawes of this realme, and by the queen's majestie's injunctions, and by thadvertisements set forthe by publique authority is appointed and prescribed.

"4. Whether your curates or ministers do publiquely in their open churches reade in manner appoynted the queene's majestie's injunctions and homilies; the advertisements lately sette forthe by publique authoritie." VISITATION ARTICLES OF 1569. IB. P. 355, 356.

In Articles No. 2, 3, 5, 8, 14, 22, he inquires whether certain things were done according to the Queen's Injunctions.

1575.] "9. Whether your Preachers set out in their Sermons the Queens Majesties Authorities over all her subjects, and in all Causes, and exhort their hearers to due obedience under the same, to the folowyng of her Majesties Injunctions, and other lawes, statutes, orders, advertisements, and decrees, set forth by common authority."

"16. Item, whether they . . . . minister the Sacraments reverently in such sort as it is set forth by the lawes of this Realm, the Queens Majesties Injunctions, and the advertisements.

"38. Item, . . . . whether your Churches and Churchyards be well repayred, adorned and fenced; whether the Roode loftes be pulled downe, and a partition made, and kept betwixt the Chancil and the Church, according to the Advertisements." VISITATION ARTICLES OF 1575, in the SECOND RITUAL COMMISSION REPORT, P. 411. Cited by PARKER, DID QUEEN ELIZABETH, &c., SECT. 5, P. 64.

But in the Advertisements of 1566, nothing is said about a partition between the Chancel and Church. There must, therefore, be other Advertisements besides those of 1566. Mr. Parker discovered in the British Museum a copy of Orders issued October 10, 1561, which makes the matter sure:

> "Provided also, that where in any Parrish Churche the sayde Roode loftes be alreadye transposed, so that there remayne a comely particion betwixte the Chauncell and the Churche, that no alteracion be otherwyse attempted in them, but be suffered in quiete. And where no particion is standyng, there to be one appoynted." Cited by PARKER, DID QUEEN ELIZABETH TAKE OTHER ORDER, &c. A POSTSCRIPT, &c., N. 8, P. 157.

In his VISITATION ARTICLES of 1569, he also inquires:

> "6. Whether the roode loft be pulled down, according to the order prescribed: and if the partition betweene the chauncell and the churche be kepte." CARDWELL, DOC. ANN., N. 73, P. 357. VOL. 1.

1569.] JOHN PARKHURST, BISHOP OF NORWICH. "Finally, ye shall diligently observe, and put in ure, all such Orders and Injunctions as have been appointed you beforetyme as well by the Injunctions of the Queen's Majesty, as by the Archbishop of Canterbury's grace, and the Bishop of the Diocese." VISITATION ARTICLES OF 1569, in the SECOND RITUAL COMMISSION REPORT, P. 404. Cited by PARKER, DID QUEEN ELIZABETH, &c., SECT. 5, P. 62.

1573.] "The Bokes of Advertisements and the canons set forth by authority." EP. 172, TO PARKER, P. 476. GORHAM, GLEANINGS, &c.

1571.] RICHARD COX, BISHOP OF ELY. "Item, that every Parson, Vicar, and Curate, shall use in tyme of the celebration of Divine Service, to weare a surplesse prescribed by the Queen's Majesties Injunctions, and the booke of Common Prayer, and shall kepe and observe all other rightes and orders prescribed in the same booke of Common Prayer and Injunctions; as well about the celebration of the Sacramentes, as also in their comely and priestlyke apparell to be worne accordyng to the precept set foorth in the booke called the Advertisements." VISITATION ARTICLES OF 1571. IB. P. 406. Cited by PARKER, DID QUEEN ELIZABETH, &c., SECT. 5. P. 62.

1571.] QUEEN ELIZABETH, in 1571, ordered Abp. Parker to preserve uniformity in Divine Service "as by the laws in that behalf is provided, and by our Injunctions also declared and explained. .... Uniformity prescribed by our laws and injunctions." EP. 292, TO PARKER, P. 386. P. C.

She says not a word about the Advertisements.

Abp. PARKER frequently alludes to the "Laws of the land" and the "Queen's Injunctions" in subsequent Epistles, but says nothing about the Queen's Advertisements:

1573.] "If the law of the land be rejected, if the Queen's Majestey's injunctions, if her chapel, if her authority be so neglected, if our book of service be so abominable," &c. Ep. 325, p. 426. P. C.

1573.] "Forasmuch as the Queen's Majesty being very careful and desirous, that one uniform order in the celebration of divine service and ministration of the sacraments shall be used and observed in all places of this her Highness' realm and dominions, according to the Book of Common Prayer set forth by public authority and her Majesty's Injunctions, without alteration or innovation," &c. Ep. 345, to Sandys, p. 451. Ib.

1575.] "The Queen's religion, stablished by law and Injunction." Ep. 369, p. 478. Ib.

5. THE ADVERTISEMENTS WERE NOT THE TAKING OF "OTHER ORDER" AS AUTHORISED BY THE ACT OF UNIFORMITY.

(1) *In 1559, and in 1560-1, the Queen issued further orders to enforce uniformity in the Church.*

Abp. PARKER, in a letter to Cecil in 1570, says expressly that the Queen, by virtue of the Act of Uniformity, did take "further order in her injunctions" of 1559. (See pages 38, 39.)

Then he adds:

"I tell them that they do evil to make odious comparison betwixt statute and injunction, and yet I say and hold, that the injunction hath authority by proviso of the statute." Ep. 283, p. 375, 376. P. C.

The commission of 1560-1, signed, sealed, and engrossed in due form, is preserved in PARKER'S REGISTER, FOL. 215 a. VOL. 1, and was executed as far as possible. (See pages 46, 47.)

In 1564-5, inasmuch as uniformity was not brought about, in spite of the efforts of the Queen, another commission was issued to Parker, to see that uniformity was enforced according to "laws already established." A contemporary copy of this letter exists among the Lansdowne MS. VIII. art. 6.

Acting under this order, in about a month, Abp. Parker and four other Bishops drew up Advertisements, which were for "his Province of Canterbury," as Cecil, Secretary of State, says, but "not authorised nor published." Parker himself complains that they were not sanctioned by the Queen, though he labored hard to that end.

Here the matter rested for about a year, when Parker, in 1566, again took up the matter, and a second draft of the Advertisements was drawn up, from he had weeded out certain things which he thought had perhaps prevented the Queen from authorising the first draft. There was now nothing in them contrary to the laws of the Realm, and Abp. Grindal, who helped draw up the Advertisements, says in 1571, that the law was neither "altered or diminished." (See page 63.)

So far as we know, the Queen never sanctioned the second draft of Advertisements. She probably left the whole matter to the Bishops. If the Advertisements had been sanctioned by law, they would not have been obeyed any more than the Rubrics were.

Parker's efforts to enforce the Laws of the Church, made him an object of hatred to the Puritans. STRYPE says:

"These being their sentiments, and our archbishop on the other hand called upon so much by the Queen also, to see her injunctions observed, and his own judgment and counsel concurring, that it was so necessary for obedience to be given to laws, he drew an extraordinary ill-will from the Puritans upon himself. The called him Papist and Pope of Lambeth, and the like. And they used all their interest to bring him into disfavour at Court, procuring the Earl of Leicester to be his fatal enemy. Who was so to the last, and did by his authority with the Queen, get almost every suit the Archbishop had with her to be disappointed or rejected." LIFE OF PARKER, OBSERVATIONS, B. 4, SECT. 4, P. 529. VOL. 2.

See PARKER, EP. 367, P. 472. P. C.

To Parker, with very little support from the other Bishops, or the Court, except the Queen, we are indebted for the preservation of the Church from Puritanism. His Epistles for the last ten years of his life bear frequent witness to the difficulties of his position, and the lack of support. In his last Epistle, to Lord Burghley, April 11, 1575, dictated from his sick bed, he expresses his intention to "plainly give over to strive against the stream." He also says that both himself and Lord Burghley were termed "great papists." EP. 369, P. 479. P. C.

During the Great Rebellion, his body was removed from its resting place and most shamefully treated, being buried in a dunghill. His monument was also destroyed. After the Restoration his bones were found and decently buried again. See STRYPE, LIFE OF PARKER, B. 4, C. 44, AN. 1573, P. 435. VOL. 2.

(2) *There is quite a marked difference between the Advertisements of 1564 and those as finally published in 1566.*

The Title of the original, is:

"*Ordinances accorded by the Archbishop of Cant. &c. in his province.*" STRYPE, LIFE OF PARKER, B. 2, C. 20, P. 314. VOL. 1.

The Title of the published copy, is:

"Advertisements partly for the due order in the publique administration of common prayers, and usinge the holy sacramentes, and partly for the apparell of all persons ecclesiasticall, by vertue of the Queene's Majestie's Letters, commaunding the same, the 25th day of January, in the seventh year of our soveraigne lady Elizabeth, &c." CARDWELL, DOC. ANN., N. 65, P. 321. VOL. 1.

As to the cause of this difference, STRYPE says:

"The matter, I suppose, was this: When these articles (by Leicester's means no question) were refused to be confirmed by the Queen's Council, the Archbishop however thought it advisable to print them under his and the rest of the Commissioners' hands, to signify at least what their judgment and will was; and to let their authority go as far as it would. Which was probable to take some effect with the greater part of the clergy; especially considering their canonical obedience they had sworn to their Diocesans. But because the Book wanted the Queen's Authority, they thought fit not to term the contents thereof *Articles* or *Ordinances*, by which names they went at first, but by a modester denomination, viz., *Advertisements*." LIFE OF PARKER, B. 1, c. 20, P. 314. VOL. I.

After speaking of the differences in the Preface, he adds:

"There be also some other small alterations. As the word *constitutions* in the MS. is changed into *temporal orders* in the Collections: and *positive laws in discipline*, is changed into *rules in some part of discipline*. I have also diligently compared the printed book with the aforesaid MS. copy, and find them different in many places, and sundry things are left out which are in the copy; the Archbishop thinking fit in that manner to published them, because of their want of the stamp of authority to oblige persons to the observance of them." IB.

(3) *The Advertisements, as we have seen, were the work of the Bishops, though they were incited thereto by the Queen, " who could not satisfy her conscience without crushing the Puritans." (Speech of Cecil, cited by Oldmixon, Hist. of England, an. 1573, p. 451.)*

But their powerful friends at Court, (among whom were Sir Francis Knolles, allied to the Queen by marriage; Dudley, Earl of Leicester; Sir Francis Walsingham; the Earl of Bedford,) took care that she should not legally sanction the Advertisements, which consequently were not binding in law; and of this fact the Puritans were well aware, as is evident from numerous contemporary Documents.

In the Synod of 1571, the Clergy were very anxious that the Advertisements should be referred to, so that they might receive some sanction from the Crown, requiring sacristans to observe all things contained in "the Royal Injunctions, and in the Book of Advertisements—regiis injunctionibus, et in libello admonitionum." CARDWELL, SYNODALIA, N. I. P. 126.

But Elizabeth refused to ratify these Canons. CARDWELL makes this note:

"The celebrated Advertisements of the year 1564, which, acting on the same principle as in the case of these canons, the queen refused to put forth with her sanction, although she had required the bishops in commission to draw them up, and afterwards insisted that they should be vigorously enforced. By this and by other synods they seem to have been considered as having the most perfect authority." I<small>B</small>.

The Canons of 1575 were ratified by the Queen, but not until she had struck out what related to the Advertisements.

It seems as if the Clergy tried to play a sharp trick on the Queen, by which they hoped to get the Advertisements approved indirectly, but they were unsuccessful. CARDWELL says:

"In the eighth article the clause 'paying nothing for the same' had been framed by the bishops in the following manner, 'paying not above four pence for the seal, parchment, writing and wax for the same, according to an article of the advertisements in that behalf.' [CARDW., DOC. ANN., N. 75, P. 324. VOL. 1.] By inserting this clause the bishops may have wished to obtain indirectly the queen's confirmation of the Advertisements; from which however she appears to have withheld her official sanction during the whole of her reign, although they were drawn up and enforced at her command." SYNOD., P. 136.

The following extracts will show that the Advertisements were not regarded by the Puritans as being sanctioned by the Queen:

Circa 1572.] A SECOND ADMONITION TO THE PARLIAMENT. "It may be that they [the Bishops] know their order when they ride in their scarlet robes before the Queen, and how to poll their clergy as they call them . . . . or how to rattle up these new fellows, these young boys, that will not obey at a beck to their Articles, Advertisements, Canons, Caveats, and such like stuff of their own forging." PAGE 23. Cited by MACCOLL, LAWLESSNESS, &c. PREF. TO THE 3D ED., P. CXI.

Circa 1584.] AN ABSTRACT OF CERTAINE ACTS OF PARLEMENT; OF CERTAINE OF HER MAJESTIE'S INJUNCTIONS: OF CERTAINE CANONS, ETC. "Though her Majestie's most excellent name be used by the publishers of the sayd Advertisements for confirmation of them, and that they affirm her M. to have commanded them thereunto, by her highness letters; yet because the booke itself commeth forth without her M. priviledge and is not printed by her M. printer, nor any in his name, therefore it carrieth no such credite and authoritie with it, as whereunto her M. subjects are necessarily bound to subscribe, having other lawes, and other Injunctions under her M. name, and authorised by her M. priviledge, contrary to the same." N. P. (Page 47, in the margin.)

Circa 1590.] THE COPIE OF A LETTER WRITTEN BY A GENTLEMAN IN THE COUNTREY, UNTO A LONDONER, TOUCHING AN

ANSWERE TO THE ARCHB. ARTICLES. "[The Advertisements] were yet neuer duelie published, as being aduertisementes, onlie in name ordinaunces, and not in deede. Forthough her Majesties' name, & commaundment by her highness Letters, be vsed by the publishers of the saide advertisementes, for the confirmation of them, yet, neuertheless because the booke it selfe commeth foorth without her Majesties priuiledge, and hath bin printed not by her Majesties printer, nor any in his name, Therefore the same caryeth as yet no such creditt and authoritie with it, as wherevnto, *propter falsitatem expressam*, or *veritatem tacitam in impetracione*, her Majesties subjects are necessarilie bounde to subscribe, especiallie having other Injunctions vnder her Majesties owne name, and authorised by her Majesties priviledge, contrarie to the same, as in the article, concerning not preaching without licenses, shall appeare." PARTE OF A REGISTER, P. 162, 163.

1605.] CONSIDERATIONS AGAINST THE DEPRIVATION OF A MINISTER, FOR THE NOT USE OF A SURPLICE IN DIVINE SERVICE. "For our partes we acknowledge, that the Queenes Highnes had authoritie by the statute with the advice of her Commissioners, &c. or Metropolitane, to take other order for ornamentes. But wee never yet understood, that any other order was taken accordingly: and especiallie in any such sorte, as that the Archbishops, Bishops and other Ordinaries might warrent their sentences of deprivation to be lawfull against the Ministers, which refuse to use the Surplice.

"For though by her Highnes letters it doth appeare, that she was desirous, as the preface to the advertisements importeth, to have advice from the Metropolitane & Commissioners, that she might take order; nevertheless that her Highnes, by her authority, with their advise, did take order & alter the ornaments: this (I say) doth nowhere appeare, no not by the advertisements them selves. Howsoever then the Metropolitane upon the Queenes mandative letters, that some orders might be taken, had conference and communication, and at the last, by assent, and consent of the ecclesiasticall commissioners did think such orders as were specified in the advertisements, meete and convenient to be used and followed; nevertheless all this proveth not that these orders were taken by her Majesties Authoritie. For the Metropolitane and Commissioners, might thinke, agree and subscribe, that the advertisements were meete and convenient, and yet might these advertisements be never of any valew, as wherennto her Highnes authoritie was never yeelded." PAGE 35, 36. Cited by PERRY, NOTES ON THE JUDGMENT OF THE JUD. COM. OF THE PRIVY COUNCIL, P. 54, 55.

Circa 1640.] JOHN COSIN, afterwards BISHOP OF DURHAM. "*Such ornaments, &c.*] By the Act of Uniformity the parliament thought fit, not to continue this last order [the Rubric of 1552], but to restore the first again [that of 1549]; which since that time was never altered by any other law, and therefore it is still in force at this day." NOTES ON THE BOOK OF COMMON PRAYER, 3D SERIES, P. 440. WORKS, VOL. 5.

1640–1.] Among the "Innovations in Discipline," complained of by the Puritans to Parliament in 1641, was this:

"10. By pretending for their innovations, the injunctions and advertisements of queen Elizabeth, which are not in force, but by commentery and imposition." CARDWELL, HIST. OF CONF., C. 7, P. 273.

DANIEL NEAL. "But the queen was firm to her former resolution; she would give no authority to the Advertisements." HIST. OF THE PURITANS, C. 4, P. 98. VOL. 1.

1713.] EDMUND GIBSON, afterwards BISHOP OF LONDON. "*Until other Order.*] Which *other* Order (at least in the method prescribed by this Act [1 Eliz. c. 2, s. 25.]) was never made: and therefore, *legally*, the Ornaments of Ministers in performing Divine Service are the same now as they were in 2 *E*. 6." CODEX, JUR. ECCL., TIT. 13, C. 1, P. 297. VOL. 1.

1763.] DR. RICHARD BURN. "For by the 1 El. c. 2, it is provided, *that such ornaments of the church, and of the ministers thereof, shall be retained and used, . . . until other order shall be therein taken,* . . . which other order as to this matter, was never taken." ECCL. LAW, word PUBLICK WORSHIP, N. 4, P. 265. VOL. 3.

1845.] DR. ARCHIBALD JOHN STEPHENS. "Which other order (at least in the method prescribed by this Act [1 Eliz. c. 2, s. 25],) was never made." ECCL. STAT., P. 370. VOL. 1. Cited by PERRY, NOTES, P. 118.

In process of time, when the facts in the case were forgotten, the Advertisements came to be looked upon as having much authority, and were sometimes joined with the Queen's Injunctions. STRYPE remarks:

"But to return to the Advertisements. At length, it seems the Archbishop's patience, and persistence prevailed, and these ecclesiastical rules (now called advertisements) recovered their first names of Articles and Ordinances: as may appear by the metropolitical visitation of the church of Gloucester, anno 1576, . . . when among the Injunctions (eight in number) given at that Church, one was this, 'Not to oppose the Queen's Injunctions, nor the Ordinations, nor Articles made by the Queen's Commissioners, (which are there said to be, Matthew, Archbishop of Canterbury; Edmund, Bishop of London; Richard, Bishop of Ely; Edmund, Bishop of Rochester; Robert, Bishop of Winton; and Nic., Bishop of Lincoln;) January, the 25th, in the seventh year of the Queen's reign. To which that Archbishop (next successor to our Archbishop) subscribed his name. Where we may observe, that these ordinations of the Queen's Commissioners are joined with her own Injunctions to be observed. Of such force they were now become." LIFE OF PARKER, B. 2, C. 20, P. 319, 320. VOL. 2.

In 1585, Archbishop Whitgift, in his Visitation Articles for the Diocese of Chichester, inquires:

"V. Whether doth your Minister in public prayer wear a surplice: and go abroad apparelled, as by her Majesties *injunctions* and *advertisements* is prescribed?" LIFE OF WHITGIFT, B. 3, APPENDIX, N. 29, P. 180. VOL. 3.

But the fact remains, that though the Archbishop was most strenuous for enforcing uniformity, as was also the Queen, she did not see fit, perhaps, because she would not in any way disallow the Vestments, although determined to enforce the Surplice, or perhaps from motives of policy, to proceed in her own name, thinking it better to let the Bishops enforce the law and bear the blame. We have an instance of this in the case of Aylmer, Bishop of London. He committed Cartwright to prison, well knowing that the Queen was much incensed against him, and sent the Lords word that he had done it by warrant from her. She was much displeased at this, wishing the Bishop himself to incur all the blame and outcry which was sure to follow from this act. STRYPE, LIFE AND ACTS OF AYLMER, C. 7. P. 76, 77.

The authorities in those days were very careful not to enforce as law anything which had not the Royal assent. Grindal refused to accept the canons of 1571 as they had not received " her Majestie's royal assent," nor were " confirmed by act of Parliament," for fear of *praemunire.* STRYPE, LIFE OF GRINDAL, B. 2, C. 2, P. 246, 247.

STRYPE gives the following account of Sir Thomas Smith, the Queen's Secretary of State:

"Speaking of the irresolutions and inconstancy of the Court, he said, that 'till the Queen had signed he durst never adventure to affirm anything, for fear of contrary winds;' the which, he said, was no news in that Court." LIFE OF SMITH, C. 18, P. 178.

6. IT IS NOW CLAIMED BY SOME THAT THE ADVERTISEMENTS WERE DIRECTED AGAINST HIGH RITUAL.

The Puritans of those times looked upon them with dismay, for they well knew that they were not intended to curtail, but rather to increase ritual. They knew that at heart the Queen was what we would call an extreme High Churchman. The Advertisements were intended to stop the lawlessness of the Puritans, who had generally given up the habits; to make binding the Surplice, and requiring the Cope only in Cathedral and Collegiate Churches; but at the same time prohibiting it nowhere. The use of the Chasuble was not forbidden. The Advertisements were very tolerant. No instance is known, I believe, where the Vestments were enforced, In Visitation Articles addressed to Cathedrals even, there is no inquiry whether the Cope is used, as required by law. Only the Surplice was required, but that even was frequently disused, and such offenders left unpunished.

1566.] COVERDALE, HUMPHREY & SAMPSON. "Our affairs are not altered for the better, but, alas! are sadly deteriorated. For it is now settled and determined, that an unleavened cake must be used in place of common bread;—that the communion must be received by the people on their bended knees;—that out of doors must be worn the square cap, bands, a long gown and tippet; while the white surplice and cope are to be retained in divine service. And those who refuse to comply with these requirements, are deprived of their estates, dignities, and every ecclesiastical office.

"Besides, as many of us as have cast out these things from the churches committed to our trust, cannot restore them without grevious offence and abominable impiety.

"The question, we confess, is nice and difficult, whether it is better to yield to circumstances, or to depart; to admit the relics of the Amorites, or to desert our post." EP. 50, TO FARELL, &c., P. 121-123. Z. L. 2D.

This letter is dated July, 1566; the Advertisements were published the last of the preceding March. See also the Letters of Beza, Zanchius, Humphrey and Sampson, and Wiburn, cited on pages 37, 38, and Section xib, (iii).

I will conclude with this Note from CARDWELL:

"These Advertisements and the proceedings consequent thereon occasioned the first open separation of the nonconformists from the Church of England." DOC. ANN., N. 65, P. 321. VOL. 1.

### 7. SUMMARY.

(1) *Circumstances attending the drawing up of the Advertisements.*

At the beginning of her reign, the Queen was much offended at the varieties used in celebrating Divine service, and at the filthiness and neglect into which Churches had fallen. Therefore, January 22, 1560-1, she addressed a letter, duly drawn up, signed and sealed, to Archbishop Parker, ordering him to correct abuses, and bring about a uniform method of celebrating Divine service in all Cathedrals and Collegiate Churches, which could better bear the expense, and even in Parish Churches "either the same" or a "like" manner of service was to be used. Thereupon, Parker and others drew up "Interpretations," suggesting the use of "only one apparel," as the Cope, with the Surplice, instead of many vestures, as ordered by the Rubric, thereby making a compromise and lightening the expense of providing many Vestments.

These "Interpretations" were never published, perhaps, because, as was evident from Convocation the next year, there was a strong opposition in certain quarters to all Vestments, even the Surplice.

But, as the evil continued to increase, in 1565, Cecil drew up a letter which he proposed that the Queen should issue, but which he as yet had not shown her for fear, among other things, that she would not think it severe enough. As a matter of fact, the Queen never did sign this letter, so far as we know. By this letter Parker was ordered to proceed,—not to enact new laws,—but by "laws already established," to bring about one manner of uniformity. Parker and four other Bishops drew up Ordinances, or, as they were afterwards styled, Advertisements, requiring the Cope in Cathedrals and Colleges, and the Surplice in Parish Churches, but not forbidding the Cope even there; and for outward apparel, the square cap and gown. Cecil informs us that these were "not authorized or published," and Parker tells us that the Queen would not sanction them. A year later, Parker again takes up the matter and "weeds" out whatever he thought prevented the Queen from approving his former book; but, as before, he could get no help from her. She wished him to make use of his own authority, to avoid all odium and unpopularity from attaching to herself. He determined to act on his own responsibility, and published the Advertisements about March 28, 1566. One month later we find him still complaining to Cecil, that though the Queen was very desirous of enforcing uniformity, he could get no direct aid from her. The Advertisements had but little effect in bringing about uniformity, as other Bishops and public men neutralised all Parker's efforts by shielding offenders. Finally, worn out in his efforts to "strive against the stream," he dies in 1575.

(2) *The Queen never signed the Advertisements; therefore, they could not have repealed or modified the Rubric of 1559.*

She never signed even the letter to Parker which is now said to be the letter authorising him to take "other order." Parker and Cecil both inform us that she would not sanction the Advertisements of 1565, and so far as we can learn from Parker himself she would never sanction those of 1566. She refused to sanction the Canons of 1571, which recognized the Advertisements, nor would she allow those of 1575 till all allusion to them had been removed. In 1571, the Queen again orders Parker to enforce uniformity by "laws and injunctions" already "provided," and says not a word as to the Advertisements. Parker himself never claimed that the Advertisements were the taking of "other order," by virtue of the Act of Uniformity, when he endeavored to enforce the Surplice, though he did make this claim for the Injunctions of 1559, when he defended the use of Wafer-bread against those who insisted upon the usual bread. Parker also tells us in 1566 that the Advertisements were "against no law of the realm." Grindal says in 1572 that the law was neither "changed or diminished;" that is, it still remained in full force. So the Advertisements could not have repealed or modified the Rubric. The Puritans always denied that they were issued by Royal authority or had any legal force, but were the sole work of the Bishops. The Privy Council decided in 1877, more than three hundred years after the event took place, that the Advertisements were the "'taking of order' within the Act of Parliament, by the Queen."

(3) *The Advertisements were not against High Ritual.*

As is well known the services in the Queen's Chapel were of an extremely Ritualistic character from the very beginning of her reign. Copes, or Chasubles, as they were sometimes called, Crucifixes, Altar Lights, Surpliced Choirs, Organs and various musical instruments had been in constant use. See Section xiv, (iii). In fact, she once told Parker that but for the Proviso in the Act of Uniformity, for ordering and publishing "further ceremonies or rites," she would never have accepted the Book of 1559, which was substantially the Book of 1552, with the Ornaments Rubric of 1549. In 1560-1, she was very desirous of having "either the same" or a "like" manner of conducting services both in Cathedrals and Parish Churches, and so late as 1573, Parker informed Sandys that the Queen was still desirous that one "uniform order" should be "observed in all places" in her kingdom.

In 1564, at the very time when the Advertisements were first drawn up, the Queen intended to advance Ritual. She told De Silva that "she had been compelled to temporize at the beginning of her reign"—it was then that she made the fatal mistake of appointing as Bishops rank Puritans like Grindal, Sandys and Parkhurst, (the two former came near being deposed), men who wore the Vestments simply in obedience to the law in order to retain their places, as they themselves confessed, while at heart they abhorred them, and shielded those who refused them,—and that she thought of restoring the Crucifix to Parish Churches. In 1565, at a christening in the Royal Chapel, at which the Queen herself was godmother, and the Archbishop one of the godfathers, the Altar was a blaze of light, being illuminated with eighty-three candles in candlesticks of gold, silver and chrystal. The Altar was loaded with jewelled fonts and incense ships garnished with precious stones, though there is no mention of the actual use of incense. All this does not look like lowering Ritual. The Puritans of that time complained bitterly of being obliged to adopt usages which they detested.

In 1572, Cartwright calls the Queen's Chapel "the pattern of all superstition," and Cathedrals "Popish dens." Bishop Cox, in defence of such services, says that the Queen did not "deviate even in the slightest degree from the law prescribed." So far as we know, Queen Elizabeth was what would now be termed a "Ritualist" as long as she lived.

But even if the Queen did sanction the Advertisements, and they did repeal the Rubric of 1559, they could not affect in the least the Rubric of 1662, adopted nearly a hundred years later.

## VIII. Prayer Book and Rubric of 1603-4.

JAMES I. succeeded to the throne May 7, 1603. The Prayer Book was reviewed and authorised to be published by a Proclamation, March 5, 1603-4. No alteration of importance was made. The Rubric of 1559 remained unaltered.

## IX. Canons of 1603-4.

THE Ornaments Rubric of the Prayer Book still remained in full force. One of the Canons expressly declares, that:

"All Ministers likewise shall observe the Orders, Rites, and Ceremonies prescribed in the Book of Common Prayer, as well in reading the Holy Scriptures, and saying of Prayers, as in administration of the Sacraments, without either diminishing in regard of preaching, or in any other respect, or adding anything in the matter or form thereof." CAN. 14, p. 21.

The Canons order Copes and Surplices for the Clergy.

"In all Cathedral and Collegiate Churches the holy Communion shall be administered upon principal feast days, . . . the Principal Minister using a decent Cope, and being assisted with the Gospeller and Epistoler agreeably according to the Advertisements published anno 7 Eliz."

"In the time of Divine Service and Prayers in all Cathedral and Collegiate Churches, when there is no Communion, it shall be sufficient to wear Surplices;" &c.

"Every Minister saying the public Prayers, or ministering the Sacraments, or other Rites of the Church, shall wear a decent and comely surplice with sleeves, to be provided at the charge of the parish." CAN. 24, 25, 58, p. 35, 37, 81.

## X. The House of Lords, 1640-1.

IN 1641, the Puritan House of Lords appointed a committee to revise the Rubrics, consisting of ten Earls, ten Bishops, and ten lay Barons. Besides, they were empowered to associate with them as many as they pleased, and they availed themselves of this permission. This Committee, in their Report, suggested:

"3. Whether the rubric should not be mended where all vestments in time of divine service are now commanded, which were used 2 Edw. VI." CARDWELL, HIST. OF CONF., c. 7, p. 274.

May 9, 1644, this Ordinance was passed by both Houses of Parliament:

"No Copes, Surplices, Superstitious Vestments, . . . shall be or be any more used in any Church or Chapel within this Realm." JOURNAL OF THE HOUSE OF LORDS, P. 456. VOL. 6; JOURNAL OF THE HOUSE OF COMMONS, P. 486. VOL. 3.

The use of the Prayer Book itself was forbidden January 3, 1645.

## XI. Prayer Book and Rubric of 1662.

THE Royal Commissioners completed their labors December 20, 1661, and the present English Prayer Book, after having been sanctioned by Convocation, passed both Houses of Parliament,—the House of Lords, April 10, and the House of Commons, May 8,—received the Royal assent May 19, and came into general use August 24, 1662.

The Rubric plainly requires the use of the Vestments, and is as follows:

"And here it is to be noted, that such Ornaments of the Church, and of the Ministers thereof, at all times of their Ministration, shall be retained, and be in use, as were in this Church of England, by the Authority of Parliament, in the Second Year of the Reign of King Edward the Sixth."

Thus at the revision of the Prayer Book in 1662, the Rubric of 1559 was adopted, with a little change in the wording to make it conform to the words of the Act of Uniformity of 1559, though the Presbyterians, at the Savoy Conference in 1661, objected that:

"Forasmuch as this rubrick seemeth to bring back the cope, albe, &c., and other vestments forbidden by the Common Prayer

Book, 5 and 6 Edw. VI., and so our reasons alledged against ceremonies under our eighteenth general exception, we desire it may be wholly left out."

The Bishops answered:

"We think it fit that the rubric stand as it is, and all to be left to the descretion of the ordinary." CARDWELL, HIST. OF CONF. c. 7, P. 314, 351. See also THE EXCEPTION OF THE PRESBYTERIAN BRETHREN AGAINST SOME PASSAGES IN THE PRESENT LITURGY, p. 13.

The Nonconformists were not satisfied with this answer of the Bishops, for in their Reply (the *italics* are in the original), they say:

"We have given you Reason enough against the Imposition of the *usual Ceremonies;* and would you draw forth these *absolute ones to encrease the burden?* AN ACCOUNT OF ALL PROCEEDINGS OF COMMISSIONERS FOR REVIEW OF THE BOOK OF COMMON PRAYER, P. 98.

BAXTER, in his account of the proceedings at the Savoy Conference, says:

"And here, because they would abate us nothing at all considerable, but made things far harder and heavier than before, I will annex the Concessions of Archbishop *Usher,* of Archbishop *Williams,* Bishop *Morton,* Bishop *Holdsworth,* and many others in a Committee at *Westminster* (before mentioned), 1641." RELIQUAE BAXTERIANAE, PT. 2, N. 241, P. 369, 371.

Then follows a list of concessions, one of which is cited above on page 77.

They complained that all the Rubrical changes were in a more Churchly direction:

"So strongly did they themselves feel this conviction, that it was proposed on their behalf in the house of lords that the existing liturgy should be continued, and all the corrections made in Convocation should be abandoned." CARDWELL, HIST. OF CONF., c. 8, P. 389.

The Earl of Northumberland, a Presbyterian, proposed in the House of Lords:

"That the old *Book of Common Prayer* might be confirmed without alteration or addition."

But it was answered that the proposition came too late, that to reject the present book "for no other Reason but because they liked better the old Book, which had been for twenty Years discontinued and rejected," was to put "an affront upon the Convocation and upon the King himself." HYDE, THE CONTINUATION OF THE LIFE, &c., P. 288.

They even asked "that those parts of it [the Liturgy] which impose any ceremonies, particularly the Surplice, the sign of the Cross, and kneeling, might be abrogated." WILKINS, CONC., P. 572, T. 4. The Church Commissioners refused to comply with this demand.

Previously, in 1660, they had the impudence to request the King to forbid his Chaplains to use the Surplice, on the ground that it gave offence to the people. The King refused to comply. IB. c. 7, P. 564, T. 4,

The twelve Bishops (CARDW., HIST. OF CONF., c. 6, P. 257) who represented the Church of England at the Savoy Conference, closed their labors July 25, 1661. The committee of eight Bishops— Cosin, Wren, Skinner, Warner, Henchman, Morley, Sanderson and Nicholson—appointed by Convocation to revise the Prayer Book (IB. c. 8, P. 370), began their labors November 21, 1661.

In 1668, BAXTER and other Puritans still regarded the Rubric as sanctioning the Vestments of 1549:

"The most necessary Alterations of the Liturgy. . . . The Rubrick for the old Ornaments, which were in use in the second Year of *Edw.* VI. [be] put out." RELIQ. BAXTER., PT. 3, N. 72, P. 39.

By some misprint there are two pages numbered 39, one a few pages beyond this.

BAXTER further says:

"And these same Men, who when Commissioned with us, to make *such Alterations in the Liturgy as were necessary to satisfie tender Consciences*] did maintain that *no alteration was necessary to satisfie them* and did moreover contrary to all our importunity, make so many new burdens of their own to be anew imposed on us, had now little to say, but that they must be obeyed, because they are imposed." IB. PT. 3, N. 80, P. 38, 39.

## XII. Attempted Revision of the Liturgy in 1689.

THE Royal Commissioners in 1689 proposed to substitute for the present Rubric the following:

"Whereas y$^e$ Surplice is appointed to be used by all Ministers in performing Divine Offices, it is hereby declared, That it is continued onely as being an Antient & Decent Habit. But yet if any Minister shall come & declare to his Bishop that he cannot satisfye his Conscience in y$^e$ Use of y$^e$ Surplice in Divine Service, In that case y'e' Bishop shall dispense with his not using it, and if he shall see cause for it, He shall appoint a Curate to Officiate in a Surplice."

"Mem: This Rubric was suggested, but not agreed to, but left to further Consideration."

On the margin of the omitted Rubric this is written:

"Mem: A *Canon* to specify y'e' Vestments." COPY OF THE ALTERATIONS IN THE BOOK OF COMMON PRAYER, PREPARED BY THE ROYAL COMMISSIONERS FOR THE REVISION OF THE LITURGY IN 1689. (PARLIAMENTRY PAPER, 2 JUNE, 1854.) Cited by PERRY, NOTES, P. 173, 174.

## XXXI. Attempted Revision of the Ornaments Rubric in 1879.

CONVOCATION OF THE PROVINCE OF CANTERBURY.

IN the Convocation of the Province of Canterbury, in the Upper House, June 27, 1879, the Bishop of Gloucester and Bristol read the report of the Committee of the whole House, recommending that the following words be added to the Ornaments Rubric:

"The minister at all times of his ministration shall wear a surplice, with the stole, or scarf, and the hood of his degree until it shall be otherwise ordered by canon of the Church, lawfully enacted, promulgated, and executed, provided always that this rubric shall not be understood to repeal the 24th and 58th Canons of 1604." Cited in the *Church Times, Supplement*, JULY 4, 1879, P. 433; GRUEBER, CANON XXX., P. 2.

The Primate, as Chairman of the whole House, stated that this was carried in Committee by a majority of 10 to 5.

The Lower House, July 1, rejected this new Rubric by 68 to 13, and proposed the following, which was adopted July 3, by 57 to 8:

" In saying public prayers or ministering the sacraments or other rites of the Church, every priest and deacon shall wear a surplice, with a stole or scarf, and the hood of his degree; and in preaching he shall wear a surplice, with a stole or scarf and the hood of his degree; or, if he think fit, a gown with hood or scarf. Nevetheless, he that ministereth in the Holy Communion may use with the surplice and stole the other vestures specified in the First Prayer Book of King Edward VI.; and that such vestures shall not be introduced into any church other than a cathedral or collegiate church without the consent of the Bishop." Cited by GRUEBER, CANON XXX., P. 2; *Church Times*, JULY 11, 1879, P. 442.

This Rubric was rejected by the Upper House, which then proposed a Conference with the Lower House. This was held in the College Hall, at Westminster, July 4. In this Conference—

"The Archbishop, having briefly reviewed the circumstances which led to a conference of both Houses, remarked that it seemed to have been overlooked, in the course of the various discussions on the subject of the Ornaments Rubric, that no one wished to bind the Church with the decisions which had been arrived at in the law courts. It was quite conceivable and possible—some might even say probable—while others would think it improbable, that in the course of time these decisions might be reversed, in which case it would be very inconvenient to have a rubric with the force of statute law which would render new interpretations impossible or impracticable. The great difficulty in the way of formulating a rubric arose from a desire not to lay down a hard-and-fast line which might prevent future reconsideration." Cited in the *Church Times*, IB. P. 446.

The Bishop of Lincoln also made the following statement:

"We must use great care and forbearance. There was a very great outcry some forty years ago against the surplice. That has passed away because we have the law on our side. So as to the cope. I have worn the cope ever since the Purchas judgment, as I felt it my duty to obey the law, and I have had no remonstrance. If there should be a case of vestments brought into use against a recalcitrant congregation—which I cannot think possible—you have given us the power to restore peace to the parish. It was for that very reason, to secure the liberties of the clergy and peace, that I was induced to abandon that which you sent up to us, and what I have thus done to promote your peace and to extend your liberties has been concurred in and accepted without a dissentient voice in the Upper House. That which we have sent to you is not merely to give you all reasonable liberty, in harmony with order and law, but also to promote that which we earnestly desire with all our hearts—namely, the establishment of peace, for the blessing of God, in this great branch of the Catholic Church of Christ. (Cheers.)" IB. P. 443.

These assurances that the Bishops did not intend to interfere with the use of Vestments where the congregation desired to have the Rubric strictly obeyed, induced the Lower House, by a vote of 39 to 24, July 4, to sanction the following addition to the Ornaments Rubric, as recommended by the Upper House:

"In saying public prayers, or ministering the sacraments or other rites of the Church, every priest and deacon shall wear a surplice, with a stole or scarf and the hood of his degree; and in preaching he shall wear a surplice with a stole or scarf and the hood of his degree, or, if he think fit, a gown with hood and scarf; and no other ornament shall at any time of his ministration be used by him contrary to the monition of the Bishop of the diocese; provided always that this rubric shall not be understood to repeal the 24th,

25th, and 58th Canons of 1604." Cited in the *Church Times*, IB. P. 443; GRUEBER, CANON XXX., P. 2.

The present Rubric was construed by Convocation the same as by the Ritualists. The Decisions of the Privy Council were virtually repudiated, as well as their figment about the Advertisements. The resolution to accept the proposal of the Upper House was passed, 39 to 24, with the express understanding that the Bishops would not interfere, if it could be avoided, with the clergy or congregations using Vestments; that the Vestments were the law of the Church, and that the only question was as to the discretion of using them, and that such discretion was ultimately to be regulated by the Bishop. But subsequently some of the Bishops refused to be bound by such a regulation.

### CONVOCATION OF THE PROVINCE OF YORK.

Convocation met July 30, 1879, and proceeded to consider the Ornaments Rubric. The Archdeacon of Chester proposed:

"That it is not desirable to make any alteration or addition at present to the Ornaments Rubric."

This was adopted in the Lower House, by 25 to 20, but rejected in the Upper House, by a vote of 4 to 1. The two Houses having come to opposite decisions, the question in regard to the Rubric remained unaltered. Cited in the *Church Times*, AUG. 1, 1879.

## XIV. The Use of Vestments in the Church of England since the Reformation.

THE Jewish Priest put on a white linen Ephod when about to officiate, and God Himself appointed the rich vesture which they should wear. EXOD. 28: 1-43, 29: 5-9, 35: 9, 39: 1-43; LEV. 8: 7-30; 1 SAM. 2: 18; EZEK. 44: 17-20. JOSEPHUS, ANTIQ. JUD., L. 3, c. 8, P. 84-87, gives an account of the Sacerdotal Vestments of the Levitical Priesthood.

I shall not enter into the history of the ministerial garments of the Christian Priesthood, referring those interested to MARRIOTT'S VESTIARIUM CHRISTIANUM, and similar works. I shall only briefly mention the Vestments named in the Rubrics of 1549.

ALB, *Alba*, a long white tunic, worn from Apostolic times. Sometimes it was slightly embroidered. A plain Alb was one without Apparels. See figures 8, 9, 10, 15, 17, 18.

CHASUBLE, *Casula*, the ancient *Pœnula* and *Planeta*. It was like a short cloak and usually made of silk, but was of various shapes. The modern Roman Chasuble differs from the ancient pattern of the Church of England. It was the usual garment used at the celebration of the Holy Communion. From being called the principal Vestment of the Church, it came at length to be known as the Vestment, and is mentioned by that name alone in the Rubric. Under the name of Vestment, it also included the Stole, Maniple, and Amice. See figures 7, 8, 9, 10.

COPE, *Cappa* or *Pluviale*. A long cape, anciently used as an out-door garment in case of rain. It was often made of some thick heavy stuff, and capable of much ornamentation. The Cope was generally used in processions and occasions of display. See figures 13, 14, 15.

ROCHETTE, *Rochetum*. This garment was anciently called *Linea*. It differed from the Surplice chiefly in having narrower sleeves. The Bishops formerly wore a scarlet Chimere under the Rochette. In the reign of Edward VI., and subsequently, they wore it over the Rochette, and in the reign of Elizabeth red was changed to black satin, which latter garment is generally used at present. See figures 22, 23, 24, 25.

SURPLICE, *Super-pellicium*. This garment is merely a large and full Alb, which can be easily worn over any other dress, a great advantage in cold climates. Although a comparatively modern vestment, it was originally the same garment as the Alb. See figures 19, 20.

TUNICLE or TUNACLE, *Tunica*, *Tunicella*. In shape it resembles the later Dalmatic. The material was rich and highly ornamented. It was worn by the Gospeller and Epistoler at the Holy Communion. See figures 7, 16.

Hooper was the first to raise disputes about the Vestments, by refusing to be consecrated Bishop of Gloucester in the proper Episcopal Habits, declaring them to be the "inventions of Antichrist," and that it was "a sin" to wear them. RIDLEY informs us, that:

"He saith that 'they be not things indifferent, but very sin, for they are things forbidden by the word of God.'" REPLY TO HOOPER, P. 375. BRADFORD'S WORKS. VOL. 2.

JOHN AB ULMIS says that at one time Hooper had lost much of his influence with the nobility—

"chiefly for being too urgent in doing away with the ministerial habits, and rashly pronouncing as impious and wicked all who are content to wear them." EP. 201, TO BULLINGER, P. 426. ORIG. LET. VOL. 2.

See BRADFORD'S WORKS, P. 373-395. VOL. 2; HOOPER, EP. 39; HILLES, EP. 124, ORIG. LET. VOL. 1; PETER MARTYR, EP. 230; MICRONIUS, EP. 263, 264; UTENHOVIUS, EP, 270; BURCHER, EP. 317, 318, IB. VOL. 2; P. MART., EP. 53; BUCER, EP. 55, 58; HOOPER, EP. 65, GORHAM, GLEANINGS, &c.; STRYPE, MEM. OF CRANMER, B. 2, C. 16, P. 301-309. VOL. 1; COLLIER, ECCL. HIST., B. 4, P. 377-384, 419. VOL. 5; BURNET, HIST. OF THE REF., PT. 2, B. 1, P. 264-266, 286. VOL. 2; IB. PT. 3, B. 4, P. 347-355. VOL. 3; FROUDE, HIST. OF ENG., C. 27, P. 320-326. VOL. 5.

But Hooper finally consented to "sin" rather than forego being made a Bishop, and was consecrated in 1550-1.

STRYPE gives the following account of Hooper's consecration:

"March 8, John Hoper was consecrated Bishop of Gloucester, just after the same manner by the Archbishop; Nicolaus Bishop of London, and John, Bishop of Rochester, assisting, clothed (say the words of the register) in linen surplices and Copes, and John [Hoper], elect of Gloucester, in like habit." MEM. OF CRANMER, B. 2, C. 24, P. 364. VOL. 1.

And when, after all that had been said, he was consecrated in the usual manner, it was, Utenhovius says:

"not without the greatest regret both of myself and of all good men, nor without affording a most grevious stumbling-block to many of our brethren." EP. 270, TO BULLINGER, P. 586. ORIG. LET. VOL. 2. See HILLES, EP. 124, P. 271. IB. VOL. 1.

Peter Martyr and Bucer, though they were opposed to the Habits, advised him to submit, inasmuch as such things were of themselves matters of indifference, and as yet ordered by law, doubtless expecting by his aid, when once Bishop, to get the Habits repealed regularly by law, and in this they partially succeeded in 1552. John à Lasco, however, was the only foreigner of any account who supported Hooper. (HOOPER, EP. 40, P. 95. ORIG. LET. VOL. 1.) But a dispute was opened which has never been closed, and great quarrels raised, owing to the obstinacy of this man, who was doubtless sincere in what he did.

During the reign of Queen Elizabeth, when the Puritans showed a disposition to obey the law, the Calvinistic Reformers often by their advice encouraged contentions and disobedience.

1571.] RICHARD COX, BISHOP OF ELY. "I wish indeed you had not lent so ready an ear to a few of our somewhat factious brethren. And it were to be desired that a man of your piety had not so freely given an opinion, before you had fully understood the rise and progress of our restoration of religion in England." Ep. 94, to Gualter, p. 234. Z. L.

"Master Gualter wrote last year (I think) a letter to my brother Parkhurst, bishop of Norwich; which, as it occasioned some excitement among men of his way of thinking [Puritans], who are always planning some innovation or other, and refuse to be subject to the ordinances established in our church, I have thought it right to admonish our brother Gualter to be more cautious, lest either in ignorance, or without intending it he may seem by his writings to encourage contentions." Ep. 78, to Bullinger, p. 194. Z. L. 2d.

See also the Letters of Peter Martyr, Sampson, Beza, Gualter, Withers, and Zanchius, cited on pages 7 and 8.

If these men had merely refused to wear the Vestments themselves, we should not find so much to blame in them, but such was their intolerance that they would not allow Churchmen to wear them or exercise their religion in peace, and stigmatised as "Popery" what the Lutheran Protestants possessed in peace and quietness.

A distinction has of late been made between the Cope and the Chasuble, on the ground that the latter was the exclusive mass-garment, and consequently is a "sacrificial garment." As a matter of fact, the dress of the Clergy was originally the same as that worn by other people in every-day life. It was the same as that made use of by our Lord and His Apostles. In the course of time the fashion of dress changed, but that of the Clergy remained substantially the same, only being made more ornamental and beautiful, or modified in shape to render it more convenient for the Divine Offices. The idea of "sacrifice" originally had no place whatever. Beauty and dignity in the worship of God were alone sought after. Gradually certain Vestments, from being better adapted for the purpose, were generally or always used in the Eucharistic Office, and thereby became associated with the idea of "sacrifice." To disprove this modern theory, it will be necessary to show:

1. The history of the Chasuble.

2. The history of the Cope, showing that it was originally identical with the Chasuble.

3. That the early Puritans never made any distinction between the Vestments, but condemned them all alike.

4. That the Cope was sometimes used as a Mass-vestment in England by the Church of Rome, both before and since the Reformation.

5. That the Armenians and Nestorians at this day use the Cope as the Eucharistic Vestment.

1. HISTORY OF THE CHASUBLE.

The Latin word for Chasuble is *Casula;* the corresponding Greek words are φαινόλιον (phainolion) and πλανήτης (planetes). We will briefly examine these words separately.

(1) φαινόλιον, φαινόλης, older form φαιλόνης or φελόνης, Latin, *Pænula* or *Penula.* This was the cloak (φηλόνην) which St. Paul left at Troas. (2 TIM. 4 : 13.) The Pænula was originally a cloak-like garment, with an aperture in the centre for the head; used as an out-door dress for protection against cold and wet by all classes. The primitive shape is probably that still retained in some parts of the East. See figures 1–5.

The Phænolion, or Phælonion has always been used in the Greek Church, as a super-vestment, under that name, but in the West it went under another name. See LITTLEDALE, THE HOLY EASTERN CHURCH, P. 58–81, for an account of the Vestments of the Greek Church.

(2) πλανήτης (planetes) ; Latin, *Planeta.* This is regarded by all as the same garment, under another name, as the Phænolion or Pænula. The fourth COUNCIL OF TOLEDO, in 671, C. 28, P. 232, BRUNS, T. 1, speaks of the Planeta as an already recognized ecclesiastical garment for Priests. Pope INNOCENT III., in the twelfth century, speaks of the Planeta as one of the six Vestments common to Bishops and Priests, and makes the Planeta and Chasuble synonymous, " Casulam vel planetam, quae significat charitatem." DE SAC. ALT. MYST., L. 1, c. 58, COL. 795. PAT. LAT. T. 217. See also MARRIOTT, PLATE XVIII.–XXI., XXV., XXVIII., XXX–XXXVI., XXXIX.

(3) *Casula*, sometimes called *infula* or *amphibalum*, Chasuble. This vestment is the Planeta under another name. ST. AUGUSTINE, DE CIV. DEI, L. 22, c. 8, N. 9, COL. 765, 766. PAT. LAT. T. 41, is the first to mention the *Casula*, and speaks of it not as an ecclesiastical garment, but as the ordinary dress of a poor man.

ISIDORE, Bishop of Seville, in Spain, about an. 600, identifies the Chasuble with the Planeta, and describes it as follows:

| | |
|---|---|
| *Casula* est vestis cucullata, dicta per diminutionem a *casa* quod totum hominem tegat, quasi *minor casa.* Unde et cuculla, quasi *minor cella;* sic et Græce Planetas dictos volunt, quia oris errantibus evagantur. ETYMOLOG., L. 19, c. 23, N. 7, COL. 691. PAT. LAT. L. 82. | The Casula is a garment with a hood, so named as a diminutive from casa, because it covers the whole man, as a little house. Whence also the hood is so called as a little chamber. So also they say that in Greek they are called Planetae, because they spread out with wavy borders. |

The hood has long since disappeared, and the shape of the garment has been modified. The *Casula* is first spoken of as an ecclesiastical vestment in the ninth century, and this name soon supplanted that of *Planeta*.

847.] RABANUS MAURUS, Bishop of Mayence.

| | |
|---|---|
| Septimum sacerdotale indumentum est quod Casulam vocant; dicta est autem per diminutionem a casa, eo quod totum hominem tegat, quasi minor casa: hanc Graeci planetam πλανήτην nominant. Haec supremum omnium indumentum est, et caetera omnia interius per suum munimen tegit et servat. Hanc ergo vestem possumus intellegere charitatem quae cunctis vestibus supereminet, et earum decorem suo tutamene protegit et illustrat. De Instit. Cleric., L. 1, c. 21, col. 308. Pat. Lat. T. 107. | The seventh Priestly garment is that called the Chasuble. It is so called as a diminutive from *casa*, because it covers the whole man as a little house. The Greeks call this garment a Planeta. This is the last of all the garments, and covers and protects all the rest within by its enclosure. This vesture we may understand as charity, which is above all vestures, and covers and adorns their beauty by its protection. |

See also Symphosius Amalarius, Priest of Metz, De Eccl. Offic., L. 2, c. 19, col. 1095. Pat. Lat. T. 105.

The Chasuble became the usual super-vestment in the Eucharistic Office in the Western Church. The shape of the present Roman Chasuble is quite modern. See figures 11, 12; Pugin, Glossary, p. 62; Blunt, Annot. B. of C. P., c. 6, n. 6, p. 588.

For ancient examples see figures 7–10, and also Marriott, Plate lxi.; Pugin, Plates 4–7; Chambers, Divine Worship, &c., p. 62–66.

2. History of the Cope; originally identical with the Chasuble.

The Latin word for Cope is *Cappa* or *Capa*. All authorities, Roman as well as Anglican, are agreed that the Cope and the Chasuble have one common origin. The primitive shape of the Cope was doubtless like that given in figure 3.

The following authorities identify the origin of the Cope with that of the Chasuble:

PIERRE Le BRUN, (Roman Catholic).

| | |
|---|---|
| La chasuble étoit autrefois si ample, qu'elle étoit pour ansi dire une petite maison dans laquelle un homme habitoit. Explic. des prieres et des cerem. de la Messe, Art. 4, Note (6), p. 52. T. 1. | The Chasuble was formerly so full, that it was, so as to speak, a little house, in which a man might live. |

AUGUSTUS WELBY PUGIN, (Roman Catholic). "The primitive form of the Chasuble was perfectly round, with an aperture in the centre for the head. In this form it covered the whole body: and according to some writers its very name is derived from casula, a small house. During the the middle ages, the shape was that of *Vesica Piscis*, as shown in Plate II. It then hung down before and behind, long and pointed, and was gathered up in a few graceful folds over the arms. . . . This may be considered as the perfection of the chasuble."

"All Liturgical writers agree that the original shape of the chasuble has been altered. Anciently as Angelus Rocca, and others, assure us, this vesture had no aperture made for the arms, but was full all round, and reached down to the feet, so that the arms could not be exerted, except by doubling the border of the vestment over the shoulder, or arranging it in folds upon the arms."

"The opinion, however, that the cope and the chasuble were originally one and the same vestment, receives great support from the fact that the Armenian Catholics use for the sacrificial vestment a *phenolion* closely resembling our cope, but without a hood. The word *phenolion* is said to be the same with the Latin *pænula*, which the above writers regard as the original, to which both cope and chasuble can be traced." GLOSSARY, P. 62, 65, 83, NOTE.

FREDERICK EDWARD WARREN. "Among the episcopal or sacerdotal vestments and ornaments alluded to in these passages as being in use in these early times we have proof of the existence of the following:—

"*The Chasuble.*—This vestment in its full circular shape, with embroidered orphreys," &c. THE LITURGY AND RITUAL OF THE CELTIC CHURCH, c. 2, N. 15, P. 112.

See PALMER, ORIG. LITURG., APP., SECT. 3, P. 312-314, and PLATES, VOL. 2; BLUNT, ANNOT. B. of C. P., c. 6, N. 6, P. 588.

The form of the Cope has been altered by being made open in front and fastened at the neck by a morse or clasp, so as to be readily thrown over the shoulders, instead of being whole with a hole in the centre to put the head through. The hood long since disappeared, an ornamental piece of flat cloth taking its place. "Copes were however, ornamented with embroidery and jewels at a very early period; and in the thirteenth century, they became the most costly and magnificent of all the ecclesiastical vestments." PUGIN, GLOSS., P. 78.

The Cope from its magnificence was usually worn in Processions and on occasions of display. Sometimes it was used as a supervestment at Mass, though not generally, as it was not as convenient a garment to celebrate in as the Chasuble. See SECTION 4. D'ARNIS' LEXICON OF MEDIÆVAL LATIN, and DUCANGE, speak of the *Capa Missalis* used in celebrating Mass, but say it is the same as the Dalmatic.

See figures 13-15; PUGIN, Plates 2, 4; HIERURGIA ANGLICANA,

p. 157, for Plate representing a Procession of Clergy in Copes, and the Choir in Surplices on St. George's Day during the reign of Charles II., taken from ASHMOLE'S ORDER OF THE GARTER.

3. THE EARLY PURITANS NEVER MADE ANY DISTINCTION BETWEEN THE VESTMENTS, BUT CONDEMNED THEM ALL ALIKE.

The Cope, and Surplice even, as well as the Chasuble, were denounced simply because they had been abused by Rome and become "tainted with superstition."

We constantly hear Copes denounced as "filthy Copes," "Babylonish garments," "sacred garments," and the "golden vestments of the Papacy."

1554.] JOHN BRADFORD. "My dearly beloved, therefore mark the word, hearken to the word, it alloweth no massing, no such sacrificing, nor worshipping of Christ with tapers, candles, copes, canopies," &c. LETTER ON THE MASS, TO HOPKINS AND OTHERS, SEPT. 2, 1554, P. 393. VOL. 1.

1560.] EDWIN SANDYS, BISHOP OF WORCESTER. "Only the popish vestments remain in our church, I mean the copes [*copas intellige*]." EP. 31, TO P. MARTYR, P. 74. Z. L.

Surplices were also denominated "Popish," "filthy vestments," "sacred garments," and "habits such as the Mass Priests," and "the Priests of Baal wear."

1566.] L. HUMPHREY & T. SAMPSON. "What the papists babble about the surplice, of how great importance the clerical dress is esteemed among them, and to what religion it is dedicated," &c. EP. 71, TO BULLINGER, P. 159. Z. L.

1566.] The Ministers and Elders of the Churches in Scotland, in a Letter to the Bishops and Pastors in England, December 28, 1566, speak of the Surplice as a "badge of idolatries," and "the dreggs of the Romish beast." Cited by STRYPE, LIFE OF PARKER, APP. B. 3, C. 51, P. 151. Vol. 3; WHITTINGHAM, A BRIEF DISCOURSE OF THE TROUBLES, &c., P. CCXII–CCXV.

Severer words could not be used of the Chasuble, than were used of the Cope and Surplice. See numerous testimonies cited below under Section (iii). The Rubric of 1552 forbade the Cope as well as the Chasuble, and allowed only the Surplice and Rochette. The Puritan Parliament in 1644 forbade the Surplice even.

4. THE COPE, AND THE SURPLICE EVEN, WAS SOMETIMES USED AS A MASS-VESTMENT BY THE CHURCH OF ROME, BOTH BEFORE AND SINCE THE REFORMATION.

(1) *Use of the Cope before the Reformation.*

We have evidence in ancient brasses of the fifteenth and sixteenth centuries that the Cope was sometimes used in England at Mass before the Reformation. We find Priests vested in Alb, girded and apparelled; Stole, crossed to denote a Celebrant at Mass; Maniple, Amice, and Cope, and sometimes carrying a Chalice and Wafer. See the admirable Letters of JOHN R. LUNN in the *Church Times*, February 24 and March 3, 1882; J. G. & L. A. B. WALLER's SERIES OF MONUMENTAL BRASSES; C. BOUTELL's MONUMENTAL BRASSES; HAINES' MANUAL OF BRASSES; J. S. COTMAN's ENGRAVINGS OF SEPULCHRAL BRASSES.

In PUGIN's GLOSSARY, Plate 4 (see figure 15), may be seen the representation of an English Priest in 1490, properly vested for Mass, wearing a Cope, from a monumental effigy.

In addition to the testimony of ancient brasses, we will add that of WALTER TRAVERS, who in 1574 published a Treatise entitled *Eccles. discip. et Angl. ab illa aberrat., plena e verb. Dei, et dilucida explicatio*. THOMAS CARTWRIGHT, the same year, translated this Treatise into English under the title of "A FULL AND PLAINE DECLARATION OF ECCLESIASTICAL DISCIPLINE," &c.

"For seeing it is manifest that Popishe Priestes received ther orders, by puttinge on off a surplice and square cappe, and that they used the coope euen to the singinge of masse [capa autem etiam ad missam canendam uterentur. TRAVERS, P. 101]." PAGE, 131.

Cartwright also calls Copes and Surplices " the preaching signes of popish priesthood, the Pope's creatures." Cited below under 𝔖ection (ib).

It may be said that these brasses represent the Priest vested for the Procession before the Mass, and that afterwards he removed the Cope, and put on a Vestment. It may be so. A mute brass cannot speak and say what it is intended to signify. But it is much more probable that a Priest would prefer to be represented as vested for celebrating Mass, rather than merely arrayed for a Procession before the Mass. Besides we have testimony that the Cope was used at Mass, and as we find brasses vested accordingly, we think, in the absence of proof to the contrary, that they intended to represent the Priest at Mass.

In the Pre-Reformation *Ordinale et Statuta* of Wells Cathedral, we find this direction:

| | |
|---|---|
| In Adventu et a Septuagesima usque ad Pascha utuntur Diaconus et Subdiaconus casulis. In aliis vero temporibus dalmaticis et tunicis. REYNOLDS, WELLS CATHEDRAL: ITS FOUNDATION, &c., P. 38. | In Advent, and from Septuagesima to Easter, the Deacon and Sub-deacon use Chasubles. But at other times Dalmatics and Tunicles. |

That is, for nearly one-fourth of the year, in penitential seasons, when a lower rather than a higher ritual would naturally be adopted, the Chasuble is worn by the Deacon and Sub-Deacon; but for the remaining three-fourths of the year, during the festive seasons, it seems that a Dalmatic or Tunicle was used. So far was the Chasuble from being solely a "sacrificial" or "sacerdotal garment," that for the greater part of the year it was outranked by the Tunicle.

(2) *Use of the Cope since the Reformation.*

It is plain from the following testimonies that either the Cope was sometimes used at Mass, or that the words Cope and Chasuble were used loosely for each other.

1562.] HENRY MACHYN. "The viij day of September whent thronghe London a prest, with a cope, taken sayhyng of masse in Feyter lane at my lade (*blank*), and so to my lorde mare, and after to the contur in . . . ; and the thursday after he was cared to the Masselsay." DIARY, P. 291, 292. CAMDEN SOC. PUBL. VOL. 42; STRYPE, ANN., C. 32, P. 545. VOL. 1, PT. 1.

1604.] EDWARD PEACOCK made the following communication to the *Church Times*, November 12, 1880, P. 744:

"I have met with several passages in late sixteenth and early seventeenth century documents which have led me to think that the word cope was occasionally—perhaps in latter times commonly—used to indicate a chasuble. I have usually neglected to make notes of these, for which I am now sorry. One instance however is familiar to me, as it occurs in a work edited by myself.

"In 'A List of Roman Catholics in the County of York in 1604,' the original manuscript of which is in the Bodleian Library (Rawlinson B. 452) we find under the parish of Sherburne that 'Agnes Rawson . . . hath had semynaries or Jesuytes dyuers tymes resorting to her house and that some of her seruants have confessed that they found dyuers thinges in her barne, as cope, challice, books and such like thinges as they vse for mass.' p. 23."

See also a similar communication from the same in NOTES AND QUERIES, SEPT. 4, 1880, P. 195, 196.

(3) *Use of the Surplice at Mass before the Reformation.*

The Surplice even was deemed sufficient for Mass in small and poor Parishes before the Reformation. See CHAMBERS, DIVINE WORSHIP, &c., c. 3, P. 44. We may infer this from the SYNODAL CONSTITUTIONS OF HENRY WOODLOKE, Bishop of Winchester, 1308, where benefices of fifty marks or more were ordered to have at least one Vestment, a Tunic and Dalmatic,—"unum ad minus vestimentum solenne, ac tunica et Dalmatica competens,"—forbidding under penalty of anathema any priest from presuming to borrow vestments from any other source to deceive the Bishop of the Diocese on his visitation. WILKINS, CONC., P. 295, 296. T. 2. See also LINDWOOD, PROVINCIALE, L. 3, TIT. 23, P. 237.

5. THE ARMENIANS AND NESTORIANS AT THIS DAY USE THE COPE AS THE EUCHARISTIC VESTMENT.

PIERRE LE BRUN, (Roman Catholic).

| La chape sans chaperon, au lieu de chasuble, quoique dans le latin on ait mis *ad casulam*. Elle est nominée en Arménien *Churtchar*. EXPLICATIO .. DES CEREM. DE LA MESSE, ART. 9, DISS. 10, N. 7, P. 80, TOME 5, VOL. 3. | The Cope without the hood, instead of the Chasuble, though in the Latin Church they say mass in the Chasuble. It is called in Armenian, Churtchar. |
|---|---|

On PAGE 58, ART. 6, is a plate of an Armenian Priest vested for Mass in an Alb, Stole, Amice, sacred Bonnet, and Cope, fastened with a morse, and with a cross and figure of our Lord on the back (figures 13, 14). On PAGE 57 is the representation of an Armenian Church with four lights and three crosses on the Altar, with two tall lights at each end resting on the floor.

See BLUNT, ANNOT. BOOK of COMMON PRAYER, c. 6, N. 6, P. 588; PALMER, ORIG. LITURG., APP., SECT. 3. P. 314. VOL. 2.

6. THE USE OF THE COPE BY THE ANGLICAN REFORMERS.

The use of vestments is not mediæval or Romish, for they are still used by the Eastern Church, by the Lutherans, and are of great antiquity in the Church. There can be no doubt that the Reformers intended to use a distinctive dress to give dignity to the Holy Sacrament. Why the Cope was allowed to be used as an alternative with the Vestment or Chasuble, by the Rubric of 1549, we know not, as has been remarked on page 48. There is a remarkable absence of documents relating to the matter. However, on Wednesdays and Fridays, when there is no Communion, the Cope alone was to be used at the Altar, which seems to imply that a Vestment was to be used when there was a Communion. Copes were of very rich material and highly ornamented, so that it was not from love of simplicity that they were made an alternative with the Vestment, or even given the preference. Both garments were originally identical. In the course of time we have two separate garments instead of one, and in the West the Chasuble became the usual Mass Vestment. In some parts of the East they use to this day the Cope as the Mass Vestment. No reason was ever assigned by the Reformers for allowing the Cope as an alternative. The Roman Catholics taunted the Reformers with rejecting Transubstantiation, pulling down Altars and setting up Tables, doing away with Saint Worship, Purgatory, &c., but never, so far as I know, attached any doctrinal significance to the use of the Cope instead of the Chasuble, or even alluded to it. The Puritans objected equally against both Vestments, calling Copes "Popish Vestments," and saying that as both "are in one predicament, it was inconsistent to reject one and retain the other." If the Cope was substituted for the Chasuble, it then became the Mass or Eucharistic Vestment, just as the Chasuble had formerly been substituted for the Planeta.

We can account for this liberty granted by the Rubric of 1549, in only one way—that it only adopted a practice in vogue before.

In the "Inventory of the ORNAMENTS and GOODS wythin the sayd county of Northumberlande," made in the second year of Edward VI., we find that in the Chapel in the Castle of Alnewyke, there was in addition to the Vestments:

"One coope with deacon and subdeacon." SURTEES SOC. PUBL., APPEND., VII., P. XCIII. VOL. 22.

In the Inventory of Church furniture in Hertfordshire in 1552, we find no Vestments at St. Albans' Parish Church, Bramfield, Willian, and Ware. For the Parish of Therfield, P. 85, we have this entry:

"Item a cope of purple veluet & ij tunacles of the same on [one] for a deacon w<sup>th</sup> Albe Stole Amys & Phanel & another for a subdeacon w<sup>th</sup> amys & Phanel."

Yet, strange to say, the Commissioners did not appoint for the use of the Church this beautiful and costly Mass Cope, but selected a

"vestment of Red taffita w<sup>t</sup> albe amys & phan w<sup>t</sup> a corporas cloth & case." PAGE 86.

They seem to have regarded a Cope as being as bad, to say the least, as a Chasuble.

July 21, 1549, Abp. Cranmer was at St. Paul's vested "in a Cope with an aulbe under it," and the "deakin and sub-decon with aulbes & tunicles." WRIOTHESLEY, CHRON., P. 16, 17. CAMDEN SOC. PUBL. N. S. VOL. 20.

In the Inventory of Church goods in Berkshire, we find a Cope only at the Church in Chyveley. According to other Inventories, Copes instead of Vestments were left for the use of the Churches. It is not very likely that between 1549 and 1552 the Vestments, which were often quite plain, would have been stolen and the richer Copes left, so that it is probable that in some Parishes Copes were used instead of Vestments.

Chasubles were sometimes made Cope fashion. COSIN speaks of "open fashioned vestments" in use at Durham Cathedral when he first came there in 1624. Perhaps the words Cope and Chasuble were used loosely and interchangably for each other. It is also a question whether Chasubles were not sometimes used in the Queen's Chapel under the name of Copes.

In 1560, SAPMSON calls the vestures used in the Queen's Chapel "the golden vestments of the papacy." SANDYS also calls Copes,—though he invents the word "*copas*" instead of using the proper word *capas* or *cappas*, unless *copas* is a mistake for *capas*,—"the popish vestments." In 1566, BULLINGER, in a letter to Humphrey and Sampson, replying to his complaints as to the kind of services in the Queen's Chapel, approves of the course of Sampson in refusing to officiate "in the appropriate dress of the mass, that is in the alb and cope." The original Latin is *casula*, and should be translated chasuble. See the testimonies cited in full below. This proves one of two things,—and the opponents of Vestments can take whichever horn of the dilemma they please,—that either the Cope is as much a sacerdotal garment as the Chasuble, or that Chasubles, properly so called, though generally spoken of as Copes, were actually used in the Queen's Chapel. Sir Thomas Smith, Elizabeth's Secretary of State, had a "Vestment and Alb for the Priest" in his private Chapel in 1569.

We have clear evidence of this use in the case of Durham Cathedral, where according to COSIN, "open fashioned vestments" were commonly worn as late as June 12, 1627, when they were sent to London to be made into a Cope, though by the Advertisements and Canons of 1604, Copes were expressly ordered to be used in Cathedrals; which proves that the Rubric of 1559 was still intact, and that though Chasubles were not expressly ordered, they were not forbidden; so that "omission" is not "prohibition."

# Plates Illustrating the Vestments.

### Stoles.

The upper figure represents an ancient English Stole of about the year 1200. The two lower figures are copies of the modern Roman "shovel-pattern" Stoles. The Roman pattern is modern. From Antiquary.

For patterns of Vestments, Surplices, Stoles, and ecclesiastical costumes, address "Antiquary," care of F. Edwards & Co., 42, Bramah Road, Brixton, London, S. W.

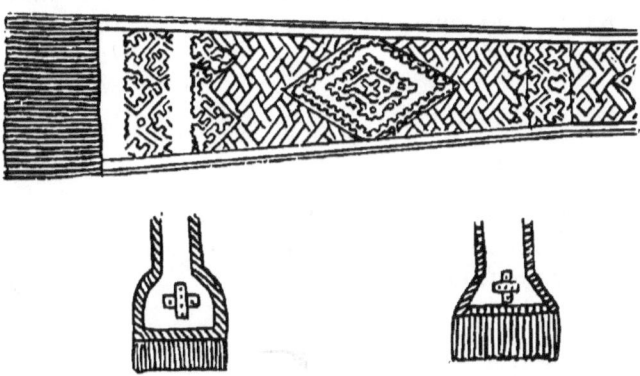

1. Praying figure dressed in a Phænolion or Pænula, answering to the *Casula* or Chasuble in the Latin Church. Fresco in the Catacomb of SS. Marcellinus and Petrus, Via Labicana. ARINGHUS, ROMA SUBTERRANEA, L. 4, C. 14, P. 39. T. 2.

2. St. Bicentius, or Vincentius, Martyr. St. Vincent is commemorated in the Church of England, January 22. He was Deacon to Valerius, Bishop of Saragossa in Spain, and suffered under Diocletian, A. D. 304. St. Augustine, St. Leo and Prudentius frequently refer to his Acts. Vested in a Phænolion and Alb. From a sculptured Sarcophagus in the Catacomb of Pontianus, Via Portuensis. This figure must be older than the middle of the fifth century, as the Catacombs ceased to be used as a burial place after the year 457. ARINGHUS, L. 2, C. 22, P. 229. T. 1.

3. St. Sampson. A Greek Priest, vested in a Phænolion, a Sticharion (answering to the Latin Alb), and Peritrachlion or Stole. MARRIOTT, PLATE LVIII.

4. A Bishop, from a Mosaic at Ravenna, made about the year 540, wearing the Omophrion or Pall, the Phænolion, and the Sticharion. PALMER, ANTIQUITIES, PLATE I, FIG. 2, P. 322. VOL. 2.

5. The Presbyter Romanus, martyred A. D. 303, wearing a Phænolion over a Sticharion. From an ancient Mosaic in St. George's Church, at Thessalonica, supposed to have been built by Constantine. MARRIOTT, PLATE XVIII.

6. The Archbishop Maximianus, vested in a Phænolion and Sticharion or Alb. He also wears a Pall and holds a jewelled cross in his hand. From a Mosaic at Ravenna. MARRIOTT, PLATE XXVIII.

7. Two English Bishops vested in a Chasuble, Dalmatic or Tunicle, Alb, Amice and the Pall. From a MS. of the twelfth century. "ANTIQUARY;" and CHAMBERS, P. 64.

8 and 9.   Front and back views of an old English Chasuble, such as is now used in the Church in accordance with the Rubric.   From "ANTIQUARY."   See also CHAMBERS, P. 62, for similar ancient examples, and P. 66 for a representation of the Chasuble of St. Thomas, which is long and Cope-like, as are these examples.   The figure is also vested in an Alb, Stole, Amice and Maniple.

10.   Statue of a Bishop in Lichfield Cathedral, twelfth century, vested in a Chasuble, Dalmatic, Alb, Stole, Amice, Gloves, Mitre, and holding the Pastoral Staff.   From "ANTIQUARY."

11 and 12.   Front and back view of the modern Roman "fiddle-back" Chasuble.   Just compare this vestment with the ancient Phænolion, Planeta and Chasuble, and it will readily be seen that they no more resemble them than a jacket does a coat.   They are Chasubles only in name.   Compare an Anglican Chasuble with ancient examples, and it will be seen how closely they agree.   An Anglican Chasuble is not a "Romish" vestment at all, but, on the contrary, is a vestment wholly unknown to that Church.   A mere glance at the figures will convince any one.   From "ANTIQUARY."

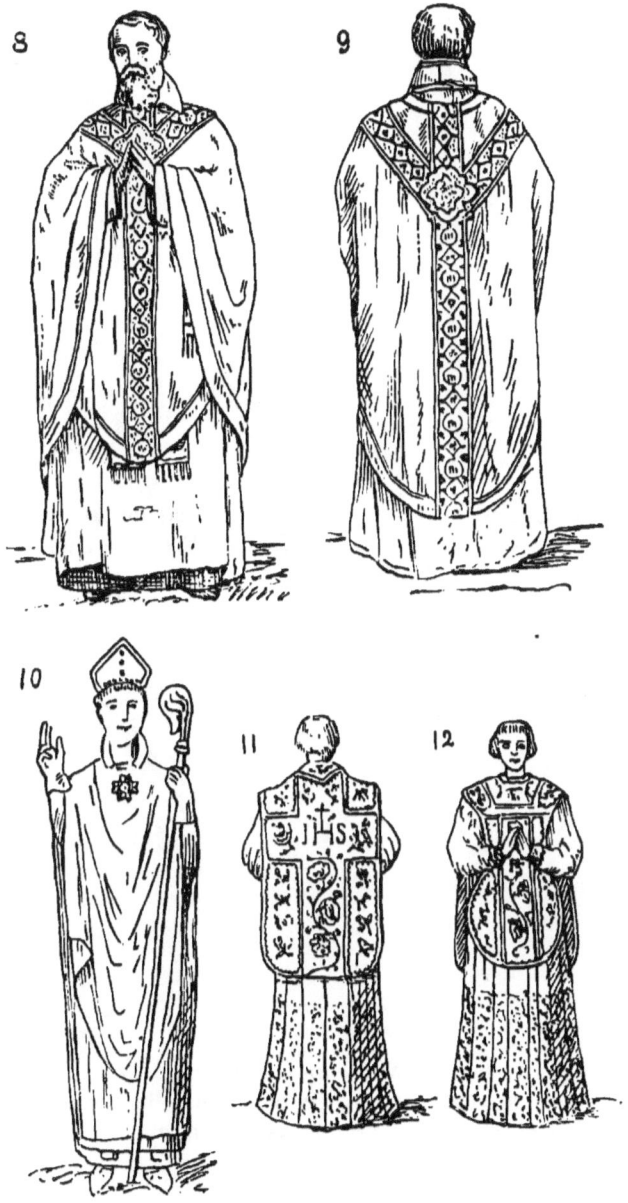

13 and 14. Front and back view of an Armenian Priest vested for Mass in a Cope, Alb, Stole, Amice and sacred Bonnet. LE BRUN, P. 58, TOME. 5, VOL. 3.

15. An English Priest, A. D. 1490, vested for Mass in Cope, Alb, Maniple, Amice, and crossed Stole. From an ancient monumental brass. PUGIN, PLATE 4.

16. St. Lawrence, Deacon, in Dalmatic or Tunicle, and Alb. From an ancient vestment, A. D. 905, found in the tomb of St. Cuthbert. PALMER, PLATE V., P. 322. VOL. 2.

17. A praying figure in an Alb, Tunic or Dalmatic. Fresco from the Catacombs of SS. Marcellinus and Petrus. ARINGHUS, L. 4, C. 14, P. 39. T. 2.

18. A praying figure in a long Alb, Tunic or Dalmatic. Fresco from the Catacomb of St. Callistus, Via Appia. ARINGHUS, L. 3, C. 22, P. 331. T. 1.

19. Priest in an ancient English Surplice, embroidered at the top. They were also sometimes embroidered at the bottom. Since the Reformation, Surplices have been embroidered in some cases. Also showing a fur Almuce or Amess over his shoulders. This was abolished by Act of Henry VIII. The use of the grey Almuce, Amess, or Amice, as it is sometimes incorrectly called, was forbidden by the Canons of 1571. (CARDWELL, SYNOD., P. 116. VOL. I.) This Amice was a scarf lined with grey fur, used in in Cathedral and Collegiate Churches, and totally distinct from the ecclesiastical vestment of that name. From "ANTIQUARY."

20. Boy in ancient English Surplice, swinging a censer. Old MS. From "ANTIQUARY."

21. Modified form of the Surplice, used in the Church of Rome, called a Cotta. Such a garment was unknown in ancient times. From "ANTIQUARY."

22. Ancient English Rochet, embroidered, with Stole and Hood, without the Chimere. Sometimes it is so used now in hot climates. From "ANTIQUARY."

23. Chimere, made properly without sleeves and worn over the Rochet. See also the portrait of Andrewes, figure 25. From "ANTIQUARY."

24. Chimere, pinched in at the back to sew on bulbous sleeves, which, not bulbous however, properly belong to the Rochet. A fearful looking garment. From "ANTIQUARY."

25. Lancelot Andrewes, Bishop of Winchester in 1618, in Rochet, Chimere, Scarf, and the square or cornered Cap so violently objected to by the Puritans. He was a very High Churchman,—a "Ritualist," if you please,—and burnt incense in his Chapel, used altar lights, wafer bread, the mixed chalice, the eastward position, all of which things have been condemned by the Privy Council. From "ANTIQUARY."

26. John Cosin, Bishop of Durham, 1660, in scarlet cloak, white fur hood and square cap. He suffered much from Puritan persecution. See Section (iii). He was also a "Ritualist." From "ANTIQUARY."

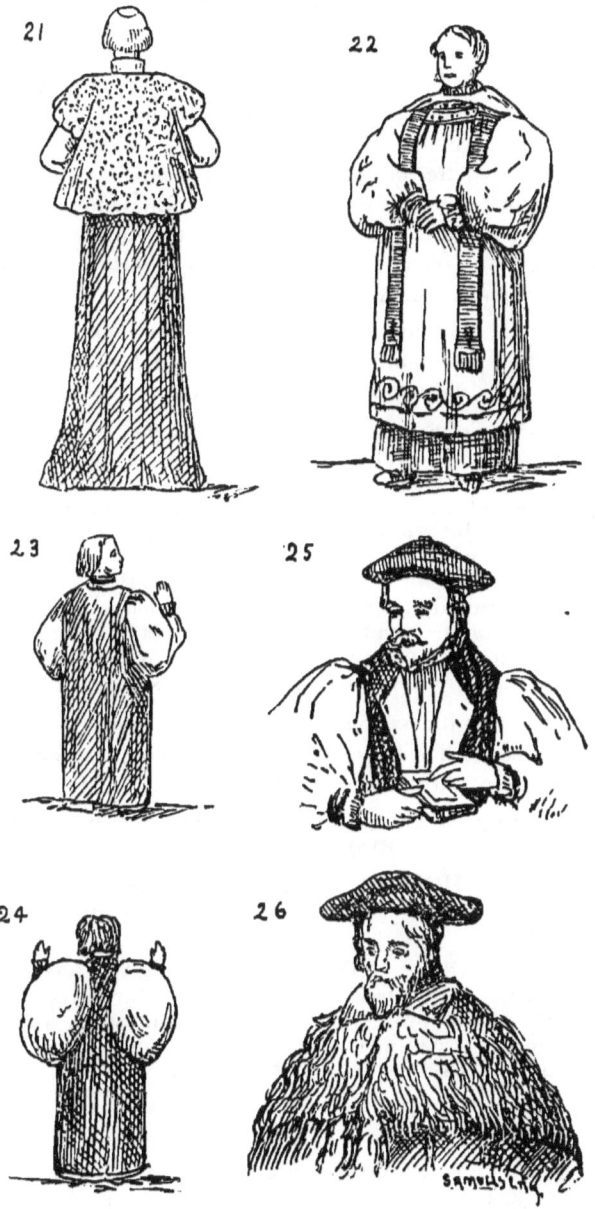

## (X). Use of Vestments under the Prayer Book of 1549.

THE Rubrics of the Book of 1549 may be seen on pages 29–30. The Duke of Somerset, in a letter to Cardinal Pole, dated June 4, 1549, (preserved in the Record Office, STATE PAPERS, DOMESTIC, EDW. VI., VOL. VII.) in reply to the Cardinal's letter of May 6, says of the new Prayer Book, that he has no doubt but that if he should come to England and see things as they really are, he would "be in all poyntes satisfied." Cited in the FIRST REPORT OF THE COMMISSIONERS APPOINTED TO INQUIRE INTO THE RUBRICS, &c., APP. K., P. 148.

EDWARD VI. and his Council sent the following reply to the demand of the Devonshire rebels for the old Latin services, upon the plea that they did not understand English:

"As for the Service in the *English* Tongue, it hath manifest reasons for it. And yet it seemeth to you a new Service, and indeed it is no other but the old. The self same words in *English* which were in Latine, saving a few things taken out, which were so fond, that it had been a shame to have heard them in *English*, as they can judge who list to report the truth. . . . If the service were good in the Church in *Latine*, it remaineth good in *English*: for nothing is altered, but to speak with knowledge that which was spoken with ignorance, and to let you understand what is said to you, to the intent you may further it with your own devotion." Cited by FOXE, ACTS AND MONUMENTS, B. 9, N. 3, P. 47. VOL. 2.

This shows that the services of the Church were to be conducted in such a manner that they would present about the same external aspect that they did before the Reformation. The doctrines of Saint Worship, Purgatory, Transubstantiation, &c., and the gross superstitions were done away with.

1549.] JOHN HOOPER. "They still retain their vestments and the candles before the altars." EP. 36, TO BULLINGER, P. 72. ORIG. LET. VOL. 1.

1549.] M. BUCER AND P. FAGIUS. "We hear that some concessions have been made both to a respect for antiquity, and to the infirmity of the present age; such, for instance, as the vestments commonly used in the sacrament of the eucharist, and the use of candles." EP. 248, P. 535. IB. VOL. 2.

1549.] RICHARD HILLES (EP. 121, P. 266) and FRANCIS DRYANDER (EP. 171, P. 351. IB. VOL. 1.) speak of "useless and perhaps hurtful" ceremonies "after the manner of the Nuremberg Churches" as being "retained" by the Book of 1549. They do not specify them, but they doubtless refer to vestments and candles.

1550.] JOHN BUTLER. "Some blemishes in respect to

certain ceremonies, such for instance as the splendour of the vestments, have not yet been done away with." EP. 293, P. 635. ORIG. LET. VOL. 2.

## (H). Use of Vestments under the Prayer Book of 1552.

**T**HE Puritans, urged on by the foreign Reformers, were not satisfied with the Book of 1549, did not obey it, but clamored for further reforms. The Book of 1552 was the result. The Rubric (see page 34) strictly forbade the use of the Vestment, Cope and Alb, and ordered the Surplice only for Priests and Deacons; but at the same time another Rubric was inserted ordering that "Chancels shall remain as they have done in the past," so that the same ornaments of the Altar were legal in 1552 that were in use previously, though the ornaments of the Clergy were curtailed. Yet the Puritans were not satisfied with the permission to use a surplice only instead of a Vestment or Cope, but still clamored for further reform, and had the King lived a little longer, it is highly probable that the Surplice even would have been abolished in the reforms contemplated. (See pages 5, 6.) Peter Martyr would never wear a Surplice while Canon at Oxford; Humphrey and Sampson say that the Eucharist was sometimes celebrated without a Surplice, and Withers tells us that no one was compelled to observe the Rubrics against his will. (See pages 6, 43.) Common bread was often used instead of Wafer-cakes as ordered by the Rubric. Nor have we any reason to think that the Rubric as to Chancels was any better observed. Ridley pulled down Altars in spite of the Book of 1549. In fact, every man did about as he pleased. The Puritans did not wear the Surplice, though strictly required to by the Rubric. Churchmen wore Vestments, Copes and Albs, though strictly forbidden to do so by the Rubric, but they did so with the express permission of the Royal Commissioners, acting under the "discretion" reposed in them, who often left "for the use" of the Church, Vestments, Copes, Tunicles, Albs, Altar Crosses, Candlesticks, occasionally Censers even, and other ornaments. The Commissioners "comytted" the goods of the Church "to the custodie of the churchwardens," or other fit persons, "savely to be kept and to be forthcomyng att all tymes when itt shalbe requyryd" (FIRST REPORT OF THE COMMISsioners, &c., App. K., p. 149), or "to keepe the same untyll such tyme as the Kings Majesties pleasure be therein ffurder known." (Inventory of Furniture and Ornaments ... of Hertf., p. 23.) If they, or the Clergy, or the Parishioners were Puritans, they assigned to the Church barely enough ornaments to carry on the services in the plainest manner.

Where the Commissioners, or the Clergy, or the Parishioners were Churchmen, and had a strong attachment for the Ornaments to which they had been accustomed, in addition to committing the Church goods to fit persons, they assigned a portion of them, including Vestments, which were forbidden by the Rubric, "for the use of the Church," "for the only maintenance of Divine Service," &c.

The word "only" in the Rubric was, as a matter of fact, regarded as not compelling the Foreign Reformers and Puritans to adopt Ornaments to which they objected. The use of Copes at the consecration of Scory and Coverdale (see page 111) seems to prove this. In no other way can I account for the manner in which assignments of Church goods are made in the various Inventories.

This may seem strange, but it must be remembered that men do about as they like in religious matters, in spite of laws, and this was especially the case in the Church of England at the beginning of the Reformation, and has been so to a great extent ever since. Bancroft, afterwards Archbishop of Canterbury, in 1593, speaking of the lawlessness of the Puritans, says:

"There is no Church established in Christendome so remisse in this point as the Church of *England*. For in effecte: euery man vseth and refuseth what he listeth." Survey of the Pretended Holy Discipline, c. 26, p. 311.

Nor do men pay any more attention to Divine than to human laws. Take one example, for instance. The Rubric, if I may so speak, in Malachi 1:11, orders that "in every place *incense shall be offered unto My name." But this prophecy remains unfulfilled. Why? Simply because the use of Incense is regarded as "Popish!" But anything ordered by Almighty God cannot be "Popish." We may not like it, or we may doubt the policy or expediency of His commands, but that is a totally different thing. Call things by their proper names. To those who think that things which have always been in the Church, and which are regarded by some, at least, as being of vital importance, can be effectually suppressed by con-

---

*It is a remarkable fact that when the wise men came from the East—Gentiles, ignorant of this prophecy—came to visit the infant Saviour, they brought, among other gifts, Frankincense. Matt. 2:11.

stant tinkering of the Prayer Book, I would suggest that they go to the bottom. and not to the surface of the matter, and make the Bible conform to their ideas, not by changing the language itself, but by " wisely and judiciously " inserting words in brackets, so that they may be no longer exposed to the taunts of "unbelievers," that they do not carry out the teachings of their own Bible. The prophecy of Malachi would then read:

*" In every place [except among Protestants] incense shall be offered unto My name."

Thus would Scripture be fulfilled.

Copes were used at the consecration of Scory and Coverdale after the Book of 1552 had been sanctioned. STRYPE says:

"August the 30th, John Scory, Ponet being translated to Winchester, was consecrated Bishop of Rochester, at Croydon, by the Archbishop of Canterbury, assisted by Nicolas Bishop of London, and John Suffragan of Bedford.

"Miles Coverdale was at the same time and place consecrated Bishop of Exon, all with their surplices and copes, and Coverdale so habited also." MEM. OF CRANMER, B. 2, c. 26, P. 389. VOL. 1.

Before giving some examples from these Inventories, I will here remark that these documents show that love for the purity of religion was far from being the cause why many espoused the Reformation. The corruptions in the Church, no doubt, made some long for a better state of things, but the restraints which the Church still imposed upon men, and a desire to possess the goods and riches of the Church, led many to be impatient of her authority, and to clamor for the confiscation and doing away with the " monuments of superstition," as the goods of the Church were called. In a Commission issued by Edward VI. in 1553, the linen ornaments and altar coverings, beyond what are actually needed, are ordered to be given to the poor "as may be most to God's glory and our honour;" but the Copes, Vestments, plate, jewels, &c.,—valuable articles,—are to be sold, not " to God's glory," but " to our own use." (PARISH CHURCH GOODS IN BERKSHIRE, INTRODUCTION, P. XXXV., XXXVII.)

This shows the character and purpose of the Commission— robbery—and the list of goods still left in the Churches shows little

---

*" In Cole's MSS. (Br. Mus. 5873, p. 82, d.) it is stated, 'that it was the constant practice on the greater Festivals at Ely to burn incense at the altar in the Cathedral, till Dr. Thomas Green, one of the Prebendaries, and now Dean of Salisbury, 1779, a finical man, though a very worthy one, and who is always taking snuff up his nose, objected to it under the pretence that it made his head to ache.'" FIRST REPORT OF THE COMMISSIONERS, &c., P. 153; WALCOTT, TRADITIONS AND CUSTOMS OF CATHEDRALS, SECT. 4, P. 160.

real desire, on the part of the Commissioners, to rid the Church of "superstition." Numerous accounts of the embezzlement and conversion to private use of Church goods may be found in these Inventories, which are now deposited in the Record Office, Fetter-lane, London. Some of them have been published.

All these Inventories were made subsequent to the publishing of the Second Prayer Book, April 6th, 1552, and that of HERTFORDSHIRE was made November 1, the very day that the Book was first used, and signed March —, 1553. PAGE 22.

STRODE, ROCHESTER, July 24, 1552. After an inventory of the goods of the Parish, occurs the following assignment for the use of the Parish:

"Out of the particulars within written the said Commissioners have appoynted and delivered unto the sayd churchwardens to the use and behoof of the sayed churche and commyn prayers to be ministred and used in the same churche theis particulars following.
 First a cope of whyte damaske.
 Item a vestment of whyte damaske.
 Item a cope of Ryd velvett.
 Item a vestment of Reyd velvett.
 Item a herse cloth.
 Item iij surplices.
 Item ij chalasses.
 Item ij alter cloythes.
 Item a cloythe to hang before the Table of yalowe and blue sylke.
 Item two of the best Towelles.
      Pr me Johen Byer
      Pr me Georglm Clarke."
FIRST REPORT OF THE COMMISSIONERS, &c., APP. K., p. 149.

ST. NICOLAS, ROCHESTER, July 18, 1552. After the inventory occurs the following assignment:

"Of which particulars aforesaid the Comysshoners have appoynted and delivered unto the Said wardens to the use and behoof of the parishoners of the said churche for y$^e$ admynystracon of y$^e$ Communyon in the same, that is to say,
 First twoo Chaleces of Silver and Gilte with the twoo covers aforeseid weyng . . . . . . xxxij ounces.
 Item one other Chalece gilded wherof the Cupp is Silver and the residue of Copper with a patten of Copper to the same weying togither . . . . . . . xj ounces.
 Item a Coope of Crymson velvett with aungells and Flowers deluces for Festyvall dayes . . . price xxx$^s$.
 Item a Cope of purpull velvett with aungells, Floweres de luces and other Floweres thereupou for Saboth dayes . price xvi$^s$.
 Item one Coope of blue damaske with Floweres for inferior dayes . . . . . . . price x$^s$.

Item a payer of orgaynes lackyng pipes.
                    By me John Burwell.
                    Pr me Johem Byer.
                    By me Thomas Swan.
                    By me George Clerke."

IB. P. 149, 150.

STUNTNEY, CAMBRIDGESHIRE, July 28, 1552.

"Playt        ffirst j chalysse of sylver with y^e paten and gilt
Ornaments     Item j vestm^t of grene bawdkyn. Item two Aulter candlesticks off latten.
Bells         Item in the steeple ij litle belles. All w^h peells above wrytten be delyvered and commytted by us the said Commyssioners unto the sayff custody and keepyng of Nycohales Shepphard William Duche and John Ckeckyte parisheners to be answered and to serve in the said chappell for the only mayntenance of Devyne Service there.
                    Henry Goderyk       Thomas Ralston
                                        Richard Wilkes
              By me Henry Shepperd
                                        William Dunch."

IB. P. 150.

Partial list of assignments of Church goods in various Counties made in 1552, as cited in the FIRST REPORT OF THE COMMISSIONERS, &c., P. 150:

|  | Copes. | Vestments or Chasubles. | Tunicles. | Albs. | Surplices. | Two Altar Candlesticks. | Standard Candlesticks. |
|---|---|---|---|---|---|---|---|
| BERKS, 13 Churches. | 2 | 4 | — | 1 | 2 | 10 | 2 |
| BUCKS, 14 Churches. | 4 | 6 | 3 | 1 | 1 | 9 | 2 |
| HAMPSHIRE. | 52 | 63 | 11 | 15 | 8 | 8 | 3 |
| ESSEX. | 96 | 29 | — | 7 | 55 | — | — |
| CAMBRIDGESHIRE. | 131 | 73 | 4 | 45 | -- | — | — |
| KENT. CANTERBURY. | 7 | — | — | 6 | 3 | — | — |

In BUCKS forty other Churches are mentioned as having each two candlesticks.

HEREFORDSHIRE. Out of the inventories of sixty-four Churches, there were "reserved to the use of the Parish:" Copes in fifty instances, Vestments in twenty-five, and Vestments to make a Cope in eighteen cases.

DORSETSHIRE. Upwards of two hundred and sixty Churches had assigned to them at least one Cope or Vestment.

HERTFORDSHIRE. The certificate of the Commissioners for Hertfordshire was made in March, 1553, but the inventories were made November 1, 1552. A few of the goods are directly assigned for the use of the Church:

"Furder We the said Commyssioners doo Sartiffie that the said Challices sartain lynnons and other thinges we haue appointed and assigned ffor thadministracon of the Sarvice in the saide Churches & Chappelles haue this writtine vppon the margints of the Saide inventories ouer agenste the things so assignede pro· ecclesia or for the Church as in the same appeareth.

"All whiche Gooddes plait Juells and Ornaments We the Saide Commyssioners haue assigned and delyuered vnto the saiff custodie and kepinge off one or ij of the most honestest and Crediblest parsonnes or men of the saide Parrysshe to be ffurth cumynge when the Kinges Majesties pleasure shalbe therin ffurder known as in the saide inuentories most plainly appeareth." INVENTORY OF FURNITURE AND ORNAMENTS .. OF HERTF., P. 15.

List of Ornaments of the Ministers assigned in the margin of the Inventories of the various Hundreds in Hertfordshire:

|  |  | No. of Churches. | Copes. | Vestments. | Tunicles. | Albs. | Surplices. | Rochets. |
|---|---|---|---|---|---|---|---|---|
| Hundred of | CAYSHO, | 43 | 1 | — | — | 4 | 6 | 2 |
| " | " HUTCHINE, | 9 | — | — | — | — | 1 | — |
| " | " BRODWATTAR, | 24 | — | — | — | — | — | — |
| " | " ODSEY, | 12 | 1 | 4 | — | 2 | — | — |
| " | " EDWINSTERE, | 20 | 5 | 9 | 2 | — | — | — |
| " | " HARTFFD, | 15 | 4 | 2 | — | — | — | — |
| " | " BRAWGHIN, | 13 | 3 | 3 | — | — | — | — |

A few other ornaments are directly assigned, occasionally, as altar cloths, towels, organs, bells, and even a sanctus bell, and most always a chalice. Perhaps the Parish made use of such goods as were assigned to "saiff custodie," where nothing was assigned for its use in the margin.

BERKSHIRE. The actual Commission for Berkshire has not been found. The Inventories were made between August 1–6, 1552. Nothing is assigned directly for the use of the Parish. It is merely said:

"And all the seid parcels safly to be kept & preserued And the same and euery parcell therof to be forthcommynge at all tymes when it shalbe of them requyred." PARISH CHURCH GOODS IN BERKSHIRE, P. 2.

LANCASHIRE. The "Inventories of Goods in the Churches and Chapels of Lancashire," for the Hundred of Salford, were made between September 27 and October 12, 1552. In the indenture made between the Commissioners and the Vicar and Church-wardens, no special assignment for the use of the Church is made of the numerous Copes, Vestments, Albs, Surplices, Candlesticks and other ornaments mentioned, neither is the use of them forbidden or said to be illegal or superstitious; but—take the Parish of Manchester for example—it is merely said:

"that the same coopes, vestimentes, forfrountes, Aulter clothes candlestickes Chalices bells w$^t$ all other ornamentes Aforesaid shall not at any tyme hereaft$^r$ be alienated imbecilled or otherwise put away from o$^r$ soui'gn lord the Kyng but shall be answercable & furthe comyng to thuse of his highnes at suche tyme and tymes as his ma$^{tie}$ or his hon'able counsell shall demaunde the same." PAGE 4, 5. CHETHAM SOC. PUBL. VOL. 107.

Similar action was taken during the reign of Henry VIII. Take for example the inventory of goods in the Chantries in the city of Durham, made in the twenty-eighth year of his reign:

"Thes particuler parcells of plate, ornaments and goods ensuying, the same savely to kepe and preserve to the King's Majesties use, and untill his Majesties pleasure in this behalf be further known." APPENDIX 3, P. XLV. SURTEES SOC. PUBL. VOL. 22.

Mr. J. FULLER RUSSELL sent a communication to the *Church Times,* JUNE 3, 1881, P. 362, containing an analysis of assignments of Church goods for eight of the Hundreds of Essex, furnished him by Mr. H. W. King, the Hon. Secretary of the Essex Archæological Society, from which I make the following abstract. Many of the Inventories have been utterly destroyed by damp and decay, so that the assignments are imperfect, but enough remain to show that Copes, Chasubles and Albs were expressly allowed to be used during the whole reign of Edward VI. There were four hundred and fifteen Parishes in Essex.

The Commissioners for the different Hundreds were not always the same persons. Surplices were invariable assigned in all the eight Hundreds. The forms of the assignment are:

"appointed for Divine Service," "for the use of the church," "for the ministration."

| | No. of Parishes. | Chasubles. | Copes. | Albs. | Rochets. |
|---|---|---|---|---|---|
| Hundred of ROCHFORD, | 24 | 14 | 19 | 2 | — |
| " " DENGEY, | 24 | 7 | 9 | 1 | 2 |
| " " THURSTABLE, | 10 | — | 7 | — | — |
| " " SENDRING, | 32 | 2 | 12 | — | 1 |
| " " CHAFFORD, | 15 | 3 | 13 | 1 | 1 |
| " " ONGAR, | 26 | — | 11 | — | — |
| " " DUNMOW, | 2 | — | 2 | — | — |
| " " BEACONTREE, | 9 | 2 | 3 | 1 | — |

Inventory in LINDSAY DEANERY, in Lincolnshire, dated August 19, 1552:

"Mem. that all the churche goodes is commytted to the saife kepyng of the saide presenters [churchwardens] savyng one challyce, one vestment, one coope, one surplysse, whych is committed to the kepynge of the Curate for the Servyng of the Churche." Cited by WALCOTT, CONST. AND CANONS OF THE CHURCH OF ENGLAND, INTRODUCTION, P. XII.

In the previous Inventories not a word is said as to the confiscation of any of the Church goods. But now all Ornaments not actually required for the services of the Church are to be sold. January 16, 1553, the following Commission was issued:

"And Wee do futher geve unto you, seven, syx, fyve, or four of you, full power, and anctorytye ymmedyatelye to collect, or cause to be collected and brought togeyther, all and singuler redye money, plate, and Juelles certyfyed by our Commyssioners aforesaid to remayne in any church, Chapell, Guild, Brothered, Fraternitye or company, in any shire, Countye, or place within this Realme of Englond, causing the said ready money to be delyvered by indenture to our use to thands of our trustie servaunt sir Edmod Peckham, Knyght, and causing the said plate and Juells to be delyvered lykewise by Indenture to our use to thandes of the maister of our Juell house for the tyme being. And to thintent the said Churches and Chapelles may be furnysshedd of convenyent and comely things mete for thadmynystracion of the holy Communyon in the same, Wee geve unto you seven, syx, fyve, or four of you, full power and auctorytye to leave or cause to be leaft out of the said plate for the same purpose and to the same use in everye Chathedrall or Collegiat Churche where Chalyces be remaynyng one or two chalyces by your discreacion, and in every small paryshe or chapell where Chalyes be remaynyng one chalyce, delyveryng or causing to be deyvered the same chalyes so appoynted to remayn to thuse aforesaid to thand the deane, Provost, Churchewardens, or other Mynysters of the said Churches and Chapells by Indenture in wryting, wherby to charge them and their successours with the same herafter. And we gyve unto you, seven, syxe, fyve, or foure of you, full power and auctory after the honest and comely furnyture of coverynges for the commnnyon table and surples or surplesses for the mynyster or mynysters in the said churches or chapells by your discrecions, to distribute or cause to be distrybuted and geven frely to the poore people in every parysh wheare the same churches and chapells stond and be, The resydue of the lynnyn, ornaments, and ymplements of the said churches and chapells in suche order and sort as may be most to Godes glory and our honor. And we gyve unto seven, syx, fyve, or four of you full powe and auctory to sell or cause to be sold to our use all and singuler copes, vestments, Aulter clothes, and other ornaments whatsoever remaynyng or being within any of the said churches or chapells not appoynted by this our Commyssion to be leafte in the said churches or chapelles, or to be dystrybuted to the poore as afore ys declared. And also to sell or cause to be sold to our use by weight all parcells or peces of metall except the metall of greatt bell, saunse bells, in every of the said churches or chapells." PARISH CHURCH GOODS IN BERKSHIRE, INTROD., P. XXXIV., XXXV.

It was to prevent the Church goods from being stolen promiscuously that this commission was issued by the Crown, confiscating the money into the Exchequer. Bishops and Priests, as well as laymen, were guilty of peculations. (See STRYPE, MEMORIALS OF CRANMER, B. 2, c. 8, 26; B. 3, c. 25. VOL. I.) There is not a single word in this or the previous commissions as to certain ornaments being superstitious or illegal, though they were all issued after the Prayer Book of 1552 had been published, and in some cases after it had come into actual legal use.

Edward VI. died the following July, and under Queen Mary, who succeeded him, the services of the Church were again conducted as they had been under Henry VIII., though not at once in all places. See TERRENTIANUS, EP. 182, P. 369. ORIG. LET. VOL. I.

## (III). Use of Vestments under the Prayer Books of 1559 and 1662.

THE Rubrics of these two Books (see pages 36 and 77) both order the use of such ornaments as were used in the second year of Edward VI. Many of the citations given below are from Puritan writers who complain bitterly of the practice of the Church. The reader is referred to HIERURGIA ANGLICANA for a multitude of testimonies.

1558–9.] Shortly after Queen Elizabeth ascended the throne, Secretary CECIL wrote to Guest, a learned man, and afterwards Bishop of Rochester, asking him to examine the different Books and prepare a new one, inquiring at the same time whether, in his opinion, certain ceremonies taken away in Edward's second Book should not be restored. Among his inquiries is this:

"IV. Whether in the celebration of the communion, priests should not use a Cope besides a surplice?" Cited by STRYPE, ANNALS, C. 4, P. 120, 121. VOL. 1, PT. 1.

GUEST replied as follows:

"Ceremonies once taken away, as ill used, should not be taken again, though they be not evil of themselves, but might be well used."

"Because it is sufficient to use but a surplice in baptizing, reading, preaching, and praying, therefore, it is enough also for the celebrating the communion." IB. APP., N. 14, P. 459, 461. VOL. 1, PT. 2; CARDWELL, HIST. OF CONF., C. 2, P. 49, 50.

But the new Book, notwithstanding the Puritan proclivities of some of the Reformers, did sanction not only the Cope, but all the Vestments used " in the second year of King Edward VI." Guest himself shortly afterwards wore a Cope at the consecration of Archbishop Parker.

1559.] At the obsequies of Henry II., King of France, September 9, at St. Paul's, London,—

" the three bishops elect in copes, and the two prebendaries in grey amices, came forth from the vestry to the table of administration." Cited by STRYPE, ANN., c. 9, P. 189. VOL. 1, PT. 1.

1559.] MATTHEW PARKER was consecrated Archbishop of Canterbury, December 17, 1559. His REGISTER contains the following account of the affair:

" These things being thus arranged in their order, in the morning about five or six o'clock, the archbishop enters the chapel by the west door, vested in a scarlet cassock and hood (toga talari coccinea caputioque indutus), preceeded by four torches, and accompanied by the four bishops who were to officiate at his consecration.

" Then, without delay, immediately they return by the north door, apparelled in this manner: the Archbishop was vested in a lawn surplice (linteo surperpellicio), as it is called; the Elect of Chichester wore a silk cope (capa serica), being prepared to perform the service, upon whom did minister and assist two chaplains of the archbishop, viz., Nicholas Bullingham and Edmund Gest, archdeacons of Lincoln and Canterbury respectively, likewise vested in silk copes.

" And being thus vested, and arranged, they proceeded to celebrate the Communion, the archbishop reverently kneeling at the lowest step of the sanctuary." Cited by LEE, VALIDITY OF THE HOLY ORDERS OF THE CHURCH OF ENGLAND, c. 18, P. 177, 178; and APPENDIX, P. 427.

1560.] HEYLIN says of Parker and the other Bishops of the period:

" These Bishops . . . never appearing publicly but in their Rochets, nor officiating otherwise than in Copes at the Holy Altar." HIST. OF THE REF., P. 295.

1561.] In the " Interpretations " drawn up by Parker and other Bishops, it is suggested that there be used " only but one apparel: as the Cope " in the Holy Communion, and " the Surplice in all other ministrations." See page 48.

1564.] PARKER defended the use of the Vestments in the Church of England against the objections of Sampson, Humphrey, Bucer, Alasco and others. STRYPE, LIFE OF PARKER, B. 2, C. 23, P. 329–345. VOL. 1.

PARKER and others drew up the following paper, the result of their deliberations:

| | |
|---|---|
| Proposito Episcoporum.<br>Ministri in Ecclesia Anglicana, in qua Dei beneficio pura Christi doctrina, et fidei Evangelicae praedicatio jam viget, quaeque manifestam detestationem Antichristianismi publice profitetur, sine impietate uti possunt vestium discrimine, publica authoritate jam praescripto, tum in Administratione, tum in usu externo, modo omnis cultus, et necessitatis opinio amoveatur. | Proposition of the Bishops.<br>The Ministers in the English Church (in which by God's favor the pure doctrine of Christ, and the preaching of Evangelical faith still flourishes, and which publicly professes manifest detestation of Antichristianism), may without impiety use the distinction of habits, now prescribed by public authority, both in service, as also in outward employment, provided only that all reverence and opinion of necessity be taken away. |

. . . "This was subscribed to by Canterbury, London, Winchester and Ely, Bishops; and by Goodman, Dean of Westminster; Robinson, a learned Doctor of Divinity in Cambridge, the Archbishop's Chaplain, and afterward Bishop of Bangor; Bickley, the Archbishop's Chaplain, and afterwards the Warden of Merton college, and Bishop of Chichester; and one Hill." IB. P. 344.

Two others subscribed conditionally.

1566.] In 1566, Parker published the Book of Advertisements, drawn up by himself and four other Bishops, making obligatory the use of Copes in Cathedral and Collegiate Churches, but forbidding them nowhere. See page 50.

1560.] THOMAS LEVER. "No discipline is as yet established by any public authority; but the same order of public prayer, and of other ceremonies in the church, which existed under Edward the sixth, is now restored among us by the authority of the queen and parliament.

"In the injunctions, however, published by the queen, after the parliament, there are prescribed to the clergy some ornaments, such as the mass-priests formerly had and still retain. A great number of the clergy, all of whom had heretofore laid them aside, are now resuming similar habits, and wear them, as they say for the sake of obedience. . . . For the prebendaries in the cathedrals, and the parish priests in the other churches, retaining the outward habits and inward feelings of popery, so fascinate the ears and eyes of the multitude, that they are unable to believe, but that either the popish doctrine is still retained, or at least that it will shortly be restored." EP. 35, TO BULLINGER, P. 84. Z. L.

1566.] A BRIEF DISCOURSE AGAINST THE OUTWARD APPAREL AND MINISTERING GARMENT, OF THE POPISH CHURCH. "As touching the ministering garmentes that are nowe enforced; how unmeete it is that we should now admit them, shall easely appeare to all that will consider whence they first come, howe they have bene used, and what shall happen unto us if we shall nowe receyve them.

"For the first they are partly Jewishe and partly Heathenishe. . . . Some parte of the Pope's ministering garments were heathenish, as is the Surplesse, the Tunicles, the Chesible, and Cope. And some mixt of both, as is the Albe, or whyte linnen garment, wherein the Priest useth to say his Masse.

"If there were no more in us therefore than a desire not to seeme to be Idolatours, sorcerers, or conjurers, it were ynough to move us to refuse to admit the Ministring garmentes of the pope's church, but there is more to move us." PAGES 28, 31. Cited by PARKER, DID QUEEN ELIZABETH TAKE OTHER ORDER, &c. A POSTSCRIPT, &c., N. 11, P. 179.

1566.] MILES COVERDALE AND OTHERS. "The white surplice and cope are to be retained in divine service." EP. 50, P. 121. Z. L. 2D.

1566.] THEODORE BEZA. "[The Clergy] will resemble also the priests of Baal in their square caps, bands, surplices, hoods, [the original Latin is *casulis*, and should be translated chasubles,] and other things of the like kind." EP. 53, TO BULLINGER, P. 130. IB.

1566.] L. HUMPHREY AND T. SAMPSON. "For not only (as our people wish to persuade your reverence) are the square cap and gown required in public, but the sacred garments are used in divine service; and the surplice, or white dress of the choir, and the cope are re-introduced.

"The cope, which was then [1552] abrogated by law, is now restored by a public ordinance.

"5. The sacred habits, namely the cope and surplice, are used at the Lord's supper.

"6. The popish habits are ordered to be worn out of church, and by ministers in general; and the bishops wear their linen garment, which they call a *rochet*; while both parties wear the square cap, tippets, and long gown, borrowed from the papists." EP. 71, TO BULLINGER, P. 158, 159, 164. Z. L.

1566.] HENRY BULLINGER. "And to repeat my sentiments in a few words, I could never approve of your officiating, if so commanded, at an altar laden, [as the Queen's was] rather than adorned, with the image of him that was crucified, and in the appropriate dress of the mass, that is, in the alb and cope, [the original Latin is *casula*, and should be translated chasuble,] on the back part of which also the same image is represented. EP. 3, to HUMPHREY AND SAMPSON, P. 345, APPENDIX. IB.

1566.] AN ANSWER FOR THE TIME TO THE EXAMINATION PUT IN PRINT WITHOUT THE AUTHOR'S NAME, PRETENDING TO MAINTAIN THE APPAREL PRESCRIBED AGAINST THE DECLARATION OF THE MINISTERS OF LONDON. "You reject the vestment, and retain the cope; you reject the alb, and retain the surplice; you reject the stole, and retain the tippet; you reject the shaven crown, and retain the square cap. And yet these, and such like, are in one predicament; why should you keep the one and refuse the other we know not, but by this rule, Quod volumus sanctum est." PAGES 29, 30. Cited by MACCOLL, LAWLESSNESS, &c., PREF. TO THE 2D ED., P. XLVII., XLVIII.

"You think that the small number can excuse them; as who they say were so few as you would have them seem to be. Cope, surplice, starch-bread, gospellers, pistlers, kneeling at Communion, crossing at baptism, baptism of [by] women, cap, tippet, and gown. Item, by authority of Parliament, albs, altars, vestments, &c. These few things are more than may be well borne with.

"By the former Book of King Edward (whereto the Act of Parliament referreth us) an alb is appointed with a vestment, for [or] a cope, for the administration of the Sacrament, and in some places the priest at this day weareth an alb." PAGES 54, 115. Cited in HIERURGIA, P. 381; PARKER, DID QUEEN ELIZABETH TAKE OTHER ORDER, &c. A POSTSCRIPT, &c., N. 11, P. 179, 180.

Circa 1566.] GEORGE WITHERS. "Altars, organs, the theatrical dress of the papists, and other things of the like kind were retained [by Edward VI.] under the name of ornaments of the church and of the ministers thereof. . . . The high parliament of the whole realm was assembled [by Elizabeth], Popery again cast out, and the second form of prayers, which Edward left behind him at his death, was restored to the church. But the ceremonies, which, as above stated, were retained in the church at the first reformation of Edward, are restored under the same name." EP. 62, TO THE PRINCE ELECTOR PALATINE, P. 159, 161. Z. L. 2D.

1567.] EDMUND GRINDAL, BISHOP OF LONDON. "But when the Bishop still told them [certain Puritan separatists] that this was no answer for their not going to church; Smith said, that he had as lief go to mass, as to some churches: and such was the parish church where he dwelt; and that he was a very Papist that officiated there. But the Bishop said that they ought not to find fault with all for a few; and that they might go to other places. . . . And when one of them charged the government, that the Pope's canon law, and the will of the Prince had the first place before the Word and Ordinances of Christ, the Dean of Westminster observed how irreverently they spoke of the Prince, and that before the Magistrates. And the Bishop asked them what was so preferred. To which another of them answered boldly, that which was upon his [the Bishop's] head and upon his back, their copes and surplices, their laws and Ministers. . . . Then they urged, that surplices and copes, which the Bishop, they saw, intended to place in the third rank, were superstitious and idolatrous; and demanded of him to prove that indifferent which was abominable. The Bishop said again, things not forbidden by God might be used for order and obedience sake. . . . When the Bishop had occasionally said, he had said mass, and was sorry for it, one of them presently said tauntingly, that he went like one of the mass-priests still. To whom he gently said, that he wore a cope and a surplice in Paul's, yet had rather minister without these things, but for order sake, and obedience to the Queen. But they presently declaimed against them, calling them *conjuring garments* of Popery, and garments that were *accursed*." Cited by STRYPE, HIST. OF THE LIFE AND ACTS OF GRINDAL, B. 1, C. 12, P. 171–175.

A full account of this matter may be found in AN EXAMINATION OF CERTAYNE LONDONNERS, written by one of their number, PARTE OF A REGISTER, P. 23–37. The copy in the Boston Public Library is incomplete. The Rev. Dr. Dexter kindly allowed me to consult his copy, as also several other rare books.

1569.] SIR THOMAS SMITH. In 1569, Smith took an inventory of the furniture in each chamber of his house:

"For the furniture in the chapel was a cupboard or altar of walnut tree; vestment and alb for the Priest;" &c. STRYPE, LIFE OF SMITH, c. 17, p. 171.

1570.] CERTAINE QUESTIONS, ARGUMENTS, AND OBJECTIONS, CONTAINING A FULL ANSWERE TO ALL THE CHIEF REASONS THAT ARE VSED FOR DEFENCE OF THE POPISHE APPAREL, &c. "Doe not the people, with the greater part of the inferiour Majestrates, euery where thinke a more greuious fault is committed, if the Minister doe celebrate the Lordes Supper or Baptisme without a surplesse or coape, than if the same through his silence should suffer an hundred soules to perishe, and many of his parishioners to die naked with colde for faulte of garments." PAGE 45.

1570.] CHARGE AGAINST THURLAND, MASTER OF THE HOSPITAL OF THE SAVOY, FOR WHICH, AND OTHER ENORMITIES, HE WAS DEPOSED. "Also he sold away the jewels, copes, vestments and other ornaments of the said house. STRYPE, LIFE OF GRINDAL, B. 2, c. 1, p. 237.

1571.] The XXXIX. ARTICLES of the Church of England were agreed upon in Convocation in 1562-3, and were revised and assumed their present form in 1571. ART. XXXVI. declares:

"The Book of Consecration of Archbishops and Bishops, and Ordering of Priests and Deacons, lately set forth in the time of Edward the Sixth, and confirmed at the same time by authority of Parliament, doth contain all things necessary to such Consecration and Ordering: neither hath it any thing, that of itself is superstitious and ungodly. And therefore whosoever are consecrated or ordered according to the rites of that Book, since the second year of the forenamed King Edward unto this time, or hereafter shall be consecrated or ordered according to the same Rites; we decree all such to be rightly, orderly, and lawfully consecrated and ordered."

"The Forme and Maner of makyng and consecratyng of Archebishoppes, Bishoppes, Priestes and Deacons," put forth in 1549, orders the use of Albs, Surplices, Copes and Tunicles. (See pages 29, 30.) Convocation did not select the Ordinal of 1552, which differs very little from that of 1549, excepting that the vestures of the Clergy are not prescribed, but passed it over and approved of that of 1549, which ordered them. So we have the Articles—the highest Protestant authority—pronouncing that there is nothing "superstitious or ungodly" in the use of the Alb, Tunicle or Cope, and that those who use them "hereafter" do so "lawfully!" That being the case, why find fault with the use of them? If the use of the Vestments was "lawful" in 1571, the Advertisements of 1566 could not have done away with them.

1571.] HIEROME ZANCHIUS. "[The Clergy wear] white linen garments that the mass-priests wear in the popish religion."

"Your most gracious majesty may believe me, that the restoration of such popish vestments will be a far greater evil than may appear at the first glance, even to those who are most sharp-sighted. For I seem to see and hear the monks calling out from their pulpits, and confirming their people in this ungodly religion by your majesty's example, and saying, 'What; why, the queen of England herself, most learned and prudent as she is, is beginning by degrees to return to the religion of the holy Roman church; for the most holy and consecrated vestments of the clergy are now resumed.' . . . What else is it then, to re-introduce at this time these filthy vestments, and the other rubbish of the popish church into the church of Christ," &c. EP. 1, TO Q. ELIZ., APPEND., P. 339, 343. Z. L. 2D.

———] PERCEVAL WIBURN. "In every church throughout England, during prayers, the minister must wear a linen garment, which we call a surplice. And in the larger churches, at the administration of the Lord's supper, the chief minister must wear a silk garment which they call a cope." STATE OF THE CHURCH OF ENGLAND, C. 29, P. 361. IB.

1572.] THOMAS CARTWRIGHT. "They ministered the sacraments plainly; we pompously, with singing, piping, surplice, and cope-wearing." AN ADMONITION TO PARLIAMENT. Cited by WHITGIFT, DEF. OF THE ANS. TO THE ADMONIT., TRACT. 15, C. 3, P. 106. VOL. 3.

WHITGIFT replies:

"This is very slender reason to prove that the sacrament of the supper is not sincerely ministered because there is singing, piping, surplice, and cope: when you show your reasons against that pomp which is now used in the celebration of that sacrament, you shall hear what I have to say in defence of the same." IB.

1573.] EDWARD DERING. "If I doe subscribe to this, howe can I subscribe to the ceremonies in Cathedrall churches, where they haue the Priest, Deacon, and Subdeacon in coopes & vestments, all as before." AN AUNSWERE VNTO 4. ARTICLES. PARTE OF A REGISTER, P. 84.

1573.] ROBERT JOHNSON. "You must yeild some reasons, why the *shauen crowne* is despised, and the square cappe receyued: why the *Tippet* is commanded, and the *Stole* forbidden: why the vestiment is put away, and the coape retayneed: why the *albe* is layde aside, and the Surplesse vsed: or why the chalice is forbidden in the Bishop of Canturburies articles: or the *gray amisse* by the canon, more then the rest: what haue they offendid, or what impietie is in them more then the rest nowe conmaunded." A LETTER WRITTEN TO MASTER EDWINE SANDES. PARTE OF A REGISTER, P. 104.

1574.] In a LETTER TO GOODMAN, DEAN OF WESTMINSTER, JOHNSON speaks of colored Vestments being used:

"Vpon Easterday you had not so manie colours uppon your body, as you had pernicious errours in your brest." PARTE OF A REGISTER, P. 116.

1586.] A pamphlet entitled "A REQUEST OF ALL TRUE CHRISTIANS TO THE HONOURABLE HOUSE OF PARLIAMENT," appeared about 1586, denouncing the services held in Cathedral Churches:

"That all Cathedral churches may be put down, where the service of God is greviously abused by piping with organs, singing, ringing, and trowling of psalms from one side of the choir to another, with the squeaking of chanting choristers, disguised (as are all the rest) in white surplices; some in corner caps and filthy copes, imitating the fashion and manner of antichrist the pope, that man of sin and child of perdition, with his other rabble of miscreants and shavelings." Cited by NEAL., HIST. OF THE PURITANS, C. 7, P. 181. VOL. 1.

1587.] One of Queen Mary's Roman Catholic attendants, describing to a friend in France the burial of her late mistress, in speaking of Peterborough, writes:

"Where has been built a very handsome church . . . where canons officiate in the same sort of dress and vestments as ours." STRICKLAND, LETTERS OF MARY, QUEEN OF SCOTS, P. 315. VOL. 2.

1588.] The effigy of Archbishop Sandys, who died in 1588, is vested in a Chasuble in Southwell Minster. MACCOLL thus describes it:

"There is in the north transept of Southwell Church a recumbent effigy of Archbishop Sandys (who died in 1588) wearing the following vestments:—a long tunic with tight sleeves, somewhat like an Alb, but falling over the feet; a chasuble; a doctor's hood, with good sized tippet; and a small ruff round the neck. The chasuble is a peculiar one. It reaches to about the middle of the leg in front, and is cut square. On the arms it comes about as far as the elbows; and it is so long behind that it would trail on the ground, and is turned back under the figure. It has no orphreys, and is fringed all round." LAWLESSNESS, &C., LETTER 2, P. 140, 141.

A fac-simile plate of Sandys' Effigy may be seen in DRAKE'S EBORACUM, opposite page 456. Sandys died at Southwell, July 10, 1588, while Archbishop of York. He was at one time so Puritanically inclined, that he came near being deposed (see page 125), but he seems to have been of a better mind in his later life, for in his will he says:

"Fourthly, concerning rights [rites] and ceremonies by political constitution authorized among us, as I am and have been persuaded that such as are now sett down by publick authority in this church of England, are no way either ungodly or unlawful, but may with good conscience, for order and obedience sake, be used of a good Christian." Cited by DRAKE, EBORACUM, P. 455.

1558–1603.] QUEEN ELIZABETH died in 1603. What kind of services " our good Protestant Queen " delighted in, the following extracts will show. Yet we are gravely told that it was to curtail ritual that in 1566, the Bishops, at her instigation, put forth the Advertisements. If she did curtail her ritual, it was left sufficiently " high " to please most any one, though she was constantly implored by the Geneva Reformers and their followers at home to make her religion " pure and Evangelical."

1558.] " On the 15th day [of January] she was crowned with the usual ceremonies at Westminster-abbey. . . . In the hall they met the bishop that was to perform the ceremony, and all the chapel, with three crosses borne before them, in their copes, the bishop mitred; and singing as they passed, *Salva festa dies*." STRYPE, ANN., C. 3, P. 44. VOL. 1, PT. 1.

1560.] THOMAS SAMPSON. " What can I hope, when three of our lately appointed bishops are to officiate at the table of the Lord, one as a priest, another as deacon, and a third as subdeacon, before the image of the crucifix, or at least not far from it, with candles, and habited in the golden vestments of the papacy; and are thus to celebrate the Lord's supper without any sermon? . . . I will propose this single question for your resolution; for I wish, my father, to employ you as my medium of correspondence with masters Bullinger and Bernardine. It is this: whether the image of the crucifix, placed on the table of the Lord with lighted candles, is to be regarded as a thing indifferent; and if it is not to be so considered, but as an unlawful and wicked practice, then, I ask, suppose the queen should enjoin all the bishops and clergy, either to admit this image, together with the candles, into their churches, or to retire from the ministry of the word, what should be our conduct in this case? . . . Certain of our friends, indeed, appear in some measure to regard these things as matters of indifference; for my own part, I am altogether of opinion, that should this be enjoined, we ought rather to suffer deprivation." EP. 27, TO P. MART., P. 63. Z. L.

See the reply of BULLINGER, cited on page 120.

1560.] EDWIN SANDYS, BISHOP OF WORCESTER. " The queen's majesty considered it not contrary to the word of God, nay, rather for the advantage of the church, that the image of Christ crucified, together with [those of the Virgin] Mary and [Saint] John, should be placed, as heretofore, in some conspicuous part of the church, where they might more readily be seen by all the people. Some of us [bishops] thought far otherwise, and more especially as all images of every kind were at our last visitation not only taken down, but also burnt, and that too by public authority; and because the ignorant and superstitious multitude are in the habit of paying adoration to this idol above all others. As to myself, because I was rather vehement in this matter, and could by no means consent that an occasion of stumbling should be afforded to the church of Christ, I was very near being deposed from my office, and incurring the displeasure of the queen." EP. 31, TO P. MARTYR, P. 73, 74. IB.

1560.] HEYLIN says of the Queen's Chapel :

"The Liturgy was officiated every day, both morning and evening, not only in the public Chapel, but in the private Closet; celebrated in the Chapel with Organs and other Musical Instruments, and the most excellent Voices, both of men and children, that could be got in all the Kingdom. The Gentlemen and Children in their Surplices, and the Priests in Copes, as oft as they attend the Divine Service at the Holy Altar. The Altar furnished with rich plate, two fair gilt Candlesticks with Tapers in them, and a Massie Crucifix of Silver in the midst thereof." HIST. OF THE REF., P. 296.

1559-65.] The Diplomatic Correspondence contained in the Historical Documents printed in the seventh volume of the "Memorias de la Real Academia de la Historia, Madrid, 1832," furnishes much important information in relation to Queen Elizabeth and the Reformation. These documents have never been translated, but Spencer Hall, in 1865, translated and published extracts from them under the title of "Documents from Simancas relating to the Reign of Elizabeth (1558-1568.) Translated from the Spanish of Don Tomas Gonzalez." From these I have made the following extracts :

1559. "On the 13th of August they removed the crosses, statues and altars from all the churches." PAGE 64.

1559, Oct. 3. "Elizabeth now ordered the cross and candles to be replaced in her chapel as before. This caused some disagreement with her Council. She said they had caused her to adopt measures which had met with general disapprobation, and that the order to burn all statues and pictures had created great discontent, especially in Wales and in the North." PAGES 64, 65.

1564, Sept 29. "De Silva exerted himself with great ability on behalf of the Catholics, and in private conference with her [Elizabeth] on the matter she said, 'She had been compelled to temporize at the beginning of her reign upon many points repugnant to her but that God only knew the heart, and that she thought of restoring the crucifixes to churches." PAGE 91.

1565. "Shortly afterwards, and it was thought with the concurrence of Cecil, Elizabeth showed some tendencies as regarded religion, which the Reformers did not take in good part. Among others was the order given as regarded placing an image in her own chapel, and the use of vestments by the Clergy." PAGE 94.

1565. "Upon Ash-Wednesday the Dean of St. Paul's [Dr. Nowell] preached, but as he condemned images and the cross [in churches] the Queen ordered him to be silent." IB.

1565.] State of the Royal Chapel at Westminster, September 30, 1565, at the christening of the child of Lady Cecile, wife of John, Earl of Friesland, Marquis of Bawden, and sister of Eric, King of Sweden:

"The back Part of the Stalles in the Royal Chappell wherein the Gentlemen of the Chappell doe sing, was hanged with rich Tapestry representing the 12 Monthes, and the Front of said Stalles was also covered with rich Arras. The upper Part of the Chappell, from the table of Administration to the Stalles, was hanged with Cloathe of Gold, and on the South Side was a rich Travers for the Queene, the Communion Table was richely furnished with Plate and Jewells, viz. a Fountayne and Basen of Mother of Pearl; a Basen and a Fountayne gylte, rayled with Gould; a rich Basen, garnished with Stones and Peerless; a shipe or Arke garnished with stones; Two great Leires, garnished with Stones and two lesser Leires, garnished with Stones and Pearles; a Bird of Agath, furnished with Stones; a Cupp of Agath, furnished with Stones and Perles; a Bole of Corall, garnished with Pearles; a Bole of Christall, with a Cover; Two Candlestickes of Christall; Two Shippes of Mother of Pearle; One Tablet of Gould, set with Diamonds; another Shipe of Mother of Pearle; Two Payre of Candlestickes of Gould; Two Great Candlestickes, double gilt, with Lights of Virgin Waxe; and a Crosse. Over the sayd Table, on the Wall, upon the Cloath of Gold, was fastened a Frount of rich Cloath of Gould sett with Pelicannes; before the sayd Table hung reaching to the Ground, another Frount of the sayd Suit. Also there was lett doune from the Roof of the sayd Chappel Ten Candlestickes in Maner of Lampes of Silver and gilte, with great Chaines, every One having Three great Waxe Lights. Over the aforesayd Table was sett on a Shelfe as high as the Windowe, Twenty-one Candlestickes of Gold and Silver double gylte, with xxiiii. Lights. On the North Side of the Quire betweene the Organes and the upper Windowe, stoode xvii Candlestickes double gilt, with xvii Lights; and on the Toppes of the Stalles were fastened certaine Candlestickes with 12 Lights, soe that the whole Lights sett there were eighty-three." Cited by LELAND, DE REB. BRIT. COLLECT., P. 691, 692. VOL. 1, PT. 2.

The Queen acted as godmother on this occasion; the Archbishop of Canterbury and the Duke of Norfolk, as godfathers.

The "shipe or arke garnished with stones," and the other "shippes" mentioned, were vessels of an oval shape, in which incense was kept.

1572.] In 1565, Richard Tracy wrote a letter to Secretary Cecil against the use of the crucifix in the Queen's Chapel. STRYPE observes:

"But I find the queen's chapel stood in *statu quo* seven years after. For thus rudely and seditiously did the Admonition to parliament charge her chapel, viz. *as the pattern and precedent of all superstition.*" ANN., C. 46, P. 200. VOL. 1, PT. 2.

1572.] THOMAS CARTWRIGHT. "As for organs and curious singing, though they be proper to Popish dens, I mean to cathedral churches, yet some others also must have them. The queen's chapel and these churches must be the patterns and precedents to the people of all superstitions." AN ADMONITION, &c. Cited by WHITGIFT, DEFENCE TO THE ANSWER, &c. TRACT. 22, 1ST DIV., P. 392. VOL. 3.

1593.] In THE CHEQUE-BOOK, OR BOOK OF REMEMBRANCE. OF THE CHAPEL ROYAL, St. James, we find the following account of Queen Elizabeth's Communion on Easter day, April 15, 1593:

"Her Majestie entred her travess moste devoutly, there knyelinge: after some prayers she came princely beffore the Table, and there humbly knielinge did offer the golden obeysant, the Bushop the hon. Father of Worcester holdinge the golden basen, the Subdean and the Epistler in riche coaps assistante to the sayd Bushop: which done her Majestie retorned to her princely travess sumptuously sett forthe, untyl the present action of the Holy Communion, contynually exercysed in earnest prayer, and then the blessed Sacrament first receyved of the sayd Bushop and administered to the Subdean, the gospeller for that day, and to the Epistler, her sacred person presented her selfe beffore the Lord's Table, Royally attended as beffore, where was sett a stately stoole and qwssins [cushions] for her Majestie, and so humbly knielinge with most singuler devocion and holye reverence dyd most comfortablye receyve the most blessed Sacramente of Christes bodye and blood, in the kinds of bread and wyne, occordinge to the laws established by her Majestie and Godly laws in Parliament. The bread beinge waffer bread of some thicker substance, which her Majestie in most reverend manner toke of the Lord Bushop in her naked right hand," &c. N. 15, P. 150. CAMDEN SOC. PUBL. VOL. 3.

1603.] NICHOLS thus describes Elizabeth's funeral, April 20, 1603:

"Gentlemen of the Chappel in Copes; having the children of the Chappel in the middle of their company, in surplices, all of them singing." PROGRESSES OF QUEEN ELIZABETH. The true order and formal Proceeding at the Funeral of . . . Elizabeth, P. 622. VOL. 3.

DANIEL NEAL. "Her majesty was afraid of reforming too far; she was desirous to retain images in churches, crucifixes, and crosses, vocal and instrumental music, with all the old popish garments.

"She would not part with her altar, or her crucifix, nor with lighted candles out of her own chapel. The gentlemen and singing children appeared there in their surplices, and priests in their copes; the altar was furnished with rich plate, and two gilt candlesticks, with lighted candles, and a massy crucifix of silver in the midst: the service was sung, not only with the sound of organs, but with the artificial music of cornets, sackbuts, &c., on solemn occasions. . . . In short, the service performed in the queen's chapel, and in sundry cathedrals, was so splendid and showy, that foreigners could not distinguish it from the Roman, except that it was performed in the English tongue." HIST. OF THE PURITANS, c. 4, P. 76, 82. VOL. 1.

She sometimes publicly showed her dislike of Puritanism. The editor of Neal's History remarks:

"Of this Dr. Warner gives the following instances: When the Dean of St. Paul's, in a sermon at court, spoke with some dislike of the sign of the cross, her majesty called aloud from her closet, commanding him to desist from that ungodly digression and to return to his text. At another time, when one of her chaplains preached a sermon on Good Friday in defence of the real presence, which, without guessing at her sentiments, he would scarce have ventured on, she openly gave him thanks for his pains and piety.—*Ecclesiastical History*, vol. ii., p. 427." IB. C. 4, P. 87. VOL. 1; HEYLIN, HIST. OF THE REF., P. 296; FROUDE, HIST. OF ENG., C. 8, P. 136, 137, 140. VOL. 8.

DAVID HUME. "But the princess herself, so far from being willing to despoil religion of the few ornaments and ceremonies which remained to it, was rather inclined to bring the public worship nearer the Romish ritual; and she thought that the reformation had already gone too far in shaking off those forms and observances, which, without distracting men of more refined apprehensions, tend, in a very innocent manner, to allure and amuse, and engage the vulgar. She took care to have a law for uniformity strictly enacted: she was empowered by the parliament too add any new ceremonies which she thought proper: and though she was sparing in the exercise of this prerogative, she continued rigid in exacting an observance of the established laws, and in punishing all nonconformity. The zealots, therefore, who harbored a secret antipathy to the episcopal order, and to the whole liturgy, were obliged, in a great measure, to conceal these sentiments," &c. HIST. OF ENG., AN. 1568, P. 117, 118. VOL. 4.

Now such services as the Queen had in her Chapel, and were in some Cathedrals and other Churches, *were never pronounced illegal or contrary to the laws of the Church*, by the most violent Puritans. They contented themselves with pronouncing such places "dens of superstition." This is a most important fact to bear in mind at the present time when such things are pronounced illegal. Better to acknowledge that they are legal but "superstitious," as the old Puritans did.

But it is sometimes said:

"We shall probably be more correct if we refer Elizabeth's proceedings to her own pleasure . . . They [altar lights] were re-established in the royal chapels by Elizabeth, not from any authority of the Church, but because of her own personal tastes." (ROBERTSON, HOW SHALL WE CONFORM TO THE LITURGY, &c., PT. 2, C. 5, (*a*.), P. 91, 92.) Or "that the chapels-royal had ways of their own." (IB. PT. 3, CONCLUS. P. 302; 3D ED. P. 77, 78, 257.)

As if Chapels-Royal were above the laws of the Church, and could have whatever services they pleased, and that what was allowable there, was unlawful and forbidden in Parish Churches. Bishop Cox, a man of Puritanical leanings, writing to Gualter 1571, anticipates and refutes this objection:

"But this is not only false, but injurious both to the queen and the ministers of the word, to wit, that we humour her royal highness, and make her more decided in ordering everything according to her own pleasure. But far be any one from suspecting any thing of the kind in so godly and religious a personage, who has always been so exceedingly scrupulous in deviating even in the slightest degree from the laws prescribed." EP. 94, P. 236. Z. L.

1571.] ROBERT HORN, BISHOP OF WINCHESTER. "For our Church has not yet got free from those *vestiarian* rocks of offence, on which she first struck. Our excellent queen, as you know, holds the helm, and directs it hitherto according to her pleasure. But we are awaiting the guidance of the divine Spirit, which is all we can do; and we all daily implore him with earnestness and importunity to turn at length our sails to another quarter. Meanwhile, however, we who stand in a more elevated situation do not act in compliance with the importunate clamours of the multitude; for it would be very dangerous to drag her on against her will, to a point she does not yet choose to come to, as if it were wresting the helm out of her hands." EP. 98, TO BULLINGER, P. 248. IB.

Horn was a Puritan, and in his opinion the Church made a mistake in the beginning in ordering vestments for the Clergy. But as it was the Queen's pleasure that the laws of the Church should be complied with, he thought it would be a dangerous thing to attempt to force her to act contrary to her will.

JEWELL informs us, in EP. 6, TO PETER MARTYR, April 14, 1559, P. 18, IB., that at the very beginning of her reign, the Queen refused to make any changes in religion "without the sanction of law;" again, in 1566, that she was still "unable to endure the least alteration in matters of religion." EP. 67, P. 149. IB.

1603–1607.] THORNBOROUGH, Bishop of Bristol, in Articles of Inquiry, in 1603, and BABINGTON, Bishop of Worcester, in 1607, name Copes among "Popish reliques and monuments of superstition." Copes fell into disuse even in Cathedrals, and in 1604 a Canon was enacted requiring the use of them. Archbishop Bancroft was a great favorer of them. (ROBERTSON, HOW SHALL WE CONFORM, &c., c. 5, (c.), P. 84. 3D ED.) COLLIER says:

"In short Bancroft's unrelenting strictness gave a new face to religion: the liturgy was more solemnly officiated; the fasts and festivals were better observed: the use of copes was revived, the surplice generally worn, and all things in a manner recovered to the first settlement under queen Elizabeth." ECCL. HIST., B. 8, P. 32. VOL. 7.

1604.] WILLIAM BRADSHAW. "If therefore men would set their wits upon the highest strain to invent an apparel to disgrace the Ministers of the Gospel, they could not invent a more odious attire than the consecrated attire of a filthy Mass-Priest, the most abominable Idolater in the earth.

"Those that abhor Idolatry as much as they do beggary and folly, cannot but hate and abhor the badges of Idolatry as much as the badges of folly and beggary, and therefore cannot but account that Priestly attire that is enjoined unto us by our Prelates an apparel more unbecoming the Minister of the Gospel than a cloak with a thousand patches," &c. A TREATISE OF DIVINE WORSHIP, &c., c. 7, N. 11, 12, p. 13.

1605.] AN ABRIDGMENT OF THAT BOOKE WHICH THE MINISTERS OF LINCOLNE DIOCESS DELIVERED TO HIS MAJESTIE UPON THE FIRST OF DECEMBER LAST. "What one Bishop is there, that in celebrating the Communion, and exercizyng every other publicke ministration, doth weare (besides his rochet) a Surplice, or Albe & a Cope or vestment, and doth hold his pastorall staff in his hand, or els hath it born by his Chapline? To all which, notwithstanding he is bound by the first book of Common prayer made in King Edward the 6 his time, and consequently by authority of the same statute whereby we are compelled to use those Ceremonyes in question." EXCEPT. 2, ARG. 4, P. 53, 54.

In the opinion of these Lincoln ministers the Advertisements had not abolished the Vestments.

1607.] ROBERT PARKER. Like the author of AN ANSWER, &c., and the Lincoln Ministers, he taunts the Bishops with inconsistency in enforcing the cross and Surplice, but not—

"The *Alba* [Alb], the *Cappa* [Cope], the *Casula* [Chasuble], the *Baculus Pastoralis* [Pastoral Staff], all which are enioyned by law, as well as the *Crosse* and *Surplice*, because named in K. *Edw.* communion booke, to which our Law and Rubric sendeth vs." A SCHOLASTICALL DISCOVRSE AGAINST SYMBOLIZING WITH ANTICHRIST IN CEREMONIES: ESPECIALLY IN THE SIGNE OF THE CROSSE, PT. 1, c. 3, P. 151.

1605-1613.] In the Chapel Royal, at least, the use of the Cope was not confined to the ministration of the Holy Communion, but was employed in churchings, baptisms, and confirmations. At a baptism, May 5, 1605; at a churching, May 19, 1605; and at confirmations, April 3, 1607, March 22, 1610-11, and April 5, 1613, the officiating Bishops and Clergy were "clothed in riche Coaps." THE OLD CHEQUE-BOOK, N. 17, P. 167-172. CAMDEN SOC. PUBL. N. S. VOL. 3.

Copes were also used in August, 1604, when the Spanish Ambassador took the King's oath; January 27, 1610-1611, when the French Ambassador took the oath; on Candlemas day, 1625, at the coronation of King Charles I. (IB. N. 15, P. 151-160); at the marriage of " Frederick Prince Elector Count Palatine of Rheine" and "Ladie Elizabeth." (IB. N. 16, P. 163-166.)

I also find this entry:

"1611. Henry Alred for many disorders and for suspicion of stealing 3 coapes out of his Maj$^{ty}$* Vestery at Greenwich was put out of his place the vii$^{th}$ of June." IB. N. 13, P. 131.

1616.] According to an "Inventory of the Plate" &c., made May 19, 1616, York Cathedral possessed:

"Two coapes of gold. One cope of white satten." THE FABRIC ROLLS OF YORK MINSTER, N. 57, P. 315. SURTEES SOC. PUBL. VOL. 35.

These Copes were still in existence in 1634, according to an Inventory made January 16, 1633-4. (IB. P. 317.) During the Great Rebellion "there was three Copes taken away by order of the committee by the sequestratours." (IB. N. 62, P. 333-4.) According to an Inventory made November 11, 1681, the Church possessed a "White Satton Cope." IB. N. 57. P. 317.

1630.] "ARTICLES, OR INSTRUCTIONS FOR ARTICLES, TO BE EXHIBITED BY HIS MAJESTIES HEIGH COMMISSIONERS, AGAINST MR. JOHN COSIN," &c. "Agreeable to it you have provided much Altar furniture, and many massing implements, crucifixes, candlesticks, tapers and basons, and copes, one taken from masspriests, adorned with images, and having the picture of the Blessed Trinity on the Cape thereof, wrought in gold very bravely," &c. COSIN CORRESPONDENCE, N. 90, SECT. 9, P. 170, 171. VOL. 1. SURTEES SOC. PUBL. VOL. 52.

NOTE BY THE EDITOR, REV. JOHN ORNSBY. "It would appear from a statement in Smart's Common-place book, which seems to be corroborated by an entry in the Chapter Books in Cosin's handwriting, that vestments, properly so called, or chasubles, had previously been in use in Durham Cathedral. Smart, of course, writes with scorn and ridicule respecting the particular vestments to which he refers, but he is clearly describing chasubles in the extract we are about to give. He says, 'that is not a decent cope which is no cope at all, but a gay curtail'd vestment, reaching scarce down to the knee, of which our Durhamers had 2, condemned and forbidden by the Bishop in his Visitation, and some other of the prebendaries, which tearmed them jackets, tunicles, herald's coats, etc., etc.' Rawl. MSS. Cosin's entry in the Acts of Chapter is as follows:—'It is further agreed that the three vestments, and one white cope, now belonging to the Vestry of this Church, shall be taken and carried to London, to be altered and changed into fair and large copes, according to the Canons and Constitutions of the church of England.' . . . An unpublished diary, kept by Gyll, a local antiquary, who was Attorney-General to Egerton, Bishop of Durham, has the following entry respecting their discontinuance:—'1759: at the latter end of July or beginning of August the old copes, (those raggs of Popery) which had been used at the communion service at the abbey ever since the time of the Reformation were ordered by the d. and ch. to be totally disused and laid aside. Dr. Warburton, one of the prebendaries and bp. of Gloucester, was very zealous to have them laid aside, and so was Dr. Cowper the dean.' No such order, however, appears amongst the Acts of Chapter." IB. P. 170.

Smart, though an intense and bitter Puritan, does not seem to have objected to the Cope *per se*,—a "decent" one, that is, a plain one,—but only to gorgeous and richly embroidered ones.

Five Copes still remain in Durham Cathedral:

"1. Purple Velvet, richly embroidered, and with a crucifix on the back; 2. Purple Silk, embroidered in Gold, with Saints on the Hood; 3. Crimson Velvet, embroidered in Gold, with Saints on the orphrey; 4. Cloth of Gold and Blue Velvet, woven together in a pattern; 5. Crimson Satin, embroidered in Gold, David with the head of Goliath on the Hood: this Cope was given by King Charles I." PERRY, NOTES, P. 49.

In reply to the charges brought against him in 1641, COSIN answered:

"At his first coming [to Durham Cathedral in 1624] he found two open fashioned vestments to be there usually worne, of which, by the late Dean's appointment, one large cope was made." ART. 2, ANS. 2, P. 219. SURTEES SOC. PUBL. VOL. 34.

This Cope made from two ancient Chasubles is still preserved in the Dean and Chapters' Library.

1634.] FATHER LEANDER, (Roman Catholic.)

Vestes praeterea clericales, superpellicia, rochettas, cappas, ... adhuc frequentanda servarunt. APOST. MISS. STAT. IN ANGLA. HYDE, STATE PAPERS, P. 197. VOL. 1.

Moreover, they have preserved to be still used, the Clerical Vestments, Surplices, Rochets, and Copes.

1634.] GREGORIO PANZANI, (Roman Catholic). "The dress of the officiating ministry only was changed to a less gaudy and less garish vesture." MEMOIRS, INTRODUCT., P. 17.

1635.] SIR WILLIAM BRERETON, BART. "When the communion is here [Durham] administered, which is by the bishop himself, here is laid upon this altar, or rather communion-table, a stately cloth of cloth of gold; the bishop useth the new red embroidered cope, which is wrought full of stars, like one I have seen worn in St. Dennis in Fraunce; there are here other two rich copes, all which are shaped like unto long cloaks reaching down to the ground, and which have round capes." TRAVELS, P. 83. CHETHAM, SOC. PUBL. VOL. 1.

1636.] HENRY BURTON. "Our Changes [Changers] doe plead that they bring in no changes, but revive those things, which ancient Canons have allowed and prescribed. . . . These [Cathedrals] bee those nests and nurceries of Superstition and Idolatry, wherein the old Belldame of Rome hath muzzled up her brood of popelings; and so preserved her *Usum Sarum* in life to this very day. . . . For these Mother Churches, to which the Daughter Churches must conforme, are they not the natural daughters of Rome? Do they not from top to toe exactly resemble her? Her pompous Service, her Altars, Palls, Copes, Crucifixes, images, superstitious gestures and Postures, all instruments of musick, &c.? . . . with their hundreds of tapers and candles. . . . What prescription can that Cathedral Church at Wolverhampton in Staffordshire plead for her goodly costly new Altar, with the Dedication thereof within these 2 or 3 years last past, in which Dedication, all the Roman rites were observed, as Censings, washings, bowings, Copes (though borrowed from Lichfield)?" FOR GOD AND THE KING, P. 158-161.

Circa 1638.] JOHN COSIN, afterwards BISHOP OF DURHAM. "*In the second year of the reign of King Edward the Sixth.*] For the ornaments of the church and of the ministers thereof, the order appointed in the second year of his reign was retained, and the same we are bound still to observe. Which is a note wherewith those men are not so well acquainted as they should be, who inveigh against our present ornaments in the church, and think them to be innovations introduced lately by an arbitrary power, against law; whereas, indeed, they are appointed by the law itself. And this Judge Yelverton acknowledged and confessed to me, (when I had declared the matter to him, as I here set it forth,) in his circuit at Durham, not long before his death, having been of another mind before." NOTES ON THE BOOK OF COMMON PRAYER, 2D SERIES, P. 233. WORKS, VOL. 5.

Circa 1640.] "*Such ornaments, &c.*] The particulars of these ornaments (both of the church and of the ministers thereof, as in the end of the Act of Uniformity) are referred not to the fifth of Edw. VI. . . . but to the second year of that king, when his first Service-book and Injunctions were in force by authority of parliament. And in those books many other ornaments are appointed; as, two lights to be set upon the altar or communion-table, a cope or vestment for the priest and for the bishop, besides their albs, surplices, and rochets, the bishop's crosier-staff to be holden by him at his ministration and ordinations; and those ornaments of the church, which by former laws, not then abrogated, were in use by virtue of the statute 25 Henry VIII." IB. 3D SERIES, P. 438, 439. IB.

1640.] WILLIAM WATS.

Usum, scilicet hujus Albae in Ecclesia Anglicana, in desuetudinem potius sponte sua (sed quomodo nescio) abiisse, quam authoritate aliqua sacerdotibus nostris aut vetitum esse aut negatum. Cum enim in Rubrica trium illarum media, quae principio Liturgiae Anglicanae prefiguntur, statutum reperiatur; &c. IN M. PARIS, VERB. ALBA, P. 268.

The use of this Alb in the Anglican Church, fell into disuse rather of its own accord, (but how I know not) than by being forbidden or denied to our priests by any authority. For seeing that in the middle of those three Rubrics which are prefixed to the beginning of the Anglican Liturgy, it may be found enacted; &c.

'Coaps' nos Angli dicimus et in liturgia adhuc iis utimur. We English call them Copes, and still use them in the Liturgy. IB. P. 276.

1641.] At the Great Rebellion, when the Church was swept away, a satirical poem entitled, "Lambeth Faire, wherein you have all the Bishop's Trinkets set to sale," appeared in 1641, wherein the Bishops are represented as selling their Vestments and the Ornaments of the Church :

" 'Come, customers, see what you lack, and buy:
Here's vestments consecrate, all sorts and sizes,'

. . . . . . .

'Wax candles, tapers,' another cries and calls,
'These brought I with me from Cathedral Paul's;' "
PAGES 1–9.  Cited in HIERUGIA, P. 254–256.

1641.] Report of the Committee of the House of Lords. See page 77.

1644.] Ordinance of Parliament. See page 77.

1661.] Then came the Restoration in 1660, after the Church had been suppressed for twenty years. Meanwhile the Vestments had to a great degree been destroyed ; yet at the coronation of Charles II., we are told by PEPYS :

"At last comes in the Dean and Prebendaries of Westminster, with the Bishops (many of them in cloth of gold copes,) and after them the Nobility, all in their Parliamentary robes, a most magnificent sight." DIARY, APRIL 23, 1661, P. 191. VOL. 1.

The Puritans, before and at the Savoy Conference, did all they could to have the Vestments done away with, but without success. See pages 77–79.

1660.] THE OLD NONCONFORMIST, TOUCHING THE BOOK OF COMMON PRAYER AND CEREMONIES. "And these faults that are in that book of Ordination which is of the last edition, and most reformed. In the former edition (which seems by the words of the 36 Article to be that we are required to subscribe unto, and which it may be some of the bishops do still use) there are other corruptions. As
1. That the Cope, Albe, Surplice, Tunicle and Pastoral staff are appointed to be used in Ordination and Consecration." PAGE 32.

1660.] VIEW OF THE PRELATICAL CHURCH IN ENGLAND, &c. Albs were worn at the consecration of Bishops in Dublin :

"The Bishops elect in their albs." PAGE 33. Cited in HIERURGIA, P. 167.

1661.] WHITE KENNET, BISHOP OF PETERBOROUGH. "As soon as he [Bishop Walton, at his enthronization in Chester Cathedral] had put on his Episcopal Robes, he hasted the Performance of his Devotions in the Quire. When he entered the Body of the Church, the Dean (Dr. *Henry Bridgman*, brother to the Lord Chief Justice *Bridgman*) and all the Members of the Cathedral, habited in their Albes, received a Blessing from his Lordship, sung the *Te Deum*, and so compassing the Quire in the Manner of a procession, conveyed him to his Chair. AN HISTORICAL REGISTER, &c., p. 537.

1680.] RALPH THORESBY. "Went afterwards to see the Abbey; viewed the exceeding rich copes and robes, was troubled to see so much superstition remaining in Protestant Churches; tapers, basins, and richly embroidered I. H. S. upon the high altar, with the picture of God the Father, like an old man; the Son, as a young man, richly embroidered upon their copes. Lord, open their eyes, that the substance of religion be not at length turned into shadows and ceremonies." DIARY, SEPT. 15, P. 60, 61. VOL. 1.

1681.] "January 1. Afternoon returned to Durham:
2. Die Dom. In the forenoon went to the Minster; was somewhat amazed at their ornaments, tapers, rich embroidered copes, vestments," &c. IB. P. 75. IB.

1683.] THOMAS DE LAUNE. "Have they [the Romans] proper, distinguishing *Habits* for their Clergy, and particular Vestments for their holy Ministrations; as *Albs, Surplices, Chasubles, Amicts, Gowns, Copes, Maniples. Zones,* &c.? So we." A PLEA FOR THE NON-CONFORMISTS, P. 49.

1699.] ABREGE DES HISTOIRES DES PLUS FAMEUX HERESIARQUES QUI ONT PARU EN EUROPE DEPUIS L'ANNE 1040, ET AU PRECIS HISTORIQUE DES CAUSES DU SCHISM DE L'EGLISE ANGLICANE. ROUEN. 1699. (Roman Catholic.)

On se sert des habits et des Ornemens à la Romaine. ... Et on a quantité de ceremonies dans leur Offices et Services retenués ou imitées des ceremonies Romains, &c. PT. 2, P. 55. Cited by MACCOLL, LAWLESSNESS, &c., LETTER 1, P. 143, 144.

They preserve the Habits and the Ornaments according to the Roman Church. ... And there are many ceremonies in their Offices and Services retained, or imitated from the Roman ceremonies, &c.

1708.] THOMAS BENNET. "From hence 'tis plain that the Parish Priests (and I take no notice of the Case of others) are obliged to no other Ornaments, but Surplices and Hoods. For these [the Advertisements and Canons] are authentic Limitations of the Rubric, which seems to require *all* such Ornaments as were in Use in the second Year of King *Edward's* reign." PARAPHRASE ON THE BOOK OF COMMON PRAYER, P. 6, 7.

1710.] WILLIAM NICHOLLS. "*Ornaments.*] This Clause as to Ornaments seems to be restrain'd to the Person of Queen *Elizabeth*, and she making no alteration in them, they remain'd at her Death the same as they were in the 2nd of *Edw.* 6. See the Rubric immediately preceeding the Morning Service in the Common Prayer Book, confirm'd by 14, C. 2. c. 4. where the Ornaments appointed for that Service, are enjoyn'd as they were in the 2nd of *Edw.* 6. (*Quest.* If the ancient Ornaments and no other, ought not to be used at this Day?) COM. ON THE BOOK OF COMMON PRAYER. Note on c. 25, Elizabeth's Act for Uniformity—not paged.

1710.] CHARLES WHEATLY. "These [the Alb, Vestment, Cope, Tunicle and Pastoral Staff] are the ministerial ornaments and habits enjoined by our present rubric, in conformity to the practice of our Church immediately after the Reformation; though at that time they were so very offensive to Calvin and Bucer, that the one in his letters to the Protector, and the other in his censure of the English Liturgy, which he sent to archbishop Cranmer, urged very vehemently to have them abolished; not thinking it tolerable to have any thing in common with the papists, but esteeming everything idolatrous that was derived from them.

"However, they made shift to accomplish the end they aimed at, in procuring a further reform of our Liturgy: for in the review that was made of it in the fifth of Edward VI., amongst other ceremonies and usages, these rubrics were left out, and the following one put in their place, viz.

"*And here it is to be noted,*" &c. [Rubric of 1552, cited on page 34.]

"But in the next review under queen Elizabeth, the old rubrics were again brought into authority, and so have continued ever since; being established by the Act of Uniformity that passed soon after the Restoration." RATIONAL ILLUST. OF THE BOOK OF COMMON PRAYER, C. 2, SECT. 4, N. 7, P. 105, 106.

1713.] EDMUND GIBSON, afterwards BISHOP OF LONDON. "Therefore, *legally*, the Ornaments of Ministers in performing Divine Service, are the same now as they were in 2 *E*. 6." CODEX JUR. ECCL., TIT. 13, C. 1, P. 297. VOL. 1.

1727-1748.] DANIEL DE FOE. "This Church [Durham] is very rich: they have excellent music. The old Vestments which the Clergy before the Reformation wore are still used on Sundays and other Holy-days, by the Residents. They are so rich with Embroidery and embos'd Work of Silver, as must needs make it uneasy for the Wearers to sustain." A TOUR THRO' THE WHOLE ISLAND OF GREAT BRITAIN, P. 214, 215. VOL. 3. [This edition is brought down to 1748.]

1732.] JOANNES GRANCOLAS, (Roman Catholic.)

| | |
|---|---|
| Presbyteri haec omnia in Templis decantant per anni cursum, superpelliceo, pluviali et casulis induti. Puerorum choros quoque habent, cantores, et organa. COM. HIST. IN ROM. BREV., L. 1, C. 12, P. 26. | The Priests sing all these things in the Churches during the course of the year, clothed with a Surplice, Cope, and Chasubles. They also have boy-choirs, singing-men, and organs. |

1733.] BERNARD PICART. "The Oath of Supremacy is taken by the King as Head of the Church, and as such on the Day of his Coronation, he puts on a Surplice, a Stole and a Dalmatic."

"Bishops, Deans, Canons, in Cathedral Churches, wear a Cope besides the Surplice, and are to put it on at the Communion Service, Administration of Sacraments, or any other religious Function which is to be performed with solemnity." RELIGIOUS CEREMONIES, P. 46, 55. VOL. 6.

1763.] DR. RICHARD BURN. "So that in marrying, churching of women, and other offices not here specified, and even in the administration of the holy communion, it seemeth that a surplice is not necessary. And the reason why it is not enjoined for the holy communion in particular, is, because other vestments are appointed for that ministration, which are as followeth: ' Upon the day,' " &c. [Rubric of 1549.] ECCL. LAW, WORD PUBLICK WORSHIP, N. 4, P. 265. VOL. 3.

1801.] An edition of the Prayer Book was published in 1801 for John Reeves, "one of the patentees of the office of King's printer." In the preface, dedicated to the Queen, we find the following:

"The rubric goes no further than to speak of their (ministers') ornaments, which are to be retained as they were used in the second year of Edward VI. Thus we are referred to the First Prayer Book of Edward VI., where we find directions for wearing various articles of ornament in dress, which are now out of use, and hardly known to us; for besides the surplice and hood, which are now used, there are the rochette or albe, cope or vestment, the pastoral staff, and tunicle. Some of these are deemed to retain in them too much of the Popish reverence for indifferent things; and it was accordingly, in the Second Book of Edward VI., directed that the minister should not at communion wear an albe, vestment, or cope; but, if a bishop, he should have a rochette, and, if a priest or deacon, a surplice only. However, in the next review under Queen Elizabeth, the rubric of the First Book was restored, which order was continued since, being, as we have just seen, referred to in our present rubric.

"The habits enjoined by the First Book, and forbidden by the Second were restored.

"Among other ornaments of the Church then in use, and therefore within the meaning of this rubric, there were two lights, enjoined to be set upon the altar, as a significant emblem of the light which Christ's Gospel brought into the world. This was ordered by the same injunction which prohibited all lights and tapers, that used to be superstitiously set before images and shrines. These two lights are still used in cathedral churches and chapels as often as divine service is performed at candle-light; and they ought also, by this rubric, to be used in all parish churches and chapels when there is service at candle-light." Cited in the *Church Times*, DEC. 12, 1879, P. 779.

1838.] FORM AND ORDER OF THE CORONATION OF QUEEN VICTORIA. "Then followeth the Litany, to be read by two Bishops, vested in Copes. . . . . The Archbishop, being still vested in his Cope," &c. SECT. 4, 19, P. 6, 28.

On the opposite page is a plate representing Queen Victoria receiving the Blessed Sacrament, after her coronation, at Westminster Abbey, June 28, 1838. From the picture by F. Winterhalter.

1843.] DR. JOHN JEBB. "The Cope, or the Vestment, specially prescribed to be used by the Clergy administering the Holy Communion, by the regulation referred to in the Rubric, and

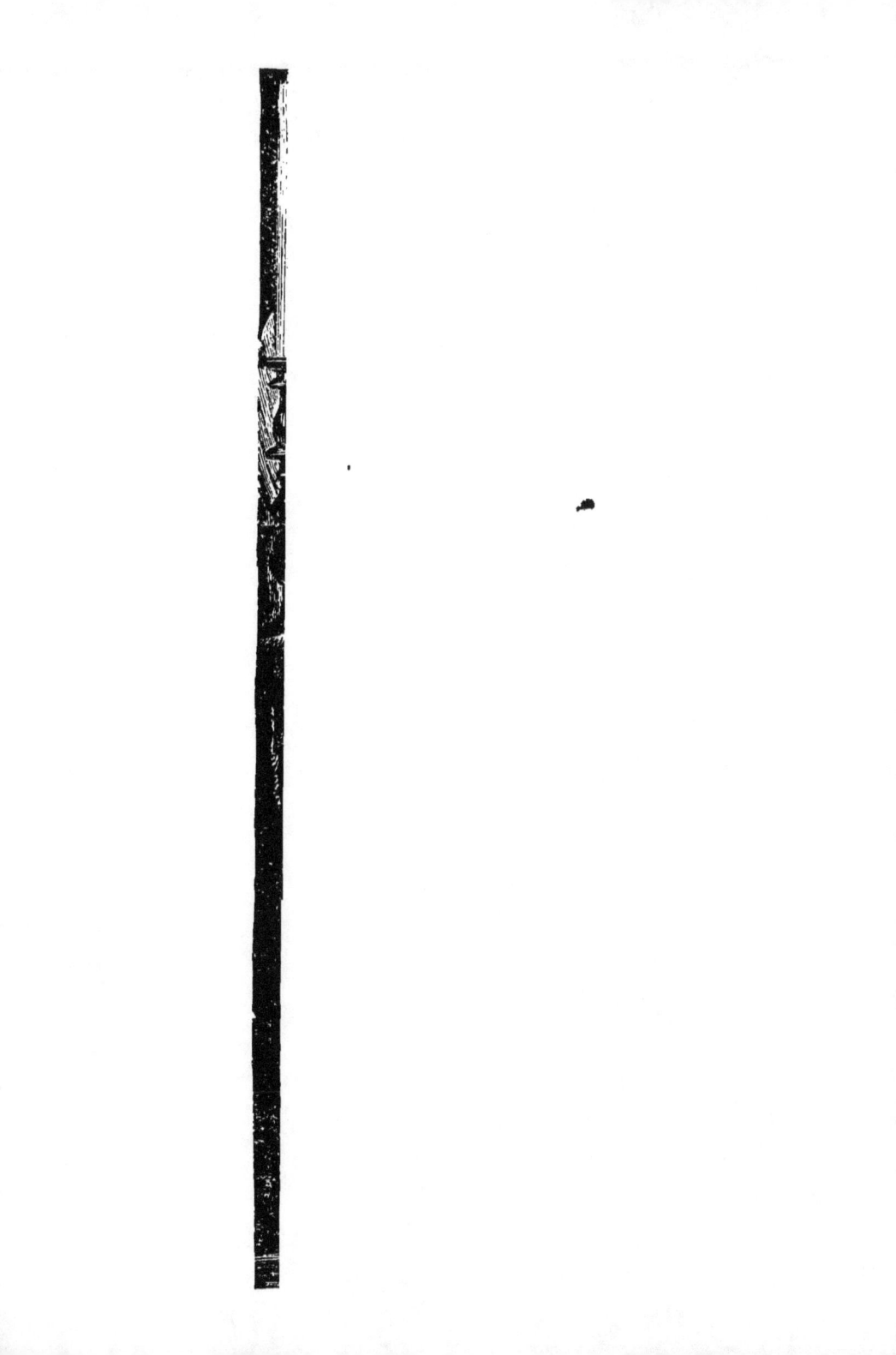

Attention Scanner:
Foldout in Book!

expressly ordered to be used in the Cathedral Churches by the twenty-fourth Canon, has now fallen into almost total disuse, being retained only at Westminster Abbey, at coronations, when all the Prebendaries are vested in Copes, as well as the Prelates who then officiate. The ancient Copes, used till some time in the last century, still exist at Durham; and at Westminster, as tradition informs us, they were used till about the same time. We have sufficient evidence from documents, that not only in Cathedrals, but also in the University Colleges, &c., they were in common use till at least the Great Rebellion.

"The Vestment and Cope were ignorantly objected to by many after the Reformation, as Popish Ornaments. It is sufficiently well known that these as well as the other ecclesiastical garments retained, or enjoined by our Church, were common also to the Eastern Church, and were as ancient as any ritual record now extant; that they are Catholic and Anglican, and therefore ought to be retained.

"I must honestly acknowledge, that I can find no argument to justify the disuse of these ancient vestments, so expressly enjoined by authorities to which all Clergymen profess obedience, except that rule of charity, which as Bishop Beveridge expressed it, is above rubrics." THE CHORAL SERVICE, SECT. 27, P. 216-217.

1844.] HENRY PHILLPOTTS, BISHOP OF EXETER. "Why have these been disused? Because the parishioners—that is, the churchwardens, who represent the parishioners—have neglected their duty to provide them: for such is the duty of the parishioners by the plain and express canon law of England (Gibson, 200). True, it would be a very costly duty, and for that reason, most probably, churchwardens have neglected it, and archdeacons have connived at the neglect. I have no wish that it should be otherwise. But, be this as it may, if the churchwardens of Helston shall perform this duty, at the charge of the parish, providing an alb, a vestment, and a cope, as they might in strictness be required to do (Gibson, 201), I shall enjoin the minister, be he who he may, to use them." Cited in the ENGLISH CHURCHMAN, NO. XCVIII. HIERURGIA, P. 388, 389.

1845.] DR. ARCHIBALD JOHN STEPHENS. "All the Rubrics just quoted were omitted in 1552, and never appeared again. The only Rubric respecting ornaments in the second Common Prayer-Book of Edward VI., confirmed likewise by Act of Parliament, was directed against the use of the Cope and Pastoral Staff. These ornaments, however, were again introduced by the Rubric of 1559, which brought us back, not to the second book of Edward VI., but to the first. And this Rubric of 1559, slightly altered was a second time authorized at the last review [in 1662].

"Copes were worn at Durham and Westminster till the middle of the last century, and copes are worn now by the bishops at the coronations; indeed, all the directions contained in the first book of Edward VI., as to the ornaments of the church and of the ministers thereof at all times of their ministration, are by stat. 14, Car. II., c. 4, the statute law of the Anglican Church." NOTES LEGAL AND HISTORICAL ON THE BOOK OF COMMON PRAYER, P. 367, VOL. 1. Cited by PHILLIMORE, THE PRINCIP. ECCL. JUDG., ELPHINSTONE v. PURCHAS, P. 177.

1851.] The writer of the article in the QUARTERLY REVIEW, "*Rubric* versus *Usage*," a strong anti-Puseyite, after citing the first and fourth Rubric of the Prayer Book of 1549, as cited on page 29, goes on to say:

"These Rubrics, besides offering some discrepancies and obscurities in other details, would allow the minister in any but the specified services to '*use a surplice or no*,' that is, '*or nothing*,' at his pleasure, while it prescribes albs, copes, and tunicles to all ministers for the Communion, and rochets, albs, copes, and croziers to the Bishop on all occasions. We need not say into what total disuse these rubrics have fallen—yet they are, as far as we can discover, the only rubrical directions for the vesture of her ministers that the Church of England now possesses.

"At all events, this clause [in the Act of Uniformity] annulled the Rubric of King Edward's second book (1552) for the exclusive use of the surplice, and restored, not all the rubrics of the first book (1549), but only those relating to the *ornaments* of the church and clergy, *surplices, albs, tunicles, vestments, copes, and croziers*; and '*that* seems to be the present state of the law—this Act of the 1st Eliz. having been confirmed by the 1*st* of *James* I., and so far as relates to the Church, made perpetual by the 5*th* of *Queen Anne*, c. 5,' and being, in fact, the first Act of Uniformity that now stands in front of our prayer-books." PAGES 219-221. VOL. 89. 1851.

1874.] CHRISTOPHER WORDSWORTH, afterwards BISHOP OF LINCOLN. "*Q*. What 'ornaments of the Church and of its Ministers, at the times of their ministration,' are allowed by the Church of England?

"*A*. Those ornaments which were in the 'Church of England, by the Authority of Parliament in the second year of King Edward.'

"*Q*. What are these?

"*A*. Such as are specified in the First Book of Common Prayer put forth in the reign of King Edward VI., and authorized by legislative sanction in the Act of Uniformity passed at that time; and as have not since been abrogated." THEOPH. ANGLIC., PT. 4, c. 1, P. 316.

Here are two contradictory decisions of the Privy Council. We give them now, and shall refer to them again hereafter.

1857.] LIDDELL *v*. WESTERTON. "The Rubric to the present Prayer Book adopts the language of the statute of Elizabeth; but they all obviously mean the same thing, that the same dresses and the same utensils or articles which were used under the First Prayer Book of Edward VI. may still be used." PRIVY COUNCIL JUDGMENTS, P. 53.

1871.] HEBBERT *v*. PURCHAS. "The Cope is to be worn in ministering the Holy Communion on high feast days in cathedral and collegiate churches, and the Surplice in all other ministrations." IB. P. 183.

## (IV). The Use of Copes and Vestments in Parish Churches.

E have just given instances of the general use of Vestments in the Church of England. We now propose to give some instances of their use in Parish Churches exclusively.

The Rubric of 1559 makes no distinction between Parish and Cathedral Churches. The Queen in her letter to Archbishop Parker, in 1560-1, (see pages 46–47), was very desirous of preserving uniformity in all Churches, especially in Cathedral and Collegiate Churches, which could better bear the expense than Parish Churches, though in the latter, the "same" or "at the least the like" manner of service was to be used. See also PARKER, EP. 345, cited on page 66. In 1561, the Archbishop drew up "Interpretations," suggesting that the Cope alone should be used in the Lord's Supper, but not forbidding the use of the Chasuble. (See page 48.)

It is now claimed that the use of the Cope, except in Cathedral and Collegiate Churches, was forbidden by the Advertisements. (See page 51.)

The Advertisements were published in March, 1566. They only order the Cope to be used in certain churches, and forbid it nowhere. (See page 50.) The Puritans of that time, as Coverdale, Humphrey and Sampson, (see page 120), say absolutely that the Cope is to be retained in divine service, and do not restrict it to Cathedrals. In the controversies between Cartwright and Whitgift, afterwards Archbishop of Canterbury, the Cope is objected to in general, and nowhere spoken of as confined to certain churches.

DR. HASTINGS ROBINSON, in the Introduction to the second series of the Zurich Letters, remarks:

"It may be well, however, to observe, that the original words rendered by the term *surplice* appear sometimes to have been used by the writers, where, according to the Injunctions, the cope, and perhaps some other habits, may have been included or intended; and indeed considerable uncertainty seems to have prevailed as to the occasions on which these vestments were respectively used, as well as to the precise meaning of some of the terms by which they were designated in the original letters." PAGE IX.

1670.] GILBERT SHELDON, Archbishop of Canterbury, in a CIRCULAR LETTER TO CATHEDRALS, June 4, 1670, says:

"Our cathedrals are the standard and rule to all Parochial Churches of the solemnity and decent manner of reading the liturgy, and administering the holy sacraments." CARDWELL, DOC. ANN., N. 154, P. 331. VOL. 2.

1564.] WYMONDHAM, NORFOLK. A correspondent sent a communication to the *Church Times*, DEC. 30, 1881, P. 910, containing an extract from a small history of Wymondham Church, published in 1853 by R. Foster, then parish clerk :

"An inventory of all the churche ornaments, remaynynge in the vestry of the churche of Wymondham, taken by Stephen Vardon, Will'm Kett, John Neve, Tho's Wyseman, churchwardens, the first day of December, Anno Dom. 1564, &c. comytted to the custody and charge of John Powle, then vrisse clarke, except such ornaments as be layed into the cheast which be then accordyngly named as appeareth.

*Imprimis.*—One vestment of redd velvett, embrodered with imagry of gold, layed into the cheast.

*Itm.*—One other like redd vestmente embrodered for a deacon, lay into the cheast.

. . . . . .

*Itm.*—One crymsen velvett cope, embrodered with gold.
*Itm.*—One whyt damask cope.
*Itm.*—One vestment of grene and tawny satten abridges embrodered.

. . . . . .

*Itm.*—One cross of latten, wh. the shaffe of latten gilted.
*Itm.*—One lytle candlestyck and ij long waterpotts of latten.
*Itm.*—One shippe of tyne and censor of latten.
*Itm.*—One great long candlestick of latten."

EDWARD PEACOCK has published a book on ENGLISH CHURCH FURNITURE, containing an inventory of the ornaments of a hundred and fifty parishes in the Diocese of Lincoln, in the year 1565-6. By the following extracts, it will be seen that not only were Copes and Vestments used in some Parish Churches, but that they were not accounted as "Popish" or "superstitious."

BASINGHAM, 18. March 1565[6.] ". . . haue a cope in the churche the wch wee ar admitted [by the injunc]tions to kepe for o' mi'ster." PAGE 42.

BILLINGBOROWE, 14. March 1565[6.]—"Itm, one cope—remayneth in or pishe churche wt a surplesse and 5 towelles w<sup>ch</sup> we occupie about the coion [communion] but all the tromperie and popishe Ornaments is sold and defaced so that ther remaynethe no supersticious monumente wt in or pish churche of Billingborowe." PAGE 49.

BLYTON, 20. April 1566.] "Ornamntes of the Priest—a cope wch remaynith, an alb whearof is made a surpless, and a vestm' of the w<sup>ch</sup> is made a covering for o' pulpit by the said churchwardens the said yeare. PAGE 52.

MARKET DEEPINGE, 18 March 1565[6.]—Itm fyve table clothes

xv towelles a fonte clothe a surples a rocket or ij for the clark and a silver coppe—Remanith in o<sup>r</sup> pishe church a° dni 1565 W<sup>m</sup> Harvie and W<sup>m</sup> affen churchwardens so that no popishe peltrie remaineth in o<sup>r</sup> said pishe church." PAGE 68, 69.

LENTON ALS LEVINGTON, 22. March 1565[6.] "Itm a cope wth all thother thinges according to thininctions [injunctions]—remaineth in o<sup>r</sup> said pish church A° dni 1565 Symon Searson and John Barleman churchwardens." PAGE 114.

LUNDONTHORP, 11. April 1566.] "Itm one Cope—remaynige in or said pische so that wee haue no monument of supersticon now remaynige." PAGE 115.

In addition to the parishes above mentioned, the Cope is spoken of as still "remayninge" in twenty-two other parishes: Belton, Bichefeld, Little Bitham, Ednam, Epworth, Ffulletbie, Hollywell, Mintinge, Market Reason, Riskington, Sibsaie, Somerbie, Stevenbie, Swaton, Swynested, Tedforth, Totill, Vffington, Welbie, Willerton, Winthorpe and North Witham.

In a few cases, a Vestment, or Alb is spoken of as remaining. In some cases the Alb had been made into a Surplice or Rochet. There are but a very few cases where mention is made of the existence of a Surplice even, in a parish.

BOMNBIE, 26. April 1566.] "Itm one alb. . . . Remaynith." PAGE 53.

GRETFORD, 4. March 1565[6.] "Itm two old vestmentes of bustion a stole and two phannele yet remayninge."
"Itm two surplesses yet remayninge." PAGE 90, 91.

GUNBIE, 18. March 1565[6.] "Itm one vestment one cope one chalice an albe w<sup>ch</sup> is nowe made a surples . . . Remaineth in o<sup>r</sup> pishe church of Gunbie." PAGE 92.

LAUGHTON JUX<sup>A</sup> STOWE, 9. April 1566.] "One vestment and one handbell wch do yet remayne." PAGE 112.

LEA, 8. April 1566.] "Itm a Rochet one crose clothe ij banner clothes and one old vestment—Remaynith in o<sup>r</sup> Church." PAGE 113.

STEVENBIE, 18. March 1565[6.] "Itm one cope and a vestment one albe and one sepulcre—the cope remaynethe in o<sup>r</sup> churche at this p'nte tyme and also the vestment and albe remaynethe there nowe and as for the sepulcre is broken and defaced." PAGE 146.

WILLERTON, 8. April 1566.] "Itm one cope iij vestmtes and an albe wth a crwet—now remaynith in the house of the said churchwardens."

". . . so that nowe their remaynith no more popish peltrie in or pish [our parish]." PAGE 162.

1566.] ASSIGNMENT OF CHURCH ORNAMENTS TO BE USED IN THE CHURCH OF ST. PETHERICK, BODMIN, COUNTY OF CORNWALL. "Thys Indentuer made at bodmynn the Sunday next after the ffeast of Seynt mygell the archangell ynn the eyght yere of the

Raygne of our Soueraygne Lady Elyzabeth by the grace of god of England ffrancie and Ireland quene defender of the ffaythe &c Between Nycholas Cory mayor of the towne of bodmyn of thone party and Richard Water & Thomas Cole tanur Wardens of the Churche of St. Petherick yn bodmynn aforesayd of thother party Wyttnesseth that the said Rychard Water and Thomas Cole Wardens & ther successors Wardens hath taken & receved into ther handes & kepyng of the sayd Nycholas Cory mayor and of all the hole paryshe aforesayd to be vsed & occupyed to the honor of God ynn the same churche from the day & yere aforesayd fourthward all suche goodes & ornaments as folowth . . . Item one vestment of grene satyn of bryddes. Item one hole sute of blew velut decon subdecon & pistholere, a pere of vestments of whyte damaske one cope of red satyn of bryddes. Item a vestment of blue velut one whyte cope of satyn. Item one whyte vestment of satyn & more toe copes used on good fryday and a obe [alb] of sylck . . . ij pere of candlestyckes . . . a lampe before the hye auter." Published by Sir John Maclean, Parochial and Family History of the Deanery of Trigg Minor in the County of Cornwall, Appendix 2, p. 341. Vol. 1.

From an account of some Churches in Cornwall, published in the *Supplement* to the *Rock*, Nov. 7, 1879, p. 902, we learn that the Parish Church of St. Mary and St. Petrock, the largest church in Cornwall, was built in 1468. Prior Vivian, Bishop of Megara, who died in 1533, is represented in full pontifical vestures on his tomb. There is a beautiful sculptured font in the Norman style, and the Altar piece and east window are very ancient. The Clergy orientate and wear white Eucharistic Vestments. The seats are free.

1571.] "Humphrey Colles, Esq., of Beerton, Somerset, was a Justice of the Peace for that County: in 1569 he, with some 800 other Magistrates, signed the Declaration of adhesion to the Act of Uniformity, in which the Signatories said, 'Neither shall any of us that hath subscribed do, or say, or suffer anything to be done or said, by our procurement or allowance, in contempt, lack, or reproof of any part of Religion established by the aforesaid Act;' and a service to which he was appointed in 1570 appears to have placed him in somewhat intimate connexion with Cecil and other Members of the Privy Council, so that he was likely to know the state of the Law touching the Goods and Ornaments of the Church. His Will is dated June 10, 8th Elizabeth, 1566, and was proved in London before Abp. Parker in 1571. . . . One of his Executors was Wm. Rowsewill the then Solicitor General, and another Sir Hugh Paulet, Kt., who signed with him the Declaration above mentioned.

"'Furthermore, I will to the Churchwardens of the Parish Church of Corff, in the County of Somerset, to the use of the same Church, and maintainance of Divine Service there, the Cope of velvet embroidered that my wife lent to the parishioners there, and all Vestments and other furniture of mine whatsoever the Churchwardens have, meet for the maintainance of Divine Service there.

"'Also I give and bequeath to the said Churchwardens, for the use and maintainance of the Ornaments, and reparations of the said Parish Church of Corff, 20s.'" Cited by PERRY, NOTES, P. 240.

Many similar bequests could be produced.

Circa 1570.] ANTHONY GILBY. Among many Popish practices still remaining in the Church, he enumerates:

"24. The Surplisse in litle Churches. 25. The Cope in great Chur." A VIEWE OF ANTICHRIST, &c., PARTE OF A REGISTER, P. 63.

1571.] JOHN STRYPE. "And what sort of popishly affected priests still officiated in the Church, the forementioned Northbroke [minister of Redcliff, in Bristol] will tell us, in his epistle to a book entituled, *A brief and pithy sum of the Christian faith*. Therein he spake 'of certain men, then ministers of the Church, who were papists, and so gave out themselves to be in their discourses. Who subscribed, and observed the order of service, wore a side gown, a square cap, a cope and surplice.'" ANNALS, B. 1, c. 11, p. 145. VOL. 2, PT. 1.

1572.] SIR EDMUND TRAFFORD was appointed one of the Commissioners to take an "Inventory of goods in the Churches and Chapels of Lancashire" in 1552. The possession of certain church goods troubled him, so when he made his will, which was proved in 1572, he gave the following order:

"I bequeth all such choops [copes] and vestiments w$^{ch}$ I haue that Wyllm Robert my fatherinlawe bought, w$^{ch}$ weare once the church goods, to be restorede againe for the servise of God unto the church wher yt shall please God my bodie to be buriede yf Gods lawe will suffer yt." LANCASHIRE AND CHESHIRE WILLS AND INVENTORIES, P. 158, 159, CHETHAM SOC. PUBL. VOL. 51.

Circa 1573.] THOMAS CARTWRIGHT, in a REPLY TO AN ANSWER OF M. DR. WHITGIFTE AGAINSTE THE ADMONITION TO THE PARLIAMENT, and in the ADMONITION, cited on page 123, objects to the Cope, Surplice, Cap, and Tippet in general; nor does his opponent, Whitgift, ever hint even that the Cope was obligatory only in certain churches, and forbidden in Parish Churches, but he defends the use of them as being ordained by the authority of the Church. CARTWRIGHT says:

"We marvel that they could espy in the last synod, that a grey amice [almuce?], which is but a garment of dignity, should be a garment (as they say) defiled with superstition, and yet that copes, caps, surplices, tippets, and such like baggage, the preaching signs of popish priesthood, the Pope's creatures, kept in the same form to this end, to bring dignity and reverence to the ministers and sacraments, should be retained still, and not be abolished. . . .

"Because that [the Amice] was used in few churches, and but of few also in those few churches, therefore, if there were cause to take away that, there was greater to take away the surplice. And to take away the amice out of the church, and leave the surplice, &c., is to heal a scratch, and leave a wound unhealed."

To this WHITGIFT replies as follows:

"The grey amice was justly taken away, because the use of it is not established by any law of this realm, as the use of the other vestures be; and in mine opinion the bishops deserved commendation in so doing; for thereby they declared that they will not suffer any rites or ornaments to be used in this church, but such only as are by public authority." Cited by WHITGIFT, DEFENCE OF THE ANSWER, &c., TRACT. 7, c. 6, p. 50, 51, 52. VOL. 2.

CARTWRIGHT again says:

"A man may find greater dissent amongst those which are united in surplice and cope, &c., than there is amongst those which wear them not, either with themselves, or with them that wear them. For how many there are that wear surplices which would be gladder to say a mass than hear a sermon, let all the world judge. And of those that do wear this apparel, and be otherwise well minded to the gospel, are there not which will wear the surplice and not the cap; other that will wear both the cap and surplice, but not the tippet; and yet a third sort, that will wear surplice, cap, and tippet, but not the cope?" IB. Cited by WHITGIFT, IB. P. 61.

"They should first prove, by the word of God, . . . that . . . wafer-cakes for their bread when they minister it, surplice and cope to do it in, . . . and other such foolish things, are agreeable to the written word of God." AN ADMONITION, &c.

WHITGIFT replies:

"Of 'wafer-cakes,' ministering in 'surplice or cope,' . . . I have spoken before: wafer-cakes be bread; surplice and cope, by those that have authority in the church, are thought to pertain to comeliness and decency. . . . The form of bread, whether it ought to be cake-bread, or loaf-bread, every particular thing that pertaineth to decency or comeliness, at what time, in what place, with what words we ought to give thanks, is not particularly written in scripture, no more than it is that you were baptized. And therefore (as I have proved before) in such cases the church hath to determine and appoint an order." DEFENCE, &c., TRACT. 21, c. 1, p. 333, 334, 335. VOL. 3.

1574.] WALTER TRAVERS. "But iff they perteine to decency and comlyness, what needeth any commandment to be giuen to a minister to vse dailie the tippet and square cappe, and a Priestes gowne, and at divine seruice the cope and the surplice." A FULL AND PLAINE DECLARATION, p. 129. CARTWRIGHT's translation.

1559-1577.] JOHN CHARLES COX, in his NOTES ON THE CHURCHES OF DERBYSHIRE, remarks:

"In the second year of Queen Elizabeth, 1559-60, we find that the church [of All Saints, Derby,] possessed *inter alia*, 'a brasse crosse,—an holy-water can of brase—a Cowpe of blak Vellyvet—and 1 fyne vestment.' In the following year, in addition to the above, mention is also made of a suit of vestments of black velvet.

In 1563-4, an albe and an amice, a cope of black velvet, three surplices, and a cope of blue chamlet. These copes are mentioned repeatedly in subsequent inventories, and an albe is enumerated year by year up to 1576." PAGE 87. VOL. 4.

"Those interested in the 'Vestment Controversy,' will find herein a remarkable corroboration of the common sense view of the question, viz., that vestments were certainly not prohibited, but understood to be sactioned by the 'Ornaments Rubric,' yet that in course of time their use *gradually* died out in all Churches, owing to the ascendancy of a puritan spirit, and the great cost necessary for their maintainance. It will be noted that vestments were used in All Saints' for more than a decade after the alleged '*Advertisements*' of Privy Council fame." NOTE, IB.

"In the 3rd of Elizabeth (1560-1) occurs the following Inventory:—
A brasen Cross & a holy water Can of brasse.
A fyne Cope of blak vellevytt.
A fyne Vestment that M$^r$ Reyd gave. . . .
Itm blak Vestmentes of vellvyt that be in the custody of M$^r$ Ward."

"In 1562-3 occurs, *inter alia*, 'a vestment y$^t$ M$^r$ Reede gave except y$^e$ albe & y$^e$ amysse,' thus demonstrating that this Elizabethan 'vestment' was the chasuble and its appurtenances.

The following is the Inventory of 1563-4:—
. . . A Coope of blacke velvet—iij surplesses—An aube & an amis—and A Coope of blew chamlet.

In 1564-5 occurs much the same Inventory.

The last year in which copes are mentioned in these Inventories is the 10th of Elizabeth (1567-8), but albes are enumerated year by year up to the 19th of Elizabeth (1576-7)." THE CHRONICLES OF . . . ALL SAINTS, C. 8, P. 173, 174.

1607.] "On a slab just in front of the altar [of Holy Trinity Church, Wensley,] is a fine brass of an ecclesiastick in sacerdotal robes of very fine execution, probably Flemish, and remarkable as being subsequent to the Reformation. The legend runs thus:— 'Oswaldus Dyke jaceo hic rector hujus Ecclesiae xx annos reddidi animam 5° Decem' 1607. Non moriar sed vivam, et narrabo opera DOMINI." ECCLESIOLOGIST, VOL. VI., P. 63. Cited in HIERURGIA, P. 381, 382.

1617.] The BOOK OF BENEFACTORS, of Christchurch, Hants, now in the Parish chest, records the gift of "a rich cope" in 1617 by Jo. Marsten, the Vicar. WALCOTT'S HISTORY OF CHRISTCHURCH, HANTS, P. 81, 2D ED. Cited by PERRY, NOTES, P. 91; WALCOTT, CONST. AND CANONS, &c., INTRODUCT., P. XII.

1636.] HENRY BURTON. See pages 133, 134.

1640.] PETER HEYLIN. "The like [persecution by the House of Commons] happened also unto *Heywood* Vicar of St. *Giles's* in the Fields, *Squire* of St. *Leonard's* in *Shoreditch*; and *Finch* of *Christchurch*. The Articles against which four and some others more, being for the most part of the same nature and effect, as namely, . . . Administering the Sacrament in Copes, Beautifying and Adorning Churches with Painted Glass, and others of the like condition, which either were to be held for Crimes in the Clergy generally, or else accounted none in them." CYPRIANUS ANGLICUS, L. 5, P. 471, PT. 2.

1643.] The Puritan House of Commons, October 3. 1643, ordered:

"That the Committee for removing of scandalous and superstitious Monuments, do take away all Copes and Surplices out of all Cathedral, Collegiate, and Parish Churches and Chapels," &c. JOURNALS OF THE HOUSE OF COMMONS, P. 262. VOL. 3.

1644.] May 9, 1644, Parliament forbade the use of Vestments, Copes and Surplices in all Churches. See page 77.

1772-83.] Extract from the Churchwarden's accounts of the Parish of Bledlow, Bucks, in 1771-2:

"'Paid him (i. e. the clerk) for washing the tablecloth, napkins, the surplice and the alb . . . 0. 7s. 0d.'"

In an inventory made in 1783, we find the following articles:

"'An alb, a short surplice for funerels and another for the clark without sleaves, 0 15 0.'" W. F. SHAW, in the *Guardian* (*Supplement*), July 26, 1871, and August 2, 1871. Cited by PERRY, NOTES, P. 105.

## (V). Summary.

WE find that the Vestments are clearly enjoined by the Rubrics of all the Prayer Books, except that of 1552, where they are expressly forbidden, and the Rochet and Surplice alone allowed. But they were extensively used notwithstanding the Rubric. They are enjoined now by Rubric. We also find that the Puritans made persistant though ineffectual efforts to have certain Rubrics repealed. It is a remarkable fact, that the old Puritans always objected against the Prayer Book, that certain Vestments, Ornaments, and Ceremonies, which they disliked, were expressly ordered; while their descendants assert that these same things are forbidden.

The fact that the Rubric was not obeyed, is not at all strange. The chosen children of Israel did not regard the Ten Commandments given them by God Himself, nor do many professed Christians now pay the slightest regard to their solemn vows and promises. If people care not for God, why should they care for what His Church teaches?

A class of men called Puritans, refused to wear a surplice even, from conscientious motives, as they said. From policy, or indifference, they were tolerated, and, with certain exceptions, the Surplice alone was made to suffice as a compromise. What was once allowed to "weak consciences," is now, with the lapse of time, claimed as a precedent and a law. It was a greater "innovation" once not to wear the Vestments, than it is now to wear them. Yet the descendants of those who were most zealous in innovating, have the most to say about what they now call innovations.

The use of the Alb was generally superseded by the Surplice. Copes, often very richly ornamented, generally took the place of the Chasuble, perhaps, because they were enjoined by name in the Advertisements and Canons; whereas the names of the Vestments were not given in the Rubric of 1559, but reference is made to the book of 1549, which had been mostly destroyed under Queen Mary. Copes were worn in Cathedrals, with hardly any exception, down to the Great Rebellion, and also to some extent for a long time after the Restoration, and are ordered by the Purchas Judgement to be used there now. They were used at the consecration of Archbishop Parker and others; at the coronation of all the English Sovereigns down to the present time, if I am not mistaken; at the funerals of some great men, and in many Parish Churches, from the time of the Reformation.

The reasoning adopted by those who oppose the Vestments is, that inasmuch as the use of them has been generally discontinued for nearly two hundred years, and as no clergyman has been called to account for violating the law, it is clear that the law was in effect repealed by the Advertisements. But a great many things are commanded by Acts of Parliament, and the Rubrics and Canons of the Church, which are not obeyed, and yet no one is punished for infraction of the law. In the Purchas Judgment it was decided that the Cope was not only a legal garment, but that its use was obligatory in Cathedrals at the Holy Communion; but a large number of the Bishops do not obey the law. The Bishops of London, Lincoln, Ripon, Peterborough, and some others, do use the Cope now. The Vestments have been used here and there, though not generally, during a large part, if not the whole, of this period during which it is claimed that they were disused. Their *legality* was never questioned till within the last few years.

## II.

# Holy Table or Altar.

## I. Name.

THE heathen word for Altar is commonly βωμός (bomos) or ἐσχάρα (eschara); the former only is used in the New Testament, and that but once, where St. Paul speaks of an altar at Athens to the unknown God (ACTS 17 : 23.) In the Septuagint Translation of the Old Testament, this word always denotes an altar erected to a false God. The heathen Celsus uses the same word when he objects that the Christians had no altars such as they had:—"βωμούς . . . ἱδρῦσθαι φεύγειν." ORIG. CONTRA CELS., L. 8, C. 17, COL. 1540. PAT. GR. T. 16.

The word θυσιαστήριον (thusiasterion), which is not found at all in classical Greek, but was probably originated by the LXX. Translators, is always used to designate an altar to the true God. St. Paul uses the word, with the same idea of sacrifice, when he speaks of the Christian Altar. The word βωμός is not used to designate a Christian Altar till the fifth century. SYNESIUS, Bishop of Ptolemais (CATASTASIS, COL. 1571, PAT.  GR. T. 66.) speaks of the "unbloody altar,—βωμόν." The above figure is a representation of a common form of a pagan altar.

In the Book of 1549, Altar, Lord's Table, and God's Board are used interchangeably. In those of 1552 and 1559, Lord's Table and God's Board are used, the word Altar being omitted to please the Puritans. *Mensa*, Table, is frequently found in the Sarum Office, used before the Reformation. "Goddes borde" was in general use in English translations of the Missal and other books long before the Reformation. The Council of Trent (SESS. XXII. C. 1, P. 117, 118.) and the Catechism of the Council of Trent (PARS 2, C. 4, Q. 55, 56, P. 201, 202.) use the words Table and Altar interchangeably. In the Book of 1662, and in the Communion Office of our American Prayer Book, Table and Lord's Table alone are used; but in the Office of Institution, however, at the end of our Prayer Book, the word Altar is always used, and Table never. In the "Form and Order of the Coronation of Queen Victoria," in 1838, prepared by Dr. Howley, Archbishop of

Canterbury, the word Altar occurs thirty-two times and Lord's Table once. In the Scottish Office, this word is generally used. It is called an Altar by reason of the great memorial Sacrifice there offered to God, and Table by reason of the Eucharist therefrom partaken. In the words of Elizabeth's Injunctions, cited below, it makes no difference whether they are called Tables or Altars, "so that the Sacrament be duly and reverently ministered." Both words are proper, and are used interchangeably in the Old and New Testaments:

EZEK. 41:22. The altar ($\theta\upsilon\sigma\iota\alpha\sigma\tau\eta\rho\iota\upsilon$, thusiasterion) of wood was three cubits high, &c. This is the table ($\tau\rho\alpha\pi\epsilon\zeta\alpha$, trapeza) that is before the Lord.

IB. 44:15, 16. And they [the Priests] shall stand before Me to offer unto Me the fat and the blood, saith the Lord God:

They shall enter into My sanctuary, and they shall come near to My table ($\tau\rho\alpha\pi\epsilon\zeta\alpha\nu$, trapezan) to minister unto Me, and they shall keep My charge.

MALACHI, 1:7. Ye offer polluted bread upon Mine altar ($\theta\upsilon\sigma\iota\alpha\sigma\tau\eta\rho\iota\upsilon$, thusiasterion); and ye say, Wherein have we polluted Thee? In that ye say, The table ($\tau\rho\alpha\pi\epsilon\zeta\alpha$, trapeza) of the Lord is contemptible.

1 COR. 10:18, 21. Behold Israel after the flesh: are not they which eat of the sacrifices partakers of the altar ($\theta\upsilon\sigma\iota\alpha\sigma\tau\eta\rho\iota\upsilon$, thusiasteriou)?

Ye cannot be partakers of the Lord's table ($\tau\rho\alpha\pi\epsilon\zeta\eta\varsigma$, trapezes), and of the table of devils.

Some say that we have no Altar, but St. Paul, in HEB. 13:10, says distinctly that we have:

"We [Christians] have an Altar ($\theta\upsilon\sigma\iota\alpha\sigma\tau\eta\rho\iota\upsilon$, thusiasterion), whereof they [the Jews] have no right to eat which serve the tabernacle."

So you have here the choice of believing an inspired Apostle or a person who is ignorant of what his Bible contains. This statement ought to silence effectually and forever such a denial. The Apostle uses the word Table only in contrast with the table of devils. The word Altar was probably in general, if not universal, use by the Apostles. St. John always uses it in the Revelation. See REV. 6:9, 8:3, 9:13, 16:7. St. Ignatius, who was martyred not long after the death of the Apostles, speaks of the Christian Altar in three different epistles. (EP. AD MEG., c. 7, P. 178; EP. AD TRAL., c. 7, P. 190; EP. AD PHIL., c. 4, P. 212.) A learned writer of the Church of England has asserted, and has never been contradicted, that for the first three hundred years after Christ, the word Table is used by writers only once, the word Altar being invariably used:

"For altar was the name by which the holy board was constantly distinguished for the first three hundred years after Christ; during all which time it does not appear that it was above once-called table, and that was in a letter of Dionysius of Alexandria to Xistus of Rome. And when in the fourth century Athanasius called it a table, he thought himself obliged to explain the word, and to let the reader know that by table he meant altar, that being then the constant and familiar name." WHEATLEY, ILLUST. OF THE BOOK OF COMMON PRAYER, C. 6, SECT. 1, N. 3, P. 262, 263.

The Fathers, St. Augustine, St. Chrysostom, St. Gregory of Nyssa, for instance, frequently call the Altar a Table, with some epithet to denote its sacred character.

371.] ST. GREGORY, BISHOP OF NYSSA.

ἐπεὶ καὶ θυσιαστήριον τοῦτο τὸ ἅγιον, ᾧ παρεστήκαμεν, λίθος ἐστὶ κατὰ τὴν φύσιν κοινός, οὐδὲν διαφέρων τῶν ἄλλων πλακῶν, αἳ τοὺς τοίχους ἡμῶν οἰκοδομοῦσι, καὶ καλλωπίζουσι τὰ ἐδάφη. ἐπειδὴ δὲ καθειρώθη τῇ τοῦ θεοῦ θεραπείᾳ, καὶ τὴν εὐλογίαν ἐδέξατο· ἔστι τράπεζα ἁγία, θυσιαστήριον ἄχραντον, κ. τ. λ.
IN BAPT. CHRIST., P. 369. T. 3.

This holy Altar even, before which we stand, is by nature common stone, differing in nothing from other stones, wherewith our walls are constructed, and our pavements beautified. But when it has been consecrated to the service of God, and has received the blessing, it is a holy Table, an immaculate Altar, &c.

Though the word Table is perfectly proper, inasmuch as ours is a "Scriptural Church," as the late Bishop Eastburn was wont to say, it is better to use Scriptural terms and say Altar, as St. Paul and St. John did.

## II. Stone or Wooden Altars.

SOME, however, erroneously think that there is a difference between stone and wooden Altars. There is no doctrinal signification whatever in stone altars. Jewish as well as Christian Altars were frequently built of wood.

EXOD. 27:1. Thou shalt make an altar of shittim wood.

Exod. 38:1. He made the altar of burnt offering of shittim wood.

1 Kings 6:20. The altar which was of cedar.

The Altars of the Greek Church, which are regarded as "sacrificial," are of wood or stone indifferently. The Holy Table in St. John Lateran, at Rome, at which St. Peter himself is said to have officiated, and which is used exclusively by the Pope, is of fir wood and movable. Wooden Altars were in use in Africa in the time of St. Augustine. (Aug., Ep. 185, an. 417, Bonif. c. 7, n. 27, col. 805. Pat. Lat. T. 33 ; Optatus, De Schism. Donatist., L. 6, n. 1, col. 1068. Pat. Lat. T. 11.) Wooden Altars were originally in common use in England. There is still preserved in the library of Durham Cathedral a small portable Altar of wood covered with silver, used by St. Cuthbert, who died in 686. (See Smith and Cheetham, Dictionary of Christian Antiquities, word Altar, p. 69. Vol. I.) Roman Altars in this country are frequently of wood.

The Council of Epaona, in France, in the year 517, c. 26, p. 170, T. 1, orders stone Altars. St. Gregory of Nyssa and other Greek Fathers speak of stone Altars.

Stone Altars were retained in the Royal Chapels and in some Cathedrals at and after the Reformation, as well as in many Parish Churches. It is said that about fifty ancient stone Altars are still to be found in English Churches. Stone Altars in Parish Churches were, so far as we know, generally plain and without ornament, being covered with a cloth. The Altar lately set up at Westminster Abbey, by Dean Stanley and the Chapter, consists of a marble slab on a wooden frame.

Stone Altars are quite common in this country.

### III. Form of Altars.

THE oldest Altars seem to have been nearly square, like Greek Altars at the present day, as is evident from a Mosaic (Figure 1) of one in the Church of St. Vitalis, at Ravenna, made in the sixth century, where Melchisedec, vested in a Chasuble, is represented as offering bread and wine. Cited by Lundy, Monument. Christ., c. 12, p. 348; Chambers, Divine

Worship. &c., c. 3. n. 17. p. 362; Martigny. Dict. des Antiq. Christ., word Messe, p. 463.

Figure 1.

And also from the Altar (Figure 2) dedicated to St. Alexander, on the Via Nomentana, Rome, probably made in the fifth century. Smith and Cheetham, p. 63.

Figure 2.

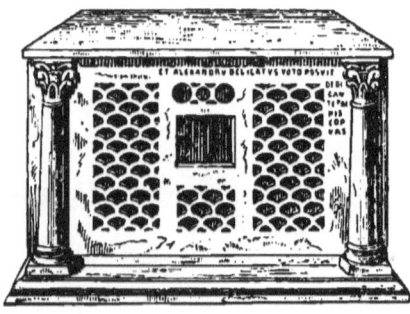

Figure 3 represents the Altar of St. Ambrose at Milan, made in the year 835. It is seven feet three inches long, four feet one inch high, and four feet four inches wide. The front is of gold; the back and ends of silver. See SMITH and CHEETHAM, p. 63, 64.

Figure 3.

Some people have an idea that a structure with legs cannot be a proper Altar, and I have heard of cases where panels had to be cut out of the Altar, so that it might appear to rest upon legs, before the Bishop would consecrate the Church. But this is a mistaken Protestant notion, as is plain from the following examples. Figure 4 is a representation of an Altar of the fifth or sixth century, found in the neighborhood of Auriol, in France, supported on one pillar or leg. See SMITH and CHEETHAM, p. 63; MARTIGNY, p. 59.

Figure 4.

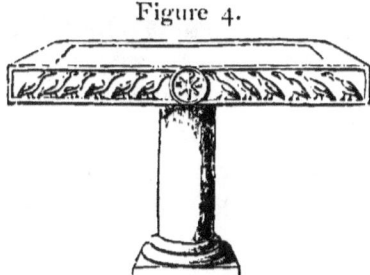

Figure 5.

Figure 5 represents the Altar of St. Eustache in the Church of St. Denis, Paris, a stone slab supported on four legs. See VIOLLET-LE-DUC, DICTIONNAIRE RAISONNÉ DE L'ARCHITECTURE.

# III.

# Position of the Priest at the Altar.

## I. The Early Christians always Prayed towards the East.

O universal was this practice, that the Pagans sometimes accused the Christians of worshipping the sun. In the Septuagint and Vulgate versions of the Scriptures, Christ, who is the true Sun of Righteousness, is often styled the East:

ZECH. 3:8. I will bring forth my servant the BRANCH (EAST, ἀνατολήν, anatolen; orientem).

ZECH. 6:12. Behold the man whose name is the BRANCH (EAST, ἀνατολή, anatole; oriens).

LUKE 1:78. Whereby the Dayspring (East, ἀνατολή, anatole; oriens) from on high hath visited us.

192.] CLEMENT, PRIEST OF ALEXANDRIA.

πρὸς τὴν ἑωθινὴν ἀνατολὴν αἱ εὐχαί. STROM. L. 7, P. 724, CD.

Prayers are directed towards the morning dawn.

200.] TERTULLIAN, PRIEST OF CARTHAGE.

Alii plane humanius et verisimilius Solem credunt deum nostrum. ... Denique inde suspicio, quod innotuerit nos ad orientis regionem precari. APOLOGIA, C. 16, P. 80. PARS 1.

Others, indeed, more kindly and more truthfully, believe that the sun is our God. ... For this reason, I suspect, because they know that we pray towards the region of the East.

230.] ORIGEN, PRIEST OF ALEXANDRIA.

Ad solam orientis partem conversi orationem fundimus. HOM. 5, IN NUM., C. 1, COL. 603. BC. PAT. GR. T. 12.

Turning to the East alone of all the quarters of heaven we pour out prayer.

370.] ST. BASIL, BISHOP OF CÆSAREA.

πρὸς ἀνατολὰς τετράφθαι κατὰ τὴν προσευχήν, κ. τ. λ. DE SP. SANCT., C. 27, N. 66, P. 75. E. T. 3, PARS 1.

We turn to the East in prayer.

398.] ST. AUGUSTINE, BISHOP OF HIPPO.

Cum ad orationem stamus, ad orientem convertimur. DE SERM. DOM. IN MONTE, L. 2, C. 5, N. 18, COL. 1277. PAT. LAT. T. 34.

When we stand at prayer, we turn to the East.

## II. Position of Ancient Churches.

CHRISTIAN Churches, from the most ancient times, have been almost universally built east and west, with the Altar at the east end. It is said that in every Church in England of any antiquity, this is always the case. The same may be said of France and Germany. In the Eastern Church the rule of orientation is always observed, there being but two exceptions, so far as known, and these are owing to peculiar circumstances. The same rule is observed among the Copts and Armenians. I was surprised to learn from HARRISON that "the general position of the early churches was exactly the reverse of that assigned to them." EASTWARD POSITION, N. 58, P. 24.

In Syria, in the Hauran, are the remains of a great many ancient Christian Churches built, according to Inscriptions in many cases still extant, from the third to the fifth centuries. Some of them, so far as we can infer from appearances, have been deserted from about the time of the Mohametan invasion. I carefully examined many at Musmieh, Edhr'a or Zorava, Kunawat, Suweidah, Um el Jemal, and at other places, and found, without exception, that the entrance was always at the west end, and the Apse and Altar in the east. So invariable was this rule that we often used the position of Churches as a ready compass to locate different parts of cities.

Dr. MERRILL, speaking of the Church at Amman, says:

"The apse of this Cathedral, according to my compass, instead of being at the east end, where it is commonly to be looked for, was at the south-east. It may have been arranged thus on account of the inconvenience arising from the channel of the stream, or from the situation of other buildings." EAST OF THE JORDAN, C. 30, P. 401.

In Rome and Southern Italy the case is frequently the other way. Some ancient Basilicas converted into Christian Churches, and some Churches built upon the foundations of heathen temples, and a few exceptional cases, have their Altars at the west end. So that it is plain that orientation is not properly a "Romish" practice. In Rome, the primitive Christians availed themselves of the existing basilicas, baths, circuses, porticos or arcades, forums, palaces, private houses, mausolea or tombs, which they converted into Churches, and perhaps for this reason, in many of the ancient Churches, the Altar is in the west. But in these cases the celebrant stood behind the Altar, which is placed upon the chord of the apse, and faced eastward, as the Pope now does at St. Peter's. In the Churches of S. Maria in Cosmedin, S. Pietro in Vincoli, S. Paolo *fuori le mura*, and S. Sabina at Rome, the Altars are orientated, but the celebrant now faces due west. Roman Catholics in this country are very indifferent as to the site of their Churches. The custom of facing east at the Altar may, therefore, be said to be universal. In ancient times there was but one Altar in a Church, as in the Anglican and Greek Churches; not many, as is the case in Roman Catholic Churches at the present day.

200.] TERTULLIAN, Priest of Carthage.

Nostrae columbae domus simplex, etiam in editis semper et apertis ad lucem, amat figuram spiritus sancti, orientem Christi figuram. Adv. Val., c. 3, p. 38. Pars 4.

The house of our Dove is simple, it is also always in places lofty and open to the light. She loves the figure of the Holy Spirit, the East the figure of Christ.

Cent. 3–5.] APOSTOLIC CONSTITUTIONS.

καὶ πρῶτον μὲν ὁ οἶκος ἔστω ἐπιμήκης, κατ' ἀνατολὰς τετραμένος, κ. τ. λ. Lib. 2, c. 57, p. 263. T. 1. Cotel.

And first, let the house be oblong, turned to the east, &c.

420.] St. PAULINUS, Bishop of Nola.

Prospectus vero basilicae non, ut usitatior mos est, ad orientem spectat, sed ad Domini mei beati Felicis basilicam pertinet memoriam ejus aspiciens. Ep. 32, ad Severum, c. 13, col. 337. Pat. Lat. T. 61.

The site of the Basilica does not, as is the more usual custom, look east, but faces towards the Basilica of my Lord St. Felix, looking out upon his tomb.

439.] SOCRATES speaks of an exceptional case:

ἐν Ἀντιοχείᾳ δὲ τῆς Συρίας, ἡ ἐκκλησία ἀντίστροφον ἔχει τὴν θέσιν, οὐ γὰρ πρὸς ἀνατολὰς τὸ θυσιαστήριον, ἀλλὰ πρὸς δύσιν ὁρᾷ. Hist. Eccl., L. 5, c. 27, p. 297.

A Church at Antioch, in Syria, has a reversed site, for the Altar does not face to the east, but to the west.

830.] WALAFRID STRABO.

Usus frequentior (secundum quod et supra memoravimus) et

The more frequent usage, as we have also mentioned above,

rationi vicinior habet in orientem orantes converti et pluralitatem animarum [maximam?] ecclesiarum eo tenore constitui. DE REB. ECCL., c. 4, COL. 923. PAT. LAT. T. 114.

and that more consonant with reason, for those engaging in prayer, is to turn to the east, and by far the largest number of Churches are constructed in that way.

### III. The Priest Stood before the Altar.

AS we have just seen, the early Christians always prayed towards the east, and Churches were constructed with the Altar at the east end; the primitive position of the Priest, therefore, was before the Altar, facing east. As worship is always directed to God, and not to the people, the Priest must, of course, face God's Altar, and not His worshippers. All the ancient Liturgies speak of the Priest standing before the Altar. It was the universal custom of the Catholic Church, and no other practice, with a few exceptions, was known for fifteen hundred years. HARRISON, a most determined foe of the Eastward Position, admits this:

"It so happens that the position of the minister now claimed by the Ritualists and others, viewed in itself, is the same as that adopted by the ministers of the early Church; but the reasons assigned for it are, as we have seen, essentially different." EASTWARD POSITION, N. 24, P. 21.

This position is essential to a due and reverent celebration of the Holy Mysteries, though not to a valid consecration. Facing South, as some do, is both unmeaning and unhistorical. The Jewish Priest always turned to the Altar when offering the lamb of sacrifice, which was a type of the sacrifice of the Lamb of God, but faced the people in the Scripture lessons. The North-end was also the proper sacrificial position at the Altar of Burnt-Offering, and has been defended on that very ground; but we make no use of victims now. We only commemorate upon the "unbloody Altar" that sacrifice which the Son of God made "once for all," when He offered up Himself as a sacrifice upon the bloody Cross, more than eighteen hundred years ago.

# IV. Position of the Altar and of the Priest in the Church of England since the Reformation.

1. THE OLD ALTARS REMOVED AND WOODEN TABLES SUBSTITUTED.

N 1550, the Puritan HOOPER first objected against Altars in a sermon before the King:

"There should among Christians be no altars. . . . It were well then, that it might please the magistrates to turn the altars into tables, according to the first institution of Christ," &c. SERMONS UPON JONAS, SERM. 4, P. 488.

The same year RIDLEY, on his sole authority, advised—for he could not order—that the Altars in his Diocese should be pulled down, and Tables put in place of them; but his action was soon confirmed by an injunction from the King (See WILK. CONC., P. 65, 66. T. 4; CRANMER, MISS. WRITINGS, APP., N. 38, P. 524):

"ITEM. WHERE as in divers places, some use the Lord's board after the form of a table, and some of an altar, whereby dissension is perceived among the unlearned; therefore wishing a godly unity to be observed in all our diocese; and for that the form of a table may more move and turn the simple from the old superstitious opinions of the popish mass, and to the right use of the Lord's Supper, we exhort the curates, church-wardens, and questmen here present to erect and set up the Lord's board, after the form of an honest table, decently covered in such place of the quire or chancel, as shall be thought most meet by their discretion and agreement, so that the ministers, with the communicants, may have their place separated from the rest of the people; and to take down and abolish all other by-altars or tables." INJUNCTIONS, BURNET, HIST. OF THE REF., PT. 2, B. 1, RECORDS, N. 52, P. 309, 310. VOL. 5.

Ridley, however, allowed the Table to stand where the Altar did in St. Paul's.

1550.] CHARLES WRIOTHESLEY. "This moneth of June in Whitson weeke, . . . all the aulters in euery parishe through London were taken away, and a table made in the quire for the receivinge of the communion. And the xiii. of June the high aulter in Pawles church was taken away, and a table satt in the quire where the aulter stode for the ministration of the holy communion." CHRONICLE, P. 41. VOL. 2. CAMDEN SOC. PUB. VOL. 20.

RIDLEY'S "REASONS" for preferring a Table to an Altar may be found in CRANMER'S MISS. WRITINGS, APP., N. 39, P. 525. Calvin, Bucer, and other foreigners labored hard for the overthrow of Altars and Chancels, and it was to defeat such sacrilege that the Rubric, "Chancels shall remain as they have done in times past," was inserted in 1552.

When Elizabeth came to the throne, she found both Altars and Tables in the Churches. In 1559 she issued Injunctions, which, after stating that the words Altar and Table were matters of indifference, order "that no altar be taken down but by oversight of the curate of the church, and the church wardens;" who, if they were Churchmen, would probably not remove them. As the Table was to stand "where the altar stood, and there commonly covered," there would be but little, if any difference, in appearance between the two.

Circa 1619.] JOHN COSIN, afterwards BISHOP OF DURHAM. "But if this were not by order of the Church, or according to the intent and meaning of the Church and State at the Reformation, how came it to pass then that from that day to this the altars have continued in the king's and queen's households after the same manner as they did before? They never dreamt there of setting up any tables instead of them; and likewise in most cathedral churches, how was it that all things remained as they did before? . . . And it will be worthy the noting, that no cathedral church had any pulling down, removing, or changing the altar into a table, no more than in the court, but in such places only where deans, and bishops, and prebends were preferred, that suffered themselves more to be led by the fashions which they had seen at Strasburg in Germany, and Geneva in France, and Zurich in Switzerland, than by the orders of the Church of England established, and continued in her majesty's family, the likeliest to understand the meaning of the Church and State than any other place. Therefore they that will not either endure we should have, or they who will not believe we have, any altar allowed or continued in our Church (howsoever as it is here, and as it is in most of the Fathers, sometimes called a table,) let them go to the king's court and most of our cathedral churches, and enquire how long they have stood there and kept that name only, as being indeed the most eminent and the most usual among Christians." NOTES ON THE BOOK OF COMMON PRAYER, 1ST SERIES, P. 85, 86. WORKS. VOL. 5.

This Series of Notes was till lately thought to be the work of Overall, Bishop of Norwich.

2. THE TABLE ALLOWED TO BE MOVED AT COMMUNION TIME.

By the Prayer book of 1549 the material and position of the Altar was unchanged. Then came wooden Tables instead of Altars. The Puritans next became much dissatisfied with fixed wooden Tables instead of the ancient Altars, so they began to move them from their ancient position, and especially at Communion time. This was but preparing the way for the Rubric of 1552, which reads:

"The Table having at the Communion time a fair white linen cloth upon it, shall stand in the body of the Church, or in the chancel, where Morning prayer and Evening prayer be appointed to be said." PAGE 265.

This was a compromise. A Churchman would let the Table remain in its proper place in the Chancel, while a Puritan would move it. The matter was entirely optional.

The variety in the service in those times was very great. The Table was placed indifferently, at the east end of the Chancel, at the entrance of the same, and even in the Nave. The Priest also faced all points of the compass.

When Elizabeth came upon the throne, in order to stop this confusion, she ordered in her INJUNCTIONS of 1559:

"Whereas her majesty understandeth, that in many and sundry parts of this realm, the altars of the churches be removed, and tables placed for the administration of the holy sacrament, according to the form of the law therefor provided; and in some other places, the altars be not yet removed, upon opinion conceived of some other order therein to be taken by her majesty's visitors; in the order whereof, saving for uniformity, there seemeth no matter of great moment, so that the sacrament be duly and reverently ministered; yet for observation of one uniformity through the whole realm, and for the better imitation of the law in that behalf, it is ordered, that no altar be taken down, but by oversight of the curate of the church, and the church wardens, or one of them at the least, wherein no riotous or disordered manner be used. And that the holy table in every church be decently made, and set in the place, where the altar stood, and there commonly covered, as thereto belongeth, and as shall be appointed by the visitors, and so to stand, saving when the communion of the sacrament is to be distributed; at which time, the same shall be so placed in good sort within the chancel, as whereby the minister may be more conveniently heard of the communicants in his prayer and ministrations, and the communicants also more conveniently, and in more number, communicate with the said minister.—And, after the communion done, from time to time the same holy table to be placed where it stood before." CARDWELL, DOC. ANN., N. 43, P. 233, 234. VOL. I. See PARKER, EP. 283, cited on pages 37, 38.

It was ordered, that when the minister could not be conveniently heard, or it was difficult for the communicants to approach, (as when a belfry interposed between the Chancel and body of the Church; or, as in the Chapel of Henry VII. in Westminster Abbey, where access to the Altar was made very inconvenient by a large erection in front of it, as in Roman Catholic Churches, a temporary Altar is sometimes erected from the same cause,) the Table was to be placed is in a convenient place in the Chancel during Communion, and afterwards moved to its proper place.

STYPE says of the Injunctions:

"This order for the table and bread was occasioned from the variety used in both, for some time, until these Injunctions came forth. For indeed in the beginning of the Queen's reign the protestants were much divided in their opinion and practice about them; which was the cause of some disturbance. And the papists made their advantage of it; laying to the charge of the protestants their mutability and inconstancy. Thus did Thomas Dorman, in his book called *A Proof*. 'This day your table is placed in the midst of the quire; the next day removed into the body of the church; at the third time placed in the chancel, again after the manner of an altar,' [that is, upon the coming forth of this before-mentioned order], 'but yet removable as there is a communion to be had. Then, your ministers face one while to be turned towards the south, and another while towards the north, that the weathercock in the steeple was noted not to have turned so often in a quarter of a year, as your minister in the church in less than one month. And at your communion, one while decreeing, that it be ministered in common bread; by and by revoking that, and bringing it to unleavened.'" ANN., c. 12, P. 242. VOL. 1, PT. 1.

The Archbishop and Bishops afterwards drew up in 1561, but never published, "INTERPRETATIONS AND FURTHER CONSIDERATIONS" of these things for the better direction of the Clergy, preserved in Parker's Papers at Cambridge:

"That the table be removed out of the choir into the body of the Church, before the chancel door; where either the choir seemeth to be too little, or at great feasts of receivings. And at the end of the communion to be set up again, according to the Injunctions." CARDWELL, DOC. ANN., N. 43, P. 238. VOL. 1; STRYPE, ANN., c. 17, P. 320. VOL. 1, PT. 1.

It will be noticed that all these concessions were permitted, not commanded. They were made to satisfy the clamors of those Puritans, who, in their zeal against Rome, went to extremes; but were not acted upon in the Royal Chapels, Cathedrals and many Parish Churches, where all things remained as before, the Rubric, "Chancels shall remain as they have done in times past," being strictly observed.

3. ALTARS OR TABLES PLACED TABLE-WISE.

Having movable wooden Tables or Altars instead of fixed ones did not long satisfy the unquiet spirits of the Puritans. They next wanted the Tables placed table-wise. Ridley at first placed the Table where the Altar stood in St. Paul's, but the next year (1551) he moved it, and set it table-wise, that is, at right angles to the ancient manner, though he had no authority for this.

1551.] CHARLES WRIOTHESLEY. "This yeare, against Easter, the Bishopp of London altered the Lordes table that stoode where the high aulter was, and he remoued the table beneth the steepps into the middes of the upper quire in Poules, and sett the endes east and west, the priest standing in the middest at the communion, on the south side of the bord, and after the creed song, he caused the vaile to be drawen that no person shoulde see but those that receaved, and he closed the iron gates of the quire on the north and south side with bricke and plaister, that non might remaine in at the quire." CHRON., P. 47. VOL. 2. CAMDEN SOC. PUB. VOL. 20.

1552.] Still another change was next made:

"After the feast of All Saintes, the upper quire in St. Pawles church, in London, where the high aulter stoode, was broken downe and all the quire thereabout, and the table of the communion was set in the lower quire where the preists singe." IB. P. 79.

1555.] At Ridley's last examination, WHITE, Bishop of Lincoln, says to him:

"A goodly receiving, I promise you, to set an oyster table instead of an alter, and to come from puddings at Westminster, to receive: and yet, when your table was constituted, you could never be content, in placing the same now east, now north, now one way, now another, until it pleased God in his goodness to place it clean out of the church." WORKS OF RIDLEY, P. 281.

The Table was called "an oyster table," because it was sometimes made by merely placing common boards on tressels.

1559.] The INJUNCTIONS of Elizabeth order the Table to stand where the Altar did, but allowed its removal at Communion time. See page 164.

1562.] By the Rubric of 1552, the Table was allowed to be moved at Communion time. According to the INJUNCTIONS Tables were allowed to take the place of the Altar, but were to stand where the Altar stood, and to be properly covered. But still the Puritans were not satisfied. What was permitted to them, they next wished to make obligatory upon all. Accordingly, in 1562, among the "General notes of matters to be moved by the Clergy in the next Parliament and Synod," we find this:

"That the table from henceforth stand no more altarwise, but stand in such place as is appointed by the Book of Common Prayer." Cited by STRYPE, ANN., C. 27, P. 475. VOL. 1, PT. 1.

As the Prayer Book then, as now, merely says that the Table " shall stand in the body of the Church, or in the Chancel," without any order as to its being placed Altar-wise or Table-wise, I am at a loss to know what the last part of the sentence means.

Later it was moved in the same Synod:

"That in all parish churches the minister in common prayer turn his face towards the people; and there distinctly read the divine service appointed, where all the people assembled may hear and be edified." IB. c. 29, P. 502.

These proposals were lost 59 to 58. Observe that this last restriction was to be confined to Parish Churches and nothing is said as to Cathedrals.

1564.] We have the following Certificate of the Archbishop's Commissary of the State of Canterbury Cathedral in 1564:

"The Common Prayer daily through the year, though there be no Communion, is sung at the communion table, standing *north* and *south*, where the high altar did stand. The Minister, when there is no Communion, useth a surplice only, standing on the east side of the table with his face towards people.

"The holy Communion is ministered ordinarily the first Sunday of every month through the year. At what time the table is set *east* and *west*. The Priest which ministereth, the Pystoler, and Gospeler, at that time wear copes.

"For ministering of the Communion we use bread [wafer bread] appointed by the Queen's Highness' Injunctions." Cited by STRYPE, LIFE OF PARKER, B. 2, C. 26, P. 365. VOL. 1.

This practice of standing east of the Altar and facing west is never mentioned as prevailing elsewhere.

1573.] Among other disorders still prevalent in this Cathedral under a Puritan Dean when Archbishop Parker visited it in 1573, we note the following:

"There were matters presented relating more especially to the Dean. As that he had consumed the church goods: which yet be denied. That he had broken the Statutes. That he had made away the copes of the church: which he confessed, *because* it had been agreed by the Chapter, that all the copes should be made away, and that he had two of them, and paid fifteen pounds for the same." IB. B. 4, C. 31, P. 301. VOL. 2. See PARKER, EP. 233, P. 303, 304. P. C.

1564-5.] Secretary CECIL has left on record a paper, dated February 14, 1564, specifying the varieties which then prevailed in the service:

"The table standeth in the body of the church in some places; in others it standeth in the chancel. In some places the table standeth altarwise, distant from the wall [a?] yard. In some others in the middle of the chancel, north and south. In some places the table is joined; in others it standeth upon tressels. In some the table hath a carpet; in others it hath none." Cited by STRYPE, LIFE OF PARKER, B. 2, c. 19, p. 302. VOL. 1.

1566.] The ADVERTISEMENTS, in order to correct these irregularities, order:

"That they shal decentlie cover with carpet, silke, or other decente coveringe, and with a fayre lynnen clothe (at the time of the ministration) the communyon table, and to sett the Tenne Commandmentes upon the easte wall over the said table." CARDWELL, DOC. ANNAL., P. 326, VOL. 1; STRYPE, LIFE OF PARKER, APPENDIX, B. 2, N. 28, P. 88, VOL. 3.

This order by implication fixes the position of the Altar at the East end against the wall.

1640.] CANONS OF 1640. "That the standing of the communion table sideway under the east window of every chancel or chapel, is in its own nature indifferent, neither commanded nor condemned by the word of God, either expressly or by immediate deduction, and therefore that no religion is to be placed therein, or scruple to be made thereon. And albeit at the time of the reforming this church from that gross superstition of popery, it was carefully provided that all means should be used to root out of the minds of the people both the inclination thereunto, and memory thereof; especially of the idolatry committed in the mass, for which cause all popish altars were demolished: yet notwithstanding it was then ordered by the injunctions and advertisements of queen Elizabeth of blessed memory, that the holy tables should stand in the place where the altars stood, and accordingly have been continued in the royal chapels of three famous and pious princes, and in most cathedral, and some parochial churches, which doth sufficiently acquit the manner of placing the said tables from any illegality, or just suspicion of popish superstition or innovation. And therefore we judge it fit and convenient, that all churches and chapels do conform themselves in this particular to the example of the cathedral or Mother churches, saving always the general liberty left to the bishop by law, during the time of administration of the holy communion. And we declare that this scituation of the holy table, doth not imply that it is, or ought to be esteemed a true and proper altar, whereon Christ is again really sacrificed; but it is, and may be called by us, in that sense in which the primitive church called it an altar, and in no other." CAN. 7, P. 549, 550. WILK. CONC., T. 4.

In the Roman Church. Altars are not placed in one regular position. Sometimes they are placed against the east end of the Church, sometimes removed a few feet from the end, and sometimes they are at the entrance or middle of the Chancel or Apse. But they are fixed to one position and not movable.

In Archbishop Laud's time, the Altars had from the time of the Reformation stood properly against the east wall, with the side towards the people, in Royal Chapels and many Cathedrals; but in a great many, and perhaps in a majority of Parish Churches, they stood table-wise, so little regard was paid by lawless men to the Queen's Injunctions.

Below will be found an exact copy of a Puritan Lord's Supper, with the Altar placed Table-wise, published by the Church Association, Tract Number 39.

This plate is "an enlarged but accurate copy from a copper plate in a small book printed in 1674, entitled 'A Course of Catechising,'" &c. This catechism purports to be gathered from sundry great divines, some of whom were High Churchmen. But this is the second edition, the first having been published in 1664, and omits many things which were of a Churchly character in the first, and is much more Puritan. Among the questions and answers are these:

"*Q. Why doth the Priest stand on the North side of the Table?*
*A.* To avoid the Popish superstition of standing towards the East."

Please notice that the sole reason given for not facing the East, is to avoid "the Popish superstition." But this is as much a Christian and a Lutheran "superstition," as it is a Popish one. It existed long before Popery existed, unless Popery is from the beginning, which we would be very unwilling to admit. If we should reject everything that Rome has, as a "Popish superstition," there would be very little of Christianity left. It is no more superstitious to face East than it is to face South. To stand at the North end, then, is a "Protestant superstition." What should we think if the Unitarians were to put forth this question and answer in a Catechism?—

"*Q. Why do Unitarians reject the belief in the Divinity of Jesus Christ?*
*A.* To avoid the Trinitarian superstition which teaches that he was God."

The cases are precisely similar, only no Unitarian would be foolish enough to give such an answer.

Notice, also, the following contradictions to the Laws of the Church:

(1) The Injunctions order the Table to stand where the Altar stood, that is, the ends to be North and South.

(2) The Celebrant is to stand at the North side, but in the picture, as we may judge from the open book, the cup, and the bread, he evidently stands at the South side, which position is also contradictory to the teaching of the Catechism itself.

(3) The Ministers wear a black Geneva gown, whereas they are commanded by the Rubric to wear a Vestment or Cope, and by the Advertisements and Canons, a Surplice at least.

Notice, also, the following, which are "abominations" to modern Protestants:

(1) As the Communicants surround the three sides of the Table, the back of the Minister is turned towards the people; yet as he

faces North or South, and not East, we hear not a word of remonstrance.

(2) The bread is also wafer-bread, as is seen in the plate. There are also several cakes which are probably to be cut up into wafers.

(3) The Ministers also wear a close-fitting cap. It is evidently not a Biretta, yet it is some kind of a cap, and a very ugly one too.

What induced the Church Association, a very Low Church Society in England, which the Bishop of Peterborough styled a "Persecution Society," to put forth a Tract so damaging to their side, is hard to see.

4. DIFFERENCE BETWEEN END AND SIDE OF THE HOLY TABLE OR ALTAR.

We have clear evidence that end and side are different things, and were so regarded by the Puritans themselves. Some have endeavored to persuade themselves and others that these words mean one and the same thing.

1627.] In 1627, HEYLIN, Vicar of Grantham, contrary to the wishes of the parishioners, removed the Table from the body of the Church to the East end of the Chancel. Williams, Bishop of Lincoln, who was Puritanically inclined, to whom the parishioners appealed, wrote a Letter to settle the dispute. He directed that the Table should at Communion time be moved into the body of the Church, but at other times stand at the East end. He regarded the position as a matter of indifference.

In 1636, HEYLIN published his "Coale from the Altar," &c., together with Williams' letter of 1627, wherein occurs the following words:

"But if you mean by Altar-wise, that the Table should stand along close to the wall, so as you be forced to officiate at one end thereof (as you may have observed in Great men's Chappels:) I do not believe that ever the Communion Tables were (otherwise than by casualtie) so placed in country Churches."

"1. You may not erect an Altar, where the Canons only admit a Communion Table.

2. This Table must not stand Altar-wise, and you at the North end thereof, but Tablewise as you must officiate at the North-side of the same." A COALE FROM THE ALTAR, &c., p. 70, 71, 77.

See also WILLIAMS' HOLY TABLE, NAME AND THING, p. 15–20.

In 1637 the Bishop replied anonymously in a treatise entitled: "The Holy Table, Name and Thing," &c. Yet the Altar in his Chapel at Bugden always stood at the East end of the Chancel, and was moreover ornamented with Candlesticks and a Crucifix. The Altar also in Lincoln Cathedral and in Westminster Abbey, of which he was Dean and ordinary, stood at the East end, and was ornamented with Candlesticks. (See also HEYLIN, CYP. ANGL., L. 4, P. 285, 286, PT. 2; HOLY TABLE, &c., P. 12.)

Williams was doubtless a Churchman at heart, but was timid and acted inconsistently at first. His animosity towards Laud, led him to incline too much to the Puritans. They afterwards distrusted and abused him. At length he saw the error of his ways and was reconciled to Laud. In his last sickness, being in want of a clergyman, he ordained a pious servant of his to give him the Sacrament, absolution, &c. LATHBURY, HIST. OF THE BOOK OF COMMON PRAYER, C. 8, 9, P. 167-169, 189-191; DRAKE, EBORACUM, P. 463.

1628.] PETER SMART. "Neither must the Table be placed along from north to south, as the altar [in Durham cathedral] is set, but from east to west, as the custom is of all Reformed Churches, otherwise the minister cannot stand at the north side, there being neither side towards the north. And I trow there are but two sides of a long table and two ends: make it square, and then it will have four sides, and no end, or four ends, and no side at which any minister can stand to celebrate." SERMON in Durham Cathedral, July 27, 1628. Cited in ACTS OF THE HIGH COM. COURT OF DURHAM, P. 216. APP. A. SURTEES SOC. PUBL. VOL. 34.

We have the following contemporary account of the Altar in Durham Cathedral in "ARTICLES, OR INSTRUCTIONS FOR ARTICLES, TO BE EXHIBITED BY HIS MAJESTIE'S HEIGH COMMISSIONERS, AGAINST MR. JOHN COSIN," &c., put forth in 1630:

"This Altar stands upon 6 stone pillars curiously polished, and fastened to the ground, having upon each black pillar 3 cherubim-faces as white as snow, and it is placed at the end of the quire, along by the wall, with neither side toward the North, al which is contrary to the Booke of Common-prayer, and Injunctions, which commanded it to be a portable table, and to stand, when the Communion is administred, in the middest of the church or chancell, where morning and evening prayers are appointed to be sayd; which evening praier is never said where the table standeth now: and that the Minister should stand at the north syde of the table, which cannot be done when neither syde of the Table standeth northward." COSIN CORRESPONDENCE, N. 90, SECT. 9, P. 169. SURTEES SOC. PUBL. VOL. 52.

Some Puritan Churchwardens, in the Diocese of Bath and Wells, did actually introduce into their Parish Church a square Table, instead of an oblong one, in order that the Minister might comply literally with the Rubric, and stand at the North side or end. According to the *Rock*, JUNE 25, 1880, the Communion Table at St.

Mary-le-Port Church, Bristol, and at Low Moor, Clitheroe, Lancashire, is now placed with the ends East and West, so " that the clergy may strictly and literally occupy the position enjoined in the rubric, 'standing at the north *side* of the table,' and ' standing *before* the table ' during the prayer of consecration."

The position of the Altar having changed, that of the Priest should change also.

5. THE RUBRICS OF THE COMMUNION OFFICE.

In accordance with the universal custom of the Church, the Rubric in the Prayer Book of 1549 is:

" The Priest standing humbly afore the midst of the Altar."

The Puritans would not obey the Rubric, but faced in every direction except East.

The Rubric of the Prayer Book of 1552 is:

"And the Priest standing at the North side of the Table,"

which was adopted without change in 1559, and again in 1662. Many of the Clergy understood by North side the North end, and stood at the North end. In the other case, when the Altar was placed table-wise, the Priest would stand at the North side facing South. Gradually the removal of the Holy Table ceased, and it was placed permanently against the East end, but so strong were the prejudices of an ignorant and bigoted populace, that many of the Clergy were afraid to resume their proper places, and remained at the North end, instead of at the North side. Wren, Cosin, and Laud, were impeached before the House of Commons for standing before the Altar.

In the Book of 1549 the Priest is ordered to turn round to the people when addressing them; in the Book of 1552, in which the term North side, as also the saying of the Ten Commandments, are first introduced, no direction is given to turn to the people, this being unnecessary, if the Priest already faced South. The Rubric, "turning to the people," as also, " standing before the Table," were first inserted in 1662, when we know that the Altars were being restored to their proper place, and the Clergy generally were resuming their proper position before the Altar.

The Bishops, at the Savoy Conference in 1661, thus replied to the objections of the Presbyterians:

"That the Minister should not read the Communion service at the Communion Table, is not reasonable to demand, since all the primitive Church used it," &c.

"The Minister's turning to the people is not the most convenient throughout the whole ministration. When he speaks to them in Lessons, Absolutions, and Benedictions, it is convenient that he turn to them. When he speaks for them to God, it is fit that they should all turn another way, as the Ancient Church ever did." CARDWELL, HISTORY OF CONFERENCES, C. 7, P. 342, 353.

The Rubric in the Scotch Office is simply:

"The Priest, standing at the Altar, shall say."

The Compilers of our American Prayer Book adopted, at first, the English Rubric, but in 1832, on the motion of Bishop Onderdonk of New York, it was changed, (JOURNAL OF THE GENERAL CONVENTION, P. 458. VOL. 2), so that we no longer have the English Rubric, which requires the Priest to stand at the North side, but,

"And the Minister, standing at the right side of the Table, . . . shall say the Lord's Prayer, and the Collect following," &c.

The Rubric says:

"Standing at the right side,"

so that there is no authority for standing at the left end. Ask any one to go to the right side of an oblong object, and he will never think of going to the left end.

"Then . . . turning to the people,"

plainly implies that he had just before been turned from them, facing the Altar. Further on we have this Rubric:

"When the Priest, standing before the Table, . . . he shall say the Prayer of Consecration, as followeth."

The Priest is represented as already standing before the Table, there being no direction for him to assume that position; for of two Rubrics immediately preceding, the one says:

"Then shall the Priest turn to the Lord's Table, and say," &c., and the other:

"Then shall the Priest, kneeling down at the Lord's Table," &c. Neither is he to go back to the end as soon as he has arranged the Bread and Wine, for the Rubric plainly implies that he is to say the Consecrating Prayer in the position he occupied just previously.

6. THE WORD "BEFORE" THE TABLE MEANS IN FRONT OF THE TABLE LOOKING EAST.

1665.] There is a Greek translation of the Prayer Book by the Dean of Peterborough, printed at Cambridge, 1665. In the Rubric,

"North side," is translated "$\pi\rho\grave{o}\varsigma\ \tau\grave{\alpha}\ \beta\acute{o}\rho\varepsilon\iota\alpha$,"—towards the Northern parts. "Before the Table," is "$\check{\varepsilon}\mu\pi\rho o\sigma\theta\varepsilon\nu$,"—in front of.

1726.] The Act of Uniformity of 1662, c. 18, as did Queen Elizabeth, in 1561, (page 47), authorized the use of the Communion Office in Latin in the Universities and some other places. In a Latin Office at Christ Church, Oxford, dated 1726, "before the table," is "*ante mensam Domini*," and "before the people" is "*coram populo.*"

1838.] In the "FORM AND ORDER OF THE CORONATION OF QUEEN VICTORIA IN 1838," we find that the terms "before" and "side" do not refer to the end:

"The Queen . . . goes to Her Chair set for Her on the South side of the Altar, where She is to kneel at Her Faldstool when the Litany begins.

"On the South side, East of the Queen's Chair, nearer the Altar, stand the Dean and the Prebendaries of *Westminster*.

"The Queen rising from Her Devotions, goes before the Altar.

"The Queen will then sit down in *King Edward's* chair placed in the midst of the *Area* over against the Altar.

"The Archbishop standing on the North side of the Altar, saith this Prayer or Blessing over Her.

"The Archbishop, standing before the *Altar*, taketh the Crown into his Hands, and laying it again before him upon the Altar, &c.

"The *Queen* being come into the Chapel, and standing before the *Altar*, will deliver the *Sceptre*." PAGES 5, 9, 12, 13, 18, 28.

7. IN 1832, THE HOUSE OF BISHOPS, AT THE REQUEST OF THE HOUSE OF CLERICAL AND LAY DEPUTIES IN 1829, PUT FORTH THE FOLLOWING DIRECTIONS TO INSURE UNIFORMITY OF POSTURE IN THE CELEBRATION OF THE HOLY EUCHARIST.

"First, with regard to the officiating Priest, they are of the opinion, that, as the Holy Communion is of a spiritually sacrificial character, the standing position should be observed by him, whenever that of kneeling is not expressly prescribed, to wit: in all parts, including the Ante-Communion and Post-Communion, except the Confession, and the Prayer immediately preceding the Prayer of Consecration.

Secondly, with regard to the people, the Bishops are of the opinion that they should observe the kneeling posture during all the prayers and other acts of devotion, except the *Gloria in Excelsis*, when standing is required by the Rubric, and except, also, during the allowed portion of the Hymns in metre, when the analogy of our services requires the same posture.

The same analogy, as well as fitness of posture for the succeeding private devotions, which are required alike by propriety and godly custom, supposes KNEELING as the posture in which to receive the final Blessing.

Analogy, also, and the expression at the close of the shorter exhortation immediately preceding the Confession, as well as the Rubric before the Confession, which suppose the posture of kneeling to be THERE assumed, indicate that that exhortation, and the longer one immediately preceding, should be heard by the people STANDING.

The postures, therefore, proper to be observed by the people, during the Communion Office, the Bishops believe to be as follows:—

KNEELING during the whole of the Ante-Communion, except the Epistle, which is to be heard in the usual posture for hearing the Scriptures, which is ordered to be heard STANDING.

The sentences of the Offertory to be heard SITTING, as the most favorable posture for handing alms, &c., to the person collecting.

KNEELING to be observed during the prayer for the Church Militant.

STANDING during the exhortation.

KNEELING to be then resumed, and continued until after the Prayer of Consecration.

STANDING at the singing of the hymn.

KNEELING, when receiving the elements, and during the Post-Communion, or that part of the service which succeeds the delivering and receiving of the elements, except the *Gloria in Excelsis*, which is to be said or sung STANDING.

After which the congregation should again KNEEL to receive the Blessing." JOURNAL OF THE GENERAL CONVENTION, P. 450, 451. VOL. 2.

## 8. THE EASTWARD POSITION.

It is not claimed that the Eastward Position has been the universal or the general custom in the Church of England since the Reformation; but that was the practice of the ancient Church, and it has been maintained in the Church in unbroken succession. The Advertisements and Canons suppose it, by ordering a Gospeller and Epistoler (Deacon and Subdeacon), in addition to the Priest, and we are told by the Puritan Neal, that in sundry Cathedrals and in the Queen's Chapel, foreigners could not distinguish the service from the Roman, except that the English language was used. As to its doctrinal signification, that has been imported into the question by its enemies. The Eastward Position does not touch the question of the Real Presence at all.

1564–5.] STRYPE gives the following account of Richard Kechyn, whom Archbishop Parker had placed in some benefice near Bocking, in Essex:

"The Archbishop had placed one Richard Kechyn in some benefice near Bocking in Essex, which seemed to be one of his Peculiars:

and upon his admission had charged him to follow the orders and rules appointed and established by law, and to make no variation, whatsoever others should or might do or persuade him to the contrary. But now this year in his ministerial course, he met with many rubs and checks by one, a neighbouring preacher, (or English Doctor, as they loved to call themselves,) who came into his pulpit, being a licensed preacher, and there openly condemned him, the incumbent, for certain things. We must know that Kechyn had in Rogation-week gone the perambulation with his parishioners; and according to the old custom and the Queen's Injunctions, had said certain offices in certain places of the parish. . . .

"He also constantly wore the surplice in his ministration, and in reading the divine service turned his face to the East.

"The Dean of Bocking, ( who, I think, was Mr. Cole,) having some jurisdiction over Kechyn and some other Ministers thereabouts, had charged him and the rest not to turn their faces to the high altar in service-saying, which was a new charge and not given before. But this Dean in his visitation usually gave new articles every year. And lastly, offence was taken at him that he used the surplice.

"Upon this occasion, the said Minister thought convenient to acquaint Peerson, the Archbishop's Almoner and Chaplain, with these things, to impart them to the Archbishop, that he might have his counsel and direction. He told the Almoner in a letter to him what his practice was, that though he turned his face upward, as he had done hitherto, yet his church was small, and his voice might be heard. That the Litany he said in the body of the church; and when he said the service he kept the chancel, and turned his face to the east; and that he was not zealous in setting forth predestination. . . . Further, that he would gladly learn what articles his Grace caused to be inquired of in his visitation; because the Dean their Visitor had every year a new scroll of articles. And this, of charging all not to turn their faces to the high altar was one; which he called a *new charge*." LIFE OF PARKER, B. 2, c. 19, P. 303–305, VOL. 1.

1565.] In a letter from King's College, Cambridge, dated Dec. 17, 1565, complaint is made of Dr. Baker, the Provost:

"That he had used one Mr. Wolwerd very roughly (he was afterwards fellow of Eaton ) because he would not officiate with his face towards the East, and his back sometimes towards ye Altar according to ye manner of ye Mass, for his refusal of w$^{ch}$ he had been expelled, was it not for an injunction from the queen and that, one of the Conducts so celebrated." LE KEUX, MEMORIALS OF CAMBRIDGE, II. 24, ED. 1841. Cited by PERRY, NOTES, P. 356; STRYPE, HIST. OF THE LIFE AND ACTS OF GRINDAL, B. 1, C. 14, AN. 1569, P. 211.

Circa 1573.] THOMAS CARTWRIGHT. "For thereupon the minister in saying morning and evening prayer, sitteth in the chauncell wyth hys backe to the people, as thoughe he had some secreate talke with God, whych the people myghte not heare. And hereupon it is likewise, that for saying another number of prayers he climeth up to the further end of the chauncel, and runneth as farre from the people as the wall wil let him as though there were some variance between the people and the ministers, or as though he were afraid of some infection of plage. And indeed it renneth the memory of the Levitical priesthode whych did withdrawe himselfe from the people into the place called the holyest place, where he talked with God, and offered for the sinnes of the people." A REPLY TO AN ANSWER, &c., p. 134.

1610.] WILLIAM BARLOW, BISHOP OF LINCOLN. Consecration of the Church at Fulmer, Bucks, All Saints Day, 1610.

"There they [the Bishop and the Founder] both kneeled, looking towards the East window of the Chancel.

"At the Celebration of the Communion, the Bishop caused the Founder to kneel by himself before the Altar, in the middle of the choir," &c. Cited by RUSSELL, ABBEY DORE CONSECRATION, APP. p. 36, 37.

Circa 1618.] LANCELOT ANDREWES, BISHOP OF WINCHESTER. Form of the Consecration of the Church of St. Mary, near Southampton.

| | |
|---|---|
| Tum flexis genibus ante sacram Mensam pergit porro. | Then kneeling before the Holy Table, he proceeds. |
| Epistolam secundus Sacellanus ante sacram Mensam stans legit. | The second Chaplain, standing before the Holy Table, reads the Epistle. |
| Itur dein ad Coenae Dominicae administrationem, Sacellanorum altero ad Australem, altero ad Septentrionalem partem sacrae mensae genu flectante et dicente. | They then proceed to the administration of the Lord's Supper, one of the Chaplains kneeling at the South part, and the other at the North part of the Holy Table, and saying. |
| Post illa Episcopus sede sua egressus, coram sacra mensa sese provolvit atque ait. | Afterwards the Bishop, leaving his seat, prostrates himself before the Holy Table, and says. |
| Episcopus . . lotis manibus, pane fracto, vino in calicem effuso, et aqua admista, stans ait. PAGE 10, 13, 14, 17. | The Bishop, having washed his hands, broken the bread, poured the wine into a Chalice, and mixed the water, says, standing. |

1632.] FRANCIS WHITE, BISHOP OF ELY. Consecration of the Chapel of St. Peter's College, Cambridge, March, 17. 1632.

| | |
|---|---|
| Tandem flexis denuo genibus ante sacram Mensam . . Episcopus pergit porro. | At length, the Bishop again kneeling before the Holy Table, proceeds. |
| Post Concionem Dominus Episcopus sede sua egressus, coram sanctissima Mensa se provolvit. Cited by RUSSELL, ABBEY DORE CONSEC. APP. P. 39. | After the Sermon, the Lord Bishop leaving his seat, prostrates himself before the most Holy Table. |

1634.] RICHARD NEILE, ARCHBISHOP OF YORK. Manner and Form of Consecrating a Church or Chapel in the Parish of Leeds, Yorkshire, 1634.

"Then the Bishop going into the middle of the church or chapel shall there kneel down with his face towards the Communion Table, and say."

Tum flexis genibus ante SS. Mensam pergit porro. In. p. 38.    Then kneeling down before the most Holy Table, he proceeds.

1634.] THEOPHILUS FIELD, BISHOP OF ST. DAVID'S. FORM AND ORDER OF THE CONSECRATION AND DEDICATION OF THE PARISH CHURCH OF ABBEY DORE. Palm Sunday, 1634. By authority of a Commission from Dr. Matthew Wren, Bishop of Hereford.

"Then turning about and there kneeling Eastward (upon a pesse [hassock] before the Table) the Founder on his left hand, and the other two behind him, he [the Bishop] saith ; " &c.

"Then all stand up, and turning Eastward, say, I believe in God," &c.

"Then the Chaplain cometh forth, and maketh a low obeisance, and stands before the Table," &c.

"The Bishop kneeling down Eastward, saith," &c.

"The Priest and the Chaplain, with due reverence, go again, one to the North part, and the other to the South part of the Table, and the Priest with a loud voice pronounceth," &c.

"Then cometh the Bishop, and worshippeth before the Table," &c.

"Then cometh the Bishop unto the Table, in the Priest's place, who is to kneel behind the Bishop," &c.

"Then the Chaplain going from the Table's end, kneeleth down in the middle at a convenient distance from the Table, and maketh the Confession. . . . And then rising, with due reverence, he goeth and kneeleth by the Priest behind the Bishop."

"Then layeth he [the Bishop] the Bread on the paten, and poureth of the Wine into the chalice, and a little water into it, and standing with his face to the Table, about the midst of it, he saith the Collect of Consecration."

"The Chaplain goeth also behind the Bishop." PAGES 10–31.

1640-1.] Among the " Innovations in Discipline " complained of by the Puritans to Parliament in 1640-1, were these:

" 1. The turning the holy table altar-wise ; and most commonly calling it an altar.

" 2. Bowing towards it, or towards the east, many times with three congees, but usually in every motion, access, or recess.

" 3. By the minister's turning his back to the west, and his face to the east, when he pronounceth the creed, or reads prayers." CARDWELL., HIST. OF CONF., C. 7, P. 272, 273.

1641.] A PARALLEL OR BRIEF COMPARISON OF THE LITURGY WITH THE MASS-BOOK, &c. "This injunction we are directed to keep, while we are not only enjoined to go as far from the people as the remotest wall and Table will permit, but to use such a posture that our back must be turned to them, that so our speech may be directed to the elements alone, and in what language you please : and no ways to the people from whom we have gone away, and on whom we have turned our back." PAGE 45. Cited in HIERURGIA, P. 205.

1641.] A LARGE SUPPLEMENT, &c. "Our men, to return to the old fashion, command the Table to be set at the east end, that in the time of the consecration the priest may stand so far removed from the people as the furthest wall of the church can permit ; and as [ if ] this distance were not enough to keep these holy words of consecration from the profane ears of laicks, our book hath a second rubrick enjoining expressly the priest in the time of consecration to turn his back on the people, to come from the north end of the Table, and to stand at such a place where he may use both his hands with more decency and ease, which is not possible but on the west side alone." PAGE 10. IB. P. 368.

1660.] THE OLD NONCONFORMIST, &c. "If what *Distinction of professors and Religion*, we answer, their worshipping towards the East, and bowing towards the Altar, prostrating themselves in their approaches into Churches." PAGE 33.

1660.] REASONS WHY THE SERVICE-BOOK WAS REFUSED BY THE CHURCH OF SCOTLAND. Complaint is made of "the Table set altarwise." REASON 2, P. 36.

"It hath. . . the Priest standing, kneeling, turning to the people, and consequently from them." REASON 3, P. 37.

1661.] ANATOMY OF THE COMMON PRAYER, BY DWALPHINTRAMIS. "Secondly, for his posture, besides the windings, turnings, and cringings, his face must be sometimes towards the people, and sometimes his back." PAGE 29. Cited in HIERURGIA, P. 76.

Cent. 17.] "A FORM OF CONSECRATION OR DEDICATION OF CHURCHES AND CHAPPELS, ACCORDING TO THE USE OF THE CHURCH OF IRELAND." Latter half of the 17th Century.

"When they [ the Bishops and Clergy ] are vested, they shall kneel down in the body of the Church, with their faces to the East, and say together."

" Then the Bishop, arising from his chair, shall kneel before the Altar or Communion Table and say."

"Then the Bishop returning to the Altar, shall with reverence and solemnity ( his face being Eastward ) lay his hands upon the plate, and say this prayer, standing." Cited by MACCOLL, LAWLESSNESS, &c., PREF. TO THE 3D ED., P. CLIX, CLX.

1703.] WILLIAM LLOYD, BISHOP OF WORCESTER. Rev. R. Tisdale, Chaplain to Bishop Lloyd, at the command of his Bishop, put forth in 1703, " A Form of Dedication and Consecration of a Church or Chapel," dedicated " to the Most Reverend Fathers in God My Lords the Archbishops ; and to the Right Reverend Fathers in God My Lords the Bishops."

The Service is substantially that used in the Abbey Dore Consecration; but the Eastward position is, if possible, asserted more emphatically. Table and Holy Table are used once each; Holy Table or Altar nine times; Altar twelve times; and Sacred Altar once.

1717.] Dr. THOMAS BRETT, a Nonjuring Bishop, held extremely high views on the sacrificial aspect of the Eucharist, and desired the Priest to stand at the North end of the Altar, as the interposition of the Celebrant's body hindered the people from joining " either in the Sacrificial or Sacramental part of the office." He acknowledges that the custom of the Church of England was the other way:

"Therefore in y$^e$ first place, I desire that y$^e$ priest may still be directed to stand at y$^e$ *north side* of y$^e$ table, and not at y$^e$ place w$^{ch.}$ we at this time call *before the Table*, that is, y$^e$ *West side*, with his back to y$^e$ people." LETTERS ON THE CHURCH OF ENGLAND. Cited by PERRY, NOTES, P. 440.

1746.] MICAJAH TOWGOOD. " I might also have asked you, sir, to what oriental deity you pay your devoirs, when, from the north, the south, the west, the worshippers in your church, on certain solemn occasions, turn reverently towards the east and make their peculiar honours? . . . This worshipping towards the East is not, I think, ordered by any canon of your church which is now generally received; but it is (if I mistake not,) its common and prevailing practice." A DISSENT FROM THE CHURCH OF ENGLAND FULLY JUSTIFIED, P. 103.

In OUGHTON'S ORDO JUDICIORUM, N. 303-308, P. 249-277, T. 2, may be found the Forms of Consecrating Parish Churches, in which the Eastward Position was used.

# IV.
# Ornaments of the Altar.

THE Rubric of 1552 orders that: "Chancels shall remain as they have done in times past." The same Rubric was retained in 1559 and 1662. Another Rubric of 1559 orders that:

"The Minister . . . shall use such Ornaments in the Church as were in use by authority of Parliament in the second year of king Edward VI."

In the Rubric of 1662, a very important alteration was made:

"Such Ornaments of the Church . . . shall be retained, and be in use, as were in this Church of England, by the Authority of Parliament, in the Second Year of the Reign of King Edward the Sixth."

What Vestments the Priest shall wear, are provided for in the Rubric of 1549; what Ornaments were in use in the second year of Edward VI., and subsequently, can be ascertained from the various Inventories made during his reign.

A Commission was appointed by Edward VI., in his second year, to inquire into the quantity and value of Church Furniture throughout England. This task not having been satisfactorily performed, another Commission was appointed four years later, and the Inventories, which seem to have been carefully made, are still preserved. In a little volume entitled, "Inventory of Furniture and Ornaments in all the Parish Churches of Hertfordshire in the last year of the reign of Edward VI.," and also in "Parish Church Goods in Berkshire, A. D. 1552," and in various other Inventories made in the 6th and 7th year of Edward VI., the reader will find Copes, Vestments, Crosses, and Candlesticks mentioned as still preserved in the Churches. These things were in use in all Royal Chapels, and many Cathedrals and Parish Churches, which evidently shows that it was the intention to retain such things, though those who objected against them, were tolerated. The Church of England was not then,—what some would make it now,—a narrow Sect, but it included men of different views in matters not essential.

The Church of England has ever professed to be a part of the Holy Catholic Church, and to reject such Ceremonies only as savor of superstition or teach false doctrine.

Art. XXXIV. declares,—and this Article was first adopted by Convocation in 1552, when the ceremonies now objected to were in use:—

"Whosoever, through his private judgment, willingly and purposely, doth openly break the Traditions and Ceremonies of the Church, which be not repugnant to the Word of God, and be ordained and approved by common authority, ought to be rebuked openly, (that others may fear to do the like,) as he that offendeth against the common order of the Church, and hurteth the Magistrate, and woundeth the consciences of the weak brethren."

Canon 30, of Canons of 1603-4, is as follows:

"But the abuse of a thing doth not take away the lawful use of it. Nay, so far was it from the purpose of the Church of England to forsake and reject the Churches of Italy, France, Spain, Germany, or any such like Churches, in all things which they held and practiced, that, as the Apology of the Church of England confesseth, it doth with reverence retain those Ceremonies, which doth neither endamage the Church of God, nor offend the minds of sober men; and only departed from them in those particular points, wherein they were fallen both from themselves in their ancient integrity, and from the Apostolical Churches, which were their first founders." PAGE 44, 45.

The Bishops, at the Savoy Conference in 1661, replied to the Presbyterians:

"Our Church doth every where profess, as she ought, to conform to the Catholic usage of the primitive times from which causelessly to depart argues rather love of contention than of peace." CARDWELL, HISTORY OF CONFERENCES, c. 7, P. 359.

Again, in the Preface to the Prayer Book of 1662, we read:

"And therefore of the sundry alterations proposed unto us, we have rejected all such as were either of a dangerous consequence (as secretly striking at some established doctrine, or laudable practice of the Church of England, or indeed of the whole Catholick Church of Christ) or else of no consequence at all, but utterly frivolous and vain."

## F. The Cross.

ST. PAUL declares: "God forbid that I should glory, save in the Cross of our Lord Jesus Christ." GAL. 6:14. Therefore, we beautify our Altars with the sign of a once-suffering, but now glorified Saviour. St. Paul makes the Cross identical with the Gospel in 1 COR. 1:17, 18, GAL. 5:11, PHIL. 3:18; and in GAL. 6:17, he perhaps alludes to being signed with the Cross: "I bear in my body the marks of the Lord Jesus." The early Christians, like St. Paul, were neither ashamed of their Lord, nor of the sign of His Cross. They made constant use of it, as TERTULLIAN tells us:

| Ad omnem progressum atque promotum, ad omnem aditum et exitum, ad vestitum et calceatum, ad lavacra, ad mensas, ad lumina, ad cubilia, ad sedilia, quaecumque nos conversatio exercet, frontem crucis signaculo | At every movement and motion, at every coming in and going out, when we dress and put on our shoes, at the bath, at the table, when we light up, when we go to bed, when we sit down, whenever we engage |

terimus. DE COR. MILIT., C. 3, p. 188. PARS 1. in conversation, we mark our foreheads with the sign of the Cross.

From ORIGEN we learn that the sign of the Cross was used in Baptism, just as we now have it in the Church:

Ecce hic Christianus dicebatur, et signo Christi signibatur in fronte, etc. HOM. 1, IN Ps. 38, c. 5, COL. 1405, B. PAT. GR. T. 12.

Behold here he was called a Christian, and was signed with the sign of Christ upon his forehead.

But the sign of the Cross meant something then. It at once marked him who employed it, as a Christian, and exposed him to torture and death. Now that it costs nothing but ridicule, people are ashamed of it. In the Baptismal Office, the Minister says:

"We receive this Child into the congregation of Christ's flock, and do sign him with the sign of the Cross, in token that hereafter he shall not be ashamed to confess the faith of Christ crucified, and manfully to fight under His banner," &c.

The Rubric directs:

"If those who present the Infant shall desire the sign of the Cross to be omitted, although the Church knows no worthy cause of scruple concerning the same, yet, in that case, the Minister may omit that part of the above which follows the Immersion, or pouring of Water on the Infant."

It always seemed to me that, by the Rubric ordering the omission of the whole declaration, instead of the part requiring the use of the sign of the Cross, the Church doubted whether a person who was ashamed of Christ's Cross at the Sacrament of regeneration, would in after life fight manfully under that banner.

The Son of God did not refuse to hang upon the Cross, "despising the shame," but His professed followers now are ashamed of it. If they do not dare to say so openly, they act as if they were. With some it is only tolerated in the form of an article of jewelry. I have frequently seen this Holy Sign, with which the Church signs the foreheads of her children, stigmatized as "the mark of the Beast," in newspapers which make great claims to be religious and Evangelical. The Protestants of Germany retain to this day, not merely the Cross, but the Crucifix even, upon their Altars. LUTHER, in his "Forms of Prayer, for Morning and Evening, to be taught to a Household," orders them to sign themselves with "the sign of the Holy Cross when retiring at night, and rising in the morning."

TYNDALE, the Martyr, approved of the sign of the Cross:

"And in like manner, if I make a Cross upon my forehead, in a remembrance that God hath promised assistance unto all that believe in Him, for His sake That died on the Cross, then doth the Cross serve me, and I not it. And in like manner, if I bear on me, or look upon a Cross, of whatsoever matter it be, or make a Cross upon me, in remembrance that whosoever will be Christ's disciple must suffer a Cross of adversity, tribulations, and persecution, so doth the Cross serve me, and I not it. And this was the use of the Cross once; and for this cause it was, at the beginning, set up in the Churches.

"And so, if I make an image of Christ, or of any thing that Christ hath done for me, in a memory, it is good, and not evil, until it be abused. . . . And to kneel before the Cross unto the word of God, which the Cross preacheth, is not evil." ANSWER TO SIR THOMAS MORE'S DIALOGUE, P. 60.

1562.] In Convocation in 1562, the Puritans complained that in the Communion:

"Some also superstitiously both kneel and knock." CARDWELL, HIST. OF CONF., C. 2, N. 10, P. 118.

BULLINGER, the Calvinist, says:

"The sign of the Cross indeed was usual among the early Christians, and they frequently marked it with the finger on their foreheads." REMARKS UPON THE LETTER OF HORN, APP. P. 357. Z. L. 2D.

1570.] ANTHONY GILBY. Among the many "Popish" practices still remaining in the Church, he enumerates:

"44. Crossing themselves in their prayers." A VIEW OF ANTICHRIST. PARTE OF A REGISTER, P. 63.

1604.] CANON 30, of CANONS OF 1603-4, says:

"The honour and dignity of the name of the Cross begat a reverent estimation even in the Apostles' time (for aught that is known to the contrary) of the Sign of the Cross which the Christians shortly after used in all their actions. . . . This continual and general use of the Sign of the Cross is evident by many testimonies of the ancient Fathers." PAGE 44.

1605.] AN ABRIDGMENT OF THAT BOOKE WHICH THE MINISTERS OF LINCOLNE DIOCESS DELIVERED, &c. "The common people in many parts of the land are known not only to retaine the superstitious vse of it (blessing themselves, there breasts, there foreheads, and everything they take in hand by it) but also to hold that their children are not rightly baptised without it." ARG. 3, EXCEPT. 2, P. 40, 41.

The Church of England, in a Rubric of the Prayer Book of 1549, left these and like practices to every man's discretion:

"As touching kneeling, crossing, holding up of hands, knocking upon the breast, and other gestures, they may be used or left, as every man's devotion serveth, without blame." PAGE 157.

## II. Altar Lights.

THE use of Lights in Divine Worship, was ordained by the Almighty Himself. Any one who reads his Bible knows this. In Exod. 26:35, 40:4; Lev. 24:2, 3; 1 Kings 7:49; Rev. 1:12, 13, we have an account of the use of Candlesticks. In Rev. 4:5, in describing the worship of Heaven, St. John speaks of the "seven lamps of fire burning before the throne" of God. These lamps could not have been for the purpose of light, for we are told in Rev. 22:5, that "they need no candle, neither the light of the sun; for the Lord God giveth them light." Surely anything that has the sanction of God, cannot be wicked or superstitious. The use of Lights throughout the East, was universal in the 4th Century, as St. Jerome tells us:

| | |
|---|---|
| Per totas orientis ecclesias, quando legendum est Evangelium, accenduntur luminaria, jam sole rutilante, non utique ad fugendas tenebras, sed ad signum laetitiae demonstrandum. Ep. 53, adv. Vigilant., c. 3, p. 160. T. 2. | Throughout all the Churches of the East, when the Gospel is to be read, lamps are lighted, while the sun is still shining, not indeed to drive away the darkness, but to show a sign of joy. |

1. The use of Altar Lights in the Church of England since the Reformation.

The use of two Altar Lights is the special legacy of the Reformation. This custom was not formerly peculiar to England, as is evident from ancient frescoes. I do not suppose that there is a Roman Altar in the whole world now, that has but two Eucharistic Lights, though I have seen but two candles lighted at Low Mass. They are to set before our eyes that Christ is the true Light of the world, and to represent to us His two natures, the human and the Divine. This custom of the Church of England in having but two Eucharistic Altar Lights, which was the general practice long before the Reformation, may have had its origin in what St. John says, when describing the worship of Heaven, in Rev. 11:4:

"These are the two olive trees, and the two Candlesticks standing before the God of the earth."

In 1547, in the first year of his reign, Edward VI. issued Injunctions, in which it was ordered that the two Altar Lights be retained:

"And shall suffer from henceforth no torches nor candles, tapers or images of wax to be set afore any image or picture, but only two Lights upon the high Altar, before the sacrament, which for the signification that Christ is the true Light of the world, they shall suffer to remain still." WILK. CONC., P. 4. T. 4; CRANMER'S MISS. WRITINGS, APP. N. 24, P. 499.

1547.] THOMAS CRANMER, ABP. OF CANTERBURY. "Item, whether they suffer any torches, candles, tapers, or any other lights to be in your Churches, but only two Lights upon the high Altar." ARTICLES OF VISITATION. WILK. CONC., P. 23. T. 4; IB. P. 155.

1549.] JOHN HOOPER. "They still retain their vestments and the candles before the altars." EP. 36, TO BULLINGER, P. 72. ORIG. LET. VOL. 1.

1549.] M. BUCER AND P. FAGIUS. "We hear that some concessions have been made both to a respect for antiquity, and to the infirmity of the present age; such, for instance, as the vestments commonly used in the sacrament of the eucharist, and the use of candles." EP. 248, P. 535. IB. VOL. 2.

1549.] ARTICLES TO BE FOLLOWED AND OBSERVED ACCORDING TO THE KING'S MAJESTY'S INJUNCTIONS AND PROCEEDINGS. "1. That all parsons, vicars and curates omit in the reading of the injunctions, all such as make mention of the popish mass, of chantries, of candles upon the altar, or any other such like thing.

"2. Item. For an Uniformity, that no minister do counterfeit the Popish mass, . . . as . . . or setting any light upon the Lord's board at any time." CARDWELL, DOC. ANN., P. 74, 75. VOL. 1.

These ARTICLES were first published by BURNET, HIST. OF THE REF., PT. 2, B. 1, RECORDS, N. 33, p. 243. VOL. 5, and the original cannot be found now, so that their authority has been denied, yet there can be no doubt but that they are genuine documents of the time. They may be the work of some Puritan Bishop, based upon some Royal Injunctions not now extant, or presuming that whatever he did would be sanctioned by authority. Ridley of his sole authority pulled down Altars in his Diocese, but his action was soon sanctioned by the King. RIDLEY also in his INJUNCTIONS, in 1550, makes use of the language employed in these Articles:

"First, That there be no reading of such injunctions as extolleth and setteth forth the popish mass, candles," &c.

"*Item.* That no minister do counterfeit the popish mass, in kissing the Lord's board; . . . or setting any light upon the Lord's board." WORKS, P. 319; BURNET, PT. 2, B. 1, RECORDS, N. 52, P. 309. VOL. 5.

Judging from his conduct in another case, perhaps Ridley had some hand in these Injunctions.

Some have thought that these Articles are an interpretation of the Book of 1549, and prove that candles were not intended to be used. No doubt it was the desire of the ultra-Reformers that they should not be used. Their intention was to gradually do away with everything ancient in favor of Calvinistic novelties. But Hooper and Bucer expressly say that Candles were allowed; these Articles by forbidding them show that they were in use. Candles are not expressly mentioned by name in the Rubric, but Queen Elizabeth understood that they were sanctioned by the Ornaments Rubric. No one doubts but that Altars, Wafer-Bread, and Vestments are expressly sanctioned by the Rubrics of 1549, and yet Ridley pulled down Altars; Fox tells us (ACTS AND MON., B. 9, N. 3, P. 47. VOL. 2) that by the end of Dec., 1549, Wafer-cakes were not ordinarily used; and Vestments, and the Surplice even, were frequently dispensed with.

1550.] CHURCHWARDENS' ACCOUNTS OF THE TOWN OF LUDLOW. "Item, to Johan Troyt, for ij tapers weyinge iij. pound for the first mas . . . . . . . . . . . ij.s.
1569.] "Item, deliveryd to Richard Halle iij. li. of candelles to burne in the churche one Christmas day. . . . ixd.
1572.] "Payd for iij. li. of Candelles agaynste Christmas. . . . . . . . . . . xd. ob."
PAGE 43, 135, 149. CAMDEN SOC. PUBL. VOL. 102.

The candles in the two last charges, judging from the price, *may* have been of an inferior quality, and used merely to light the Church at the early Celebration, though from the similarity in weight they may have been for the Altar.

1550.] RETURN OF CHURCH UTENSILS IN DORSET. In the Dorchester Deanery, Parish of Faringdon, we find a "a cross and censer, and II candlesticks appointed to the parish" by the Commissioners. HUTCHINS, HIST. AND ANTIQ. OF THE COUNTY OF DORSET, APPEND., P. 526. VOL. 2.

1554.] KNOX, and the Scottish Reformers were accused of using Lights in 1554, as appears from Calvin, who objects against them for following the customs of England:

Conquesti enim apud me amici quidam fuerunt, vos ita praecise ceremonias Anglicanas urgere, ut satis constaret, vos plus aequo esse patriae addictos. . . . Certe luminaria, cruces et ejus farinae nugas ex superstitione manasse, nemo, ut arbitror, sano judicio praeditus negabit. Unde constituo, qui eas in libera optione retinent, nimis cupide ex faece haurire, nec video, quorsum attineat Ecclesiam frivolis et inutilibus ceremoniis, ne proprio nomine noxias appellem, onerari, ubi puri et simplicis ordinis libertas nobis permittitur.

Certain friends have complained to me, that you so rigidly insist upon the English ceremonies, that it is very evident that you are too strongly attached to that Country. . . . Surely that Lights, Crosses, and trifles of that sort, had their origin in superstition, no one of a sound mind, as I think, will deny. Wherefore, I determine, that they, who of their own free choice retain them, draw too eagerly from the dregs; nor do I see why the Church should be burdened with frivolous and useless ceremonies, not to call them by

Ep. *Cnoxo et Gregal., p. 98.     their proper name, hurtful, when
col. 2. T. 9.     we have the liberty of a pure and simple order.

This Letter of Calvin had reference to the troubles among the English and Scotch exiles at Frankfort, alluded to on pages 6 and 7. It seems that Calvin had either been deceived by the party of Knox, or that he accused the exiles of having things which he knew they might have by the Prayer Book of 1549, but which they did not have. David Whitehead and others thus reply:

"These friends of yours complain that 'we are too precise in enforcing the English ceremonies, and unreasonably partial to our own country.' These, indeed, we pertinaciously retain, as knowing them to be very godly: this, however, has never been done by us in a precise manner; for we have abandoned some of them for the sake of your friends, which might at that time have been piously adopted. . . . And you might justly have been offended, had no concession been made. But as this is a barefaced and impudent falsehood of theirs, you can judge for yourself in what light they must have regarded you. You object to us 'lights and crosses.' As for lights, we never had any; and with respect to crosses, if we ever made use of them, these friends of yours have not imposed upon you. . . . But it is no wonder that our ceremonies appear redundant, and even burdensome, to those persons who exclaim against the public reading of the word of God as an irksome and unprofitable form." Ep. 358, p. 756–758, Orig. Let. Vol. 2. See Whittingham, A Brief Discours of the Troubles Begonne at Franckford, p. LI.–LV.; Cox and Others to Calvin, Ep. 357, p. 753–754. Orig. Let. Vol. 2.

It is a fact, although it may seem incredible now, that the extreme Puritans once objected to the public reading of the Bible in Church. (See page 9.) They preferred sermons,—human compositions,—to the Word of God. No wonder that they hated God's Church.

The Rubric of 1559, as also that of 1662, cited above, order such Ornaments to be in use, as were in use in the second year of Edward VI.; and two Altar Lights were without doubt in use. They were used in Queen Elizabeth's Chapel during her whole reign, in spite of the clamors of the Puritans. (See pages 125–130.) It is a very important fact that they objected to them as being "Popish" or "superstitious" but never as being illegal. They are in all King's Chapels, and many Cathedrals, Private Chapels, Colleges, and Parish Churches to this day. Lord Treasurer Burleigh used them constantly, and so did Bishop Andrewes and others.

---

*I am convinced that there is a mistake here. In the Amsterdam Edition from which I quote, and also in that of Lausanne, this letter is wrongly addressed to Knox instead of Cox,—Cnoxo instead of Coxo.

1605.] CERTAIN DEMANDS WITH THEIR GROUNDS, DRAWN OUT OF HOLY WRIT, &c. "But as for Copes, Surplices, Crosses, Candles at noone dayes, and such like superstitious ornaments, rites and ceremonies, because there is neither nature, neither necessitie, neither vtilitie, neither decencie, neither any good order that require the same; ... we affirme that they ought as a menstruous cloth be cast away, and be bidden get ye hence." PAGE 29.

Circa 1621–30.] DR. JOHN DONNE, DEAN OF ST. PAUL'S. "The oblation of this day's purification is light; so the day names it, Candlemas-day, so your custom celebrates it, with many lights.

"I would not be understood to condemn all use of candles by day in divine service, nor all churches that have or do use them; for, so, I might condemn even the primitive church, in her pure and innocent estate.

"We must not therefore be hasty in condemning particular ceremonies; for in so doing, in this ceremony of lights, we may condemn the primitive church, that did use them, and we condemn a great and noble part of the reformed church, which doth use them at this day." SERMON 8. ON CANDLEMAS DAY, P. 150, 156, 157. VOL. 1.

"And so did we in the Reformation, in some ceremonies which had been of use in the primitive church, and depraved and corrupted in the Roman. For the solemnizing of this day, Candlemas-day, when the church did admit candles into the church, as the Gentiles did, it was not upon the reason of the Gentiles, who worshipped therein the God of darkness, Februus, Pluto; but because he who was the light of the world, was this day presented and brought into the temple, the church admitted lights." SERM. 10. IB. P. 191. IB.

1625.] NICHOLAS FERRAR. "The Communion-table itself was furnished with a silver paten, silver chalice, and silver candlesticks with large wax candles in them." MS. Cited in TRANS. OF THE CAMBRIDGE CAMDEN SOCIETY, PART 1, P. 42. IN HIERURGIA, P. 29.

1633.] "Within her [Mrs. Ferrar's] Chapel was a rich Altar, Crucifix, and wax-candles, and before the reading of prayers, they bowed thrice to the Altar, as they went up and came down." Cited by FOSBROKE, BRIT. MONACH., c. 62, P. 298.

1636.] JOHN COSIN, afterwards BISHOP OF DURHAM. "Agreeable to it you [Cosin] have provided [in Durham Cathedral] much Altar furniture, and many massing implements, crucifixes, candlesticks, tapers," &c. ARTICLES OR INSTRUCTIONS, &c., N. 90, SECT. 9, P. 170. COSIN CORRESPONDENCE, VOL. 1. SURTEES SOC. PUBL. VOL. 32.

Circa 1640.] "*Such ornaments*, &c.] Among other ornaments of the church also then in use, in the second year of Edw. VI. there were two lights appointed by his injunctions (which the parliament had authorized him to make, and whereof otherwhiles they made mention, as acknowledging them to be binding,) to be set on the high-altar, as a significant ceremony of the light which Christ's Gospel brought into the world; and this at the same time, when all other lights and tapers superstitiously set before images, were by the same Injunctions, with many other absurd ceremonies and superfluities, taken away. These lights were (by virtue of this present rubric, referring to what was in use in the second of Edw. VI.) afterwards continued in all the queen's chapels, during her whole reign; and so are they in the king's, and in many cathedral churches, besides the chapels of divers noblemen, bishops, and colleges to this day.

"It was well known, that the Lord-treasurer Burleigh (who was no friend to superstition or popery) used them constantly in his chapel with other ornaments of fronts, palls and books, upon his altar. The like did Bishop Andrewes, who was a man who knew well what he did, and as free from popish superstition as any in the kingdom besides." NOTES ON THE BOOK OF COMMON PRAYER, 3D SERIES, P. 440, 441. WORKS, VOL. 5.

The REV. GEORGE ORNSBY, Editor of the COSIN CORRESPONDENCE, relates that this remarkable statement was made to him—

"A few years ago, by an aged clergyman, who was at Durham School for some time in the early part of this century, and constantly in the habit of attending the services of the Cathedral, who assured him that he had the most distinct remembrance of the altar-candles being then lighted every Sunday morning, in anticipation, no doubt, of the celebration of the Holy Communion." INTRODUCTION, P. XXVII. VOL. 1. SURTEES SOC. PUBL. VOL. 52.

1640-41.] Among the "Innovations in Discipline," complained of by the Puritans to Parliament in 1640-41, were these:

"3. Advancing candlesticks in many churches upon the altar so called.

"19. By standing up at the hymns in the church, and always at *Gloria Patria.*" CARDWELL, HIST. OF CONF., C. 7, P. 272, 273.

1641.] Accordingly, Sept. 9, 1641, the House of Commons, without the consent of the House of Lords, made this declaration:

"That all Crucifixes, scandalous pictures of any one or more Persons of the Trinity, and all images of the Virgin Mary, shall be taken away and abolisht, and that all Tapers, Candlesticks, and Basins be removed from the communion-table.

"That all corporal bowing at the Name (Jesus) or towards the East End of the Church, Chapel, or Chancel, or towards the Communion Table, be henceforth forborne." Cited by NALSON, IMPART. COLL., P. 481, 482. VOL. 2.

1643.] JOHN MILNER. "By virtue of an ordinance, which had passed in 1643, all crosses, crucifixes, representations of saints and angels, copes, surplices, hangings, candlesticks, basins, organs, &c., were carried out of the cathedral and other churches." HIST. OF WINCHESTER, P. 411, 412. VOL. 1.

Circa 1665.] A VOYAGE TO ENGLAND, CONTAINING MANY THINGS RELATING TO THE STATE OF LEARNING, RELIGION, AND OTHER CURIOSITIES OF THAT KINGDOM. BY MONSIEUR SORBIERE. DONE INTO ENGLISH FROM THE FRENCH ORIGINAL. LONDON, 1709. "That which the Presbyterians still find more fault with is, that the church has festival days (some of which are dedicated to the Blessed Virgin), as also altars, consecration of churches, bowing to the name of Jesus, burning of candles, kneeling, mitres, surplices, copes, crosses, music, and baptising with the sign of the cross." PAGE 22. Cited in the *Church Times*, MARCH 14, 1879, P. 166.

1698.] In 1698, the Parish of All Saints, Derby, paid twelve shillings for "A pair of large brasse candlesticks." COX, CHRONICLES, &c., C. 9, P. 180.

When the Church was rebuilt in 1723–5, the Altar "consisted of a large slab of white marble supported on a handsome wrought-iron frame, painted and gilded." This costly Altar was used till 1873, when it was taken down by the Low-Church Vicar, and a wooden Table took its place. IB. P. 181, 182.

A wood cut of this marble Altar may be seen in c. 10, P. 227.

1703.] WILLIAM LLOYD, BISHOP OF WORCESTER. While the Bishop is placing the Candlesticks "upon the Altar," the Chaplains are directed to say: "Thy word is a lantern unto my feet: and a light unto my paths." FORM OF CONSECRATING CHURCHES. Cited by MACCOLL, LAWLESSNESS, &C., PREF. TO THE 3D ED., P. CLXXX.

1707.] In the early part of the eighteenth century, Candlesticks and bowing to the Altar were so common in England, that a Scottish Presbyterian writer objected to the Scottish union on the ground that these things would be introduced among them from England. In his tract, "Lawful prejudices against an Incorporating union; or, considerations on the Sinfulness of this union," he says:

"We shall have blind lights, altars, and bowing to the altar." Cited by LATHBURY, HIST. OF THE BOOK OF COMMON PRAYER, C. 16, P. 427.

1710.] CHARLES WHEATLY. "I must observe still further, that among other ornaments of the church then [1549] in use, there were *two lights* enjoined by the injunctions of king Edward VI. (which injunctions were also ratified by the act of parliament here mentioned) to be set upon the altar, as a significant ceremony to represent the light which Christ's Gospel brought into the world. And this too was ordered by the very same injunction which prohibited all other lights and tapers, that used to be superstitiously set before images or shrines, &c. And these lights used time out of mind in the Church, are still continued in most, if not all the, cathedral and collegiate churches and chapels, so often as divine service is performed by candle-light; and ought also, by this rubric, to be used in all parish churches and chapels at the same times." RATIONAL ILLUST. OF THE BOOK OF COMMON PRAYER, C. 2, SECT. 4, N. 8, P. 106.

1716.] CHARLES OWEN. "6. THERE is no Command of the Church for setting up of Candles upon Communion-Tables; and yet we see unlighted Candles plac'd on Collegiate and Cathedral Altars, which some inferior Churches awkwardly ape.

"NOTHING is more rediculous than this Practice, and is even grosser than the *Romish* Ceremony they pretend to imitate, for in the Church of *Rome* they put up lighted Candles, which are of some use, if not to themselves, to the Chandeler at least; But what our *unlighted Tapers* serve for, I can't conceive, unless they be Emblems of the darken'd Understandings of the superstitious Innovators." PLAIN-DEALING, &c., c. 2, p. 37.

1736.] FRANCIS DRAKE. "In winter, from All-saints to Candlemas, the choir [of York Minster] is illuminated at evening service by seven large branches. Besides a wax candle fixed at every other stall. . . . These, with two large tapers for the altar, are all the lights commonly made use of. But on the vigils of particular holy days the four grand dignitaries of the church have each a branch of seven candles placed before them at their stalls." EBORACUM, P. 524.

In an "Inventory of the Plate, &c., belonging to York Cathedral," made January 16, 1633-4, is this entry:

"One paire of guilt candlesticks, weighing 98¾ oz., price 32*l.* 18*s.* 4*d.*" THE FABRIC ROLLS OF YORK MINSTER, N. 57, P. 316. SURTEES SOC. PUBL. VOL. 35.

These Candlesticks were taken away during the Great Rebellion (IB. N. 62, P. 333). In an Inventory made November 11, 1681, mention is made of "2 silver candle sticks." IB. N. 57, P. 317.

1830.] BELL'S LIFE IN LONDON, AND SPORTING CHRONICLE, SUNDAY, JULY 18, 1830, No. 433, VOL. 9, contains a "Representation of his Majesty George the fourth lying in State, in Windsor Castle." There are three large Candlesticks with lighted candles on each side of the coffin. "Six large massive Silver-gilt Candlesticks of the richest chased workmanship, three on each side, elevated upon black cloth pedestals of three feet high. These beautiful candlesticks were removed from the Altars of Whitehall Chapel, the German Chapel of St. James, and St. George's Chapel, Windsor. They stand about three feet high, and their present elevation is upwards of six feet."

1843.] JOHN JEBB. "The ornaments of the church, besides those stated before, may be considered as consisting of the two lights on the Communion Table, which immemorial custom had always prescribed, at least in Cathedrals, and Collegiate and Royal Churches and Chapels. In many of these places they are still retained; in many where they are disused, the disuse could be shown to be modern: and some parish churches and private chapels of Noblemen have uniformly retained them: they always stood on the Altar, and were lit when the service was performed by candle-light.

"The seven lights used in Romish Churches, were not it is believed, employed in England, where there were but two, even before the Reformation." THE CHORAL SERVICE, SECT. 27, P. 212, 213.

1844.] JAMES CRAIGIE ROBERTSON. "To speak only of such things as are not uncommonly done by those who are accounted among the most regular of the clergy—perhaps most of us have to charge ourselves with having, at some time or other, deviated from what is said to be our duty in some of the following particulars:—Omitting the performance of daily service; . . . celebrating the Holy Communion without setting two lights on the Altar;" &c. HOW SHALL WE CONFORM TO THE LITURGY, &c. INTRODUCTION, P. 5.

"The Bishop of London observes, (p. 48) 'I see no objection to candles on the communion-table, provided they are not burning, except when the church is lighted up for evening service.' The order, however, is for *lights*; Fuller argues on the word, that 'these being termed *lights*, shews they were not *lumina caeca*, but burning,' (Ch. Hist. b. vii. p. 374); and we have abundant proof that they *were* burning. . . . To have candles without lighting them is but *half*-conformity; indeed, it appears to take away the symbolical meaning for which the lights are said to be prescribed—'the signification that Christ is the very true Light of the world.'" IB. PT. 2, c. 5, (*a*), P. 79.

Robertson, however, believes that there is no authority for these Lights now, nor, if there was, would it be wise to have them. IN. PT. 3, CONCLUS., P. 312.

1859.] THOMAS LATHBURY. "We find that the 'two lights' were in use in Edward's first Book, and consequently they were lawful at that time. Though they were subsequently prohibited, yet Elizabeth's rubric, which was adopted in 1662, and which is still our rule in Church ornaments, takes us back to the first Book established in Edward's second year." HIST. OF THE BOOK OF COMMON PRAYER, C. 15, P. 353.

1872.] MACKENZIE E. C. WALCOTT. "Lighted candles on the altar were still in use after the Restoration, as Hickeringill in 1682 speaks of them, and cringing to the east to the altar. [Black Nonconformist, Works, ii. 87.] A large contemporary print of the coronation of William and Mary at Westminster in 1689, shows 28 tapers burning on the altar, and eight upon the retable. An engraving in 1689 shows the altar of St. Paul's with two lighted candles, in accordance with a view in Gunton's 'Peterborough' of the altar of that Cathedral previous to 1643. There is a tradition that the four standard candlesticks now in the choir of Ghent, once belonged to St. Paul's. They were made at Antwerp, and bear the arms of the Tudors and their donor, Bishop Trieste; having been sold in the Great Rebellion. The altar candlesticks at Bristol, now kept only in store, were taken from the Spaniards at the siege of Vigo in 1709. At Exeter, as at Salisbury, the altar had two candlesticks of brass, and a cushion with a service book on it: the pall was of red velvet; and upon a second cushion were a basin and ewer and two chalices. At the back were Moses and Aaron and the second monogram. So at Bristol, in 1635, Moses stood bareheaded whilst Aaron wore a cardinal's cap. Candlesticks still stand on the altars of Canterbury, Manchester, St. Paul's, Oxford, Hereford, (two sets, ferial and dominical), Durham, Wells, (of the time of Queen Anne), Westminster, Rochester, Chichester and York; but the tapers are only lighted on dark afternoons. As a trace of old usage they are placed on the altar only at the time of celebration at Salisbury, Ely, Lichfield, Exeter, St. Patrick's, and Christ Church, Dublin. At the beginning of this century they were regularly lighted on Sunday mornings at Durham as if in anticipation of a celebration." TRADITIONS AND CUSTOMS OF CATHEDRALS, SECT. 4, P. 161, 162.

The print representing the coronation of William and Mary was on exhibition at the South Kensington Museum, in the Crace Collection, in 1880.

The use of *lighted* candles in the Church of England since the Reformation, though sanctioned by Injunctions, the Ornaments Rubric, and the practice in high places, must have been rather of an exceptional character. The use of *unlighted* candles has been much more common, though far from the general practice. The use of lighted candles, though complained of by the Puritans as "superstitious," but not as illegal, has never been forbidden by the Church.

In CHAMBERS' "Divine Worship in England in the Thirteenth and Fourteenth Centuries," &c., may be found fac-simile plates taken from old devotional works principally, wherein the Altar is ornamented with two lighted candles:

"The Orthodox Communicant," 1726; a view of St. Paul's Cathedral in "The Holidays of the Church of England throughout the year," London, 1719 (printed below), and a similar engraving in Thomas De Laune's "The Present State of London, London, 1681;" Burnet (Dr.), "Of the State of the Dead and of those that are to Rise, translated by Matthias Earbery, Presbyter of the Church of England, second edition, 1728, 8vo," a view of the Altar of Magdalen College, Oxford; "The Introduction to the Sacrament. By Launcelot Addison, D. D., Dean of Lichfield," fourth edition, 1693; "The Communicant's Guide," 1682. The "Formae Precationum Piarum," of Melancthon, printed at Wittenberg, 1563, gives a view of the communion of the Protestants at Wittenberg, with two lighted candles on the Altar. PT. IV., C. 2, N. 9, P. 284, 286, 290, 292; and c. 6, N. 9, P. 402; c. 6, N. 6, P. 396. See HIERURGIA ANGLICANA, P. 194, for a view of the Altar of Peterborough Cathedral in 1643, taken from GUNTON's HISTORY OF THE CHURCH OF PETERBOROUGH, P. 334.

The Court of Arches in Liddell *v.* Westerton held that:

"Candlesticks and unlighted candles may be lawfully retained." PRIVY COUNCIL JUDGMENTS, P. 44.

The Privy Council affirmed this decision in 1857. IBID. P. 53.

In Martin *v.* Mackonochie, in 1868 (PAGES 124-128), it was only the use of lighted candles which was condemned. It has been seen that Edward VI. and Cranmer ordered Lights, and not merely candles to be placed on the Altar, which plainly shows that the candles were to be lighted, in order to signify "that Christ is the true Light of the world."

The Altar in St. Paul's Cathedral, in 1719.

On the next page is a representation of the Altar of the Chapel Royal of St. George, Windsor, showing the two Altar lights and the ancient gold plate.

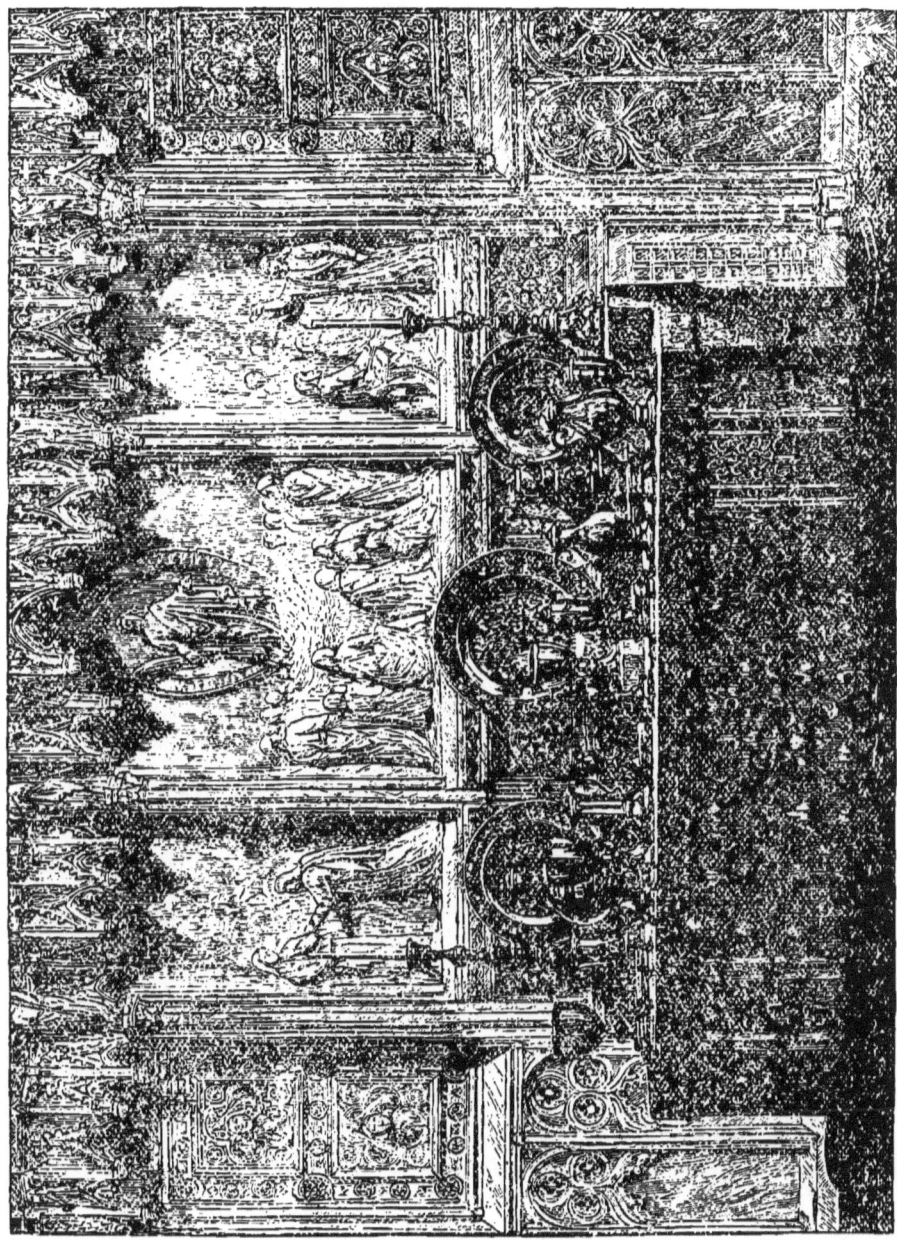

## 2. THE USE OF ALTAR LIGHTS, VESTMENTS, &c., AMONG THE LUTHERANS.

In the Reformation brought about by Luther in Germany, very little change was made in the dress of the Minister and the Ornaments of the Altar. Vestments are still retained in Denmark, Norway and Sweden, but gradually fell into disuse in Germany, though they were still in use, at least in some places, when WESLEY visited that country in 1738:

"The Minister's habit was adorned with gold and scarlet, and a vast cross both behind and before." JOURNAL, JULY 28. 1738. P. 107. VOL. 1.

Among the Lutherans, the Churches are arranged much as they are with us; the Pulpit, though, is often placed over the Altar. In Denmark, Norway and Sweden, there was very little change made at the Reformation. In Saxony, and most of Prussia, the Altar is still handsomely vested, having a super-altar, upon which are vases of flowers, with a Crucifix, and large Candles, which are always lighted at the Communion. In Churches nearer the Rhine, where through Calvinistic influences the Vases and Candlesticks have disappeared, the Crucifix still remains. In the Lutheran Church at Alexandria, in Egypt, there are two Candles and a Crucifix upon the Altar.

We learn from the preceding pages what the English services were at the Reformation; now we will give an account of what services the Lutheran Protestants enjoyed, in the language of Luther himself, as cited by DROOP, an opponent of the Vestments:

"The Lutherans, in fact, retained vestments and the eastward position, and others of the pre-Reformation externals of religious worship, for prudential reasons, to avoid shocking the prejudices of the laity. . . . Luther writes (*Briefe*, vol. v. p. 340):

"'Our churches are, thank God, so arranged in neutral things that a layman, whether Walloon or Spaniard who could not understand our preaching, if he saw our mass, choir, organs, bells, chasubles, &c., would be constrained to say that it was a truly popish church, and no difference, or but little, against those they have among themselves.'" THE EDWARDINE VESTMENTS, P. 44–46.

In THE SWEDISH ORDINAL may be found the following Rubrics:

"How a Bishop shall be installed in office.

"At the end of Divine Service, the ceremony commences with a Psalm, during which first a Priest, vested in Mass-robes, goes to the Altar, bearing the Cope and other Episcopal insignia; next the Bishop who shall be installed in office, also thereafter the Archbishop and his Assistants, vested in Mass-robes." CHAP. 13, P. 5.

"Of ordination to the Preacher-Office.

"At the end of Divine Service a Psalm is sung, during which

those to be ordained, vested in Surplices, the Assistants and the Bishop proceed to the Altar and arrange themselves in the accustomed manner. The Chasubles are laid out on the Altar rails according to the order in which they that are to be ordained stand.

"The Bishop, with the Assistants, during the singing places the Chasubles upon those ordained." Chap. 14, p. 16, 18.

"How a Church Pastor shall be installed in a Congregation.

"Before the Public Service, the ceremony is begun with a Psalm, during which the Introducendus—vested in Mass-robes,—after him the Assistants, and last the Bishop, or he that acts in his stead, proceed to the Altar." Chap. 15, p. 22.

John Wesley thus describes a visit to a Lutheran Church in August, 1738:

"*Sun. 6.*—We went to church at Bertholdsdorf, a Lutheran village about an English mile from Hernhuth. Two large candles stood lighted upon the altar: the last supper was painted behind it; the pulpit was placed over it; and over that a brass image of Christ on the cross. . . . At nine began a long voluntary on the organ, closed with a hymn, &c. . . . Then the Minister walked up to the altar, bowed, sung those Latin words, '*Gloria in Excelsis Deo:*' bowed again, and went away. This was followed by another hymn. . . . Then the Minister went to the altar again, bowed, sung a prayer, read the Epistle, and went away. After a third hymn was sung, he went a third time to the altar, sung a versicle, (to which all the people sung a response,) read the third chapter to the Romans, and went away. The people having then sung the Creed in rhyme, he came and read the Gospel, all standing." Journal, p. 109. Vol. 1.

Did Wesley denounce this "Popery?" Far from it. He spent a whole week in the neighborhood, and upon leaving, he made the following entry in his Journal:

"I would gladly have spent my life here; but my Master calling me to labor in another part of the vineyard, on *Monday,* 14, I was constrained to take my leave of this happy place. . . . O when shall this Christianity cover the earth as the 'waters cover the seas?'" Ib. p. 113.

A correspondent of the *Rock,* an ultra-Protestant paper published in England, in No. 585, p. 736, September 29, 1876, writes as follows:

"Sir,—I trust both you and 'Danophilus' will forgive my saying that I have read his letter with extreme surprise, taking as it does a favorable view of the Scandinavian communion from the Protestant standpoint. It is completely the reverse of my own conclusions, arrived at after a tour in Norway, Sweden, and Denmark this year, that I plead to be heard in reply to your correspondent. If, sir, gorgeously embroidered chasubles, with in some instances actual crucifixes (not crosses) embroidered on the back; if low monotonous chanting of the services; if turning of the 'priest's' back to the people; if the constant use of the sign of the cross; if bishops arrayed in mitre, elaborate copes, albs, &c.; if lighted candles on the 'altar;'—if all these and many other similar unprotestant ceremonies are to be encouraged, then indeed let us copy the Lutheran churches of the North, for there we find all these abominations in as full vogue as in the great Harlot of the Seven Hills herself. No, sir; if as Protestants we repudiate the Roman heresy and the Eastern picture-worship, so too, let us be consistent, and repudiate the idolatries of Protestantism, when these alas! are found, as they are, in Norway, Sweden, and Denmark. 'Danophilus' says crucifixes are not now erected in Danish churches. This town alone supplies an answer: in the modern Danish church built here is to be seen over the pulpit such a crucifix as the Pope himself might bless.

"Hull. No Surrender.

"P. S.—I could send you a photograph of Roskilde Cathedral since the restoration which would make your hair stand on end."

The Rev. Dr. J. P. Tustin, in his report on the Church of Sweden, to Bishop Williams, Chairman of "The Joint Committee on Ecclesiastical Relations and Religious Reform," published in the *Church Journal*, November 16, 1876, says:

"The mode of rendering the service is very much like the Roman in their great churches, in the large towns. But it is always in the vernacular, never in the Latin. The priest wears as gorgeous a dress during the communion Office, as the Latin priest does at the celebration of Mass. There are no thurifers, incense burnings, nor processions. But the people have very much the habitudes and modes which the Roman Catholic congregations have—at least, so far as the common people are concerned. In fact, while so intensely anti-Roman as the Swedes are, the Swedish service is only the old Mass cut down, with some alterations. Indeed the service is called 'High Mass,' with the usual distinction of 'Matins and Vespers,' called by us Morning and Evening Prayer. Offensive as these terms are to Protestant ears, the Swedes innocently enough speak of their Mass, or High Mass, as if such things had never been known among the Roman Catholics.

"Nearly every church has a fine altar piece, and this is generally the best feature in the building. A conspicuous crucifix is always present."

The Rev. Wm. Michell gives the following description of the services in an ordinary country Church in South East Prussia at the present day:

"On Communion Sunday the blessing is not given after the sermon, but while the Minister retires, the Altar is prepared, the candles are lighted, &c. He returns to his place,—the non-communicants, if they retire at all, retiring now—and sings the remainder of the service, always facing Eastwards, the organ occasionally accompanying. In consecrating the Bread and Wine the sign of the Cross, delivers the Bread into the hand, or more frequently into the mouth, and so with the Chalice, with words of prayer and blessing. After, as well as before kneeling to receive either kind, a genuflection is made. . . . The Minister concludes the service with prayers intoned at the Altar, and gives the blessing; &c.

"Wafer bread for Communion is the almost universal rule. In country districts also the rule of fasting Communion is still extensively observed.

"The colours for vesting the Altar are ordinarily red, with blue or violet for Lent, and black for Good Friday." WHAT DID LUTHER TEACH? P. 27.

In many Lutheran Churches in this country similar services may be witnessed.

The popular idea is that the Reformers were all Puritans. The above citations, together with the previous ones, it is to be hoped, will dispel this idea. If those who speak so enthusiastically of the Protestant Reformation, only knew the truth of the matter, and that the word Protestant once meant something very different from what it does now, they would speak quite otherwise than they do. Only a few of the Reformers were Puritans. They originated among the Zwinglian and Calvinistic Reformers, who infected the English exiles during the reign of Queen Mary, so that upon their return, they set about to reform their Church, after the manner they had seen abroad.

There can be no doubt but that it was the intention of the English Reformers, though they were greatly interfered with by Foreigners, as it is evident from the numerous documents which we have cited, to conduct their Reformation, as regards externals, on the same plan that the Lutherans did.

By what right do some Protestants call the Lutheran Protestants "idolators," "superstitious," and "Papists?" Surely Luther knew by experience what "Popery" was, as well as those Protestants do, at the present day, who never read a Roman Catholic book in their lives, and who know nothing of that Church, except by hearsay. They may not like such things; but that is another thing. Why not grant others the same liberty in their worship that they claim for themselves? especially when Protestants boast "the right of every man to worship God according to the dictates of his own conscience." So far as my own experience goes, these Northern Protestants are just as honest, upright, moral, and in every way as good citizens as those who, to use a slang expression, "have Popery on the brain."

On the next page is a plate representing the interior of a little country Church at Molmen, in Norway, taken from PRITCHETT'S RAMBLES AND SCRAMBLES IN NORWAY, p. 128. See also PAGE 193.

The Church probably presents about the same appearance that it did before the Reformation. English country Churches doubtless exhibited a similar appearance. On the Chancel wall is the Rood or Crucifix, and under it the arms of King Christian V. In this Church are still preserved the ancient silver chalices and curious cases for the sacred wafers. There is also a fine old Vestment with a large purple cross on the back, and in the centre, a brass crucifix, which has been in constant use since the Reformation.

I will give a few extracts showing how the Calvinists were regarded by the Lutherans:

1554.] PETER MARTYR. "Our friend à Lasco as I have informed you before, had gone into Denmark with his [congregation of] foreigners, but was received there with much harshness, not to say barbarity: not indeed, as I suppose, through the fault of the king, but of the doctors and ministers of the church, by whose preaching and attacks he and his friends were at length driven away from that kingdom." Ep. 240, to Bullinger, p. 512, 513. Orig. Let. Vol. 2.

Note by the Editor. "Westphalus, a Lutheran divine, called the wandering church of à Lasco the martyrs of the devil; and Burgenhagius declared they should not be considered as Christians." Ib.

See also Strype, Mem. of Cranmer, B. 3, c. 15, an. 1554. Vol. 1; A Lasco, Ep. 102, p. 314-316, Gorham, Gleanings, &c., and the Note by Gorham.

1566.] RICHARD HILLES. "It is to be lamented, that certain Lutherans, as you write, though they offer peace, yet do not desist from their annoyance of you. But here the Martinists, (as the Lutherans in general choose to be called, rather than Lutherans,) cease not openly to censure and reprove their orthodox fellow-ministers, (whom also they denominate Calvinists,) in their public discourses, and with the utmost boldness." Ep. 74, to Bullinger, p. 174. Z. L.

1574.] RODOLPH GUALTER. "For, not contented with what Luther long since wrote rather intemperately against our teachers, they now exclaim that we are all Arians, and worse than Mahomet." Ep. 100, to Cox, p. 253. Z. L. 2d.

1575.] RICHARD COX, Bishop of Ely. "I am exceedingly grieved at the persecutions that have lately taken place in Saxony. That Lutheran party is very cruel." Ep. 126, to Gualter, p. 315. Z. L.

Let a few firebrands and mischief-makers go into any peaceful parish in Norway or Sweden, and aided by a few malcontents, who are to be found in every community, this peaceful parish would soon become a perfect pandemonium.

### III. Flowers.

How can we better adorn God's House than by decorating His Altar with the beautiful works of his hands? Some people are so superstitious that they object to the use of flowers, and yet find no fault with evergreen trimmings at Christmas. Flowers are used to decorate Protestant pulpits, and the people, instead of objecting to them, admire their beauty. Their use in the Church is very ancient. St. JEROME praises Nepotianus for his care, while living, for the Altar, and for adorning the Churches with flowers:

| | |
|---|---|
| Qui basilicas ecclesiae, et martyrum conciliabula diversis floribus et arborum comis, vitiumque pampinis adumbrarit. EP. 3, AD HELIOD., EPITAPH. NEPOT., P. 9, B. T. 1. | He adorned the Basilicas and Churches, and the Shrines of the Martyrs, with various flowers and leaves of trees, and the tendrils of vines. |

St. AUGUSTINE tells us of a Christian, who, after finishing his devotions, took from the Altar a flower:

| | |
|---|---|
| Deinde abscedens, aliquid de altari florum, quod occurit, tulit. DE CIV. DEI, L. 22, C. 8, N. 13, COL. 767. PAT. LAT. T. 41. | Then departing, he took a flower which was before him, from off the Altar. |

## V.

## The Eucharist a Memorial Sacrifice.

N MALACHI 1 : 11, is recorded this prophecy:

"From the rising of the sun to the going down of the same, My Name shall be great among the Gentiles; and in every place Incense shall be offered unto My Name, and a pure offering; for My Name shall be great among the heathen, saith the Lord of hosts."

Throughout the whole world, from our Lord's time, this "Pure Offering" has been offered in the Catholic Church. Go where you will,—to the frozen regions of Russia, to the burning sands of Africa, to the ancient Basilicas in Rome and the damp Catacombs underlying her soil, to the little Parish Churches in England and America, and everywhere "we have Altar," as St. Paul says, bare and humble though it be, before our eyes. But among Protestants, except the Lutherans, we see nothing of the kind. The Pulpit has usurped the place of the Altar; the Preacher has supplanted the Priest.

The House of Bishops, in 1832, declared the Holy Communion

to be of a "spiritually sacrificial character," that is, the Priest pleads before God the Sacrifice which His Son once offered upon the Cross, while at the Altar he makes a Memorial of that Sacrifice, as the Fathers teach:

390.] St. CHRYSOSTOM, Bishop of Constantinople.

Ἐπὶ δὲ τοῦ Χριστοῦ τοὐεναντίον· ἅπαξ προσηνέχθη, καὶ εἰς τὸ ἀεὶ ἤρκεσε. . . . τί οὖν. ἡμεῖς καθ' ἑκάστην ἡμέραν οὐ προσφέρομεν; Προσφέρομεν μὲν ἀλλ' ἀνάμνησιν ποιούμενοι τοῦ θανάτου αὐτοῦ. καὶ μιὰ ἐστὶν αὕτη, καὶ οὐ πολλαί. . . . Οὐκ ἄλλην θυσίαν, καθάπερ ὁ ἀρχιερεὺς τότε, ἀλλὰ τὴν αὐτὴν ἀεὶ ποιοῦμεν. μᾶλλον δὲ ἀνάμνησιν ἐργαζόμεθα θυσίας. Hom. 17, in Heb. 10, c. 3, p. 240, 241, 242. T. 12.

But in Christ it is just the opposite; He was once offered, and it suffices forever. . . . What then, do we not offer daily? we do offer indeed, but we celebrate the memory of His death; and this is one and not many. . . . We do not offer another sacrifice, as the Priest did then, but we always offer the same; or rather, we make a memorial of the sacrifice.

398.] St. AUGUSTINE, Bishop of Hippo.

Unde jam Christiani, peracti ejusdem sacrificii memoriam celebrant, sacrosancta oblatione et participatione corporis et sanguinis Christi.

Hujus sacrificii caro et sanguis ante adventum Christi per victimas similitudinum promittebatur; in passione Christi per ipsam veritatem reddebatur; post ascensum Christi per sacramentum memoriae celebratur. Contra Faust. Manich., L. 20, c. 18, 21, col. 383, 385. Pat. Lat. T. 42.

Wherefore Christians now celebrate the memorial of that same sacrifice which was completed, by a holy oblation, and the participation of the Body and Blood of Christ.

The flesh and blood of this sacrifice before the advent of Christ, was promised by victims of resemblance; in the Passion of Christ, it was rendered by the truth itself; after the Ascension of Christ, it is celebrated by the Sacrament of remembrance.

As some deny that ἱερεὺς (hiereus) is to be found at all in the New Testament, I will give a few examples:

Rom. 15:16. That I should be the minister of Jesus Christ to the Gentiles, ministering (ἱερουργοῦντα, hierourgounta) the Gospel of God.

1 Peter 2:9. But ye are a chosen generation, a royal priesthood (ἱεράτευμα, hierateuma), &c.

In Rev. 1:6; 5:10; 20:6, the word "Priests" is in the original Greek ἱερεῖς, Hiereis.

Some also make a distinction between Presbyter and Priest; but both the Greek and the Latin churches use the word Presbyter for Priest in their Ordination Services. It is also very frequently used for Priest by the writers of those Churches.

In the Scotch Office the words Presbyter and Priest are used interchangeably.

Let us examine our Lord's words recorded in LUKE 22:19, and 1 COR. 11:24:

"This do (ποιεῖτε, poieite) in remembrance (ἀνάμνησιν, anamnesin) of Me." From these words, "do" and "remembrance," the Jews, who were acquainted with the Septuagint, would naturally infer the idea of sacrifice, they being used in the translation to denote sacrifice. The word translated "do," is in more than fifty places in the Scriptures translated "offer," which means offer sacrifice. I will give a few examples of this use of the word:

LEV. 9:7. And Moses said unto Aaron, Go unto the Altar, and offer (ποίησον, poieson) the sin offering, and thy burnt offering, and make an atonement for thyself, and for the people: and offer (ποίησον, poieson) the offering of the people, &c.

IB. 23:19. Then ye shall sacrifice (ποιήσουσι, poiesousi) one kid of the goats for a sin offering, &c.

NUM. 10:10. . . . and over the sacrifices of your peace offerings; that they may be for a memorial (ἀνάμνησις, anamnesis) before your God.

See LEV. 2:5, 9; 4:20; 24:7; JOSHUA 22:23; Ps. 66:15; HEB. 11:28.

## VI.

# Reverence for God's House.

IN LEVITICUS 19:30, GOD says:

"Ye shall . . . reverence My sanctuary: I am the Lord."

From the earliest times, the greatest reverence has been bestowed upon God's House by Jews and Christians alike. Moses and

Aaron did reverence at the door of the Tabernacle (NUM. 20: 6), and King Hezekiah and those with him bowed and worshipped before the Altar (2 CHRON. 29: 29). Nothing appears so irreverent to a Churchman, as to see men in the various bodies around the Church, go into meeting with their hats on, and kept on sometimes even after they have taken their seats. The Puritans invented this irreverent custom for the purpose of showing outward disrespect to the House of God, claiming that reverence should be inward and in the heart, and not consist in outward ceremonies.

But bodily worship was practised among the Jews:

2 CHRON. 29:29. And when they had made an end of offering, the king and all that were present with him bowed themselves, and worshipped."

Ps. 95:6. "Oh come, let us worship and bow down: let us kneel before the Lord our Maker.

CANON 18, of CANONS OF 1603-4, directs that:

No man shall cover his head in the Church or Chapel, in the time of Divine Service, except he have some infirmity; in which case let him wear a nightcap or coif. PAGE 26.

CONVOCATION in 1661, ordered:

"That all men, at their entrance into the Church, or Chapel, or any other place of public worship, shall in honour of Almighty God, Who is there served, reverently uncover their heads, and so continue all the time of the Divine service, sermon, or homily." CAN. 3, P. 575. WILK. CONC. T. 4.

## Bowing towards the Altar.

IT is also an ancient Christian custom to slightly bow towards the Altar upon entering and leaving the Church. In England, when a Peer of the Realm passes in or out of the Throne Room in Parliament, he bows to the throne, even when the Monarch is absent. If such reverence is shown to an earthly Ruler, how much more should it be shown to the King of Kings! By her Canons, the Church of England leaves such practices to every man's discretion. See also the Rubric to the Prayer Book of 1549, cited on page 185.

1565.] JOHN JEWELL, BISHOP OF SALISBURY. In reply to HARDING, who says:

"This requisite assent and conforming of themselves to the

priests they declare by sundry outward tokens and gestures: . . . by bowing themselves down and adoring at the sacrament, . . . and by other like signs of devotion in other parts of the service."

JEWELL replies:

"Kneeling, bowing, standing up and other like, are commendable gestures and tokens of devotion, so long as the people understandeth what they mean, and applieth them unto God, to whom they be due." REPLY UNTO M. HARDING'S ANSWER, ART. 3, DIV. 29, P. 96, 97. VOL. 2.

1634.] THEOPHILUS FIELD, BISHOP OF ST. DAVID'S. "Then the Chaplain cometh forth, and making a low obeisance, turns and stands before the Table." FORM AND ORDER OF THE CONSECRATION OF ABBEY DORE, P. 21.

1635.] PETER HAUSTED. "But our *bowing before the Altar*, towards the *East* end of the Church, troubles our *standing Pharisees* very much.

"It is a scandall and an ignorance, grosse as Ægyptian darkness, which may be felt, to say that we *bow* to the *Altar* or *Table*: No, we *bow* to *God*, and the having that Table in my sight when I bow (putting me in minde of the mercies and Sufferings of my Saviour) cannot chuse but make me bow the lower.

"But I heare another object. Will not *presently Kneeling* downe in my seate when I come into the Church, and saying a *private Prayer* lifting up a *private Ejaculation* to the Lord, serve the turne, without first bowing and prostrating my selfe before the Altar?

"I answer; doe but so, and no man shall finde fault with thee: thou doest well in doing it, but yet he who does the other too, and does it truly from his heart, and withall knows the reason why he does it, does a great deale better.

"And this very method doe we observe at our entrance into God's House: we do not immediately fall downe to our Prayers, for that were to worship God in respect of *our selves*: but first of all before we come to lay any *claime* unto him by *our Prayers*, we humbly prostrate our selves before the Altar, as acknowledging him to be the *great God*." SERMONS. SERM. 10, P. 216, 221, 222, 223, 224.

This book was licensed Nov. 10, 1635, by William Bray, Domestic Chaplain of the Archbishop of Canterbury.

Circa 1636.] JOHN COSIN, afterwards BISHOP OF DURHAM. "Denieth any frequent bowing at all to the said table, and holdeth it altogether unlawful to be done. But hath used gesture of humility, abbaisance, or bowing of the body at going out or coming into the church in reverence to God Almighty, as he found it in practice at his first coming thither, and as he hath been credibly informed constantly used for diverse years before, by the Bishop, Dean, and prebendaries that were there, and hath been since approved and practiced by all their successors. Never required or moved any one thereto." ACTS OF THE HIGH COM. COURT OF DURHAM, P. 217, 218, APP. A., SURTEES SOC. PUBL. VOL. 34.

1640.] CANONS OF 1640. "Whereas the Church is the House

of God, dedicated to His holy worship, and therefore ought to mind us both of the greatness and goodness of His Divine Majesty; certain it is that the acknowledgment thereof, not only inwardly in our hearts, but also outwardly with our bodies, must needs be pious in itself, profitable unto us, and edifying unto others. We therefore think it very meet and behoveful, and heartily commend it to all good and well-affected people, members of this Church, that they be ready to tender unto the Lord the said acknowledgment, by doing reverence and obeysance, both at their coming in and going out of the said Churches, Chancels, or Chapels, according to the most ancient custom of the Primitive Church in the purest times, and of this Church also, for many years of the reign of Queen Elizabeth. The reviving therefore of this ancient and laudable custom we heartily commend to the serious consideration of all good people, not with any intention to exhibit any religious worship to the Communion Table, the East, or Church, or anything therein contained in so doing, or to perform the said gesture in the celebration of the Holy Eucharist, upon any opinion of a corporal presence of the Body of Jesus Christ on the Holy Table, or in the mystical elements, but only for the advancement of God's majesty, to give Him alone that honour and glory that is due unto Him, and no otherwise: and in the practice or omission of this rite, we desire that the rule of charity prescribed by the Apostle may be observed, which is, that they which use this rite, despise not them who use it not; and they who use it not, condemn not those that use it." CAN. 7, P. 550. WILK. CONC., T. 4.

Circa 1660.] AN EXPEDIENT HUMBLY PRESENTED TO THE KING AND PARLIAMENT FOR THE HAPPY SETTLEMENT OF ECCLESIASTICAL AFFAIRS. "Doubtless the Papists have as much ground for Holywater, as we for bowing before an Altar." PAGE 43.

1665-6.] SAMUEL PEPYS. "It [St. George's Chapel] is a noble place indeed, and a good Quire of voices. Great bowing by all the people, the poor Knights in particularly, to the altar." DIARY, FEB. 26, P. 370. VOL. 2.

1716.] CHARLES OWEN. "3. BOWING and cringing to the East and Altar, is a Practice nowhere commanded by the Church, and yet nothing more frequent among your Ceremonialists, those pretended Monopolizers of Decency and Order." PLAIN-DEALING, &c., C. 2, P. 37.

1725-1776.] HENRY BOURNE published his ANTIQUITATES VULGARES at Newcastle, in 1725. He says:

"We may observe the generality of old people among the commonalty, as they enter into the church, to turn their faces towards the altar, and bow or kneel that way. This no doubt is the remains of that ancient custom of the church of worshipping towards the east. For in the ancient church they worshipped that way upon several accounts." ANTIQ. VULG., C. 5, P. 44.

In 1776 JOHN BRAND republished this book with OBSERVATIONS, &c.:

"We may add to Mr. Bourne's remarks, that the custom is *still* retained in many churches, of turning to the altar while the congregation are repeating the creed.—The forms are both derived to us from the same origin. We need not hesitate to pronounce as well the *bowings* as the *turnings about* to the east, or altar, to be superstitious. . . . I have observed this practice in college chapels at Oxford." PAGE 50, 51.

1838.] FORM AND ORDER OF THE CONSECRATION OF QUEEN VICTORIA. "The Queen in the mean time passes up through the Body of the Church. . . . She makes Her humble Adoration, and then kneeling at the Faldstool," &c. SECT. 1, P. 4.

1842.] CHARLES JAMES BLOMFIELD, BISHOP OF LONDON. "Although I do not consider the Canons of 1640 to be binding upon the Clergy, I see no very serious objection to the custom therein commended, as having been the ancient custom of the Primitive Church, and of this also for many years in the reign of Queen Elizabeth, of doing obeisance on entering and leaving Churches and Chancels; not, as the Canon expressly declares, 'with any intention to exhibit any religious worship to the Communion-table, the East, or Church, or anything therein contained, in so doing, or to perform the said gesture in the celebration of the Holy Eucharist from any opinion of the corporal presence of the Body of Christ upon the Holy Table, or in the mystical elements, but only for the advancement of God's glory, to give Him alone that honour and glory that are due unto Him, and no otherwise.' But that the Clergy, although they are at liberty to use this custom, are not obliged to do so, even if that Canon be in force, is clear from the words of the Canon itself, which heartily commends, but does not enjoin it. . . . If those persons, who practice these obeisances towards the Holy Table, do so under the notion of a bodily presence of Christ in the consecrated elements, or if the people are led to suppose them to do so, then I consider the custom to be objectionable, and at variance with our Reformed Church. If otherwise, the Clergy, who observe it, are bound to explain it to the people in the sense in which it is explained by the Canon." CHARGE TO THE CLERGY OF THE DIOCESE OF LONDON, 1842, P. 27, 28.

1843.] HENRY PHILPOTTS, BISHOP OF EXETER. "'The bowings to the altar' may be the bowings recommended in the seventh canon of the synod of 1604, which says that, 'Whereas the church,' &c. Now if 'the bowings to the altar' enumerated among your 'grievances' be of this kind, I must decline issuing any directions to the rector which may induce him to discontinue them. I do not understand that he attempts to impose them on his people. He performs them, it seems, himself, thereby exercising his christian liberty, with which I have no right or inclination to interfere. I do not indeed practice this obeisance myself, 'in coming in and going out of church,' but I respect the freedom of others, and I from my heart subscribe to the wise and charitable language with which the canon last cited by me concludes,—'In the practice or omission of this rite, we desire that the rule of charity prescribed by the Apostle may be observed, which is, that they which use this rite despise not them which use it not; and that they who use it not, condemn not those who use it.'" REPLY TO A MEMORIAL OF THE INHABITANTS OF FALMOUTH. ENGLISH CHURCHMAN, No. 29, p. 450. Cited in HIERURGIA, p. 63.

## VII.

## The People Kneeling.

OBSERVE, the Rubric requires the people to kneel, not stoop, as is too generally the custom. CANON 18 of the CANONS OF 1603-4, thus expresses it:

"All persons then present shall reverently kneel upon their knees." PAGE 26.

Infirmity, or some error in the construction of the pews, may sometimes prevent us from obeying this Rubric, but unless reasonably hindered, we should always strictly observe it. A kneeling congregation appears reverent. But if a congregation sits, looks about, or engages in whispering, while Prayer is being offered to Almighty God, it looks as if the people took very little interest, or had very little faith in their worship.

## VIII.

## The Apostles' or Nicene Creed.

ARTICLE VIII. declares that—

"The Nicene Creed, and that commonly called the Apostle's Creed, ought thoroughly to be received and believed."

The custom of turning to the Altar when saying the Creed is a very ancient one in the Church, and is a very common practice in every Low Church Cathedral, and in many Parish Churches in England.

## I. Bowing at the Name of Jesus.

**S**T. Paul tells us—

"That at the Name of Jesus every knee should bow, of things in heaven, and things in earth, and things under the earth." Phil. 2:10.

Surely, if the Angels in Heaven bow at Jesus' adorable name, we on earth cannot refuse Him like homage when we are openly confessing Him to be the true and eternal Son of God! This reverent custom has been handed down in the Church from Apostolic times. It was enjoined by Queen Elizabeth in her Injunctions of 1559:

"Whensoever the name of Jesus shall be in any lesson, sermon, or otherwise in the church pronounced, that due reverence be made of all persons young and old, with lowness of curtsey, and uncovering of heads of the menkind, as thereunto doth necessarily belong, and heretofore hath been accustomed." Cardwell, Doc. Ann., n. 43, p. 231.

Canon 18, of Canons of 1603–4, orders that—

"When in time of Divine Service the Lord Jesus shall be mentioned, due and lowly reverence shall be done by all persons present, as it hath been accustomed." Page. 26.

Observe, that by this Canon we are required to reverence the Name of Jesus whenever spoken, and not merely in the Creed. This custom was at first in use among the Calvinists.

1572.] Thomas Cartwright thus scurrilously speaks of the custom of the Church in his time:

"When Jesus is mentioned, then off goeth the cap, and down goeth the knees, with such a scraping on the ground that they cannot hear a good while after." An Admonition, &c. Cited by Whitgift, Defence of the Answer, &c. Tract. 21, c. 7, 2d Div., p. 384. Vol. 3.

Bowing at the *Gloria* is another very ancient custom of the Church, introduced some fifteen hundred years since, when the false doctrine of the Arians, who denied the eternal Godhead of the Son, began to prevail. It is also enjoined by an ancient Canon of the Church of England.

## II. The Word Catholic.

**O**UR Divine Master, when upon earth, established a visible Church, against which the gates of Hell should not prevail (Matt. 16:18), which was to be the teacher of mankind, and to last forever. This Church has ever been known by the name of Catholic, a word derived from the Greek καθολικός (katholikos), which means general or universal, because our Lord intended it to be the one and only Church, and to embrace all mankind within its fold. St. POLYCARP, the disciple of St. John, and a Martyr of the second century, while on his way to death, begged a few moments to pray for the "whole Catholic Church throughout the world,—ἁπάσης τῆς κατὰ τὴν οἰκουμένην καθολικῆς ἐκκλησίας." MART., c. 8, p. 280.

The Denominations which have separated from the Church have invariably named themselves after their founders or leaders, or after some particular doctrine to which they give special prominence. But the Church has always retained the venerable name of Catholic. By not adhering to this name, we have furnished Romanists with the charge of inconsistency against us. Thus MILNER speaks of some members of the Church of England:

"Every time they address the God of truth, either in solemn worship or in private devotion, they are forced, each of them, to repeat: I believe in the Catholic Church; and yet if I ask any of them the question; Are you a Catholic? he is sure to answer me: No, I am a Protestant! Was there ever a more glaring instance of inconsistency and self-condemnation among rational beings!" END OF CONTROVERSY, LET. 25, P. 158.

There is all the difference in the world between Catholic and Roman Catholic. A Catholic, following the famous rule of VINCENTIUS of Lerins, believes "that which has been believed everywhere, always, and by all,—quod ubique, quod semper, quod ab omnibus creditum est." (COMMONIT., c. 2, COL. 640. PAT. LAT. T. 50.) But a Roman Catholic, we may know what he believes to-day, but we cannot tell what he will be ordered to believe to-morrow. In KEENAN'S DOCTRINAL CATECHISM, published some years since, and approved by Archbishop Hughes, of New York, as well as by two Vicars Apostolic in Scotland, you will find, on PAGE 305, this Question and Answer:

"*Q. Must not Catholics believe the Pope in himself to be infallible?*
"*A.* This is a Protestant invention; it is no article of the Catholic faith."

There is a later edition, published by the "London Catholic Publishing Co." In C. 9, N. 2, P. 112, this Question and Answer is quietly dropped.

And yet, would you believe it! this very "Protestant invention," was in 1870 made an "article of the [Roman] Catholic faith." So with the doctrine of the Immaculate Conception, made an Article of faith in 1854, of which, together with some other doctrines, MILNER said a few years ago, that the Roman Catholic Church did not define them as articles of faith,—

"Because she sees nothing absolutely clear and certain concerning them either in the written or the unwritten word."

In the Roman Church there is now no certainty of Belief. The rule of Vincentius has been discarded, and what is heresy to-day, may be an Article of faith to-morrow. Their latest novelty, strongly advocated by Archbishop Manning, is the worship of the Sacred Heart.

The name of Protestant was at first given to those Lutherans who protested against a certain decree put forth by the Diet of Spires in 1529. In 1817, the Prussian Government prohibited the further use of the term Protestant, as being obsolete and unmeaning. and substituted for it Evangelical. The name was afterwards imported into England by the Marian exiles, and at length, with many, came to mean a member of the Church of England, in distinction from a Roman Catholic, or a Dissenter. But now it includes the aggregate of all heresy and unbelief. In Convocation, in 1689, the Lower House refused to acknowledge any connection between the Protestant Churches in general and the Church of England. CARD., HIST. OF CONF., c. 10, N. 5, P. 444-451; LATHBURY, HIST. OF THE CONVOC., C. 11, P. 273-275.

Any one who hates the belief and practice of the primitive Church is a Protestant. If a man professes to be a Protestant, we cannot tell whether he is a free-thinking Unitarian, a Universalist, a Swedenborgian, a Spiritualist, or an Orthodox Congregationalist. If he declares himself to be a Catholic, no matter whether he is a Greek, Roman or Anglican, we know this much for certainty, that he believes in our Lord's Divinity, in His one Holy Church, in the Priesthood, in certain Sacraments, &c. Let Protestants first agree among themselves as to what they believe, before they attempt to teach others. Some Protestants believe in the Trinity and everlasting punishment; others believe that Christ was a mere man, and that all sin is punished in this world. Some attach a high value to the Sacraments, while others do not regard them at all. Both cannot be right. In the mere matter of ceremonies, we find the same diversity of opinion. The Protestants of Germany, Denmark, Norway and Sweden, (which latter country is so intensely Protestant, that, till within a few years, a Roman Catholic was not allowed to publicly exercise his religion,) still enjoy the Vestments, Crucifixes, Crosses, Altars, Altar Lights, the Mass, Wafer Bread, &c., all of which are an abomination to other Protestants. It will be found that education,—or rather the want of education,—natural prejudice, and custom, have a great deal to do in making a thing seem to be right or wrong.

## III. Belief in the Creed.

LOW Churchmen profess to hold the Articles in high esteem. ARTICLE VIII. declares that the Creeds are to be "thoroughly," not partially, "received and believed." In the Creed we profess to believe "one," not three or four different Denominations, but "one Catholic and Apostolic Church;" in the Litany, we pray for deliverance from "all false doctrine, heresy and schism;" on Good Friday, we pray God to "have mercy upon "Infidels," that is, those who do not believe in Christianity at all, "and Heretics," that is, those who hold doctrines condemned by the Church; in GAL. 1:8, we hear the Apostle Paul twice repeating: "But though we, or an Angel from Heaven, preach any other Gospel unto you than that which we have preached unto you, let him be accursed," and again, telling us in TITUS 3:10: A man that is a heretic, after the first and second admonition, reject;"— (See also ROM. 16:17; GAL. 5:19-21; EPH. 5:11; 1 TIM. 6:3-5; 2 PET. 2:1; 2 JOHN 10:11; REV. 2:15;)—and yet people who call themselves Churchmen, tell us that it makes no difference what a man believes. Why then did our Lord found a Church at all, and not rather leave every man free to profess whatever religion best suited him? If a person does not believe in the Church, why does he come into it or remain in it for the respectability it may give him, constantly annoying others who do believe in it, and misrepresenting its teaching? Such conduct would not be regarded as being honest in any Society outside of the Church.

## IX.
## Notice of Holy Days.

THE Rubric orders:

"Then the Minister shall declare unto the people what Holy days, or Fasting days, are in the week following to be observed."

Some of the Clergy persistently violate this plain Rubric. They not only refuse to observe the appointed Days, but do not even give notice of their occurrence. There is a "Table of Feasts to be observed in this Church throughout the year;" as also a "Table of Fasts," given in the Preface to the Prayer Book.

## X.

# "Then Shall Follow the Sermon."

**FIRST.** The Sermon is directed to follow the Creed. There is, therefore, no Rubrical authority for a Hymn before the Sermon. It only has the sanction of custom. The House of Bishops, in 1814, permitted Anthems taken from Scripture to be sung in Church at the discretion of the Minister:

"Anthems taken from Scripture, and judiciously arranged, may, according to the allowance of this Church, be sung in congregations at the discretion of their ministers." JOURNAL OF THE GENERAL CONVENTION, P. 434, 435. VOL. 1.

The General Convention of 1874 passed this Canon:

"The selections of the Psalms in metre and Hymns which are set forth by authority, and Anthems in the words of Holy Scripture, are allowed to be sung in all congregations of this Church, before and after Morning and Evening Prayers, and also before and after Sermons, at the discretion of the Minister, whose duty it shall be by standing directions, or from time to time, to appoint such authorized Psalms, Hymns, or Anthems, as are to be sung." *Daily Churchman*, P. 228.

Authorized Hymns, Psalms, and Anthems can now be sung during any part of the Service at the discretion of the Minister.

**Second.** There is no authority whatever for putting on a Black Gown at the Sermon. Such a garment is nowhere mentioned in any of the Rubrics of any of the Prayer Books. It is only an Academical dress, introduced into the Church by graduates, or in a spirit of opposition to the Church.

## XI.
## Presentation of Offerings.

THE Rubric orders that fit persons shall receive the Offerings of the people in a decent Basin, "and reverently bring it to the Priest, who shall humbly present and place it upon the Holy Table." The Rubric requires the Offerings not only to be "placed" upon the Altar, but to be "presented" as well. To merely "place" them carelessly and indifferently, as is the usual custom, is not sufficient, and does not meet the requirements of the Rubric. The Priest, therefore, on behalf of the people, who then rise,—it being their gift,—"humbly presents" the Offerings to God by elevating them, and then "places" them upon the Holy Table. Formerly it was customary to stand during the whole Offertory, but the House of Bishops, in 1832, thought it more fitting for "The Sentences of the Offertory to be heard sitting, as the most favorable posture for handing alms, &c., to the person officiating."

## XII.
## Invitation to the Holy Communion.

THERE is no authority whatever for extending an invitation, here or elsewhere, to any one, whether strangers or members of "other Denominations," to partake of the Communion, except what follows in the regular service. The Rubric at the end of the Order for Confirmation peremptorily and expressly says:

"And there shall none be admitted to the Holy Communion, until such time as he be confirmed, or be ready and desirous to be confirmed."

This leaves the Priest no discretion. The Rubric may be very illiberal, but still it is the law, and the Priest cannot break it without violating his Ordination vows. If, however, such persons should present themselves, he is to receive them for the time, if he knows nothing against their character, not knowing the motives which led them to take the step, but he must confer with them as soon as possible, and inform them how the case stands. If they are unwilling to submit to so simple a Rite as Confirmation, to which all the children of the Church are obliged to submit, they have no one to blame but themselves if they are debarred from one of the Sacraments of the Church. No one but a Mason is entitled to a Masonic funeral, no matter how good a man he is. The cases are precisely similar.

We notice a double violation here. First, in giving any invitation at all; and, secondly, in inviting when the Church forbids.

## XIII.

# Placing the Elements upon the Altar.

THE Rubric directs:

"And the Priest shall then place upon the Table so much Bread and Wine as he shall think sufficient."

The Rubric requires the priest to "then," that is, after presenting the offerings, and not before the service begins, as is the practice of some, place the Elements upon the Holy Table. Those who do otherwise, violate a plain Rubric.

## I. The Mixed Chalice.

THE Rubric to the Prayer Book of 1549, orders the "putting thereto [the Chalice] a little pure and clean water." This was the universal practice of the whole Christian Church from our Lord's time down. JUSTIN MARTYR, in his APOLOGY for the Christians, directed to the Roman Emperor Antoninus Pius, N. 65, 67, COL. 428, 429. PAT. GR. T. 6., speaks of this custom.

1618.] LANCELOT ANDREWES, BISHOP OF WINCHESTER. See his testimony cited on page 178.

1619.] JOHN COSIN, afterwards BISHOP OF DURHAM. "Our church forbids it not, for aught I know, and they that think fit may use it as some most eminent among us do at this day." NOTES ON

THE BOOK OF COMMON PRAYER. 1ST SERIES, P. 154. WORKS, VOL. 5.

1634.] FORM AND ORDER OF THE CONSECRATION AND DEDICATION OF THE PARISH CHURCH OF ABBEY DORE. "Then layeth he [the Bishop] the Bread on the paten, and poureth of the Wine into the chalice, and a little water into it," &c. PAGE 29.

1710.] CHARLES WHEATLY. "And indeed it must be confessed, that the mixture has in all ages, been the general practice, and for that reason was enjoined, as has been noted above to be continued in our own Church, by the first reformers. And though in the next review the order for it was omitted, yet the practice of it was continued in the king's chapel royal, all the time that bishop Andrews was dean of it; who also in the form that he drew up for the consecration of a church, &c., expressly directs and orders it to be used." RATIONAL ILLUST. OF THE BOOK OF COMMON PRAYER, C. 6, SECT. 10, P. 281.

1832.] WILLIAM PALMER. "In the English Church it has never been forbidden or prohibited; for the rubric which enjoins the Priest to place bread and wine on the table, does not prohibit him from mingling water with that wine." ORIG. LITURG., C. 4, SECT. 9, P. 76. VOL. 2.

The Rubric in the Scotch Office, is:

"The Presbyter shall then offer, and place the Bread and Wine prepared for the Sacrament upon the Lord's Table."

Prepared, means mixed with water, and the practice of the Scotch Church since 1637, has been to mix water with the Sacramental wine.

## II. Wafer Bread.

WAFER BREAD was ordered by the Prayer Book of 1549. Those of 1552, 1559, and the present English Prayer Book, declare that common bread of the best quality shall suffice, where the people are contentious or superstitious. Our American Prayer Book gives no direction whatever on this point.

The Rubric to the Order of Communion of 1548 is as follows:

"Note, that the Bread that shall be consecrated shall be such as heretofore hath been accustomed. And every of the said consecrated Breads shall be broken in two pieces, at the least, or more by the discretion of the Minister, and so distributed." PAGE 8.

The Rubric to the Prayer Book of 1549, is:

"For avoiding of all matters and occasion of dissension, it is meet that the bread prepared for the Communion be made, through all this realm, after one sort and fashion: that is to say, unleavened, and round, as it was afore, but without all manner of print, and something more larger and thicker than it was, so that it may be aptly divided in diverse pieces:" &c. PAGE 97.

The Rubric of the Prayer Book of 1552, is:

"And to take away the superstition, which any person hath, or might have in the bread and wine, it shall suffice that the bread be such, as is usual to be eaten at the table with other meats, but the best and purest wheat bread, that conveniently may be gotten." PAGE 283.

The Rubric of the Book of 1559 is the same as that of 1552, and the present English Prayer Book differs from it only at the beginning:

"And to take away all occasion of dissension, and superstition, which," &c.

By the Rubric, both Common Bread and Wafer Bread can be used.

1559.] The INJUNCTIONS of Queen Elizabeth order the Communion Bread to be—

"Somewhat bigger in compass and thickness, as the usual bread and wafer, hertofore named singing cakes, which served for the use of the private mass." CARD. DOC. ANN., N. 43, P. 234. VOL. 1.

1560.] PETER MARTYR. "With regard to the unleavened bread which is used at the holy Supper, none of our [Calvinistic] churches, as you are well aware, have any contention about it, nay indeed, they all everywhere make use of it." EP. 17, TO SAMPSON, P. 40. Z. L. 2D.

1566.] MILES COVERDALE AND OTHERS. "It is now settled and determined, that an unleavened cake must be used in place of common bread." EP. 50, P. 121. IB.

———.] PERCEVAL WIBURN. "In the administration of the [Lord's] supper, for the greater reverence of the sacrament, little round unleavened cakes are re-introduced by the queen, which had heretofore been removed by the public laws of the realm, for the taking away superstition." STATE OF THE CHURCH OF ENGLAND, N. 28, P. 361. APP. IB.

1570-1.] MATTHEW PARKER, ABP. OF CANTERBURY. "For it is a matter of much contention in the realm: where most part of protestants think it [the Communion] most meet to be in wafer-bread, as the injunction prescribeth; divers others, I cannot tell of what spirit, would have the loaf-bread, &c.

"I tell them that they do evil to make odious comparison betwixt statute and injunction, and yet I say and hold, that the injunction hath authority by proviso of the statute. And whereas it is said in the rule [Rubric], 'that to take away the superstition which any person hath or might have in the bread and wine, it shall suffice that the bread and wine shall be such as is usually to be eaten at the table with other meats, &c.;' 'it shall suffice,' I expound, where either there wanted such fine usual bread, or superstition be feared in the wafer-bread, they may have the communion in fine usual bread: which is rather a toleration in these two necessities, than is in plain ordering, as in the injunction.

"This I say to shew you the ground which hath moved me and others to have it in the wafer-bread; a matter not greatly material, but only obeying the Queen's Highness, and for that the most part of her subjects disliketh the common bread for the sacrament." EP. 283, TO CECIL, P. 375, 376. P. C.

1572.] THOMAS CARTWRIGHT. See his testimony, and also that of Whitgift, cited on page 148.

1573.] JOHN PARKHURST, BISHOP OF NORWICH. There arose in this Diocese a violent dispute as to the use of Wafer Bread or Common Bread. The Bishop wrote to Parker, January 21 :

"Shewing him, how men were hereby in doubt what to do; especially remembering what the Queen had said to the Archbishops and other Bishops, when they had been not long before in her presence, in exposition, as it seems, of her own injunctions; which was in effect to continue the use of the wafer-bread. And accordingly, in obedience hereto, he did use that sort of bread in his church at Ludham." STRYPE, LIFE OF PARKER, B. 4, C. 35, P. 343. VOL. 2.

Archbishop PARKER, May 17, 1574, replied as follows:

"You would needs be informed by me whether I would warrant you either loaf-bread or wafer-bread, and yet you know the Queen's pleasure. You have her injunctions, and you have also the servicebook; and furthermore, because I would deal brotherly with you, I wrote in my last letters, how I used in my diocese for peace sake and quietness." EP. 351, P. 458. P. C.

And again June 14:

"And as for their contention for wafer-bread and loaf-bread, if the order you have taken will not suffice them, they may fortune hereafter to wish they had been more conformable: although I trust that you mean not universally in your diocese to command or wink at the loaf-bread, but, for peace and quietness, here and there to be contented therewith." EP. 353, P. 460. IB.

1580.] See the testimony of the Jesuit SANDERS, as to the general use of Wafer Bread in the Church of England, cited on page 41.

Circa 1640.] JOHN COSIN, afterwards BISHOP OF DURHAM. "*And to take away superstition*, &c." It is not here commanded that no unleavened bread or wafer-bread be used, but is said only 'that the other bread shall suffice.' So that though there was no necessity, yet there was a liberty still reserved of using wafer-bread, which was continued in divers churches of the kingdom, and Westminster for one, till the 17th of King Charles." NOTES ON THE BOOK OF COMMON PRAYER, 3d SERIES, P. 481. WORKS, VOL. 5.

WAFER BREAD WAS USED BY THE CALVINISTS AT GENEVA, AND AMONG ALL THE REFORMED UPON THE CONTINENT AT THAT TIME, AND BY THE LUTHERANS TO THIS DAY.

On the subject of Wafer Bread the people of Geneva had a dispute with Calvin, and at last drove him from the city. He became wiser in his exile, and persuaded his friends who remained in the city to make no more contention on a matter of indifference, and the use of Wafers was continued without further opposition.

COSIN remarks:

"The first use of the common bread was begun by Farel and Viret at Geneva, 1538, which so offended the people there, and their neighbors at Lausanne and Berne, (who had called a synod about it) that both Farel and Viret, and Calvin and all, were banished for it from the town, where afterwards the wafer-bread being restored, Calvin thought fit to continue it, and so it is at this day. *Vid. Vitam Calvini per Bezam ad an.* 1538, *et Ep. Calv.*" NOTES ON THE BOOK OF COMMON PRAYER, 3D SERIES, P. 481. WORKS, VOL. 5.

1567.] AN EXAMINATION OF CERTAYNE LONDONNERS.

"*Bishop* [*Grindal*]. Howe say you to the Church of *Geneua?* They communicate with wafer cakes which you are so much against.

"*Nixson.* Yea but they doe not compell to receyue so, and with no other.

"*Bishop.* Yes in their parish churches.

"*W. Wh.* The English congregation did minister with loafe bread there.

"*Bishop.* Because they were of another language." PARTE OF A REGISTER, P. 29.

## XIV.

## Disposal of the Consecrated Elements.

IN the earlier Prayer Books there are no directions as to how the consecrated Elements which remain, are to be disposed of. The Rubric to our American Prayer Book, and that of the English Book is the same, reads:

"And if any of the consecrated Bread and Wine remain after the Communion, it shall not be carried out of the Church; but the

Minister and other Communicants shall, immediately after the Blessing, reverently eat and drink the same."

The Rubric, however, to the Communion of the Sick, in the Book of 1549, is:

"And if the same day there be a celebration of the Holy Communion in the church, then shall the Priest reserve (at the open Communion) so much of the sacrament of the body and blood, as shall serve the sick person, and so many as shall communicate with him (if there be any); and so soon as he conveniently may, after the open Communion ended in the church, shall go and minister the same, to those that are appointed to communicate with the sick (if there be any), and last of all to the sick person himself." PAGE 141.

In 1560, Queen Elizabeth put forth a Latin Prayer Book for the use of the Universities and the great public schools. Her letters patent call it a mere version of her English Book, (convenientem cum Anglicano nostro Publicarum precum libro. PAGE 301), but it differs from it in many places, with the intention, probably, of bringing back the observances of the Book of 1549, to which, it is known, she was much attached. This Book was the work of Walter Haddon, who, however, made great use of the version of Aless. In some places this Latin Book was not received with much favor, being styled "the Pope's Dreggs." The Rubric to the Communion of the Sick, is much the same as that of Edward VI.:

| | |
|---|---|
| Quod si contingat eodem die Coenam Domini in Ecclesia celebrari, tunc sacerdos in coena tantum sacramenti servabit, quantum sufficit aegroto: & mox finita coena, una cum aliquot ex his qui intersunt, ibit ad aegrotum, & primo communicabit cum illis, qui assistunt aegroto, & interfuerunt coenae, & postremo cum infirmo. COM. INFIRM., P. 404. | But if it shall happen that the Lord's Supper shall be celebrated upon the same day in the Church, then the Priest shall reserve at the Supper so much of the Sacrament, as shall suffice for the sick person; and straightway, when the Supper is finished, he shall go to the sick person with some of those who were present, and shall first communicate with those who assist the sick person, and were present at the Supper, and lastly with the sick person. |

The word Priest in this version is *Sacerdos*, the very worst word, from a Protestant stand-point, that could be used. The same word is also frequently used in the Communion Office.

The Rubric of the Scotch Office directs:

"According to the universal custom of the Church of Scotland, the Priest may reserve so much of the Consecrated Gifts as may be required for the communion of the sick, and others who could not be present at the Celebration in Church."

## XV.

# The Decisions of the Privy Council.

HAVING examined the Rubrics of the Communion Office, it seemed best to also examine the Decisions of the Privy Council, which have an important bearing on the subject, and which are very little understood, though we read so much about them in the papers. They were not made to interpret the law on certain doubtful points,—for the very persons who instigated them, and the very Judges who made them, do not regard or obey them,— but to "put down" a certain class of Churchmen. They are not only false in plain matters of fact and history, but are inconsistent with each other. A person could not obey them if he would. If he should obey one Decision, he would be sure to be condemned for violating another. Especially of the Purchas Judgment we may say that a greater perversion of justice never existed. In reviewing it we can have but one opinion, that the Judges were either grossly ignorant of the whole subject, or were too biased to render a just judgment, for we must acquit them of knowingly saying what is untrue. The very Bishops who complain most of the "lawlessness of the Ritualists," and persecute them most, do not obey the Judgment and wear a Cope, as commanded; the Low Church Clergy do not obey it, by giving up the Stole and Black Gown, and by wearing the Surplice in the Pulpit. One of the leading Evangelical Bishops thought it so unfair, that he told several of his Clergy, who were liable to prosecution, that he would not enforce it upon them.

The disregard which some Bishops have for their own Judgments is well illustrated in the case of Dr. HARVEY GOODWIN, Bishop of Carlisle. When Dean of Ely, he published a book entitled A GUIDE TO THE PARISH CHURCH. In it he stated that—

"'This rule,' that is, the Ornaments' Rubric, 'if carried out, would involve the use of several vestures of which the greater number of attendants at the Parish Church have never heard, such as the vestment, the cope, the tunicle, the albe; some of these are even now used upon very special occasions, and strictly speaking they ought to be used in all Parish Churches.'" Cited in the PREFACE TO THE NEW EDITION, P. IV, V.

This book having been cited by the Ritualists as authority on the subject of Vestments, the Bishop thereupon stated that his views had undergone a change, and put forth a new edition of his book, recalling the old! In it he gives no reason for his change of opinion, except that the Judicial Committee had declared that his "interpretation of the Ornaments Rubric, as above given, is incorrect," and that "my own examination of the subject has guided me to the conclusion, that the interpretation which the Courts have put upon the Ornaments' Rubric is most probably the true one." (PREFACE, P. VI.) That is, he has simply obeyed the ruling of the Court, which he thinks to be, not certainly, but most probably true. He then (P. 180, NEW ED.) says of the Stole, that it "is so generally worn . . . that it cannot be and will not be abolished." Yet he acknowledges that "the stole has been declared by high authority to be illegal." The same Court that pronounced the Vestments illegal, whose opinion the Bishop adopts, also pronounced the Stole to be illegal, but the Bishop does not in this case adopt their opinion for the simple reason, that, as it is a very popular garment, the use of it "will not be abolished," but will be retained in spite of the Court. That is, popularity takes the precedence of legality. The use of the Chasuble is not yet popular, and so it must be abolished. If it were popular, it would be retained, as is the Stole. Such inconsistency is shameful.

After the Mackonochie case, the Ritualists were generally giving up practices which they knew were lawful, for the sake of peace; but this Judgment convinced them, as well as High Churchmen, that an attempt was being made to crush them both out by all means, whether fair or foul, and so they resisted it. And yet for doing just what Low Churchmen did, they are called "lawless!"

## 1857.] *Liddell v. Westerton.*

(I.) "At the date of the First Prayer Book of Edward VI., the doctrine of the English Church as to the Real Presence and the nature of the Holy Communion was undecided; the book therefore spoke of the rite itself as the Lord's Supper, commonly called the High Mass." PRIVY COUNCIL JUDGMENTS, P. 68.

But the word "High" is not used at all. The title of that Book is, "The Supper of the Lord, and the Holy Communion, commonly called the Mass."

(II.) "But by the time when the Second Prayer Book was introduced, a great change had taken place in the opinion of the English Church. . . . The Prayer for consecration of the elements was omitted, though in the present Prayer Book it is restored." PAGES 68, 69.

But the Prayer was not omitted, although altered in some respects, and is precisely the same as in the present Book, with this trifling exception: "We most humbly beseech Thee," instead of "We beseech Thee."

This gross error of the Judges was immediately and mercilessly exposed by the public press, but without a single word of regret or acknowledgment, the blunder was amended in the Report by Brodrick and Freemantle, the last sentence being changed, and made to read as follows: "Material alterations were introduced into the Prayer of Consecration."

The Act of Uniformity authorizing the Book of 1552, calls the Book of 1549 "a very Godly order" for the "administration of the Sacraments, agreeable to the word of God." And yet we are now told that it contained "undecided" doctrine. We are told, further on, that the reason for the changes made is due to "the curiosity of the minister and other mistakers." (Page 34.) This is a very different reason from that given by the Judges.

1868.] **Martin v. Mackonochie.**

(III.) "The various stages of the Service ['at and after the Reformation'] are, as has already been shown, fenced and guarded by directions of the most exact kind as to standing and kneeling." PAGE 120.

Whereas in the first Book of Edward VI., no less than eight places, out of eleven requiring direction, are left without any at all; and about the same is true of the Books of 1552 and 1662. The Judges immediately enter upon a long argument to prove that the Celebrant is to kneel when he communicates himself, the Rubric being silent.

(IV.) "It is assumed that all [ceremonies] are abolished which are not expressly retained. ... The use of lighted candles, if a ceremonial act or part of a ceremony, would be prohibited by Queen Elizabeth's Act of Uniformity, 1 Eliz. c. 2, sec. 4, which is now applicable to the present Prayer Book, and which makes it penal to use any other rite, ceremony, order, form, or manner of celebrating the Lord's Supper ... than is mentioned and set forth in the said Book.

"The use of lights as a ceremony or ceremonial act, was abrogated or repealed by the Act 1 Eliz., c. 3, particularly by sec. 27, already mentioned, and by the present Prayer Book, and Act of Uniformity." PAGES 125, 126.

Unlighted Candles, and lighted ones when necessary for light, are legal. Mr. Mackonochie was condemned for—

"Using lighted candles on the Communion Table, during the

celebration of the Holy Communion, when such candles are not wanted for the purpose of giving light.

"There is a clear and obvious distinction between the presence in the church of things inert and unused, and the active use of the same things as a part of the administration of a sacrament, or of a ceremony." PAGES 122, 124.

But Lights, or lighted candles, as a ceremony, are ordered by Edward VI. and Archbishop Cranmer. They were ordered as an ornament in the "Ornaments" Rubric of 1559 and 1662 (pages 36, 77); and it was declared in Liddell *v.* Westerton, that—

"The same utensils or articles which were used under the First Prayer Book of Edward VI. may still be used." (Page 142.)

Lights were used by Elizabeth (see pages 125–130),—who would not have retained them if she had abrogated them,—and especially in Cathedrals, as late as the middle of the last century, and, for aught I know, much later. (See page 186–196.)

In Liddell *v.* Westerton, it is also said:

"In the performance of the services, rites, and ceremonies ordered by the Prayer Book, the directions contained in it must be strictly observed; that no omission and no addition can be permitted; but they are not prepared to hold that the use of all articles not expressly mentioned in the Rubric, although quite consistent with and even subsidiary to, the service is forbidden. Organs are not mentioned, yet, because they are auxiliary to the singing, they are allowed. Pews, cushions to kneel upon, pulpit-cloths, hassocks, seats by the Communion Table, are in constant use, yet they are not mentioned in the Rubric." PAGE 74.

In Martin *v.* Mackonochie, PAGE 128, the same opinion is affirmed. But cloths on the pulpit are no more auxiliary to the service, than Lights on the Altar. Both are merely ornaments. Cushions do not aid devotion, but only minister to comfort. Pews are of modern origin, and are not used by the Easterns. Organs are not regarded as auxiliary to singing, by the Scotch Presbyterians.

As the Judges themselves acknowledge that "omission" is not "prohibition" we will say nothing of a multitude of things in the Church, which are not directly prescribed. These may be found in two pamphlets, published by the Rev. C. S. Grueber, entitled: "'Omission' not 'Prohibition,'" and "How am I to perform Matins, Evensong, Holy Communion," &c. We will pass to a case right to the point. In 1573, Robert Johnson, an extreme Puritan, and Chaplain to the Lord Keeper Bacon, was accused before Elizabeth's Commissioners, comprising Sandys, Bishop of London; the Lord Chief Justice; Goodman, Dean of Westminster, and others. When celebrating the Communion, the Wine failing, he delivered to the people unconsecrated Wine, by omitting to repeat the words of Institution. The Prayer Book then contained no Rubric ordering more Bread and Wine to be consecrated if needful, the Priest being supposed to provide sufficient in the beginning. In defence of his conduct, Johnson urged that "the booke appointed no such order." When the Dean of Westminster said to him, "You are not forbidden in anie place to vse the repetition," he replied, "Neyther yet am I commanded." The Bishop of London's words are: "You stande stubburnlie against vs all, and no learning will satisfie you." He was thereupon pronounced guilty, and, to use his own words, "condemned to a yeares imprisonment." THE EXAMINATION OF MASTER R. JOHNSON, PARTE OF A REGISTER, P. 107, 108, 111.

CANON 14 of CANONS OF 1603-4 enjoins:

"All Ministers likewise shall observe the Orders, Rites, and Ceremonies, prescribed in the Book of Common Prayer, . . . without either diminishing in regard of preaching, or in any other respect, or adding anything in the matter or form thereof." PAGE 21.

Yet in CANON 21 it is ordered:

"Furthermore, no bread or Wine, newly brought, shall be used; but first the words of Institution shall be rehearsed, when the Bread and Wine be present upon the Communion-table." PAGE 31.

This direction was first inserted in the English Prayer Book in the form of a Rubric in 1662. Had omission been then regarded as prohibition, Johnson would have been acquitted. He only anticipated the Privy Council.

(v.) A distinction is made between the "Sacrificial Altar," previous to the Reformation, and the "Communion Table," after the Reformation. PAGE 126.

But "Sacrificial Altar," is never found in any Missal used in the Church of England previous to the Reformation, nor is "Communion Table" now used in the present Book.

1870-1.] *Hebbert v. Purchas.*

(VI.) "The Canons of 1603-4, adopting anew the reference to the Rubric of Edward VI., sanctioned in express terms all that the Advertisements had done in the matter of vestments, and ordered the Surplice only to be used in Parish Churches.

"They [the Judges] think that in prescribing the Surplice only, the Advertisements, meant what they said, the Surplice only." PAGES 176, 178.

The word "only" is not in the Advertisements or Canons at all, but was foisted into the text. This was an act of downright dishonesty, though it may have been unintentional. To insert such an important word in a legal document, would mislead any one If a mistake was made unintentionally, by confounding the Advertisements and Canons with the Rubric of 1552, where the word "only" is used, why not candidly acknowledge the mistake, especially when it has been so often pointed out by the press? A legal document should be strictly accurate. To condemn a man upon a misquotation, is not justice. The Advertisements and Canons are cited on pages 50, 76.

Besides, if the "Surplice only" is to be used, the Black Gown is clearly illegal.

(VII.) "The Bishops in their answer [at the Savoy Conference] show that they understand the Surplice to be in question, and not the vestments. . . . The Bishops determined that the Rubric should continue as it is. But after this they did, in fact, recast it entirely." PAGE 174.

The request of the Puritans and the answer of the Bishops may be found on pages 77-78, and any one can judge whether the Bishops understood that the Surplice only was in question. Such men as Cosin, Heylin, Sparrow, and others, would not have abandoned the Vestments. The Puritans say in effect: "The Rubric, if restored, will bring back the Vestments." The Bishops reply: "We are well aware of that, but for the reasons which we have given in our defence of ceremonies, we desire the Rubric to continue as it is." They allowed the very things to which the Puritans objected.

Again, the Bishops at the Savoy Conference, and the Committee appointed to revise the Prayer Book in 1662, were two different bodies, though many of the Bishops were members of both. (See page 79.) Many of the objections of the Presbyterians which were conceded at the Savoy Conference, were rejected by the Revision Committee. In fact, the Puritans complained that all Rubrical changes were made in a more Churchly direction.

The Rubrics of 1559, and 1662, are cited on pages 36 and 77. The reader can judge whether the Rubric was recast in an unchurchly direction. Had the Bishops intended to do away with the Vestments, they would have substituted a new Rubric, which would have abrogated them in plain language.

(VIII.) "If the Minister is ordered to wear a Surplice at all times of his ministration, he cannot wear an Albe and Tunicle when assisting at the Holy Communion; if he celebrate the Holy Communion in a Chasuble, he cannot celebrate in a Surplice." PAGES 178, 179.

Except in the Rubric of 1552, the Minister is not "ordered to wear a Surplice in all times of his ministration." The word "Surplice" is interpolated. By the Rubric of 1549, to which we are referred in that of 1559, and that of 1662, it is enacted that the Clergy shall wear at the "ministration of the Holy Communion, ... a white Albe plain, with a Vestment or Cope." Instead of an Alb, a Surplice was sometimes used under the Chasuble. In another Rubric of 1549 (page 29), the Bishop is ordered to wear " besides his Rochette, a Surplice or Albe, and a Cope or Vestment."

(IX.) "With regard to the suggestion attributed to the House of Lords 'whether the Rubric should not be mended where all vestments in time of Divine Service are not commanded which were used by Edward VI.' (Cardwell, Conferences, p. 274), the learned Judge has overlooked the fact that this applies to the earlier Rubric; and the suggestion did not emanate from the House of Lords, nor was it ever adopted by that body. And the learned Judge omits to observe, that the Rubric of James, which was objected to, was amended after the suggestion." PAGE 175.

But in Liddell *v.* Westerton, in was decided that both Rubrics "obviously mean the same thing." (PAGE 53.) By reference to page 77, it will be seen that both Houses of Parliament did adopt that suggestion. The citation from Cardwell is very inaccurately quoted, "not" is substituted for "now," and "by" is used instead of "2." The meaning is thereby exactly reversed.

(X.) "There does not appear to have been any return to the vestments in any quarter whatever.

"They [the Judges] have already observed that the Chasuble, Alb, and Tunicle were swept away with severe exactness in the time of Queen Elizabeth, and there was no trace of any attempt to revive them." PAGES 179, 182.

Why, then, did Dr. Wats, in 1640, say that the Alb had never been forbidden by any authority? (See page 134.) Why, then, did Parliament in 1641 regard the Vestments as "now commanded?" The citations on pages 117–150, many from Puritan writers, disprove this assertion. See testimony of Johnson, An Abridgment, &c., and Parker, cited on pages 123, 124, 131.

Chasubles were commonly used in Durham Cathedral as late as 1627. See pages 94, 133.

(XI.) "The Cope is to be worn in ministering the Holy Communion on high feast days in cathedral and collegiate churches, and the Surplice in all other ministrations." PAGE 183.

In 1857, in Liddell *v.* Westerton, Lord Cranworth, Lord Wensleydale, Mr. Pemberton Leigh, Sir John Patteson, Sir William Maule, Archbishop Sumner, and Dr. Tait, Bishop of London, but now Archbishop of Canterbury, decided:

"That the same dresses and the same utensils or articles which were used under the First Prayer Book of Edward VI. may still be used." Page 53.

In 1871, Lord Chelmsford, Lord Hatherly, Dr. Thomson, Archbishop of York, Dr. Jackson, Bishop of London, decided just the contrary, " that the same dresses may " not "still be used," and Mr. Purchas was punished for obeying the Decision of the same Court made in 1857. In excuse of such inconsistency, they say—

"That this question of the Vestments was not before the Court." Page 184.

Whether the question of Vestments was before the Court or not, does not affect the matter in the least. The Judges decided that the Vestments were legal, even though they went out of their way to do so.

The Archbishop of York does not wear a Cope, as commanded by his own Decision, though the Bishop of London does. Nor do the Low Church Bishops, or the Archbishop of Canterbury, who have so much to say about the disloyalty of others, wear them. If those in whose interest this Decision was made, do not obey it, how can they expect others to obey it, who know that it was made for the sole purpose of crushing them out, in utter disregard of the plainest facts of history, and of consistency itself?

(xii.) "The learned Judge in the Court below has decided that it is illegal to mix water with the wine at the time of the Service of Holy Communion; but he decides that water may be mixed with the wine ' provided that the mingling be not made at the time of the celebration.' (Law Rep., 3 Ad. and Eccl., p. 102.)
" But neither Eastern or Western Church, so far as the Committee is aware, has any custom of mixing water with wine apart from and before the Services." Page 185, 186.

Yet this very practice is the rule of the Eastern Church, and the custom of a great part of the Western Church. It was the practice of the Cathedrals, and Parish Churches of England under the Sarum Use, employed previous to the Reformation.

(xiii.) " As the learned Judge has decided the act of mingling water with the wine in the Service is illegal, the private mingling of the wine is not likely to find favour with any." Page 187.

So Mr. Purchas was condemned for obeying the Court below. Whether the practice of mingling water with the wine is illegal or not, it has the sanction of some great men in the Church of England. See pages 220–221.

(xiv.) " But it has been argued by some that the phrase ' it shall suffice,' implies a permission—that the words mean ' it shall be sufficient, but another usage is allowed, and might even be better.' On the other hand, it has been argued, that in other places in the

Liturgy, 'it shall suffice' must be construed into a positive direction; that if 'it shall suffice' to pour water on a sickly child, this ought to restrain the Clergyman from immersing a child known to be sickly; &c.

"Their Lordships are therefore inclined to think, . . . that the Rubric contains a positive direction to employ at the Holy Communion the usual bread." PAGES 189, 190.

Archbishop Parker, in 1570-1, (pages 222-223), expounded "it shall suffice," to mean that the common or usual bread, which it seems most people then disliked, was only to be tolerated in exceptional cases. Whitgift, afterwards Archishop of Canterbury, tells us that "Wafer-cakes be bread." See page 148.

(xv.) In Martin v. Mackonochie, in 1868, the Judges made this Decision:

"They think that the words, 'standing before the Table' apply to the whole sentence." PAGE 197.

Yet in the Purchas Judgment it was decided just the opposite:

"The learned Judge reads it as if it ran, 'They think that the words 'standing before the Table,' apply to the whole sentence, and that before the Table means between the Table and the people on the west side.' But these last words are a mere assumption. The question of position was not before their Lordships; if it had been no doubt the passage would be conceived differently and the question of position expressly settled." PAGE 198.

It was, therefore, decided that the Priest was to stand at the North end of the Table throughout the Communion Service.

No matter whether the "question of position" was before the Judges or not, they took the liberty to pass judgment upon it. To say that if it had been, they would have decided differently, is to impeach their honesty.

(xvi.) "Upon the whole, then, their Lordships think that the words of Archdeacon, afterwards Bishop, Cosin in A. D. 1687, expresses the state of the Law." PAGE 198.

Cosin died in 1672, and to make him an interpreter of the Rubric of 1662, which was not drafted till thirty-four years after his Visitation Articles, from which the Judges quote, is simply absurd. In the *Errata* we told that 1687 is a mistake for 1627. Nothing is easier than to make a mistake in figures, whether in printing or writing. But if we accept 1627 as the correct date, it does not help the matter any, for a man cannot interpret a Law long before it is made. Probably, by some mistake the date was incorrectly given, and as the language happened to meet the views of the Judges, they eagerly adopted it without noticing the error.

(xvii.) Mr. Purchas, being a poor man, was unable to procure counsel, and was therefore condemned upon an *ex parte* hearing.

After the trial, his friends furnished money to procure counsel. A Remonstrance to the Judgment was also published March 8, 1871, for signatures by the Clergy, which received 4,761 signatures. (See PERRY, NOTES, P. 444, 445.) He thereupon appealed, but his appeal was refused for these reasons:

"Considering the great public mischief which would arise on any doubt being thrown on the finality of the decision of the Judicial Committee, their Lordships are of opinion, that expediency requires that the prayer of the Petitions should not be acceded to, and that they should be refused with costs." PAGE 207.

That is, the Court condemned a man unheard, and then refused to allow him to defend himself, lest its dignity should suffer. Perhaps the Judges were aware by this time of the untenableness of their position. The only effect of these proceedings was to kill Mr. Purchas. But "Ritualism" must be "stamped out" at any cost!

## 1876.] Clifton and Others v. Ridsdale.

(XVIII.) This was the first suit under the Public Worship Regulation Act of 1874. Judgment was delivered by Lord Penzance, February 3, 1876. Mr. Ridsdale was condemned and ordered to desist from certain Ritualistic acts, but he preferred to obey the Church rather than a secular Judge.

## 1877.] Ridsdale v. Clifton and Others; or the Ridsdale Appeal Case.

(XIX.) Mr. Ridsdale appealed from the Decision of Lord Penzance. His case was again heard and Judgment delivered May 12, 1877:

"Their lordships will now proceed to consider the first charge against the appellant—namely, that of wearing an alb and chasuble. They will however premise that they do not propose to express any opinion upon the vestures proper to be worn by Bishops, as to which separate considerations may arise." PAGE 46, 47.

Why may "separate considerations" arise in the case of Bishops? In Hebbert v. Purchas they were required to wear Copes, but it is notorious that many of them, and some the very Assessors of this Court, transgress their own Judgment by not wearing the Cope as required. It would not sound very well to condemn those very Vestments as superstitious when worn by the inferior Clergy, which are enjoined upon the superior Clergy.

(xx.) When referring to the Ornaments Rubric of 1662, the Judges speak of it as the "rubric-note of 1662."

Why is this Rubric alone singled out as a "rubric-note?" It must be to cast a slur on its clear testimony, and to weaken its force by implying that its value is less than that of the other Rubrics in the Prayer Book.

(xxi.) The Judges maintain (PAGES 47, 54) that if the Ornaments Rubric is to be interpreted as it reads, without being explained away, every Clergyman celebrating the Holy Communion without the Vestments, is liable to heavy penalties. (See page 51). They also say:

"If the rubric is not imperative as to the alb, and the chasuble and cope, in the communion office, it cannot be imperative as to the surplice in the other services, or any of them." PAGE 47.

The Judges appear to forget that when the Presbyterians at the Savoy Conference in 1661, objected to the Rubric as bringing back the Vestments, the Bishops allowed the Rubric to remain, but the use of them was "to be left to the discretion of the ordinary." (See page 78). To be sure the Clergy may have been liable for the violation of the law, for neglect to enforce a law cannot repeal it; but as no one sought to enforce the law, they went unpunished. The law simply became a dead-letter, like many laws on the statute book. The Rubric itself is imperative, but has never been enforced, even as to the Surplice.

(xxii.) "But their lordships are clearly of opinion that the Advertisements . . . of Elizabeth, issued in 1566, were a taking of order, within the Act of Parliament, by the Queen, with the advice of the Metropolitan." PAGE 49.

Had the Queen signed the Advertisements, they would doubtless have been preserved among the State Papers, but it is believed that the only MS. copy in existence is that preserved among the papers of Archbishop Parker. See pages 50–76, where this matter is fully discussed.

(xxiii.) "After 1556 [1566?], vestments, albs, and tunicles, (copes also, in parish and non-collegiate churches) are mentioned in the official acts of the Bishops and others, performed in the public exercise of their legal jurisdiction, only as things associated with superstition, and to be defaced and destroyed." PAGE 52.

Why after 1566? The Vestments—Surplices and Copes, as well as Chasubles—were regarded as superstitious and Popish as well before as after 1566. And why is a thing more an object of superstition in Parish Churches than in Cathedrals? That Copes were *worn* in Parish Churches, notwithstanding they were frequently denounced as " superstitious," see pages 143-150.

None of the Visitation Articles between 1566 and 1600, so far as known even mention the Cope. But it may be said that Copes were not enjoined after 1566; neither were they before 1566, when they were confessedly legal. They were never enforced in Cathedrals nor even inquired after in Visitation Articles addressed to Cathedrals, nor are they now enforced although they have been declared obligatory by the Privy Council. Copes were destroyed on pretence of being superstitious, not as being *illegal*. The Ridsdale judgment attempts to show from the infrequent mention of copes that the use of them was abolished, In the Purchas case, on the contrary, the frequent mention of Cope and Surplice is cited to prove that the use of the Chasuble and Alb had been abolished. It is impossible to reconcile these different conclusions. After citing numerous documents, the Judges go on to say:

"Now all the Tracts above cited are dated within ten years after the date of the advertisements, and the complaints so bitterly made as to the Cope and Surplice would certainly have been extended to the Alb and Chasuble, had they not then ceased to exist." PAGE 173.

(xxiv.) "In a Visitation held in 1569, **Bishop Parkhurst, of Norwich**, inquired, &c. . . . That he was referring to the Advertisements and ' by public authority ' meant the authority of the Queen, seems clear from one of his ' Injunctions to the Clergy ' (the fourth), at the same Visitation, about perambulations, where he orders the clergy, on those occasions, not to use surplices or superstitious ceremonies, but only give good thanks, and use such good order of prayers and homilies as be appointed by the Queen's Majesty's authority in that behalf.' The use of homilies at perambulations was prescribed, not by the Injunctions of 1559, but by the Advertisements." PAGE 52.

Parkhurst was a noted Puritan. (See page 43). His testimony proves too much. He here classes Surplices with " superstitious ceremonies." So also GRINDAL, Archbishop of York, another noted Puritan (see page 45), in his VISITATION ARTICLES in 1571, speaking of perambulations, forbids the use of any other ceremonies except such " as be appointed by the queen's injunctions, . . . without wearing any surplice, carrying of banners, . . . or such like popish ceremonies." CARDWELL, DOC. ANN., N. 76, P. 372. VOL. I.

But what is the use of citing against the vestments the charges of noted Puritan Bishops? Every student of history knows that they were opposed to the Vestments, including the Surplice, and only wore them themselves to retain their offices, while they shielded those who refused them. (See pages 44, 45.) It was a great mistake to put such persons in office, but we must remember that the nation had just shaken off for the second time the power of the Roman Church, which was so generally hated, that those who railed against "Popery" often reached high positions.

Then why must it be thought that Parkhurst necessarily refers to the Advertisements when he speaks of the use of Homilies at Perambulations. In the second book of Homilies put forth in 1563, there is a Homily entitled, "An Homily for the days of Rogation Week," in four parts. (PAGE 206–245, VOL. 2.) The fourth part is entitled: "An exhortation to be spoken to such Parishes where they use their Perambulations in Rogation Week." PAGE 238–245.

(XXV.) "The minister is to order the elements ' standing before the table:' words which, whether the table stands ' altar-wise ' along the east wall or in the body of the church or chancel, would be fully satisfied by his standing on the north side and looking towards the south; but which also, in the opinion of their lordships, as tables are now usually, and, in their opinion, lawfully placed, authorize him to do those acts standing on the west side and looking towards the east. Beyond this and after this there is no specific direction that, during this prayer, he is to stand on the west side, or that he is to stand on the north side. He must, in the opinion of their lordships, stand so that he may, in good faith, enable the communicants present, or the bulk of them, being properly placed, to see, if they wish it, the breaking of the Bread and the other manual acts mentioned. He must not interpose his body so as intentionally to defeat the object of the rubric and to prevent this result." PAGE 67.

The Eastward Position is here conceded, provided that the manual acts, which are now a piece of Protestant Ritual, are not intentionally concealed.

(XXVI.) "Their lordships will now proceed to the charge as to wafer [wafers?] or wafer-bread. The charge as to this is ' that the appellant used in the Communion service and administration wafer-bread or wafers—to wit, bread or flour made in the form of circular wafers such as is usual to be eaten.'

"The charge, in their opinion, is consistent with the possibility of it having been the fact that bread, 'such as is usual to be eaten,' but circular, and having such a degree of thinness as might justify its being termed wafers, was what was used. And if this is what was used, their lordships do not think it could be pronounced illegal.

"Their lordships think that if it had been averred and proved that the wafer, properly so called, had been used by the appellant, it would have been illegal." PAGE 68, 70.

That is, Wafer Bread, if leavened, is legal; if unleavened, illegal.

(XXVII.) The Lord Chief Baron, Sir F. Kelley; Sir R. Phillimore; and Sir R. Amphlett, were not present when the Judgment was delivered, and it is generally understood that they dissented from it. The Archbishop of Canterbury alone of the Episcopal

Assessors was present; the others, the Bishops of Chichester, St. Asaph, Ely, and St. Davids were absent, and, it is believed, also dissented. It was also rumored that Sir James Hannen and Lord Coleridge were actually prevented from taking their seats by a strongly worded letter from a high official quarter.

(XXVIII.) It having been commonly reported in the newspapers that the Lord Chief Baron had pronounced the Ridsdale Judgment "an iniquitous one—a Judgment based not upon law, but upon policy," he wrote a letter to P. Constable Ellis, October 25, 1877, saying:

"My attention has been called to a newspaper in which you are reported to have said that I had described the Ridsdale judgment as 'an iniquitous one,' and had added that 'it was not a judgment based upon law, but upon policy.' Your memory is inaccurate as to my having used the expression 'an iniquitous judgment.' If I had done so, it certainly should not have been repeated, and I should have much regretted that by any inadvertence such an expression should have fallen from my lips. I may here hazard the expression that there was much of policy rather than of law, though perhaps unconsciously to themselves, in the judgment of the majority of the judges. I certainly authorized you to say as publicly as you thought fit, that I dissented from the majority of the judges, and I expressed the regret which I felt, and shall feel to the last moment of my life, that my earnest request to the court to declare my dissent from the Judgment, whenever it should be pronounced, was disregarded and rejected. . . .

"I had and have one strong and decisive reason for desiring that my dissent from the Judgment in the Ridsdale case should be publicly known, and it was this:—

"In July, 1866, a body of gentlemen called the 'English Church Union' submitted a case to myself, and I believe eight other counsel, all then at the bar, upon the precise question, of the legality of the vestments under the rubric in the Prayer Book, which arose in the Ridsdale case. And we all, without doubt or hesitation, declared it to be our decided opinion that the wearing of the vestments was authorized by the rubric in the Prayer Book. We all considered that the language of the judgment of five of the most eminent and distinguished judges that ever adorned the bench, as pronounced in Liddell *v.* Westerton, was decisive upon that question. And this opinion was subscribed by the authoritative names, among others, of the late Lord Chief Justice Bovill, of the present Lord Chief Justice of the Common Pleas, Lord Coleridge, of the now Lord Justice James, of the President of the Probate and Divorce Court, Sir James Hannen, of Sir Robert Phillimore, Judge of the Admiralty Court (all Privy Councillors), and Dr. Deane, Mr. Prideaux and Mr. Cutler. This Opinion was printed and published, and extensively circulated throughout England, and I cannot doubt that it must have induced a great many clergymen of our Church to believe implicitly in the legality of the vestments, and it may be in many cases to assume and wear the vestments accordingly. And I do not hesitate to say that if at any time before the

Judgment in the Ridsdale case was about to be delivered, I had changed my opinion, or entertained the slightest doubt of its correctness, upon this important question; still more, if I had thought that a single clergyman of the Church of England, could have been convicted of a criminal offence for having acted upon that Opinion, I should never have forgiven myself, if I had not immediately taken measures to warn the clergymen of the Church of England, whom that Opinion might have reached, and actuated in their performance of Divine service in their respective churches, that the Opinion was erroneous, or even open to question, and that they must no longer believe it to be a true and correct statement of the law." Cited in the the *Church Times*, Nov. 2, 1877, p. 614.

(xxix.) It was for these reasons that these men were condemned.

(1.) They used the VESTMENTS, as they were commanded by the Rubrics, pages 29, 34, 36, 77. They were also declared to be legal in 1857, in Liddell *v.* Westerton, page 232, 233. After 14 years of legal use, it is not to be expected that the Vestments would be given up willingly.

(2.) They used LIGHTED ALTAR LIGHTS AT THE HOLY COMMUNION, as commanded by Edward VI., and Archbishop Cranmer, pages 186, 187, and by the Ornaments Rubric of the Prayer Book, pages 77, 182. It had also been declared in 1857, in Liddell *v.* Westerton that "the same utensils or articles used under the First Prayer Book of Edward VI. may still be used." Page 232, 233.

Dr. Phillimore allowed them in his Decision in the Court of Arches, in 1868, in Martin *v.* Mackonochie, PAGE 108, but upon appeal, they were not allowed.

(3.) They STOOD BEFORE THE TABLE DURING THE PRAYER OF CONSECRATION, as ordered by the Rubric, page 174. They were ordered to do so in Martin *v.* Mackonochie, page 234. In Hebbert *v.* Purchas, they were ordered not to do so. By the Ridsdale appeal case they were again allowed the Eastward Position, page 238.

(4.) They used WAFER BREAD in the Holy Communion. The Rubric allows either kind of Bread, page 222. The Injunctions of Elizabeth order Wafer Bread, page 222. Most of the English people at the Reformation desired it. The Lutherans and Calvinists universally used it. By the Ridsdale appeal case Wafer Bread, if leavened, was allowed, page 238.

(5.) They used the MIXED CHALICE. In the Book of 1549, they were ordered to, page 220. The Dean of the Arches Court had decided that this mingling of the water was legal, provided that it was "not made at the time of the celebration." PAGE 185.

For doing just what the Church, and some of the Courts ordered, these men are called lawless. The way to make men lawless, is to try to enforce upon them Decisions which they know to be untrue historically, as well as unjust. These men were condemned solely for obeying the Church in preference to the contradictory Decisions of a secular Court. They were not persons guilty of gross immorality, neglect of their flocks, refusal to use the Church Service, or the Creeds, or unbelievers in the Prayer Book. Had they been guilty of most of these things, they would never have been molested. They were men of unblemished lives and hard workers, as their bitterest enemies willingly acknowledged.

(xxx.) These are the reasons why Churchmen refused to obey the Decisions of a secular Court.

ARTICLE XX. declares:

"The Church hath power to decree Rites or Ceremonies, and authority in Controversies of Faith."

ARTICLE XXXIV. declares:

"Every particular or national Church hath authority to ordain, change, and abolish, ceremonies or rites of the Church ordained only by man's authority, so that all things be done to edifying."

Now the Judicial Committee of the Privy Council is not the Church, and its Decisions, instead of supporting the Church, tamper with and destroy her teaching.

War against what is popularly called Ritualism began in 1855, and has been carried on ever since. The result is a vast increase of Ritualism, and the condemning of one man for doing just what another was condemned for not doing. The Lord Chancellor says that the law is as yet undetermined. Twenty-seven years, with contrary decisions of the Highest Tribunal, have failed to "interpret the law." The fact is, the law of the Church is plain enough already, and all the efforts made, have been made to force the law in an opposite direction. The developments which a few have made in a Romeward direction, though this was doubtless far from their intention, would otherwise be checked. The positions they now hold are due to the persecutions to which they have been subjected. They know that they will be condemned if they adopt the Ritual allowed by the Church, and so they adopt a kind of fancy Ritual, oftentimes not in accord with the Church. If, instead of persecuting the Clergy for mere matters of Ritual which are allowed by the Church, certain Bishops would devote their attention to inculcating sound and correct views of the doctrine and discipline of the Church, those whom they look upon as "lawless," would be their stanchest defenders. Few, if any, would refuse to obey the "godly admonitions" of their Bishops, but they do refuse to obey them when they attempt to force upon them the contradictory and false Decisions of the Privy Council. Besides, the Bishops differ very widely in their views. What one Bishop gladly sanctions, another will not tolerate.

## XVI.

# Ritualism Not Necessarily Romanism.

ONE would not think of calling the Lutherans Romanists, and yet their Service is as gorgeous as the Roman. The Irvingites are extremely Ritualistic. The Masons, Odd Fellows, Good Templars, and, in fact, all secret Societies, employ much Ritual in their Offices. Invocation of Saints, Mariolatry, Purgatory, the Immaculate Conception, Papal Infallibility, and similar errors, which are utterly contradictory to the teaching of the Primitive Church, are not Ritualism. To be sure Ritualism may be associated with Romanism as well as with anything else, but it is only when made to cover up Roman doctrine, that it becomes Romanism. Popular misconception has made Ritualism synonymous with Romanism, and thus covered an innocent word with suspicion and obloquy. The writer of the Article on Mediævalism, in the *Church Journal*—a paper which cannot be suspected of Ritualism—December 7, 1876, holds such sound views on this subject, that I shall quote largely from him:

"(1.) The distinctive terms of these systems should not be confounded—if for no other reason, to keep our ideas from confusion.

"(2.) It is a mistake to apply the term Mediæval to Popery. As well call a full-grown man juvenile, because once he was young. Popery matured—that is, in its true self and substance—is eminently modern.

"(3.) Neither is Ritualism to be called Popish, inasmuch as the whole Ritual System, from the first century to the nineteenth, contains not a trace of that principle—the *fons et origo mali*—namely, the absorption of the Catholic Church into the Papal Community; the absolute dependence of each believer directly upon the Pope.

"(4.) That Popery has availed itself of Ritual in establishing its dominion over mankind, gives it no right to pilfer the name.

"(5.) Popery, Mediævalism, and Ritualism are distinct systems, in date, in history, and in principle; and the advocate of truth will best advance her claims by consenting to no transfer or exchange of terms that is not philosophically valid, and in accordance with historic fact.

"9. It were not worth while to write this with any hope of effecting an immediate change in the popular use of terms. The multitude repeat them with no idea beyond the usage of the day. But there may be a hope of inducing those who think and write for others, and are more or less leaders of the popular mind, to consider the gain it would be to all parties, if the broad and deep distinctions between the things in question were not only discerned, but kept in view by accuracy in the names employed to designate them. There may be some, indeed, who for mere party ends seek to confuse terms, finding their gain in the prejudice thereby excited. Perhaps this motive has some influence in impeding the recovery of the word Catholic to its true ecclesiastical sense. If there are any who, in lieu of argument, or as subsidiary to it, find Popish and Ritualistic conveniently obnoxious epithets, they may still insist upon applying them where they will stick to the outside, even though there be no inward and natural attraction. Not on this account is it lost labor to appeal to the sense of fairness, or even to the mere intellectual perception of the fitness of words.

"Let, then, the terms Popish and Popery be strictly confined and faithfully applied to that which grows out of or exists for the Papacy.

"Turn now to an instance of a false cry raised when there is no object fairly in view. We have it in the very words that have been so frequent in these pages—catholic, popish, ritualistic. As popularly used, they tend not only to the hopeless confusion of ideas, but, what is even worse, the exceeding embitterment of controversy. They are utterly perverted in their use; linguistically degraded; taken hold of as mere pokers to stir the fires of party zeal. For general and immediate effect, an odious name is worth a volume of argument. It takes all for granted. It is the symbol of the argument concluded, and the case decided on 'our' side and against the other. It is the court-seal to the claim for damages; the writ of execution flourished in our opponent's face. Would there were some Judge to grant a stay to such proceedings and enjoin the triumphant party from further step till the accuracy of the proceedings could be reviewed! Then would many an innocent piece of ritual be rescued from hands bent on tearing it in pieces as a popish rag. The great principle of truth indicated by the word Catholic, would not be smirched over with the stains of popish corruption. Some precious tokens of the primitive ages would not be discredited as the product of mediæval superstition." Chap. 9, p. 776, 777.

If a person prefers a plain Service, by all means let him have one. His opinions should be respected. It is idle to expect that a person who has no ear for music, or has a dislike for it, should enjoy a choral service. There are many Churches, and it is to be hoped that there will ever be such, where people can have plain Services. On the other hand, let not such find fault with those who prefer more ornate ones.

But a large majority of those called Low Churchmen would not be content with the Prayer Book carried out in its integrity without Ritual. Disbelief in the Prayer Book itself is at the root of their trouble, and Ritual but serves as a pretext. That is why Low Churchmen, whenever they have an opportunity, seek to alter their Prayer Book. The Reformed Episcopalians exchanged the old Book for a new one, which they soon modified. As soon as the Irish Church was disestablished, the Low Churchmen set about tinkering their Prayer Book. If they really believed in it, they would not have tried to alter it.

There is in England a "Prayer Book Revision Society," whose object is to eliminate from that Book "every alleged support of Auricular Confession and Priestly Absolution and the doctrines of the Roman Mass." If the Prayer Book contains no such things, how can they be eliminated?

## XVII.

## The Ritualists.

I AM no "Ritualist," and I regret as much as any one the excesses of some who, by inconsiderate actions, have raised needless prejudice against sound Church principles. But I think that every one, even a "Ritualist," should have justice done him, and should not be obliged to suffer from mere popular prejudice. In fact, I hate religious persecution in any manner or shape. When very young, my feelings were so harrowed up by recitals of the atrocities of the Inquisition, that I conceived a strong aversion for it. I then innocently thought that the Church of Rome was the only persecuting body of Christians, and did not know that the boasted Protestant rule of "Liberty to worship God according to the dictates of every man's conscience," existed mostly in theory and not in practice. Great, then, was my surprise to learn that Calvin had Servetus burnt as a heretic; that our Puritan forefathers, who left England to enjoy liberty of conscience in the wilds of America, went far ahead of their alleged persecutors, and punished with death those who differed from them; that the Protestant mob, as Wesley testifies (pages 25, 26), surpassed the Popish, in stoning and annoying him and his followers; that Simeon, and the leaders of the Evangelical movement, were maltreated in various ways; that scarcely twenty-five years ago, in London, rotten eggs and similar arguments were hurled at the Minister by the Protestant mob, during Divine Service, for merely preaching in a Surplice. *In the Victorian persecutions, as late as 1880, we beheld aged Priests, men of unblemished character, imprisoned in a felon's cell for cele-

---

*The Rev. A. Tooth was imprisoned January 22, 1877; the Rev. T. Pelham Dale, October 30, 1880; the Rev. R. W. Enraght, November 27, 1880; the Rev. Mr. Green, of Miles Platting, March 19, 1881, and still remains in jail. In addition to being a "Ritualist," he is a poor man, with a large family

brating the Services as the Prayer Book directs, and their flocks scattered. Had one of the old Pagan persecutors witnessed such disgraceful scenes, he could no longer have said, except in bitter irony: "See how these Christians love one another." Shame alone should prevent such acts. It should be borne in mind what the "unconverted" think of such things. They think that Christianity is a religion of hate, and not of "peace and good will towards men."

A few years ago, in the city of Rome, if a person wished to publicly worship God in a manner different from the rites of the Roman Church, he was obliged to go outside the city walls. Such intolerance was severely commented upon by Protestants. Yet in New England, only a few years since, a large congregation was broken up and driven outside of the city limits into an adjoining town in order to worship God, by the bigotry and intolerance of people who called themselves Churchmen and boasted of being Protestants. It must be said in extenuation of such unchristian conduct, that those people driven out of town belonged almost wholly to the laboring class,—poor people, the "masses" about whom we *hear* so much in Church Congresses, but for whom we see so little *done*,—who are accordingly looked upon as of little account. These proceedings were not for "the glory of God and the salvation of souls," for they not only severely tried the religious faith of many, but, in some cases, broke it up. Ritualism was, of course, the pretence, but, as a matter of fact, other things were at the bottom of the movement.

I have also seen so many professed Christians who differed from those who did not pretend to be Christians, only in empty professions; who do nothing to make those around them better; who are always finding motes in the eyes of others, apparently unconscious of the beam in their own; who are constantly talking about others and fomenting quarrels and dissensions, instead of allaying them, and tending to their own affairs, that I sympathise with all, no matter what their Creed is, who strive to benefit their fellow men. We may not approve of the methods used, but we respect them for their work's sake. It is not necessary to be narrow-minded to enter the straight and narrow way. A person who is charitable towards others, though he may differ widely from the

---

dependent upon him, and his congregation is composed of poor working people. The Rev. Knox Little's Church is not far from Mr. Green's, but though an advanced "Ritualist," he is a greater man, and therefore has more influential friends; consequently he has recently been made Canon of Worcester Cathedral. For precisely the same "crime," one man is lodged in jail, it may be for life, and another elevated to a Canonry in the Church. One of Mr. Green's advocates has been made Dean of Carlisle.

views they entertain, is as likely to enter the Kingdom, as one who is always gossiping and finding fault with others. Such persons misrepresent religion. St. James, 1: 26–27, says:

"If any man among you SEEM to be RELIGIOUS, AND BRIDLETH NOT HIS TONGUE, but deceiveth his own heart, this man's RELIGION IS VAIN.

"Pure religion and undefiled before God and the Father is this, To visit the fatherless and widows in their affliction, and to keep himself unspotted from the world."

Some twenty years ago, an English merchant wished to endow a Church in London where it would do the most good. He asked the chief of Police to point out the worst place in that city, which he did after some delay. A Nobleman gave the site, and the merchant built a magnificent Church. It was endowed, by the same merchant, with the paltry sum of £150 a year. This worst district of London, among the poorest of the poor, with its Church and slender endowment, was handed over to a single clergyman in 1862. But he soon associated with him three or four more Priests who were willing to work for the good of others without regard to pay. Would the chief of Police to-day point out St. Alban's, Holborn, as the worst district in London?

One would naturally expect that such self-denying labors among Christian heathen—for there are worse heathen in London than in many nominal heathen lands—would at least elicit sympathy from Christians; but, as a fact, being a poor people, that congregation has been more annoyed and persecuted than any other one in London. And it is a fact, that in every case, so far as I know, poor Churches, just able to struggle along, are selected for persecution, while rich ones, like All Saints, Margaret Street, where the Princess of Wales frequently attends, are let alone. A poor man has a soul to be saved just as much as a rich man, for God is no respecter of persons. A poor man has as much right to worship his God, as a rich one has, and to put him in some obscure corner of the Church, is contrary to the teachings of Christianity. There should be no spirit of caste in the House of God.

I have frequently attended St. Alban's, and always found it crowded with devout worshippers. In the service I saw some things of which I did not approve, not that they were wrong in themselves, but they were of questionable taste, and served to overload, and to detract from the beauty and dignity of the Service, instead of adding to it. As the congregation seemed to enjoy their worship, it was not for me to find fault, especially, when I knew that very many of them were once steeped in crime, and were doomed to pass their lives in cheerless rookeries, and had no bright firesides, books, pictures, &c., to make home happy. To them the Church, with its lively and cheerful services, its music and flowers, its words of instruction and counsel, is the only bright spot in their lives. I have also attended some of the very Low Churches, where the Services were bald enough to suit most any one; where the congregation was a mere handful, and not very reverent in their behavior. I thought that the thousands of pounds wasted in breaking up the Ritualistic Churches, with their crowded congregations, many of whom had been rescued from the lowest depths of degradation, might be more advantageously spent in inducing that class to fill the vacant pews. When a person not long since complained to the Bishop of London that Ritualism drove people away from certain Churches, he replied that there were plenty of Churches with plain services and thin congregations, where Ritualism could not be urged as an excuse for staying away from Church.

But it is said that certain things are offensive to the people. Doubtless they are to some people; and so is the Gospel. It is for this reason that more than one-half of the population of our manufacturing towns habitually absent themselves from public worship on Sundays, and the same may be said of most of our country towns. It cannot be because there is no sect with which they can sympathise, for in every large place a dozen different sects can be found. Many who do attend public worship, are willing that the preacher should denounce the sins of the "wicked Jews," but if he denounces the sins of the present age, they think he is personal.

There is nothing immoral in "Ritualism," whether people like it or not. But immorality, profanity and drunkenness, are severely condemned in the Bible, and those guilty of such crimes, are excluded from the Kingdom of Heaven. Yet, for all that, persons guilty of such things are often elected to high places in the Church of God. Do such things help or injure the cause of Christ? What consistency is there in an immoral, drunken, swearing Christian, finding fault with such as are guilty of none of these things, but are only accused of little acts of Ritualism, such as bowing at the name of Jesus, or crossing themselves, &c.? Such practices may do no good, but they surely do no harm. "Ritualism" is often spoken of as a "soul-destroying error." But is it more "soul-destroying" than the sins that I have just mentioned?

It is also asked whether the Ritualists could not do as much good if they should give up their Vestments, Lights, and other ceremonies, that is, by ceasing to be Ritualists. Perhaps they could. Perhaps the Jewish religion would have been just as good without its Incense, Lights, Vestments, and other ceremonies, which God Himself commanded, and which would be very offensive to people now. Doubtless God could have redeemed the world sooner than He did, and without the sacrifice of His only Son. But we have to take things just as they are, not as we think they ought to be.

It was only about a century ago, that Wesley was misrepresented as the Ritualists are now, and called a "Papist," and similar names. He was even obliged by the Surrey Magistrates to take an oath against "Popery." These things are carefully kept out of sight now, because in the light of subsequent history, they appear so ridiculous. All now deprecate and wonder at the ill treatment which, though it did not drive Wesley away from the Church, did drive away his so-called followers, and made them her bitterest enemies. When the present generation has passed away, and with it the present quarrels and heart burnings, people will wonder at and deprecate the narrow-mindedness, ignorance, and intolerance, which drove off so many, who might have been ornaments to their Church, either into hostile Communion or into indifference and infidelity.

## XVIII.

## Why Churchmen Are Tenacious of Small Things.

CHURCHMEN are often called "bigoted." But this charge amounts to nothing. Every one who has a mind of his own may be said to be more or less bigoted. Those who have the most to say about bigotry in others, are just as bigoted in the other extreme. The only difference between the two, so far as I can see, is this: One firmly believes that the Church of Christ cannot be wrong, and believes implicitly in her; the other that the Church may be wrong, but that he cannot. If a person should now make use of the language of St. Paul, cited on page 217, he would be regarded as extremely bigoted. It would hardly do to condemn the Apostle himself, but such language would be condemned in others. Christianity was always exclusive. The Roman Emperors, Hadrian and Alexander Severus (AELIUS LAMPRIDIUS, VIT. ALEX. SEV., c. 43, p. 290. T. 1.) once deliberated whether Christ should be enrolled among the state gods, and His religion among the state religions; but the proposition was rejected for the sole reason that

Christianity would not tolerate any other religion. It is absurd to expect a man who honestly tells God in the Creed that he believes "one Catholic and Apostolic Church," to welcome every new Sect that may arise, as part of the Church of God. The Creed and the Church may be very intolerant, but they have existed for eighteen centuries, and we should not blame those who prefer their teachings to modern novelties. There are nearly two hundred different religious Sects in America, almost all of which profess to take the Bible as the sole rule of faith. Of course the Bible cannot teach two hundred different religions.

Churchmen know by experience that if they give up things which seem to be of little or no importance, truths of great importance will in time follow. Dr. DONNE, the eloquent Dean of St. Paul's, once said:

"Ceremonies are nothing; but where there are no ceremonies, order, and uniformity, and obedience, and at last (and quickly) religion will vanish." SERMON 120, preached at St. Paul's, p. 134. VOL. 5.

At the English Reformation, Churchmen wished to retain what was primitive and Catholic, and to remove only the errors and corruptions which had crept in meanwhile. The Puritans, on the other hand, in their zeal against Rome, sought to overthrow her by discarding whatever they disliked in her system, whether primitive or not. They were agreed as to what they did not want, but were seriously divided as to what they did want. Cranmer's opinion of these men is cited on pages 34, 35.

The more moderate and sober among the Calvinists deeply deplored and lamented the excesses of those whom they were unable to control. BURCHER, in 1550, (see page 31) says that—

"Our men of learning delight in novelty and change."

In the Article on Ceremonies in the present English Prayer Book, first inserted in the Book of 1552, we read:

"Some be so new-fangled, that they would innovate all things, and so despise the old, that nothing can like them but that is new."

BULLINGER, in 1567, speaking of Sampson, one of the leading English Puritans, says:

"While he resided among us at Zurich, and after he returned to England, he never ceased to be troublesome to master Peter Martyr of blessed memory. He often used to complain to me, that Sampson never wrote a letter without filling it with grievances: the man is never satisfied; he has always some doubt or other to busy himself with. As often as he began, when he was here, to lay his plans before me I used to get rid of him in a friendly way, as well knowing him to be a man of a captious and unquiet disposition. England has many characters of this sort, who cannot be at rest, who can never be satisfied, and who have always something or other to complain about. I have certainly a natural dislike to men of this stamp." Ep. 59, to Beza, p. 152. Z. L. 2d.

In another Letter, BULLINGER sends Beza the Letters of certain Bishops in England, in order that he may hear something " besides the clamours of Sampson." NOTE, IB.

1573.] EDWIN SANDYS, Bishop of London. " The people are fond of change, and seek after liberty." Ep. 114, to Bullinger, p. 295. Z. L.

See also the Testimonies cited on pages, 6-10.

The result of every man's claiming to make a religion that suited him, was general anarchy and confusion, and a constant departure from former practices. We will mention a few.

Baptism was at first regarded as so sacred a thing, that women were not allowed to administer it in case of necessity, but now it is regarded of little importance,—oftentimes not necessary to Communion,—and women are now allowed to act as pastors. The communion in the Lord's Supper was insisted upon, whereas now it is generally celebrated but once a quarter. One of the greatest contests at the Reformation, was that the wine as well as the bread, should be given to the laity; now water, or raisin juice, is frequently used. Neither of these is wine, which our Lord commands. The Presbyterian form of Church Government was adopted, in preference to the Episcopal, which in turn passed into the Congregational. Ordination is generally looked upon now as a mere form. The Black Gown was worn instead of the Vestments prescribed by the Church, but that is generally given up now. No one who has not read the original writings of the Puritans can form an idea of the scurrility and invective used by them against things which Churchmen hold most dear.

The religion of Geneva to-day is not that taught by Calvin, but that of Servetus, whom he had burnt as a heretic. Most of the three hundred Chapels originally built for the Nonconformists, in England, are said to be in the hands of those who deny the Saviour's Divinity. At one time there was but one Society in Boston that adhered to the teachings of the Puritans.

One of the most popular preachers of the Puritan faith in Boston, recently declared that the religion of the future would not be that of the 13th century, or of the present, but would be something different. What it would be, he did not attempt to say. Can we wonder then that scepticism is on the increase, when those who claim to be teachers of the Gospel, acknowledge that they are all at sea, and do not know, but can only speculate, as to what the religion of the future will be?

Among the changes for the better, we notice these. Organs were once looked upon as rank Popery, and to this day are generally rejected by the Scotch Presbyterians. In this country they are almost universally used by all Denominations. Whereas the Puritans once broke and defaced the ornaments of Churches, and destroyed the stained glass windows of the Cathedrals; what they once styled " Meeting Houses " from principle their descendants now call Churches. In point of architecture, their buildings would often be mistaken externally for Roman Catholic Churches. The interior is also profusely ornamented, and the Pulpits are decorated with flowers. Many of them make a partial use of a Liturgy in their Services. In Marriages and Funerals, the Church Service is frequently used.

Churchmen believe that the Christian Religion was established once for all, eighteen centuries ago, and that if they once begin to drift from the ancient moorings, no man can tell where they will stop. That is why they are so tenacious of their faith. They *believe* in it.

## XIX.

## Conclusion.

WE have briefly examined the Rubrics of the Communion Office, and also certain ceremonies and practices connected therewith, solely from an historical point of view, and we find that those things which are objected against, are expressly ordered, commended, or allowed by the Rubrics and Canons of the Church. Whether such things are right or wrong, does not enter into the question at all. I have only endeavored to show the practices and teachings of the Church. Many of them were retained by the Lutherans, the original Protestants, and are in use among them at the present day, though this fact is carefully kept out of sight. Those who talk about the principles of the Reformation, should be careful to state whether they mean Puritan, or Church principles. The Churchman ought not to be blamed for adhering to the teachings of his Prayer Book. Let those who break its Laws, be content with that, and not blame those who observe them. No organization can long maintain its integrity, unless its rules and regulations are strictly obeyed. If the Prayer Book contains errors, then go to the root of the whole matter, and have it altered; but while it remains as it is, do not blame those Churchmen who prefer Cranmer to Calvin, and the teachings of the whole Church from the beginning, to modern novelties, which are subject to further change at any moment. It will be impossible to "stamp out Ritualism,"—mind the word, it is not "convert or convince the Ritualist," but "stamp out" his religion,—for it has always existed in the Church. Queen Elizabeth, and Luther himself, would now be denounced as extreme Ritualists.

High Churchmen never clamor for changes in the Prayer Book. They are content with its teachings as handed down by the Reformers. Such clamors always come from the other side. They originated, at the Reformation, with the Puritans, who never would obey the Rubrics, and who always did, and always will trouble the Church. No sooner was one concession made to them than they demanded another. Says CRANMER: "If such men should be heard, although the Book were made every year anew, yet it should not lack faults in their opinion." Such was their uncharitableness and ignorance, that Lord BACON, himself almost a Puritan, was forced to say of them in 1589:

"Let them take heed that it be not true which one of their adversaries said, *that they have but two small wants, knowledge and love.*" ADV. TOUCHING THE CONT. OF THE CH. OF ENG., c. 4, N. 4, P. 94. VOL. 1.

And now a few words about religious controversy. Never engage in it from mere love of dispute. To talk intelligently on any subject requires careful reading and study. In Theology, however, an ignorant person looks upon himself as just as competent, to say the least, as those who are more learned. The most learned will sometimes make a mistake, but there is no excuse, now that books are so accessible, for the gross ignorance often displayed on the simplest subjects; the arguments frequently used are childish and absurd. A little study would enable people to understand things of which they are profoundly ignorant. Some prefer to remain in ignorance. They neither know nor care what the commonest terms really mean. They attach a meaning of their own to them and it is useless to try to show them that they are wrong. Others talk so intelligently and sensibly, that it is a pleasure to differ from them, when we cannot agree with them.

"Would it not be well," said Canon RYLE, now Bishop of Liverpool, a leading Low Churchman, in a recent Church Association paper, " to remember that now-a-days Evangelical Churchmen have no monopoly of grace, and faith, and holiness, and self-denial and love to Christ, the Bible, and souls, and that biographies like that of Catherine Tait show plainly that there is some good outside our own camp? I wish some people read a little more then they do. Want of reading is the mother of ignorance, and ignorance is the mother of narrowness and intolerance." Cited in the *Church Times*, JANUARY 2, 1880, P. 7.

# Index of Authors.

**I**N this Index I have specified the Library where the books made use of may be found, in hopes of promoting independent research. Many of the books in my own library are common enough in other Libraries. Dr. Dexter's work on "The Congregationalism of the last three hundred years," contains an excellent list of books relating to the Reformation.

The following abbreviations indicate the Library where the books may be found: *A.*, Author's Library; *Ath.*, Athenæum, Boston; *B.*, Boston Public Library, Boston; *Bod.*, Bodleian Library, Oxford, England; *B. M.*, British Museum, London, England; *C.*, Congregational Library, Boston; *H.*, Harvard University Library, Cambridge; *P.*, Private Libraries; *Pr.*, Prince Library, in keeping of the Boston Public Library.

| BORN. | DIED. | FL'D. | NAMES. | EDITION. | VOLS. | LIB'Y. |
|---|---|---|---|---|---|---|
| 1559 | 1617 | 1615 | Abbot, Robert, Bp. of Salisbury. | London, 1613 | | Bod. |
| | 1569 | 1566 | Abel, John. | Zurich Letters, 2d | | A. |
| | | 1699 | Abrege des Histoires, &c. | Ap. MacColl. | | A. |
| | | 1605 | Abridgment (An) of that Booke, &c. | n. p. 1605 | | Pr. |
| | | 1584 | Abstract (An) of certaine Acts of Parlement, &c. | n. p. n. d. | | Pr. |
| | | 1662 | Accompt (An) of all proceedings, &c. | n. p. n. d. | | Ath. |
| | | 1566 | Advertisements of 1566. | Wilk. Conc. T. 4 | | B. |
| | | 293 | Aelius Lampridius. | Hist. Aug. Script. | | H. |
| | | 830 | Amalarius, Symphosius, Priest of Metz. | Pat. Lat. T. 105 | | B. |
| | | 1661 | Anatomy of the Common Prayer. | Ap. Hierurgia. | | A. |
| 1565 | 1626 | 1605 | Andrewes, Lancelot, Bishop of Chichester; trans. to Ely, 1609; to Winchester, 1618. Form of the Consecration, &c., | n. p. 1675 | | H. |
| | | 1566 | Answer (An) for the Time, &c., | Ap. MacColl. | | A. |
| | | Cent'y 3-5 | Apostolic Constitutions. | Cotelerus, T. 1 | | H. |
| | | 1676 1650 | Aringhus, Paulus. Roma Subterranea. | Lutet. Paris. 1659 | 2 | A. |
| | | 1630 | Articles, or Instructions for Articles, &c., | Surtees Soc. V. 52 | | Ath. |
| | | 1549 | Articles to be followed and observed according to the King's Majesty's Injunctions and proceedings. | Card. Doc. A. V. 1 | | B. |
| 1515 | 1568 | 1562 | Ascham, Roger. | Zurich Letters, 2d | | A. |
| | | 1566 | Assignment of Church Ornaments, &c. | Ap. Maclean. | | B. |
| 354 | 430 | 398 | Augustine, Aurelius, Bp. of Hippo. | Pat. Lat. T. 32-47 | 16 | A. |
| 1514 | 1594 | 1576 | Aylmer, John, Bishop of London. | Strype, Life of A. | | Ath. |

| BORN. | DIED. | FL'D. | NAMES. | EDITION. | VOLS. | LIB'Y. |
|---|---|---|---|---|---|---|
|  | 1610 | 1591 | Babington, Gervase, Bishop of Llandaff; trans. to Exeter, 1594; to Worcester 1597. | Ap. Robertson. |  | A. |
| 1561 | 1626 | 1589 | Bacon, Sir Francis. (Ed. Spedding.) | London, 1861–74 | 7 | Ath. |
| 1544 | 1610 | 1597 | Bancroft, Richard, Bishop of London; trans. to Canterbury 1604. | London, 1593 |  | P. |
|  | 1613 | 1605 | Barlow, William, Bishop of Rochester; trans. to Lincoln, 1606. | Ap. Russell. |  | A. |
| 1532 | 1587 | 1566 | Barnes, Richard, Bp. of Carlisle; trans. to Durham, 1575. | Cheth. Soc. V. 22 |  | Ath. |
|  |  | 1567 | Barthelot, John. | Zurich Letters, 2d |  | A. |
| 329 | 380 | 370 | Basil, Bishop of Cæsarea. | Parisiis, 1839 |  | H. |
| 1615 | 1691 | 1668 | Baxter, Richard. Reliq. Baxter. | London, 1696 |  | B. |
|  |  |  | " Def. of the princip. of love. | London, 1871 |  | Bod. |
|  |  |  | " Saints Rest. | London, 1669 |  | B. |
| 1512 | 1570 | 1550 | Becon, Thomas. Works. | Cambridge, 1844 |  | Ath. |
|  | 1830 |  | Bell's Life in London. | London, 1830 |  | P. |
|  | 1708 |  | Bennet, Thomas. | London, 1709 |  | A. |
| 1519 | 1605 | 1566 | Beza, Theodore. | Zurich Letters, 2d |  | A. |
| 1786 | 1857 | 1824 | Blomfield, Charles James, Bishop of Chester; trans. to London, 1828. | London, 1843 |  | H. |
|  |  |  | Blunt, John Henry. | London, Oxford, & Camb. 1866 |  | P. |
|  |  | 1725 | Bourne, Henry. (See Brand, John.) | New Castle, 1725 |  | Ath. |
| 1510 | 1555 | 1554 | Bradford, John. Works. | Camb. 1848–53 | 2 | B. |
| 1571 | 1618 | 1604 | Bradshaw, William. | Cam. & Oxf. 1660 |  | P. |
| 1593 | 1663 | 1634 | Bramhall, John, Bp. of Derry; trans. to Armagh, 1661. Works. | Oxford, 1842–45 | 5 | A. |
| 1743 | 1806 | 1777 | Brand, John. | London, 1810 |  | Ath. |
| 1604 | 1660 | 1627 | Brereton, Sir William, Bart. | Cheth. Soc. V. 1 |  | Ath. |
| 1667 | 1743 | 1716 | Brett, Thomas, Nonjuring Bishop. | Ap. Perry. |  | A. |
|  |  | 1566 | Brief (A) Discourse against the Outward Apparell, &c. | Ap. Parker. |  | B.M. |
|  |  |  | Bruns, Herm. Theod. Concilia et Canones. | Berolini, 1839 | 2 | A. |
| 1491 | 1550 | 1549 | Bucer, Martin. | Orig. Let. Vol. 2 |  | A. |
| 1504 | 1575 | 1566 | Bullinger, Henry. | Zurich Letters, 2d |  | A. |
|  |  | 1550 | Burcher, John. | Orig. Let. Vol. 2 |  | A. |
|  | 1785 |  | Burn, Dr. Richard. | London, 1809 | 4 | B. |
| 1643 | 1715 | 1689 | Burnet, Gilbert, Bp. of Salisbury, Hist. of the Ref. (Ed. Peacock.) | Oxford, 1865 | 7 | Ath. |
| 1579 | 1648 | 1636 | Burton, Henry. | n. p. 1636 |  | B.M. |
|  |  | 1550 | Butler, John. | Orig. Let. Vol. 2 |  | A. |
| 1509 | 1564 | 1550 | Calvin, John. Opera. | Amstel. 1667–71 | 9 | H. |
|  |  |  | " " | Orig. Let. Vol. 2 |  | A. |
|  |  |  | Cambridge Camden Society Transactions. | Ap. Hierurgia. |  | A. |
|  |  |  | Camden Society Publications. | London, 1838–72 | 109 | Ath. |
|  |  |  | " " " New Series. | London, 1871–81 | 29 | Ath. |

| BORN. | DIED. | FL'D. | NAMES. | EDITION. | VOLS. | LIB'Y. |
|---|---|---|---|---|---|---|
| 1551 | 1623 | 1615 | Camden, William. Annal. Eliz. | London, 1615 | | Ath. |
| | | | Canons of the Church of England, | | | |
| | | 1571 | "         " 1571. | Card., Synod. | | B. |
| | | 1575 | "         " 1575. | "         " | | B. |
| | | 1604 | "         " 1603-4. (Ed. Walcott.) | Oxf.&Lond.1874 | | A. |
| | | 1640 | "         " 1640. | Wilk. Conc. T. 4 | | B. |
| 1787 | 1863 | | Cardwell, Edward. Hist. of Conf. | Oxford, 1841 | | A. |
| | | | "         " Doc. Annal. | Oxford, 1844 | 2 | B. |
| | | | "         " Synodalia. | Oxford, 1842 | | B. |
| 1534 | 1603 | 1573 | Cartwright, Thomas. Reply to an Answer. | n. p.      n. d. | | Ath. |
| | | | "         Works of Whitgift. | Camb. 1851-53 | 3 | Ath. |
| 1521 | 1598 | | Cecil, William. Lord Burleigh. | Parker Corresp. | | A. |
| | Century 2 | | Celsus. | Pat. Gr. T. 16 | | B. |
| | | 1605 | Certain Demands with their grounds, &c. | n. p.      1605 | | Pr. |
| | | 1597 | Certaine Questions, Arguments, &c | Parte of a Reg. | | P. |
| | | | Chambers, John David. | London, 1877 | | B. |
| 1630 | 1685 | 1660 | Charles II. | | | |
| 1514 | 1557 | | Cheke, Sir John. | Strype, Life of C. | | Ath. |
| | | | Chetham Society Publications. | Manch'r,1844-80 | 109 | Ath. |
| 354 | 407 | 390 | Chrysostom, John, Bp. of Constantinople. | Parisiis, 1839 | 26 | H. |
| | | | Churchwarden's Accounts of the town of Ludlow. | Camd.Soc.V.102 | | Ath. |
| | | 192 | Clement, Priest of Alexandria. | Coloniae, 1688 | | A. |
| 1650 | 1726 | 1713 | Collier, Jeremy. Nonjuring Bp. | London, 1852 | 9 | P. |
| 1549 | 1634 | 1606 | Coke, Sir Edward. | State Trials, V.1 | | H. |
| | | | "  Speech at the Assizes. | London, 1607 | | Bod. |
| | | 1636 | Consecration and Dedication of the Parish Church of Abbey Dore. (Ed. J. F. Russell.) | London, 1874 | | A. |
| | | 1605 | Considerations against the deprivation, &c. | Ap. Perry. | | B.M. |
| | | 1661 | Convocation of 1661. | Wilk. Conc. T. 4 | | B. |
| | | 1590 | Copie (The) of a Letter, &c. | Parte of a Reg. | | Pr. |
| 1595 | 1672 | 1660 | Cosin, John, Bishop of Durham. Works. | Oxford, 1843-55 | 5 | A. |
| | | | "       "   Correspondence. | Surtees Soc'ty, Vols. 52, 55. | 2 | Ath. |
| 1627 | 1686 | 1670 | Cotelerus, Joannes Baptista. | Amstel. 1724 | 2 | H. |
| 1486 | 1567 | 1551 | Coverdale, Miles, Bp. of Exeter. | ZurichLetters,2d | | A. |
| | | | Cox, John Charles. Notes. | Chesterfield, 1875-79 | 4 | B. |
| | | | "    "    "    and W. H. St. John Hope. Chronicles. | London, 1881 | | A. |
| 1499 | 1581 | 1559 | Cox, Richard, Bishop of Ely. | Zurich Letters. | | A. |
| 1489 | 1556 | 1533 | Cranmer, Th., Abp. of Canterbury. | Wilk. Conc. T.4 | | B. |
| | | | "    "    "    "    " | Orig. Let. Vol. 1 | | A. |
| | | | "  Writings and Disputations | Cambridge, 1844 | | Ath. |
| | | | "  Miss. Writings. | Cambridge, 1846 | | Ath. |

| BORN. | DIED. | FL'D. | NAMES. | EDITION. | VOLS. | LIB'Y. |
|---|---|---|---|---|---|---|
| 1663 | 1731 | 1627 | De Foe, Daniel. | London, 1748 | 4 | B. |
| | 1683 | | De Laune, Thomas. | Boston, 1763 | | Ath. |
| | 1576 | 1573 | Dering, or Deering, Edward. | Parte of a Reg. | | Pr. |
| | | 1590 | Description (A) of the State civil and Ecclesiastical of the County of Lancaster. | Cheth. Soc. V. 96 | | Ath. |
| | | | Dexter, Rev. H. M. | New York, 1880 | | Ath. |
| | | | Documents from Simancas. (Ed. Spencer Hall.) | London, 1865 | | Ath. |
| 1573 | 1631 | 1621 | Donne, Dr. John. Dean of St. Paul's. | London, 1839 | 6 | Ath. |
| | | 1876 | Droop, Henry Richmond. | London, 1876 | | A. |
| | 1770 | 1736 | Drake, Francis. | London, 1736 | | Ath. |
| 1515 | | 1549 | Dryander, or Enzinas, Francis. | Orig. Let. Vol. 1 | | A. |
| 1538 | 1553 | 1547 | Edward VI. | Wilk. Conc. T. 4 | | B. |
| 1533 | 1603 | 1558 | Elizabeth, Qu. of Eng. Advertis'm'ts | " " " " | | B. |
| | | | " " " Injunctions. | Card. Doc. A.V. 1 | | B. |
| | | 517 | Epaona, Council of. | Bruns, Vol. 1. | | A. |
| | | 1567 | Examination (An) of Certayne Londonners, &c. | Parte of Reg. | | P. |
| | | 1661 | Exceptions of the Presbyterian Brethren, &c. | n. p.    n. d. | | Ath. |
| | | 1660 | Expedient (An) humbly presented, &c. | Old Non-Conf. | | Ath. |
| | | | Fabric (The) Rolls of York Minster. | Surt. Soc. V. 35 | | Ath. |
| 1504 | 1550 | 1549 | Fagius, Paul. | Orig. Let. Vol. 2 | | A. |
| 1593 | 1637 | 1625 | Ferrar, Nicholas. | Ap. Hierurgia. | | A. |
| | 1636 | 1619 | Field, Theophilus, Bp. of Landaff; trans. to St. David's, 1627; to Hereford, 1635. | London, 1874 | | A. |
| | | 1877 | Finlason, W. F. The Judgment of the Judicial Committee in the Folkstone Ritual case. | London, 1877 | | A. |
| | | 1876 | Folkstone (The) Ritual Case. (Ridsdale) | London, 1876 | | A. |
| | | | " (The) Ritual Case. (Ridsdale Appeal Case.) See Finlason. | London, 1877 | | A. |
| | | 1838 | Form and Order of the Coronation of Queen Victoria in 1838. | London, 1875 | | A. |
| | | Cent'y 17 | Form of Consecration or Dedication of Churches and Chappels, according to the use of the Church of Ireland. | Ap. MacColl. | | A. |
| | | 1549 | Forme and Maner of Makyng and Consecratyng Archebishoppes, &c. | Prayer B'k, 1549 | | A. |
| 1770 | 1842 | 1820 | Fosbroke, Thomas Dudley. | London, 1843 | | B. |
| 1517 | 1587 | 1554 | Foxe, John. Acts & Monuments. | London, 1684 | 3 | B. |

| BORN. | DIED. | FL'D. | NAMES. | EDITION. | VOLS. | LIB'Y. |
|---|---|---|---|---|---|---|
| 1818 | | | Froude, James Anthony. | London, 1856-70 | 12 | Ath. |
| | | 1562 | General notes of Matters to be moved, &c. | Strype, Annals. | | Ath. |
| 1669 | 1748 | 1715 | Gibson, Edmund, Bp. of Lincoln; trans. to London, 1723. | Oxford, 1761 | 2 | H. |
| | 1585 | 1570 | Gilby, Anthony. | Parte of a Reg. | | Pr. |
| 1816 | | 1878 | Goodwin, Harvey, Bp. of Carlisle. | Cam. & Lon. 1878 | | A. |
| | | 1848 | Gorham, George Cornelius. Gleanings, &c. | London, 1857 | | A. |
| 1660 | 1732 | 1732 | Grancolas, Joannes. | Venetiis, 1734 | | B.M. |
| 396 | | 371 | Gregory, Bishop of Nyssa. | Parisiis, 1838 | 3 | H. |
| 1519 | 1583 | 1559 | Grindal, Edmund, Bishop of London; trans. to York, 1570; to Canterbury, 1573. | Zurich Letters. | | A. |
| | | 1876 | Grueber, C. S. "Om." not "Prohib." | Oxf.&Lond.1876 | | A. |
| | | | "   Canon XXX. | Oxf.&Lond.1879 | | A. |
| | | | "   How am I to perform,&c. | London, n. d. | | A. |
| 1518 | 1686 | 1565 | Gualter, Rodolph. | ZurichLetters,2d | | A. |
| 1806 | 1875 | 1841 | Guéranger, Prosper, Abbé de Solesmes. | Paris, 1841 | 2 | P. |
| | | 1559 | Guest, (Gest, or Gheast) Edmund, Bp. of Rochester; trans. to Salisbury, 1571. | Strype, Annals. | | Ath. |
| | | 1552 | Haddon, James. | Orig. Let. Vol. 1 | | A. |
| | | | Hall, Spencer. | London, 1865 | | Ath. |
| | | 1876 | Harrison, John. | London, 1876 | | A. |
| | | 1636 | Hausted, Peter. | London, 1636 | | P. |
| 1678 | 1735 | | Hearne, Thomas. (Ed. Leland.) | | | Ath. |
| 1600 | 1662 | 1627 | Heylin, Peter. A Coale, &c. | London, 1636 | | B.M. |
| | | | "   Hist. of the Presb. | Oxford, 1670 | | P. |
| | | | "   Hist. of the Reform. | London, 1674 | | B. |
| | | | "   Cyprianus Anglicus. | London, 1668 | | H. |
| | | | Hierurgia Anglicana. | London, 1848 | | A. |
| | | 1566 | Hilles, Richard. | ZurichLetters,2d | | A. |
| | | | Historiae Augustae Scriptores sex. | Bipont., 1786 | 2 | H. |
| | | | Homilies. | London, 1816 | 2 | A. |
| 1495 | 1553 | 1550 | Hooper, John, Bp. of Gloucester. | Orig. Let. Vol. 1 | | A. |
| | | | "   "   Writings. | Cambridge, 1843 | | A. |
| | | 1580 | 1560 Horn, Robert, Bp. of Winchester. | Zurich Letters. | | A. |
| | | | House of Commons. Journals. | [London], n. d. | 90 | Ath. |
| | | | House of Lords.   " | [London], n. d. | 50 | Ath. |
| 1711 | 1776 | 1754 | Hume, David. Hist. of England. | Philadelphia, n.d | 6 | P. |
| 1526 | 1590 | 1566 | Humphrey, Lawrence. | Zurich Letters. | | A. |
| 1696 | 1773 | | Hutchins, John. | London, 1774 | 2 | B. |
| 1608 | 1674 | | Hyde, Edward, Earl of Clarendon. | | | |
| | | | State Papers. | Oxford, 1767-86 | 3 | Ath. |
| | | | "   Life. | Oxford, 1759 | 3 | Ath. |
| | 107 | 105 | Ignatius, Bishop of Antioch. | Patr. Apost. | | A. |

| BORN. | DIED. | FL'D. | NAMES. | EDITION. | VOLS. | LIB'Y |
|---|---|---|---|---|---|---|
|  | 1217 | 1199 | Innocent III., Bp. of Rome. | Pat. Lat.T.214–7 | 4 | B. |
|  |  | 1552 | Inventory of Furniture and Ornaments in all Parish Churches of Hertfordshire. | Oxf.&Lond.1873 |  | A. |
|  |  | 1552 | Inventories of Goods in the Churches and Chapels of Lancashire. | Cheth.Soc.V.107 | 2 | Ath. |
|  |  | 1552 | Inventory in Lindsay Deanery in 1552. | Walcott,Cons. & Canons. |  | A. |
|  |  | 1549 | Inventory of the Ornaments and Goods in Northumberlande. | Surt. Soc. V. 22 |  | Ath. |
|  |  | 1564 | Inventory of all the Ornaments in Wymondham Churche. | *Church Times.* |  | A. |
|  |  | 1552 | Inventory of Parish Goods in Berkshire. See Parish Goods in Berkshire. |  |  |  |
|  |  | 1616 | Inventory of the Plate, &c., in York Cathedral. | Surt. Soc. V. 35 |  | Ath. |
|  | 636 | 596 | Isidore, Bishop of Seville. | Pat. Lat.T.81–84 | 4 | B. |
|  |  | 1843 | Jebb, John. | London, 1843 |  | B. |
| 331 | 420 | 378 | Jerome, Priest. | Col. Agrip.,1616 | 9 | A. |
| 1522 | 1571 | 1559 | Jewell, John, Bishop of Salisbury. | Zurich Letters. |  | A. |
|  |  |  | "        "     Works. | Oxford, 1848 | 8 | B. |
|  |  | 1573 | Johnson, Robert. Letter to Sandes. | Parte of a Reg. |  | Pr. |
|  |  | 1573 | "     The Examination of. | "     "     " |  | Pr. |
|  |  | 1574 | "     Letter to Goodman. | "     "     " |  | Pr. |
| 38 | 93 | 67 | Josephus, Flavius. | Genevae, 1611 |  | Ath. |
|  |  |  | Journal of the General Convention. | Claremont, 1874 | 3 | B. |
| 89 | 168 | 150 | Justin Martyr. | Pat. Gr. T. 6 |  | B. |
|  |  |  | Keenan, Rev. Steph. Doct. Catech. | New York, n. d. |  | A. |
|  |  |  | "     "     "     "     " | London, 1874 |  | A. |
| 1660 | 1728 | 1718 | Kennet, White, Bp. of Peterboro' | London, 1744 |  | H. |
|  |  | 1641 | Lambeth Faire. | Ap. Hierurgia. |  | A. |
|  |  |  | Lancashire and Cheshire Wills and Inventories. | Cheth. Soc. V. 51 | 2 | Ath. |
|  |  | 1641 | Large (A) Supplement, &c. | Ap. Hierurgia. |  | A. |
| 1798 |  | 1859 | Lathbury, Thomas. Hist. of the Book of Common Prayer. | Oxf.&Lond.1859 |  | A. |
|  |  |  | "    Hist. of the Convocation. | London, 1842 |  | A. |
| 1470 | 1555 | 1535 | Latimer, Hugh, Bp. of Worcester. Works. | Camb., 1844–45 |  | B. |
| 1573 | 1645 | 1621 | Laud, Wm., Bp. of St. David's; trans. to Bath and Wells, 1627; to London, 1628; to Canterbury, 1633. |  |  |  |
|  |  | 1707 | Lawful prejudices, &c. | Ap. Lathbury. |  | h. |
|  | 1667 | 1634 | Leander, Father. | Hyde,St'ePapers |  | Ath. |
|  |  | 1869 | Lee, Frederick George. | London, 1869 |  | A. |

| BORN. | DIED. | FL'D. | NAMES. | EDITION. | VOLS. | LIB'Y. |
|---|---|---|---|---|---|---|
| | | 1710 | Le Brun, Pierre. | Paris, 1777-78 | 8 | B. |
| 1784 | 1846 | | Le Keux, John. | Ap. Perry. | | A. |
| | 1552 | 1533 | Leland, John. (Ed. Hearne.) | London, 1770 | 6 | Ath. |
| | 1577 | 1566 | Lever, Thomas. | Zurich Letters. | | A. |
| | 1446 | 1434 | Lindwood, William, Bp. of St. David's. Provinciale. | Oxon., 1679 | | B. |
| 1776 | 1851 | | Lingard, John. | Boston, 1853 | 13 | P. |
| | | | Littledale, R. F. Holy Eastern Ch. | London, 1870 | | A. |
| 1627 | 1717 | 1680 | Lloyd, William, Bp. of St. Asaph; trans. to Worcester 1699. | Ap. MacColl. | | A. |
| | | | Lundy, John P. Monum'nt. Christ. | New York, 1876 | | P. |
| 1483 | 1546 | 1521 | Luther, Martin. | | | |
| | | | MacColl, Malcom. | London, 1875 | | A. |
| 1550 | | 1562 | Machyn, Henry. | Camd. Soc. V. 42 | | Ath. |
| | | | Maclean, Sir John. | London, 1873-79 | 3 | B. |
| | | | Magnum Bullarium Romanum. | Lugd., 1654-73 | 5 | H. |
| | | | Marriott, Wharton B. Vest. Christ. | London, 1868 | | A. |
| | | | Martigny, Joseph Alexander. Dict. | Paris, 1877 | | B. |
| | | Cent'y 17 | Meldenius, Rupertus. | Baxter, S'ts Rest. | | B. |
| | | | Merrill, Selah. | New York, 1881 | | A. |
| | | | Michell, Rev. William. | London, 1870 | | A. |
| | | 1552 | Micronius, Martin. | Orig. Let. Vol. 2 | | A. |
| 1752 | 1826 | 1800 | Milner, John. End of Controversy. | New York, n. d. | | A. |
| | | | "    "    Hist. of Winchester. | Winchester, 1809 | 2 | B. |
| 1638 | 1686 | | Nalson, John. | London, 1683 | 2 | B. |
| 1678 | 1743 | 1732 | Neal, Daniel. | New York, 1855 | 2 | P. |
| 1562 | 1640 | 1608 | Neile, Richard, Bp. of Rochester; trans. to Coventry, 1610; to Lincoln, 1613; to Durham, 1617; to Winchester, 1627 ; to York, 1632. | Ap. Russell. | | A. |
| 1664 | 1712 | 1710 | Nicholls, or Nichols, William. | London, 1710 | | A. |
| 1744 | 1826 | | Nichols, John. Progresses. | London, 1823 | 3 | Ath. |
| | | 1880 | Notes and Queries. (Sept. 1880.) | London, 1880 | | Ath. |
| | | | Old (The) Cheque-Book of the Chapel Royal. | Camden Soc. N. S. Vol.3 | | Ath. |
| 1673 | 1742 | | Oldmixon, John. | London, 1739 | | B.M. |
| | | 1660 | Old (The) Non-Conformist, &c. | London, 1660 | | Ath. |
| | 380 | 365 | Optatus, Bp. of Milevis. | Pat. Lat. T. 11 | | B. |
| 185 | 253 | 230 | Origen, Priest of Alexandria. | Pat. Gr. T.11-17 | 7 | B. |
| | | | Original Letters. | Camb., 1846-47 | 2 | A. |
| | | | Ornsby, George. (Ed. Cosin Cor.) | Surt. Soc. V. 52 | | Ath. |
| | | | Oughton, Thomas. | London, 1788 | 2 | Ath. |
| 1559 | 1619 | 1604 | Overall, John, Bp. of Coventry; trans. to Norwich, 1615. | | | |
| | | 1712 | Owen, Charles. | London, n. d. | | C. |
| 1803 | | 1839 | Palmer, William. | Oxford, 1839 | 2 | A. |

| BORN | DIED | FL'D | NAMES | EDITION | VOLS | LIB'Y |
|---|---|---|---|---|---|---|
| | | 1634 | Panzani, Gregorio. | Birmingh., 1793 | | B.M. |
| | | | Parallel (A), or Brief Comparison, &c. | Ap. Hierurgia. | | A. |
| | | 1552 | Parish Goods in Berkshire, A. D. 1552. | Oxf.&Lond.1879 | | A. |
| | | 1878 | Parker, James. Did Queen Elizabeth? &c. | " " 1878 | | A. |
| | | | " Ib. Postscript. | " " 1879 | | A. |
| 1504 | 1575 | 1559 | Parker, Matthew, Abp. of Cant. | Parker Corresp. | | A. |
| | | | Parker Correspondence. | Cambridge, 1853 | | A. |
| | 1614 | 1607 | Parker, Robert. | n. p. 1607 | | Pr. |
| 1511 | 1574 | 1560 | Parkhurst, John, Bp. of Norwich. | Zurich Letters. | | A. |
| 1564 | 1610 | 1606 | Parsons, Robert. Ans. to Coke. | n. p. 1606 | | A. |
| | | | " Leycester's Commonwealth. | n. p. 1641 | | A. |
| | | 1590 | Parte (A) of a Register. | n. p. n. d. | | Pr. |
| | | | Patrologiae Graecae curs. complet. | Parisiis, 1857–66 | 160 | B. |
| | | | Patrologiae Latinae " " | Parisiis, 1844-55 | 217 | B. |
| | | | Patrum Apostolicorum Opera. (Ed. Hefele.) | Tubingae, 1855 | | A. |
| 353 | 431 | 420 | Paulinus, Bishop of Nola. | Pat. Lat. T. 61 | | B. |
| | 1866 | | Peacock, Edward. | London, 1866 | | A. |
| 1632 | 1703 | | Pepys, Samuel. | London, 1828 | 5 | B. |
| | | 1877 | Perry, Thomas Walter. | London, [1877] | | A. |
| 1500 | 1562 | 1560 | Peter Martyr. | ZurichLetters,2d | | A. |
| | | | | Orig. Let. Vol. 2 | | A. |
| 1810 | 1876 | | Phillimore, Sir Robert. | Oxf.&Lond.1876 | | A. |
| 1777 | 1869 | 1831 | Phillpotts, Henry, Bp. of Exeter. | Ap. Hierurgia. | | A. |
| 1673 | 1733 | 1730 | Picart, Bernard. | London, 1733-37 | 6 | Ath. |
| 1520 | 1575 | 1560 | Pilkington, James, Bp. of Durham. | Zurich Letters. | | A. |
| 1504 | 1572 | 1566 | Pius V., Bishop of Rome. | Mag. B. R. T. 5 | | H. |
| | | 96 | Polycarp, Bishop of Smyrna. | Patr. Apost. | | A. |
| | | 397 | Possidius, Bishop of Calama. | Pat. Lat. T. 32 | | A. |
| | | | Prayer Book of 1549. | Cambridge, 1844 | | A. |
| | | | " " 1552. | " 1844 | | A. |
| | | | " " 1559. | " 1847 | | A. |
| | | | Pritchett, Robert Taylor. | London, 1879 | | P. |
| | | | Privy (Six) Council Judgments. (Ed. Wm. G. Brooke.) | London, 1874 | | A. |
| 1811 | 1852 | | Pugin, Augustus Welby. Glossary. | London, 1846 | | B. |
| | | 1851 | Quarterly (The) Review. Vol. 89 | London, 1851 | | Ath. |
| | 856 | 847 | Rabanus Maurus, Bp. of Mayence or Mentz. | Pat. Lat. T. 107–112. | 6 | B. |
| | | 1660 | Reasons why the Service-book, &c. | Old Non-Conf. | | Ath. |
| 1752 | 1824 | 1801 | Reeves, John. (Ed. Prayer Book.) | Ap. *Church Times* | | A. |
| | | 1865 | Report of Her Majesty's Commissioners appointed to consider the Subscriptions, &c. | London, 1865 | | A. |
| | | 1867 | Report (First) of the Commissioners appointed to inquire into the Rubrics, &c. | London, 1867 | | Ath. |

| BORN. | DIED. | FL'D. | NAMES. | EDITION. | VOLS. | LIB'Y. |
|---|---|---|---|---|---|---|
| | | | Report (Second) of the Commissioners appointed to inquire,&c. | Ap. Parker. | | A. |
| | | 1586 | Request (A) of all true Christians. | Ap. Neal. | | P. |
| | | | Reynolds, Herbert Edward. Wells Cathedral. | [Leeds, 1881] | | B. |
| 1500 | 1555 | 1547 | Ridley, Nicholas, Bp. of Rochester; trans. to London, 1550. Works. | Cambridge, 1841 | | Ath. |
| | | | Ridsdale, Rev. C. J. See Folkstone | | | |
| 1813 | 1882 | 1844 | Robertson, James Craigie. 2d Ed. | London, 1844 | | A. |
| | | | " " " 3d Ed. | London, 1869 | | A. |
| 1793 | 1866 | 1845 | Robinson, Hastings. | Cambridge, 1845 | | A. |
| | | 1875 | Russell, J. Fuller. Cons. & Dedication of Abbey Dore. | London, 1874 | | A. |
| 1517 | 1589 | 1560 | Sampson, Thomas. | Zurich Letters. | | A. |
| | 1581 | 1580 | Sanders, Nicholas. Jesuit. | Ingolst., 1588 | | A. |
| 1519 | 1588 | 1559 | Sandys, Edwin, Bp. of Worcester; London, 1570; York, 1576. | Zurich Letters. | | A. |
| | | 1661 | Savoy Conference. | Card. H. of Conf. | | A. |
| | | 1572 | Second (A) Admonit'n to Parliam't | Ap. MacColl. | | A. |
| 1598 | 1677 | 1660 | Sheldon, Gilbert, Bp. of London; trans. to Canterbury 1663. | Card. Doc. A.V. 2 | | B. |
| | 1654 | | Smart, Peter. | Surt. Soc. V. 34 | | Ath. |
| 1512 | 1577 | 1567 | Smith, Sir Thomas. | Strype, Life of S. | | Ath. |
| | | | Smith, (Wm.) & Cheetham, (Sam.) Dictionary. | London, 1875-80 | 2 | B. |
| | | 439 | Socrates. | Cantab., 1720 | | H. |
| | | | State Papers. | Ap. MacColl. | | A. |
| | | | State Trials. | London, 1742-66 | 10 | H. |
| | | | Statutes at Large. | { Camb. & Lond. 1762-1864. | 104 | Ath. |
| | | | Stephens, Archibald John. | Ap. Phillimore. | | A. |
| 1525 | 1605 | | Stowe, John. Survey of London. | London, 1618 | | Ath. |
| | | | " " Memoranda. | { Camden Soc. N. S. Vol. 28 | | |
| 1806 | | | Strickland, Agnes. Letters of Mary Queen of Scots. | London, 1845 | 2 | Ath. Ath. |
| 1643 | 1737 | | Strype, John. Life & Acts of Parker | Oxford, 1821 | 3 | Ath. |
| | | | " Annals. | " 1824 | 7 | Ath. |
| | | | " Eccl. Mem. | " 1822 | 3 | Ath. |
| | | | " Life of Grindal. | " 1821 | | Ath. |
| | | | " " T. Smith. | " 1820 | | Ath. |
| | | | " Mem. of Cranmer. | " 1840 | 2 | Ath. |
| | | | " Life & Acts of Whitgift. | " 1822 | 3 | Ath. |
| | | | " Life of Sir John Cheke. | " 1821 | | Ath. |
| | | | " Life & Acts of Aylmer. | " 1821 | | Ath. |
| | | | Surtees Society Publications. | { Lond. & Durh. 1835-1880. | 71 | Ath. |
| | | | Swedish (The) Ordinal. | London, 1879 | | A. |
| | 430 | 410 | Synesius, Bishop of Ptolemais. | Pat. Gr. T. 66 | | B. |
| | | 1553 | Terentianus, Julius. | Orig. Let. Vol. 1 | | A. |
| | 216 | 200 | Tertullian, Priest of Carthage. | Lipsiae, 1839-41 | 4 | A. |

| BORN. | DIED. | FL'D. | NAMES. | EDITION. | VOLS. | LIB'Y. |
|---|---|---|---|---|---|---|
| 1658 | 1725 | 1681 | Thoresby, Ralph. | London, 1830 | 2 | B. |
| 1552 | 1641 | 1603 | Thornborough, John, Bp. of Limerick, 1593; trans. to Bristol, 1603; to Worcester, 1615. | Ap. Robertson. | | A. |
| | | 671 | Toledo, Fourth Council of. | Bruns, Vol. 1. | | A. |
| 1700 | 1792 | 1746 | Towgood, Micajah. | Newry, 1816 | | B. |
| | | | Tract 39. Church Association. | n. p. n. d. | | A. |
| | | 1574 | Travers, Walter. | Rupellae, 1574 | | P. |
| | | | "   " Ed. of Cartwright | n. p. 1574 | | Pr. |
| | | | Trent, Catechism of the council of. | Lipsiae, 1856 | | A. |
| | | 1545 | Trent, Council of. | "   1857 | | A. |
| | | 1876 | Tustin, Rev. J. P. | Church Journal. | | A. |
| 1477 | 1536 | 1530 | Tyndale, William. | Cambridge, 1850 | | A. |
| 1597 | 1672 | 1657 | Twysden, Sir Roger. | London, 1657 | | A. |
| | | 1550 | Ulmis, John ab. | Orig. Let. Vol. 2 | | A. |
| | | 1551 | Utenhovius, John. | Orig. Let. Vol. 2 | | A. |
| | | 1660 | View of the Prelatical Church of England. | Ap. Hierurgia. | | A. |
| | 445 | 434 | Vincentius, Monk of Lerins. | Pat. Lat. T. 50 | | B. |
| 1814 | | | Violett-le-Duc, Eugene Emmanuel. | Paris, 1858–68 | 10 | B. |
| | | 1665 | Voyage (A) to England, etc. | Church Times. | | A. |
| | 849 | 830 | Walafrid Strabo. | Pat.Lat. T.113-4 | 2 | B. |
| 1822 | 1880 | 1872 | Walcott, Mackenzie Edward Chas. Trad. and Customs of Cathedrals. | London, 1872 | | A. |
| | | | "   Const. and Canons of the Church of England. | Oxf.&Lond.1874 | | A. |
| | | | Warren, Frederick Edward. Liturgy & Ritual of the Celtic Church. | Oxford, 1881 | | B. |
| 1536 | 1590 | 1588 | Walsingham, Sir Francis. | Ap. Collier, T. 7 | | P. |
| | | 1640 | Wats, William. (Ed. M. Paris.) | London, 1840 | | B.M. |
| 1708 | 1788 | 1748 | Wesley, Charles. Journal and Letters. | London, 1849 | 2 | A. |
| 1703 | 1791 | 1760 | Wesley, John. Journal. | London, 1867-75 | 4 | A. |
| | | | "   " In company with High Churchmen. | London, 1872 | | A. |
| 1686 | 1742 | 1710 | Wheatly, Charles. | London, 1848 | | A. |
| | | 1557 | Whitehead, David. | Orig. Let. Vol. 2 | | A. |
| 1530 | 1604 | 1577 | Whitgift, John, Bp. of Worcester; trans. to Canterbury, 1583. | Camb., 1851–53 | 3 | Ath. |
| 1577 | 1637 | 1626 | White, Francis, Bp. of Carlisle; trans. to Norwich, 1629; to Ely, 1631. | Ap. Russell. | | A. |
| 1511 | 1566 | 1554 | White or Whyte, John, Bp. of Lincoln; trans. to Winchester, 1557. | Bradford's Wrks | | B. |
| | | 1579 | 1575 | Whittingham, William. (Reprint). | London, 1846 | | Ath. |

| BORN. | DIED. | FL'D. | NAMES. | EDITION. | VOLS. | LIB'Y. |
|---|---|---|---|---|---|---|
|  |  | 1564 | Wiburn, Perceval. | ZurichLetters, 2d |  | A. |
| 1685 | 1745 | 1737 | Wilkins, David. Conc. Mag. Brit. | London, 1737 | 4 | B. |
| 1582 | 1650 | 1621 | Williams, John, Bp. of Lincoln; trans. to York, 1841. Holy Table, &c. | n. p. n. d. |  | H. |
|  |  | 1566 | Withers, George. | ZurichLetters, 2d |  | A. |
|  |  | 1308 | Woodloke, Henry, Bp. of Winchester. | Wilk. Conc. T. 2 |  | B. |
| 1807 |  | 1869 | Wordsworth, Christopher, Bishop of Lincoln. | Lon. Oxf. & Camb. 1874 |  | B. |
| 1508 | 1561 | 1551 | Wriothesley, Charles. | Camden Soc. N. S. V. 11, 20 | 2 | Ath. |
| 1516 | 1590 | 1571 | Zanchius, Hierome. | ZurichLetters, 2d |  | A. |
|  |  |  | Zurich Letters. | Cambridge, 1842 |  | A. |
|  |  |  | "      "      Second Series. | Cambridge, 1845 |  | A. |

The Bishops' Pastoral, and the Proceedings of the General Convention in 1874, are cited from the *Daily Churchman*.

# Index of Subjects.

ADVERTISEMENTS of 1564, note, 50; not authorized or published, 61; A. of 1566, 50–76; circumstances attending drawing them up, 51–61, 73–74; difference between those of 1564 and those of 1566, 67–68; the work of the Bishops alone though incited thereto by the Queen, 56–62; published about March 28, 1566, 60; Parker left to enforce them himself, 58, 61; use in official documents, 63–66; in course of time came to be regarded as being of much authority, 71; the Queen never signed them, 74, 75; this fact well known to the Puritans, 69–71; she refused to ratify the Canons of 1571, and those of 1575 till all reference to the Advertisements was left out, 68, 69; object of the A. to enforce the Injunctions of 1559, and to oblige the use of the Surplice in Church, and for outward apparel the Gown and Square Cap, Parker, Stowe, 59–60; against no law of the land, 62, 63; did not repeal the Rubric of 1559, Gibson, Burn, Reeves, Phillpotts, Wordsworth, Quarterly Review, Privy Council in 1857, 137, 138, 141, 142; not against high ritual, 72, 74, 75; claimed now by the Privy Council that they modified the Rubric of 1662, 51, 236. See FURTHER ORDER.

ALB ordered by the Rubrics of 1549, 29, 30; by the Ornaments Rubric of 1559, 1662, 36, 77; description of, Figures 8, 15, 16, 17, 18, pp. 83, 100–105; use of, Brief Discourse, Bullinger, Smith, Wats, View, Kennet, Lincolnshire Parishes, Bodmin, Derby, Bledlow in 1783, 119, 120, 122, 134, 135, 136, 146, 149, 150; use gradually died out and the Surplice took its place, 151.

ALTAR. *Name*—Heathen name, 152; Christian name, 152; Protestants say we have no Altar, St. Paul says we have, 153; Altar or Table, name used indiscriminately in the Old and New Testaments, in the primitive and the Roman Church, 152, 153, 154; Altar called Table by the Jesuit Sanders, 41. *Stone or Wooden*—No doctrinal significance in the material of the Altar, stone or wood used indifferently under the Old Testament, in the primitive Church and in the Roman, 154, 155. *Form of Altars*—Ancient Greek, Roman, Italian and French Altars, illustrations, 156, 157; Pagan Altar, illustration, 152; mistaken Protestant notion that a structure with legs cannot be an Altar, 157. *Altars in the Church of England since the Reformation*— Hooper first objected to Altars, 162; Ridley overthrows them, 109, 162; three different changes made by him at St. Paul's, 162, 166; attempt made in Convocation in 1562-3 to place the Altar table-wise, 166, 167; allowed to be moved at Communion time, Rubric of 1552, Injunctions of 1559, Interpretations, 163-165; placed table-wise, illustration, 165-171; not moved in Cathedrals except by Puritan Deans, 163; the Altar in Canterbury Cathedral in 1564, 167; in Durham Cathedral in 1630, 172; in St. Paul's in 1719, illustration, 196; in St. George's Chapel, illustration, 197; Lutheran Altar, illustration, 203.

ALTAR-LIGHTS. Use of Lights in Divine Service ordered by God Himself, 186; two Candlesticks before the throne of God, 186; early use in the Church, 186; use in the Church of England since the Reformation, with illustrations, 186-199; authorized by the Rubric of 1549, testimony of contemporaries, 186-188; two lights ordered by Edward VI., and Cranmer, 186, 187; the seven lights of the Roman Church not used in England even before the Reformation, two—or even one in poor Churches—being the rule, Jebb, 193, 194; said to have been forbidden in 1549 by Royal Injunctions, 187; forbidden by Ridley in 1550, 187, 188; used at Ludlow in 1550, 188; used under the Rubric of 1552 where Chancels were ordered to remain as before, 109, 181, 182; used by Elizabeth in the Royal Chapels, Sampson, Heylin, State of the Royal Chapel in 1565, (when 83 lights were used), 125, 126, 127; Robertson's theory that they were used at the Queen's pleasure and not according to law, refuted by the contemporary testimony of Cox, Horn, and Jewell, 129, 130; use of lighted Candles, Certain Demands, Donne, Burton, Durham Cathedral, Ornsby, Voyage, Robertson, Chambers, St. Paul's Cathedral in 1719, 134, 190-196; unlighted, Lawful prejudices, Owen, 192, 193, 195; used among the Lutherans, illustration, 199-203.

ARMENIANS use the Cope as a Eucharistic Vestment, 92.

AUGUSTINE, St., on charity, famous saying attributed to him, 26. See MELDENIUS.

BACON, LORD. His opinion of the Puritans, 252.

"BEFORE THE TABLE" means in front of, looking east, 174, 175.

BELIEF in the Creed required by the XXXIX. Articles, 213, 217.

BIGOTRY, charge of, 248.

BOWING towards the Altar, 209–213; objected to by the Puritans, 179; left to every man's discretion by the Canons of 1640, 211; at the *Gloria*, 214; at the name of JESUS, 214; forbidden by the House of Commons in 1641, 191.

CALVINISTS used Wafer Bread, 224; hated by the Lutherans, 205.

CANDLESTICKS on the Altar at Bodmin in 1566, Derby in 1698, York in 1634–1736, Walcott, 146, 192, 193, 194, 195; illustrations, 139, 196, 197; allowed under the Rubric of 1552 by the Royal Commissioners, 113; Westminster Abbey in 1705, Addenda, XVIII.

CANONS of 1604 order Copes in Cathedrals, but forbid neither them nor Vestments elsewhere, 76; ratify the Rubric of 1559, which orders them everywhere, 76.

CANONS of 1640 recommend bowing towards the Altar, 211.

CAP, SQUARE, objected to by the Puritans, illustrations, 60, 106, 107, 120, 123.

CASULA, 86. See CHASUBLE.

CATHEDRALS the standard for Parish Churches in the method of conducting service, 143, 144; called Popish dens, &c., by the Puritans, 124, 127, 128, 134.

CATHOLIC, meaning of the word, 214–217; difference between Catholic and Roman Catholic, 215, 216; inconsistency of some Churchmen in refusing the name Catholic, 215.

CENSER appointed to the Church at Faringdon in 1550, 188; left for the use of the Church by the Commissioners in 1552, 109.

CEREMONIES of the Church not to be departed from, 182, 183; used under Edw. VI., restored by Elizabeth under the same name, Lever, Withers, 119, 121; necessary to the existence of a Church, Donne, 249.

CHASUBLE, derivation of, 86, 87; originally identical with the Cope, 87, 88; did not signify sacrifice but charity, 86, 87; description of, Figures 7, 8, 9, 10, pp. 83, 98–101; Roman pattern differs wholly from the Anglican, Fig. 11, 12, pp. 100, 101; Vestment or Chasuble ordered by the Ornaments Rubrics of 1549, 1559, 1604, 1662, 29, 36, 76, 77; forbidden with other vestures by the Rubric of 1552, but assigned to Churches by the Royal Commissioners, and used, 112–116; made Cope-fashion or open-fashioned, and used in Durham Cathedral till 1627, 93, 132, 133; possibly used in the Queen's Chapel, 94; used in Derby in 1563, 149; in Parish Churches in Lincolnshire after the Advertisements, 145; at Bodmin in 1566, 146; use gradually died out, 149; use of the Chasuble among the Lutherans, 199–203. See VESTMENT.

CLIFTON AND OTHERS *v.* RIDSDALE, 235.

CONCESSIONS, partial, never successful, Earl of Clarendon, 14.

CONFORMITY. Some of the Bishops at the beginning of Elizabeth's reign conformed to the ceremonies merely to retain their offices, 44, 45; Grindal deposed for neglect to enforce uniformity, 45; efforts of Queen Elizabeth, 45, 46, 47, 53–55, 65, 66; Parker's efforts brought upon him the ill will of the Puritans, 67.

CONSECRATED ELEMENTS, disposal of the, 224, 225.

COPE. Originally identical with the Chasuble, 87–89; description of, Figures 13, 14, 15, pp. 83, 102, 103; ordered to be used by the Rubrics of 1549, 1559, 1604, 1662, 29, 36, 76, 77; Canons of 1604, 76; use as a Eucharistic Vestment by the Anglican Reformers, 92, 93; suggested as such in 1561, 48; always used by the Bishops at the beginning of Elizabeth's reign, Heylin, 118; used in the Chapel-Royal, 125, 126, 128; used there at Baptisms, Churchings, Marriages, &c., 131, 132; at the Coronation of Queen Victoria in 1838, illustration, 138, 139; used in Durham Cathedral till the middle of the eighteenth century, 133, 136, 137; description of Copes there still, 133; objected to as Popish by the Puritans, Humphrey, Sampson, An Answer, Grindal, Zanchius, Thornborough, 120, 121, 123, 130; attempt to abolish them in Convocation in 1563, 49; abolished by Parliament in 1644, 77; ordered now to be worn in Cathedrals by the Privy Council, but not generally worn, 151, 232. *Use in Parish Churches*—Pronounced illegal in Parish Churches by the Privy Council, 232; no distinction originally between Parish Churches and Cathedrals in matters of vesture, 143–150; Elizabeth wished to have the same or similar manner of service everywhere, 46, 47; Lincolnshire Churches, 144–145; Bodmin, Gilby, Strype, Cartwright, 145–148; willed to Corff in 1571, Hants in 1617, 146, 149; distinction lately made between the Cope and the Chasuble on the ground that the latter is the exclusive "sacrificial garment," 85; the Cope is as much a sacrificial garment as the Chasuble, 94; used as a Mass-Vestment by the Roman Church in England before and since the Reformation, 89–91, 102, 103; used by the Armenians and Nestorians to this day, 92, 102, 103; use by the Reformers instead of the Chasuble, 48, 92, 93; use of the Cope with Tunicles for Deacon and Sub-deacon, 93.

COTTA, a Roman garment, illustration, 106, 107.

CRANMER, Thomas, Abp. of Canterbury. Labors on the Liturgy, 2; on the "Unquiet Spirits" of the ultra-Reformers, 34, 35;

opinion of the Prayer Book of 1549, 28, 29; wore a Cope and Alb in 1549, 93.

CREED, Apostles' or Nicene, to be thoroughly believed, 213, 217.

CROSS. Use of the Cross in the Church of England evident from the Inventories of 1552, 182; appointed to the Parish of Faringdon in 1550, 188.

CROSS, SIGN OF, constantly used by the early Christians, 183, 184; use ordered by Luther, 184; use in the Church of England, 184–185; left to every man's discretion by a Rubric of 1549, 185.

CRUCIFIX, use of the, in the Church of England evident from the Inventories of 1552, 182; authorized by the Ornaments Rubrics of 1559, 1662, 181, 182; by the Privy Council in 1857, 229; in Elizabeth's Chapel, Bullinger, Sandys, Neal, 120, 125, 128; Elizabeth thought of restoring them to Parish Churches, 126; in Durham Cathedral in 1630, 190; ordered to be removed from Churches by the House of Commons in 1641, 191; Westminster Abbey in 1705, Addenda, XVIII.; *use by the Lutherans*, 199–201; Church at Molmen, Norway, illustration, 203.

DALMATICS, or Tunicles, ordered by the Rubrics of 1549, 29.

"Do this in remembrance of Me." "Do" means to offer, 208.

DURHAM Cathedral, Chasubles commonly used at, till 1627, 94, 132, 133; Crucifix in 1630, 190; Altar in 1630, 172; Copes, Brereton, Thoresby, DeFoe, 133, 136, 137; superstition in 1680, 136; Copes still remaining, 133.

EASTWARD POSITION. Early Christians always prayed towards the East, 158, 159; position of ancient Churches, 159, 160; the Priest always stood before the Altar, 161. *Eastward Position in the Church of England*, Rubric of 1549, 173; of 1552, 1559, 1662, 173; the Advertisements and Canons of 1604 suppose the Eastward Position by ordering Gospeller and Epistoler, 50, 76, 176; Scotch Office, 174; Canons of 1640 order it, 168; in Laud's time the Altar stood table-wise in most Parish Churches, 168; great variety of position in the reign of Edward VI. and Elizabeth, Strype, White, Cecil, 165, 166, 167, 168; unsuccessful attempt by the Puritans in the Convocation of 1563 to abolish the Eastward Position in Parish Churches, 167; use in Elizabeth's Chapel, Sampson, Old Cheque-Book, 125, 128; use in the Church of England since the Reformation, 176–181; allowed by the Privy Council in 1868, 234, condemned in 1870-1, 234. allowed in 1877, 238.

EDWARD VI., a mere boy, and wholly under Puritan control, 33; intended further and more sweeping reforms, but prevented by death, 6; his opinion of the Prayer Book of 1549, 28.

ELIZABETH, Queen of England, a High Churchman or Ritualist, 252; had a clause expressly inserted in the act of uniformity to aid her in carrying forward higher ritual, 36; but for this clause she would not have adopted the Book of 1559, Parker, 37, 38; her coronation in 1558, 125; services in her chapel in 1560, Sampson, 125; thought of restoring the Crucifix to Parish Churches in 1564, 126; god-mother at a christening in 1565, (83 Lights on the Altar), 127; her Chapel called the "pattern of all superstition" in 1572, 127, 128, Parker, 65; Easter, 1593, 128; funeral in 1603, 128; very careful not to deviate in the least from the law, 129, 130; services pronounced superstitious but never illegal by the Puritans, 129; so showy as to be hardly distinguished from the Roman, Neal, 128; thanks her Chaplain for preaching the Real Presence, 129; rebukes the Dean of St. Paul's for speaking against the Cross in Churches, 126, 129; caused the Bishops to draw up the Advertisements, but refused to sign them, 69-72, 74, 75; complains of the neglected condition of Chancels and Churches, 46; and of the non-observance of rites and ceremonies, 53-55; desires the same or a similar manner of services in all Churches, 46, 47, 54; disliked the Puritans, 12, 13, 68; regarded them as dangerous as the Papists, 12; her excommunication by Pius V. in 1570, the beginning of the Roman Schism in England, 42, 43; the Pope is said to have offered to acknowledge the Church of England and the Prayer Book if she would acknowledge his claims, 40.

EUCHARIST, or Holy Communion, "of a spiritually sacrificial character," General Convention in 1832, 175, 207; a memorial sacrifice, SS. Chrysostom and Augustine, 207.

FAULT-FINDING, 21, 22.

FLOWERS in Church, antiquity of, 205, 206.

FRANKFORT, troubles at, in 1554, 7.

FURTHER ORDER taken by Elizabeth in 1559, 38, 66; again in 1561, 46, 47, 66; claimed by the Privy Council to have been also taken in 1566 in the Advertisements, 50; not taken in 1566, 51-55, 66-72.

GOSSIP forbidden by St. James, 245, 246. See FAULT-FINDING.

GOWN, BLACK. No Rubrical authority for it in the Church services, 218; attempt of Convocation in 1563 to substitute it for the Surplice, 49; attempt in 1689, 79, 80; illegal according to the

271

Privy Council in 1870-1, where the Minister is ordered to wear a Surplice at all times of his ministration, 231.

GOSPELLER AND EPISTOLER, or Deacon and Subdeacon, in addition to the Priest, ordered by the Ornaments Rubric of 1549, the Advertisements of 1566, and the Canons of 1604, 29, 50, 76; Wiburn, Addenda, Dering, XVII., 123; in the Queen's Chapel, 125, 128.

HEBBERT v. PURCHAS, 230–235.

HIEREUS, Sacrificing Priest. Use of the word in the New Testament, 207, 208.

HIGH CHURCHMEN, genuine and spurious, 15; never clamor for changes in the Prayer Book, 252.

HOLY DAYS. Observance required by the Rubric, 217, 218.

HOLY WATER can at Derby in 1560, 148.

HOOPER, John, the first to raise disputes about the Vestments, 83; accounted it a "sin" to wear them, 83; lack of support, 83, 84; opinion of the Book of 1549, 30.

HYMNS AND ANTHEMS, when to be used, 218; standing at the Hymns objected to by the Puritans, 191.

ILLEGAL. Use of Vestments, Altar-Lights, &c., now pronounced illegal; by the Puritans superstitious or Popish, but never illegal, 129, 150, 151, 195.

IMMACULATE CONCEPTION, made an Article of Faith in 1854, why not before, Milner, 215, 216.

IMMORALITIES of the ultra-Reformers, 31, 32.

INCENSE, use of, commanded to be used in every place by God Himself through Malachi, 110, 206; how Protestants can fulfill this prophecy, 111; offered to the Saviour by the wise men, 110; legal by the Rubrics of 1559, 1662, 36, 77; used by Bp. Andrewes, 106; at Wolverhampton about 1633, 134; in Ely Cathedral till near the end of the 18th century, note 111. See SHIPPE, and CENSER.

INCONSISTENCY, Bishops taunted with, in enforcing certain vestures and rejecting others equally endorsed by the Rubric, An Answer, Johnson, Abridgment, Parker, 120, 123, 131.

INFALLIBILITY OF THE Pope pronounced a Protestant invention in Keenan's Catechisms, passage left out in subsequent editions, 215.

INTERPRETATIONS and further Considerations drawn up in 1561, suggest the Cope as the Eucharistic vestment in all Churches, 48.

INVITATION to the Holy Communion, no authority for, 219, 220.

JEWISH Priests ordered to wear splendid Vestments by God Himself, 82.

KNEELING. The Rubric requires kneeling, 213.

LAMP, appointed for the high Altar at Bodmin in 1566, 146; in the Queen's Chapel, 127,

LAWLESSNESS. Low Churchmen and even Bishops do not obey the Decisions of the Privy Council any more than the Ritualists do, case of the Bishop of Carlisle, 226, 227.

LIDDELL *v.* WESTERTON, 227, 228.

LIGHTS. See ALTAR-LIGHTS.

LOW CHURCHMEN. Some are Churchmen, and some are no Churchmen at all, the feelings of the former should be respected, 15, 243; do not believe in the Prayer Book, and seek to change it, 243, 252; Prayer Book Revision Society in England, 244; Evangelical Churchmen now have no monopoly of grace, &c., Canon Ryle, 252, 253.

LOYALTY TO THE PRAYER BOOK, 1–3.

LUTHER orders the use of the sign of the Cross, 184; preserved the Mass, Chasubles, &c., 199; would be called a Ritualist now, 252.

LUTHERAN SERVICES, 199–203; use of the Vestments, Altars, Altar-Lights, Mass, Wafer Bread, these things carefully kept out of sight, 199–203, 251; Lutheran Church at Molmen in Norway, illustration, 203; dislike for the Calvinists, 205; Lutheranism regarded by the Calvinists as being almost as bad as Popery, Gualter, 39.

MANUAL acts a piece of Protestant Ritualism, 238.

MARTIN *v.* MACKONOCHIE, 228–230.

MASS. The Communion Service called the Mass in the Prayer Book of 1549, 227; some Churches in London in 1567 objected to by the Puritans as being as bad as to go to Mass, 121; called Mass among the Lutherans, 199–201.

MASS-VESTMENT. The Chasuble the usual Vestment used at Mass before the Reformation, 87; the Cope sometimes used as such, 88; used since the Reformation by Roman Catholics in England, 89–91; used by the Armenians and Nestorians now, 92; use by the Anglican Reformers, 92–94.

MIXED CHALICE, the, in the Church of England, 220, 221; condemned by the Privy Council in 1870-1, 233.

NORTH SIDE. First ordered by the Book of 1552, 173; a distinction made between North side and North end by the Puritans themselves, 171-173; North side when the Altar was placed table-wise, illustration, 169; North side changed to Right side in the American Prayer Book in 1832, 174.

OFFERINGS, presentation of, 219.

OMISSION NOT PROHIBITION, case of Johnson, and Canons of 1604, 229, 230.

ORGANS regarded as Popish by the Puritans, Withers, A Request, Cartwright, Milner, Luther, 121, 124, 127, 191, 199, 251; used in Queen Elizabeth's Chapel, Heylin, Neal, 126, 128.

ORNAMENTS, meaning of, note, 36; of the Altar, Rubric of 1552 ordered Chancels to remain as in times past, 109, 181; Rubrics of 1559 and 1662; order such Ornaments as were in use in 2d Edw. VI., 36, 77; can be known from the Inventories made in 1552, 182.

ORNAMENTS RUBRIC. See RUBRIC.

OTHER ORDER. See FURTHER ORDER.

PÆNULA, 86.

PAPIST, a common term applied by Protestants to their opponents instead of argument, Abp. Parker and Lord Burleigh called great Papists, 67; the Wesleys called Papists, Jesuits, &c., 24-26, 248; clergy called "Papists," 39.

PARKER, Abp., consecrated in a Cope, 118; efforts made to enforce the discipline of the Church brought upon him the hatred of the Puritans, 67; great debt due him for upholding the Church against the Puritans, 67; draws up the Advertisements, 56.

PARLIAMENT. The House of Lords in 1641 acknowledged the Rubric of 1559 to be still in force, 77; abolished Copes, Surplices and Vestments in 1644, 77; the Prayer Book in 1645, 77.

PASTORAL STAFF, ordered by a Rubric of 1549, 30.

PERSECUTION by Protestants, 22-26, 244; High Church services broken up by mobs, and the Priests imprisoned, 244, 245; congregation broken up and the people forced to build a church in an adjoining town, 245; poor Churches always selected for persecution, 246; Protestant rule of "Liberty to worship God according to the dictates of every man's conscience" exists mostly in theory and not in practice, 244.

PERSUASION and not force to be used in influencing men, Adkinson, note, 13.

PETERBOROUGH Cathedral in 1586 used the Vestments, 124.

PHÆNOLION, 86.

PLACING the elements upon the Altar, 220-224.

PLANETA, 86.

POSTURE, directions for, put forth by the American Bishops in 1832, 175, 176.

PRIEST, Hiereus used in the New Testament to signify Priest, 207-208; *Sacerdos* in the Latin Prayer Book of Elizabeth, 225.

PRAYER BOOK of 1549. Same as the old book, only in English, with the gross superstitions left out, 108; drawn up by the aid of the Holy Ghost, according to Edward VI. and his Council, 28; opinion of Latimer, 34; Cranmer, 28, 29; Dryander, 29; Duke of Somerset, 108; Hooper, 30; not used everywhere, 28.

*Prayer Book of* 1552—Its foreign origin, never submitted to Convocation, 33; forbids Albs, Vestments, Copes, Tunicles, and allows only the Surplice and Rochet, 34; further reforms contemplated, 6, 35; Cranmer opposed to constant tinkering of the Prayer Book, 34, 35.

*Prayer Book of* 1559—Elizabeth would not have agreed to this Book, but for a clause inserted in the Act of Uniformity, 38; re-enacts the Rubric of 1549 and all the Ornaments used in the second year of Edward VI., 36; Catholic character of the Book, De Quadra, Abp. Parker, 39; called Popish by the Puritans, Wiburn, 39, 40; the Pope is said to have been willing to confirm it, 40; abolished by Parliament in 1645, 77.

*Prayer Book of* 1604—Substantially the same as the Prayer Book of 1559, 76.

*Prayer Book of* 1662—Re-enacted the Ornaments Rubric of 1559, which adopted the Ornaments of the Book of 1549, 77; testimony of Baxter and others that all changes made were in a more Churchly direction, 77-79.

*Prayer Book* Revision Society in England, 244.

PRIVY COUNCIL. Decisions, 226-240; not made to interpret the law, but to crush out High Churchmen, 226; could not be obeyed, 226, 241; not obeyed by those in whose interest the Decisions were made, the Bishop of Carlisle, 226, 227; refused to listen to the appeal of Mr. Purchas, why, 235; refused to give any opinion in regard to the vestures of the Bishops, 235; acknowledge that the Rubric of 1662 of itself makes Vestments obligatory, 51, 236; many of the Judges dissented from the Ridsdale Judgment, 238, 239; the Lord Chief Baron pronounced the Ridsdale Judgment one of policy rather than law, 239, 240.

*Misquotations*—High Mass instead of Mass, 227; word "only" interpolated, 230, 231; "not" substituted for "now," and "by" for "2," 232.

*Misstatements*—Change in the Prayer of Consecration in 1552, 227; exact directions as to kneeling and standing, 228; lighted candles forbidden by Elizabeth's Act of Uniformity, 228, 229; "omission" not "prohibition" in the case of Johnson, 229, 230; Bishops recast the Rubric of 1559 in 1662, 231; Alb and Chasuble swept away, 232; Eastern and Western Church have no custom of private mingling of wine with water, 233; mistake as to Cosin, 234.

*Misleading statements*—Speak of Vestments as being accounted superstitious after 1566, 236; speak of the Ornaments Rubric as the "rubric-note of 1662," 236; speak of Perambulations as being ordered by the Advertisements in 1566, whereas they were ordered by the Homilies in 1563, 238.

*Contradictions*—"Omission" is "prohibition," and is not "prohibition," 229, 230; same dresses and utensils used under Edward VI. "may" and "may not" be used, 232, 233; Eastward Position allowed, condemned, and allowed, 234, 238.

PROTESTANT. Name does not mean what it did once, 216; name refused by Convocation in 1689, 216; abolished by the Prussian Government in 1817; difference of belief among Protestants, 216, 217; Protestant mobs worse than Popish, Wesley, 25, 26; Protestant rule of "liberty to worship God according to the dictates of every man's conscience," exists mostly *in* theory and not in practice, 244.

PURITANS at the beginning of the Reformation, 4; under Edward VI., 5, 6; under Queen Mary, 6; under Queen Elizabeth, 7-14; under Edward VI. and Elizabeth refused to wear the Surplice, 43, 44; few in number, 7; quarrel among themselves, 9-11, 31; objections to the Church, 3, 4; contentions encouraged by the Calvinists, 84, 85; advised by foreigners to retain their offices in the Church, 8; some honorably gave up the Ministry, 13; objected to the public reading of the Holy Scriptures, 9, 189; Lord Bacon's opinion of them, 252.

PURITANISM as dangerous to Church and State as Popery, 11-13.

REFORMATION. Many joined it for the sake of wealth and power, 4, 5; further reform intended, but prevented by the death of Edward VI., 5, 6; principles of the, Church or Puritan, 251.

REFORMERS not all Puritans, 202; ultra-Reformers often immoral, 31, 32; never could keep quiet, but always changing, 34, 249, 250; foreigners wrote to Edward VI. in behalf of further reform, 33; wrote to Queen Elizabeth, 7, 8.

RESERVATION of the Blessed Sacrament ordered by the Rubric of 1549, 225; Latin Book of Queen Elizabeth in 1560, 225; Scotch Office, 225.

REVERENCE for God's House, 208, 209.

REVISION. See RUBRIC.

RITUALISM in the General Convention of 1874, 16-19; not necessarily Romanism, 242, 243; offensive to some people, so is the Gospel, 247; nothing immoral in it, 247.

RITUALIST. Queen Elizabeth and Martin Luther would be called Ritualists now, 252; same language now applied to the Ritualists in the newspapers that was used towards the early Methodists, 24; some of them unprincipled, 16; deserve justice and fair treatment, 244-248; St. Alban's, history of, 246, 247; poor Churches always selected for persecution, but rich ones let alone, 246; could they not do as much good by giving up their ceremonies? 247, 248; reason why they were condemned, 240, 241.

ROCHET ordered by the Ornaments Rubric of 1549, 29; description of, Figures 22-25, pp. 83, 106, 107.

ROMAN CATHOLICS not hardly dealt with by Elizabeth, 7; bulk of them conformed to the Church of England for ten or eleven years of the reign of Elizabeth, 40-42.

ROMANISM, reasons for the increase of, Parker, Baxter, 20.

ROME, secession to, 19, 20.

RUBRIC. Ornaments Rubric of 1549, 28-30; of 1552, 30-35; not obeyed, 109; of 1559, 35-37; of 1603-4, 76; of 1662, 77-79; attempted revision in 1689, 79, 80, Addenda, XVII.; in 1879. 80-82; Rubric of the Communion Office, 173, 174.

RYLE, Canon, Evangelicals have now no monopoly of grace, &c., 252, 253.

SACERDOS used for Priest in the Latin Prayer Book of Elizabeth, 225.

SACRAMENT, irreverent language towards the, forbidden by Edward VI., 5.

SANDYS, Archbishop, effigy of, vested in a Chasuble, 124.

SCORY consecrated in a Cope in 1552, after it had been forbidden by Rubric, 111.

SCRIPTURES, public reading of the, not practiced by the early Puritans, Cox, Whitehead 9, 189.

SERMON, 218.

SERVICES, separation of the, 27.

SHIPPE or SHIP, or Incense boat on the Altar of Elizabeth's Chapel in 1565, 127.

SMITH, Sir Thomas, had an Alb and Chasuble in his Chapel for the Priest in 1569, 122.

STOLE included under the word Vestment, 29, 93; ancient pattern of the year 1200, illustration, 95; pronounced illegal by the Privy Council, but worn because popular, Goodwin, 226.

SUPERSTITION. The Queen's Chapel and Cathedrals denounced as dens of superstition and Popish by the Puritans, 124, 127, 128, 133, in Durham Cathedral in 1680, 136; not to get rid of superstition, but robbery the reason why Church goods were confiscated in 1552, 111, 112, 116, 117; nothing superstitious or ungodly in the use of the Vestments according to Article XXXVI., 122.

SURPLICE, description of the, Figures 19, 20, pp. 83, 104, 105; use ordered by the Rubrics of all the Prayer Books, 29, 34, 36, 77; disused by the Puritans under Edward VI. and Elizabeth, 43, 44; required in all ministrations, preaching even, according to Guest, 117; attempt of the Puritans in Convocation in 1563, as also in 1689, to abolish it and substitute the Gown, 49, 79, 80; abolished by Parliament in 1644, 77; used sometimes as a Mass-Vestment before the Reformation, 91, 92; the word Surplice as used by the early Puritans may have included other vestures, Robinson, 143; the Surplice as well as other vestures objected to by the Puritans as Popish, Brief Discussion, Beza, Zanchius, 119, 120, 123; according to Guéranger the more liberal Roman Clergy in Germany officiate in ordinary clothes, 44; Surplice riots, 244.

TUNICLES or Dalmatics ordered by the Rubrics of 1559, 29; description of, Figures 7, 16, pp. 83, 99-103.

UNIFORMITY, Act of in 1559, contained a proviso for further rites and ceremonies, 36; Puritans at first hoped it would be used to curtail ritual, 36; but it was inserted expressly by Elizabeth to enable her to adopt higher ritual, and the Puritans feared lest she should exercise it, 37, 38.

UNIVERSITIES. Revenues invaded, 5.

"Unquiet Spirits" of the Puritans, Cranmer, Prayer Book of 1552, Bullinger, Sandys, 9, 10, 34, 35, 249, 250.

Vincentius of Lerins. His famous rule, 215.

Vestments ordered by God Himself to be used by the Jewish Priesthood, 82; the Vestments ordered by the Ornaments Rubric of 1549, 29; the word Vestment properly means the Chasuble, Stole, Amice and Maniple, 29, 93, 149; attempt to abolish it by the Puritans in Convocation in 1563, 49; left to a a Parish Church by Sir Edmund Trafford in 1572, 147; abolished by Parliament in 1644, 77; the early Puritans never made any distinction between the different Vestments, but regarded them all alike as being superstitious, 89; their legality never denied till lately, 150, 151; colored Vestments, Inventories, Johnson, Cox, 112, 113, 124, 149; Alb, Vestment, Dalmatic, and Cope disallowed in Parish Churches, and the Cope only allowed in Cathedral and Collegiate Churches by the Privy Council, 232; See Chasuble.

Wafer Bread ordered by the Rubrics of 1548, 1549, and Injunctions of 1559, 48, 221, 222; left optional by the Rubrics of 1559 and 1662, 222; use in the Church of England since the Reformation, 222, 223; general use testified to by Sanders the Jesuit, 41; the common bread disliked by most people in 1571, Parker, 223; used by Queen Elizabeth, Easter, 1593, 128; decided by the Privy Council as legal if leavened, illegal if unleavened, 233, 234, 238; used by the Lutherans, 202, 203, 224; by the Calvinists, 224.

Wesley, John and Charles. Both persecuted by Protestants as Papists and Jesuits, 24-46; obliged to take an oath against Popery, 248; how ridiculous these proceedings seem now, 248.